80002726

# A–Z

## Contents

A–Z entries ..... 1

Appendices

Physics revision lists ..... 277

Physical quantities and their units ..... 289

Useful formulae and equations ..... 292

Physical constants ..... 296

Useful data ..... 297

Preparing for the examination ..... 299

Examiners' terms ..... 303

Synoptic questions in A-level physics ..... 305

# How to use this book

Physics, like many other subjects of study, is built up from a large number of interlinked concepts. From your previous studies you will have started to construct your own mental map of physics. A-level physics requires many new concepts to be added to this map so that, at times, you may find it hard to see how everything links together. The *A–Z Physics Handbook* is an alphabetical textbook designed to show these connections.

Each entry begins with a one-sentence definition. The entry then opens out with explanations, diagrams and examples. If relevant, the initial definition is followed by a word equation, a definition of the unit and the symbols for the quantity and its unit.

Entries vary in length according to the amount of detail needed. *Magnet* requires little more than a clear statement, whereas a topic such as *displacement–time graph* or *photoelectric effect* needs an introduction, annotated diagrams, and some development of the principles, along with worked examples. The intention has been to offer a focused account of the subject without leaving out any of the essential steps towards a new concept.

Entries contain cross-references in italics to other entries; these support or extend the ideas in the entry, and will encourage you to deepen and expand your knowledge of the subject by tracing a pathway from an initial area of interest to something that may be less familiar. The compactness of the book gives a clearer view of the whole subject than does a longer, heavier and more detailed text, and this helps to speed up the difficult processes of learning and understanding.

Since the entries are in alphabetical order, this is a book that has no beginning. Just open it anywhere and start reading, then move forward or backward by several letters, or let the cross-references guide you. Occasional browsing can be a profitable and interesting enterprise.

You should find the appendices useful when examinations are approaching. Along with the website that accompanies this handbook, the appendices provide you with ideas for tackling revision, as well as helping you to be aware of the nature of exam papers and what examiners are looking for.

## A–Z Online

This new digital edition of the *A–Z Physics Handbook* includes free access to a supporting website and a free desktop widget to make searching for terms even quicker. Log on to

**www.philipallan.co.uk/a-zonline** and create an account using the unique code provided on the front inside cover of this book.

Once you are logged on, you will be able to:

- search the entire database of terms in this handbook
- print revision lists specific to your exam board
- get expert advice from examiners on how to get an A* grade
- create a personal library of your favourite terms
- expand your vocabulary with our word of the week

You can also add the other *A–Z Handbooks (digital editions)* that you own to your personal library on A–Z Online.

We hope that the *A–Z Physics Handbook* will be an invaluable study aid, from the beginning of your course to its successful completion.

*David Sang and Michael Chapple*

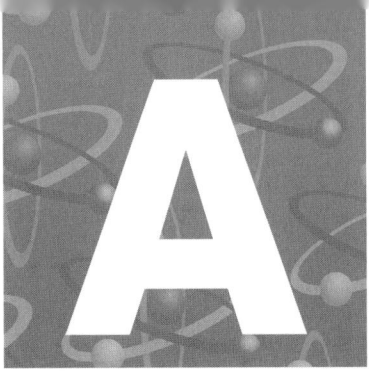



**abscissa:** the *y* coordinate of a point on a graph. (See *ordinate.*)

**absolute temperature scale:** a theoretical temperature scale based on a theorem in thermodynamics concerning the efficiencies of heat engines. It is sometimes called the absolute thermodynamic temperature scale. It is identical to the ideal gas scale of temperature. The numerical values are fixed by setting the triple point of water at 273.16 K above *absolute zero.*

Thermometers are calibrated against the *International Practical Temperature scale.* This scale of temperature has legal force. It is defined by setting numerical values to several reproducible temperatures such as the triple point of water, the boiling point of water and the melting points of a number of pure metals and by defining how intermediate temperatures are to be measured.

Temperatures may be measured either from absolute zero (giving a temperature in K on the *Kelvin scale*) or from the freezing point of water (giving a temperature in °C on the *Celsius temperature scale*). Temperature differences are given in kelvins on either scale. (See *centigrade temperature scale.*)

**absolute zero** is the lowest temperature on the *absolute temperature scale.* It is unachievable in practice.

Absolute zero is the temperature at which it becomes impossible for a body to release energy to its surroundings. It is incorrect to say that the atoms of a body have no energy at this temperature; they retain a certain zero-point energy, but this energy cannot be extracted from them.

Experimental methods have been devised which can achieve temperatures within $10^{-10}$ K of absolute zero.

**absorption coefficient:** see *attenuation.*

**absorption spectrum:** the dark absorption lines seen across a *continuous spectrum* after it has passed through a cool gas. The wavelengths corresponding to these lines are identical to the wavelengths in the *emission spectrum* for the same gas. The diagram on page 2 underlines the correspondence between the emission spectrum of hydrogen gas in a discharge tube and the absorption spectrum for cool hydrogen. The 'spectral lines' are images of the slit, with each line having its particular wavelength. All the focusing paraphernalia has been left out of the diagram.

The spectrum of a star is an absorption spectrum. The continuous spectrum is the *total radiation curve* associated with the temperature of the hot surface of the star. The absorption spectrum, seen as a mass of dark lines against this background, is composed of the various line spectra of the elements which are present in the cooler gases some distance above the star's surface. These gases absorb particular frequencies from the outward-travelling light, and this produces the absorption lines.

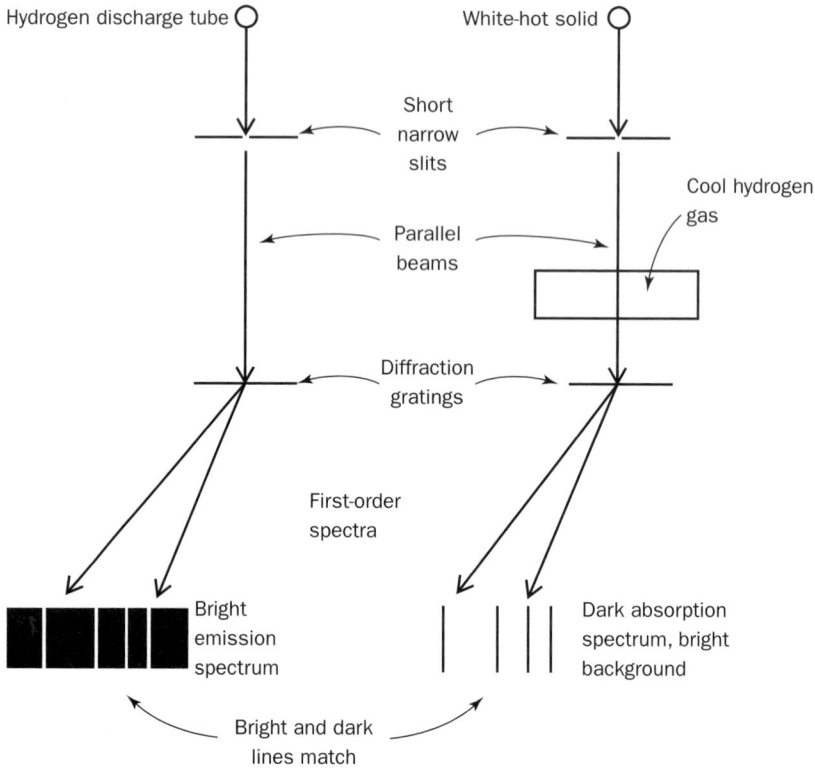


**acceleration** is rate of increase of *velocity*. It is a vector quantity represented by the symbol $a$ and its SI unit is metre per second squared ($m\,s^{-2}$). The word equation definition is:

$$\text{acceleration} = \frac{\text{increase in velocity}}{\text{time interval}}$$

$$m\,s^{-2} = \frac{m\,s^{-1}}{s}$$

This word equation defines acceleration; however, we need to distinguish between instantaneous acceleration and uniform acceleration. Instantaneous acceleration is the limiting value of the acceleration calculated over a very short time interval at the appropriate instant of time; it equals the *gradient* of the *velocity–time graph* at the same instant of time.

*Displacement*, velocity and acceleration are related quantities. They are all vectors and all measured positively in the same direction. The three graphs on page 3 show how they relate to one another. A stone is thrown vertically upwards from the ground with an initial speed $29.4\,m\,s^{-1}$. It takes three seconds to rise just over 44.1 metres and another three seconds to return to the ground. Displacement is measured in the upwards direction from the ground; the first graph shows the changing values of the displacement during the six seconds. Velocity must be measured upwards too; the second graph shows the linear change with time from positive $29.4\,m\,s^{-1}$ to negative $29.4\,m\,s^{-1}$. Velocity in the upwards direction decreases steadily in value. The upwards acceleration (measured in the same direction as displacement) is constant and negative.

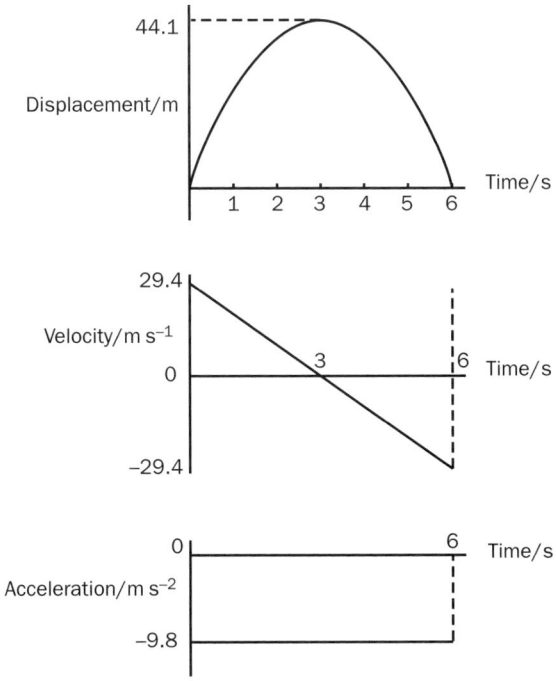


Acceleration is uniform (constant) if the velocity changes by equal amounts in equal times. These changes in velocity must be in the same direction and equal in magnitude. This can happen only if the body is moving along a straight line. The magnitude of a uniform acceleration is calculated from the following word equation:

$$\text{uniform acceleration} = \frac{\text{final velocity} - \text{initial velocity}}{\text{time taken}}$$

$$a = \frac{v - u}{t}$$

$$\text{or, rearranged, } v = u + at$$

The last equation is one of the *equations of motion*. It is an implicit definition of uniform acceleration.

An understanding of acceleration is essential in *straight line motion*, *circular motion* and *simple harmonic motion*. At A-level, acceleration is uniform for straight line motion. For circular motion, acceleration is constant in magnitude but not in direction.
For simple harmonic motion, the magnitude of the acceleration changes constantly and the direction switches twice each cycle. Acceleration plays a key role in *Newton's laws of motion*.

Rate of change of *speed* is a scalar quantity which has no special name. It should not be called acceleration. Acceleration is a vector quantity — it is the rate of change of velocity.

**acceleration due to gravity:** see *acceleration of free fall*.

**acceleration of free fall** (symbol $g$) is also known as *acceleration due to gravity.* It is the *acceleration* of a body towards the Earth's surface when it is acted on by one force only — its weight. Close to the Earth's surface, it has a typical value of

$$g = -9.81\,\mathrm{m\,s^{-2}}$$

and this is the value that you will usually be required to use in examination calculations.

When a body falls freely under gravity (i.e. without any other forces acting on it), its condition is described, curiously, as 'weightlessness'. A satellite in orbit is acted on by one force only, namely its weight, and this weight is employed in providing the centripetal force.

If the Earth is treated, for the moment, as a perfect sphere of mass $M$ and radius $R$, then the gravitational force $F$ on a small mass $m$ near the Earth's surface is given by

$$F = G\frac{Mm}{R^2} = mg$$

where $G$ is the universal gravitational constant and $g$ is the *gravitational field strength*. The unit for $g$ defined by this equation is $\mathrm{N\,kg^{-1}}$.
We can also write

$$F = mg$$

where $F$ is still the gravitational force on the mass $m$ but $g$ is now the acceleration of the mass under the action of this force. Here $g$ is called the acceleration of free fall and its unit is $\mathrm{m\,s^{-2}}$. Since the Earth is spinning, the equation would more correctly be written as

$$F = \text{centripetal force} + mg$$

The *centripetal force* on an object of given mass is strongest at the equator.

The measured value for the acceleration of free fall increases from the equator to the poles for two reasons. First, the Earth is not a perfect sphere — its radius is smaller at the poles (the Earth is said to be an 'oblate spheroid', i.e. flattened near the poles, with radius greater at the equator), so the gravitational field strength increases towards the poles. Second, the centripetal force on an object gets smaller towards the poles.

Acceleration of free fall does not differ much from $9.8\,\mathrm{m\,s^{-2}}$ the world over. Except near mountainous masses, its direction is towards the Earth's centre. If $\phi$ represents latitude and $H$ the height in metres above sea level, then the value for $g$ is given empirically by the equation

$$g = 9.780\left(1 + 0.0053\sin^2\phi\right) - \left(3.086 \times 10^{-6}H\right)$$

For York, $\phi$ is 54°. Put $H = 0$ (which cannot be far wrong near a wide river) and we find that $g = 9.814\,\mathrm{m\,s^{-2}}$. For London, $\phi$ is 51.5° and we get $g = 9.812\,\mathrm{m\,s^{-2}}$. The table lists some measured values for $g$.

| Location | Latitude | $g$ / $\mathrm{m\,s^{-2}}$ |
|---|---|---|
| Equator | 0°N | 9.780 |
| Chennai | 13°N | 9.783 |
| Calcutta | 23°N | 9.788 |
| Sydney | 34°S | 9.797 |
| New York | 42°N | 9.803 |
| London | 51°N | 9.812 |
| St Petersburg | 60°N | 9.819 |
| North Pole | 90°N | 9.832 |

**acceleration of free fall — measurement:** Experiments to measure the acceleration of free fall in the laboratory may be direct or indirect. A direct method involves using an object which is falling freely. An indirect method hinges on something like a *simple pendulum* or helical spring the period of which depends on *g in a known way.* Read the question; if you describe the wrong method you will generally be awarded no marks!

The direct measurement is a popular question and the time allowed usually about ten minutes. You would be expected to draw and label a diagram, list and describe all the relevant measurements and explain how the answer is worked out. The points that will be looked for in the diagram are the precise distance for which the fall time is measured and the circuitry for measuring fall time. Both elements should be clearly labelled. A skeleton circuit is usually sufficient for the time measurement.

**Experiment to measure the acceleration of free fall using an object in free fall**

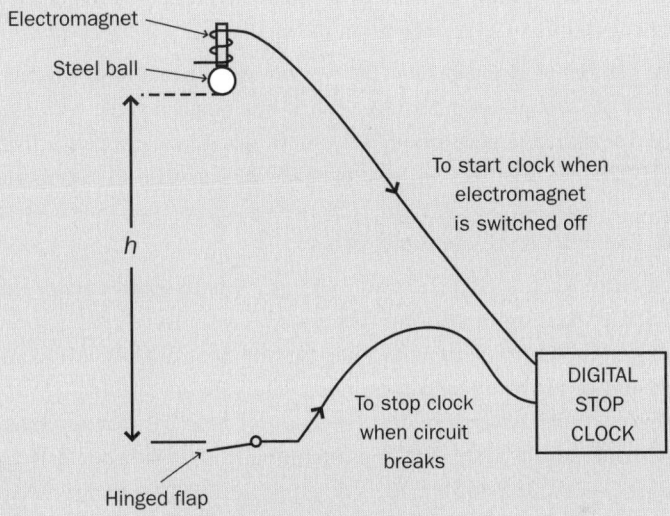


**Apparatus**

Set up the apparatus as shown in the diagram. The distance $h$, the fall distance for the steel ball, must be labelled precisely. The digital clock is arranged to start when the electromagnet circuit supporting the steel ball is broken. It stops when the steel ball strikes the hinged flap at the bottom of its fall.

**Measurements**

Use a metre rule to measure the fall distance. Repeat this measurement twice and calculate the average value $h$. Measure the fall-time for one fall distance three times and calculate the average value $t$ of these three measurements. Repeat this procedure for a range of heights between 50 cm and 2 metres.

**Conclusion**

Use the relationship $s = ut + \frac{1}{2}at^2$ . Put $u = 0$, $s = h$ and $a = g$.

This gives us $h = \frac{1}{2}gt^2$ . Draw a graph of $2h$ against $t^2$. It will be a straight line through the origin and the gradient will equal $g$.

**Comments**

Notice that repeating the measurements reduces random errors such as some $h$ values being slightly too large and others being slightly too small. But repetition does nothing for systematic errors like a clock that is too slow or a steel ball that sticks too long to the electromagnet so that it starts to fall only a short time after the clock has started. Systematic errors must be identified and minimised some other way.

You should add a word or two to explain how you minimise any parallax error when measuring $h$.

**accuracy** is a way of describing how close a measurement is to the true value. It should only be used in a descriptive sense. For example, you might say that a *micrometer screw gauge* was used in an experiment to improve the accuracy. (See also *error, uncertainty.*)

**acoustic impedance** is a measure of the extent to which a surface transmits or reflects sound or ultrasound. It is usually denoted by $Z$ and is the product of the density $\rho$ of the medium and the speed $c$ of ultrasound within the medium: $Z = \rho c$. (See *ultrasound.*)

**activity** is the number of disintegrations per second which occur in a radioactive source. It is a measure of the strength of the source. The SI unit of activity, the *becquerel* (Bq), is defined as one disintegration per second. When new, school sources give activities in the region of 200 kBq. Some older sources have their activities marked in microcuries; however, the curie (which is equal to $3.7 \times 10^{10}$ Bq) should no longer be used. (See *count rate, frequency, fundamental law of radioactive decay.*)

**adiabatic change** occurs when a system either gains or loses energy through working but not by heating or cooling. The usual reason for a change being adiabatic is that something happens too fast for any heat to flow. An example is the sudden expansion of air when a balloon pops. The *first law of thermodynamics* states that any increase in *internal energy* $\Delta U$ is the sum of heat $\Delta Q$ flowing into the system and work $\Delta W$ done on the system. When a balloon pops, the work $\Delta W$ done by the surroundings on the expanding air is negative, and $\Delta Q$ is zero. So $\Delta U$, like $\Delta W$, must be negative — there is a loss of internal energy. The air mass cools down not because of heat transferred to the surroundings (driven by a temperature difference) but because of energy released when the expanding gas works on its surroundings. Similarly, a large mass of warm air rising from the ground expands adiabatically (because it is so big); it cools down, condensation follows and a cloud forms. It is sometimes convenient to resolve a change in the state of a gas into two component changes: one adiabatic and the other isothermal. (See *isothermal change.*)

The pressure and volume of a fixed mass of gas vary during an adiabatic change in such a way that the expression $pV^{\gamma}$ is constant, where $p$ is gas pressure, $V$ is gas volume and $\gamma$ is the ratio of the specific heat capacities of the gas measured at constant pressure and at constant volume. Its value is 1.67 for a monatomic gas and 1.40 for a diatomic gas.

**aeroplanes** are supported in the air by an upward thrust on the wings called *lift*. There are two ways to think of the origin of this force. The first one is that because the wings are tilted, as the aeroplane moves forwards the wings will push air downwards. The downward force on the air results in an equal and opposite upward force on the wings (a consequence of *Newton's third law of motion*).

Alternatively, we can picture the lift as being generated by the different airflow rates over the upper and lower wing surfaces. The shape of the wing encourages the air speed $v_U$ over the upper surface of the wing to be faster than the air speed $v_L$ under the lower surface of the wing. This sets up a pressure difference and, therefore, a resultant thrust at right angles to the wing, directed upwards.

The *free-body force diagram* below relates lift to the other forces acting on an aeroplane in horizontal flight at constant speed. The lift balances the weight. The frictional force of the air on the plane is called the *drag*. The drag balances the forward thrust from the propellers or jets. Archimedean upthrust is assumed to be small compared with the weight.

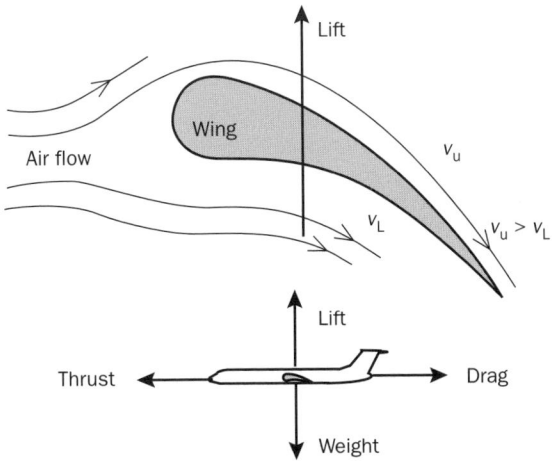


**air bags** are safety devices fitted in most modern cars. In a collision, the car decelerates suddenly. A sensor called an accelerometer detects the high magnitude of *acceleration* and electrically triggers the explosive inflation of the air bag. Without the air bag, the person in the car would strike the windscreen or another hard surface, receiving a serious blow. The air bag provides a softer, protective surface.

The operation of the air bag can be understood in terms of *momentum*. The person in the car has momentum while the car is moving. This must be reduced to zero when the car stops. If the person's momentum is reduced to zero in a very short time, the force on the person's body must be very high; this follows from the relationship between force and momentum as described by *Newton's second law of motion* (force = rate of change of momentum). The air bag extends the interval of time over which the person's momentum is reduced to zero, so that the rate of change of momentum (and hence the force) is reduced. (See also *crumple zones*.)

**albedo:** the fraction of the radiation falling on the surface of a planet (or moon etc.) which is reflected.

**algebraic sum:** the simple addition of two magnitudes. The sum of two scalar quantities is their algebraic sum, provided that the quantities in question can be added together. Mass (5 g + 8 g = 13 g) and electric charge (9 C + 7 C = 16 C) are added together algebraically. Electric charge, though a scalar quantity, can be either negative or positive.

Temperatures measured on the absolute scale can only be positive but temperature differences may be positive or negative. An equation like 300 K − 8 K = 292 K needs careful reading. The value 8 K is probably a temperature difference; 300 K and 292 K are probably temperatures. But we could be wrong and would need to know the context.

For some quantities, such as density or thermal conductivity, algebraic addition makes no sense. Vector quantities have directions as well as magnitudes and this makes their addition more complicated. (See *parallelogram law.*)

**alloys** are metals with new or enhanced properties formed by melting together and cooling two or more metals to form a mixture rather than a chemical compound. The physical properties of an alloy depend on the metals chosen, the proportions combined and the process by which the alloy is formed. Brass is an alloy of copper and zinc. Steel is an alloy of iron and carbon, usually with the addition of other elements.

**alpha decay** is the spontaneous emission of an alpha particle from a nucleus. An alpha particle is a stable particle formed from two protons and two neutrons. It is identical to the nucleus of the helium atom. The general equation for alpha particle decay is

$$^{A}_{Z}\mathrm{X} \rightarrow {}^{A-4}_{Z-2}\mathrm{Y} + {}^{4}_{2}\alpha + \text{energy}$$

where X is the parent nuclide and Y the daughter nuclide. The source of the energy released is the excess mass of X compared with [Y + $\alpha$]. It is released in the form of kinetic energy which is shared by the two emergent particles in the inverse ratio of their masses. Since alpha decay is characteristic of heavy nuclei, the alpha particles carry off most of the energy. All alpha particles from a pure source have the same initial energy, characteristic of the source. (See also *alpha radiation, radiation detectors, N–Z curve for stable nuclei.*)

**alpha particle scattering experiment:** the classic experiment leading to the discovery of the nucleus, carried out by Geiger and Marsden under the direction of Rutherford. The essential features of the apparatus are shown in the diagram below. The alpha particle beam is narrow and parallel. The vacuum is essential; alpha particles travel no more than a few centimetres in air. The gold foil has to be very thin. The detector was a zinc sulfide screen, and scintillations were observed through a microscope.

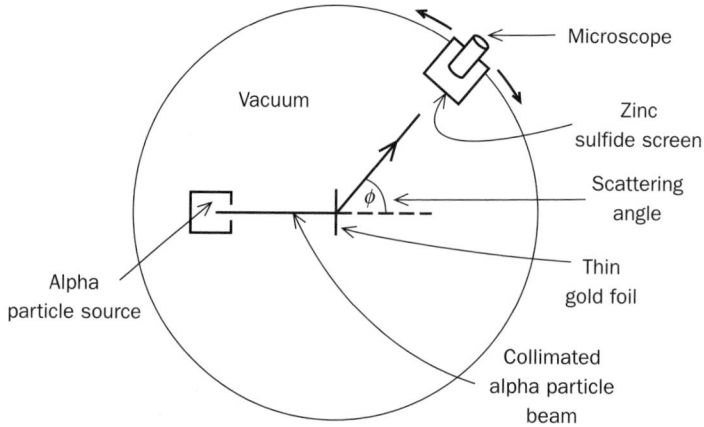


The work involved three wholly distinct stages:

***Stage 1***. Having discovered that alpha particles pass freely through thin metal sheets, Geiger and Marsden checked the possibility of reflection. This was at Rutherford's suggestion. They found that a tiny fraction of the alpha particles were reflected.

***Stage 2***. This was the theory stage. Rutherford had shown a few years earlier that alpha particles are doubly ionised helium atoms with enormous kinetic energy for their size. How could they pass through thin gold foil in their millions without producing any discernible effect in the foil. Equally, how could an atom of gold reflect an alpha particle without being torn from the foil?

Rutherford had been working on the idea that the positive charge in an atom, and almost all of its mass, are concentrated within a small central nucleus. Electrons were somehow located near the edges, so most of the atom would be empty space. An alpha particle which approached a nucleus head on would be slowed down to a stop and turned back by the repulsion between their positive charges, provided the nucleus of the gold atom were only about $10^{-14}$ m across; a larger nucleus would be broken up by the alpha particle. An alpha particle is identical to the nucleus of a helium atom and therefore very small. These ideas led Rutherford to the (simplified) scattering equation:

$$N_{\delta\phi} \propto \frac{1}{\sin^4(\phi/2)} \cdot \delta\phi$$

where $N_{\delta\phi}$ is the number of alpha particles scattered into the element of angular width $\delta\phi$ at the angle $\phi$.

***Stage 3***. Geiger and Marsden checked this result by counting $N_{\delta\phi}$ for different angles $\phi$, starting near zero and going up to almost 180°. They used different materials, different thicknesses and alpha particles of different energies. It was a demanding few months. The outcome was the verification of Rutherford's nuclear model of the atom and a close estimate of the nuclear diameter.

This experiment should be seen also as an early example of a 'scattering experiment' in which the nucleus is probed and its diameter measured. In the decades which followed, particle accelerators were built which have provided beams of electrons, protons and other *subatomic particles* to explore matter down to the details of proton structure. (See *nuclear radius.*)

**alpha particle:** a stable particle formed from two protons and two neutrons. It is identical to the nucleus of the helium atom. Some radioactive materials of high atomic number emit alpha particles and the emergent flux of alpha particles is known as *alpha radiation.*

**alpha radiation** is the outward flow of alpha particles from a radioactive source. Rutherford called it alpha radiation to underline the difference between the penetrating powers of this and the much more penetrating component, beta radiation. Gamma radiation was discovered some time later.

Rutherford used a spectroscopic technique to show that alpha particles are doubly ionised helium atoms or, as we would now say, helium nuclei. They consist of two protons and two neutrons in a tight, stable bundle.

Alpha particles from a given source have roughly equal amounts of kinetic energy and therefore approximately equal ranges in air. Alpha particles from different sources have different energies and different ranges in air. Ranges in air are never more than a few centimetres. Alpha particles are stopped altogether by thin card or a thin sheet of aluminium.

Although alpha particles are highly energetic, their comparatively large mass (about 8000 times the electron mass) ensures a much lower speed which gives greater opportunity for interactions to take place with any atom in its path. Energy absorption is strong and penetrating power low. Although a strong burst of alpha radiation could cause skin burns, a more likely hazard is deep body damage to particular tissues if an alpha particle radiator were to be ingested.

Although their charge enables them to be deflected by electric or magnetic fields, the comparatively large mass and momentum of alpha particles ensure that any deflection is slight unless the field strength is high.

The most convenient way of detecting alpha radiation is with a *GM tube* attached to a scaler. The window of the GM tube must be made of thin mica, otherwise alpha particles cannot reach the detecting gases inside the tube. (See also *attenuation*.)

**alternating current and voltage:** the word 'alternating' implies frequent change of direction. In practice, the word is mostly used in connection with mains frequency currents and voltages. Although the term could include square (or any other shape) waves in which the current or the voltage varies between positive and negative values, it is normally assumed to imply a simple sine or cosine wave variation.

Typical equations describing an AC current and an AC voltage are:

$$I = I_0 \sin \omega t = I_0 \sin 2\pi ft$$
$$V = V_0 \sin \omega t = V_0 \sin 2\pi ft$$
$$\text{where } \omega = 2\pi f \text{ and } f = \frac{1}{T}$$

Here $T$ is the period of the signal in seconds, $f$ is the frequency in Hz, $\omega$ is the angular frequency in radians per second, $I$ and $V$ are the instantaneous values of current and voltage, respectively, and $I_0$ and $V_0$ are their peak values.

The equations shown above are written in terms of sine functions, which implies that the initial (i.e. when $t = 0$) value of $I$ or $V$ is 0. If the equations were written in terms of cosine functions, the initial values of $I$ and $V$ would be $I_0$ and $V_0$, respectively.

**ammeters** measure electric current. Digital ammeters are accurate and cheap. There is no point in wondering how they work unless you have a special interest. They must be placed in series with the current to be measured, so that all the current flows through the ammeter and none bypasses it. The diagram below shows how a voltmeter and ammeter should be connected when measuring the current in, and the potential difference across, a resistor $R$.

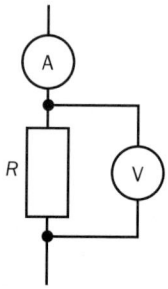

The presence of meters in a circuit can have an effect on the quantities being measured. An ammeter inevitably adds *resistance* to the circuit, thereby reducing the current it is intended to measure. An ammeter must therefore have a low resistance.

**amorphous solids** are either dust-like substances which lack any ordered structure at the atomic level, or substances such as *glasses* and some polymers which are known to have no ordered structure at the atomic level. Some *polycrystalline solids* consist of crystals so small that they are effectively amorphous on a slightly larger-than-atomic scale. Amorphous means without form.

**ampere:** the *SI* unit of current. It is one of the seven SI *base units*. The symbol for the ampere is A.

The definition of the ampere is the end point of a sequence of ideas. Picture two infinitely long, straight and parallel conductors carrying currents $I_1$ and $I_2$ a distance $d$ apart in vacuum. The current in each wire results in a magnetic field which exerts a force on the current in the other wire. The force of attraction per unit length, $F$, is found to be as follows:

$$F = \left(\frac{\mu_0}{2\pi}\right)\frac{I_1 I_2}{d}$$

where $\mu_0$ is the permeability of free space.

Now look at the SI definition of the ampere:

> 'The ampere is that constant current which, when flowing in two straight, parallel conductors of infinite length, of negligible circular cross-section, and placed one metre apart in vacuum, produces a force between the two wires of $2 \times 10^{-7}$ newtons per metre of length.'

If these values are substituted into the above formula, we find that

$$\mu_0 = 4\pi \times 10^{-7}\,\mathrm{H\,m^{-1}}$$

The ampere is thus defined by setting a particular and exact magnitude for the permeability of a vacuum, $\mu_0$. (See also *permeability of free space, permittivity of free space, speed of light.*)

**amplitude** is the maximum displacement from its rest position of a body in *simple harmonic motion*. When the definition is extended to wave motion, it means the maximum displacement of the medium when a wave flows through it. The definition can be carried beyond this to the maximum value of any oscillating quantity. The energy associated with either a simple harmonic oscillation or a wave form is proportional to the square of the amplitude. (See also *loudness.*)

**amplitude modulation** (AM) means linking an information wave to a carrier wave by simple addition of their amplitudes in preparation for transmission. The process was originally used when mounting a sound frequency wave on to a radio frequency carrier wave for radio transmission. (See *modulation.*)

**analogue signal:** a signal whose *amplitude* can take any value between reasonable limits and which can vary with time. This changing amplitude with time carries information. A *sound wave* is an analogue signal. The term is used mostly to describe a voltage that varies continuously with time, recording the time variation pattern of some other physical quantity that the voltage signal represents. The output voltage of a *thermocouple*, for example, suitably amplified, will trace the temperature variations with time to which the thermocouple is exposed.

**analogue-to-digital conversion** (A to D conversion) describes the action of a type of integrated circuit used to convert an *analogue signal* to a *digital signal*. The converter first samples the voltage levels of an analogue input signal at fixed (and very short) intervals of time. This timing is governed by a clock which drives two switches in antiphase. The *sampling* is usually achieved by charging a small capacitor to the instantaneous voltage level of the signal. This happens when the first switch is active. Next, the clock opens the first switch and closes the second switch. The voltage pulse from the charged capacitor is applied to a logic circuit whose output encodes the magnitude of the charge stored in the form of a binary number. An encoded binary number is illustrated in the diagram.

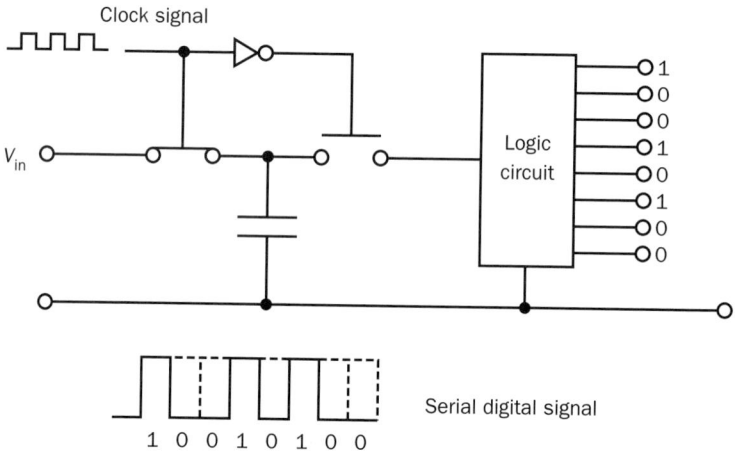


An 8-bit *digital signal* like that shown in the diagram can represent any integer of magnitude from 0 to 255 (i.e. 256 values) but not the fractional values in between. This means that the analogue signal has been 'quantised'. One consequence of this is that low voltages are represented with greater relative error than larger voltages: a digital signal of 233 units, say, is known to ±½ unit, i.e. 1 part in about 250. But a digital signal of amplitude 3 units, also known to ±½ unit, is known with an accuracy of about 1 part in 3 only. This disadvantage of the encoding process can be improved by *companding*.

The diagram shows the output of an analogue-to digital converter as the parallel output from eight pins. The signals are usually converted to serial form for transmission. The two ends of the serial signal must be defined by coded start and finish pulses.

**analogue transmission systems** rely on the *amplitude* of the transmitted wave being a faithful copy in time of the amplitude of the original voltage signal. The advantage compared with digital transmission is simplicity; the disadvantage is the increased *noise* imposed by the transmission process, especially at the reception stage.

**angle** is the inclination of one line relative to another. The magnitude of an angle can be given in one of two units. The commonly used unit, the degree, is defined as one complete rotation divided by 360. The diagram below defines the magnitude of an angle in *radians*:

$$\text{angle in radians} = \frac{\text{arc length}}{\text{radius}}$$

$$\theta = \frac{AB}{r}$$

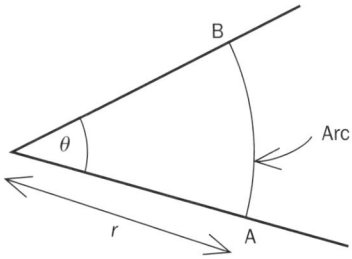


Care must be taken when using trigonometric functions (sine, cosine etc.) on a calculator — make sure that the calculator is set to work with the appropriate unit of angle. Most calculators offer three options: degree, radian and grad (where there are 100 grad in a right angle).

**angular acceleration** is the rate of increase of *angular velocity*. The symbol used is $\alpha$. The SI unit is rad $s^{-2}$. At A-level you will work only with constant angular acceleration, and in these circumstances the defining word equation is constructed by analogy with the definition of uniform acceleration:

$$\text{uniform angular acceleration} = \frac{\text{final angular velocity} - \text{initial angular velocity}}{\text{time interval}}$$

$$\alpha = \frac{\omega_2 - \omega_1}{t}$$

where $\omega_1$ and $\omega_2$ are, respectively, the initial and final angular velocities and $t$ is the time interval for which the uniform angular acceleration operates. (See *angle, rotational motion (equations of), radian, angular speed, torque.*)

**angular displacement** is the *angle* through which a body turns; it is usually measured in *radians*. The diagram shows a body before and after it has turned through an angle of 0.8 radians; the angular displacement is 0.8 radians. (See *rotational motion (equations of), angular velocity.*)

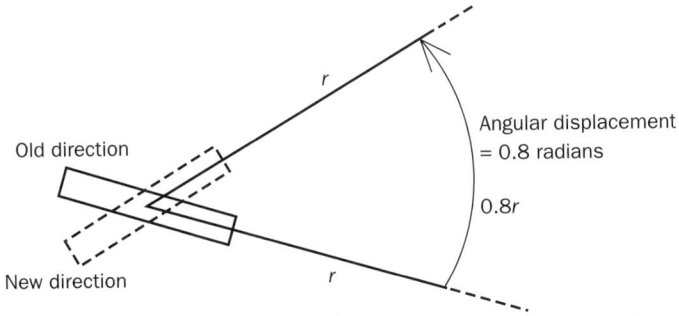


**angular frequency** is the frequency of a sinusoidal motion, whether mechanical, electrical or electromagnetic. It is measured in radians per second (not cycles per second), and is denoted by the symbol $\omega$ (Greek letter omega).

Because there are $2\pi$ radians in a complete circle, the angular frequency in radians per second is related to the frequency $f$ in cycles per second by the relation $\omega = 2\pi f$.

**angular kinetic energy:** another name for *rotational energy.*

**angular momentum** is the product of *moment of inertia* and *angular velocity.* It is a special kind of vector quantity known as a 'pseudo-vector'. Most elementary particles have an intrinsic angular momentum and another component of angular momentum linked to nearby force fields. The latter component for electrons in atoms explains the splitting of spectral lines when the source is placed in an intense magnetic field. Angular momentum is a conserved quantity.

**angular speed** is the rate of change of the angular direction of a radius joining a point on a rigid body to the axis about which it is rotating. The angular speed of a body moving along a circular path is the angular speed of the radius joining the body to the circle's centre. Angular speed is a scalar quantity; its SI unit is radians per second, rad $s^{-1}$. The symbol used is $\omega$.

Angular speed is defined by the word equation

$$\text{angular speed} = \frac{\text{angle turned}}{\text{time interval}}$$

$$\omega = \frac{\theta}{t}$$

$$\text{unit of angular speed} = \frac{\text{radian}}{\text{second}}$$

Also

$$\text{angle turned in radians} = \frac{\text{arc length}}{\text{radius}}$$

$$\frac{\text{angle turned in radians}}{\text{time interval}} = \frac{\text{arc length}}{\text{time interval}} \times \frac{1}{\text{radius}}$$

$$\omega = \frac{v}{r}$$

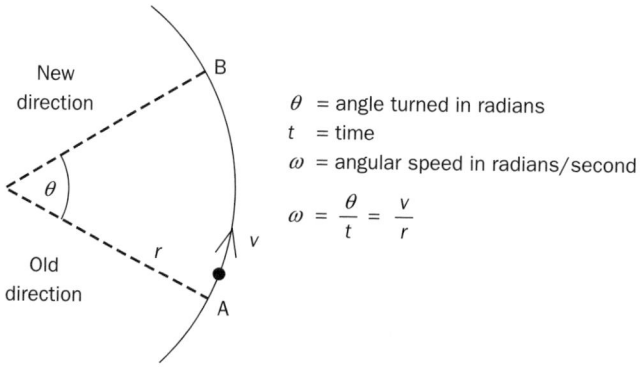


This last equation is an important relationship linking the angular speed $\omega$ for a body moving along a circular path of radius $r$ to the speed $v$ of the body along the circular path. Notice that the quantity in the equation is speed, not velocity. Angular speeds should not be in degrees per second and certainly not in revs per anything. (See *angle, radian, angular velocity, angular acceleration, rotational motion (equations of), centripetal force.*)

**angular velocity** is a vector quantity used in A-level physics to define angular momentum and angular acceleration. Even then, the vector qualities of angular velocity and angular momentum are ignored. Several books use the term 'angular velocity' when they really mean *angular speed.*

**annihilation** occurs when a particle meets its antiparticle. For example, if an *electron* meets its antiparticle, a *positron*, the two disappear and their mass energy reappears in the form of two gamma photons. These photons must travel in opposite directions if momentum is to be conserved. (See *antimatter.*)

Electron–positron annihilation is made use of in *PET scanning*, where the source of each pair of gamma photons can be traced, allowing an image to be constructed that shows where a positron-emitting tracer is located in a patient's body.

**antimatter** is a collective term for antiparticles. An antiparticle has mass in the ordinary sense — it will move in the direction of the force which pushes it. The special property of an antiparticle is that it will annihilate when it meets a corresponding particle. The combined rest mass energy of the particle–antiparticle pair is released in the form of two photons travelling in opposite directions. The quantum numbers allotted to an antiparticle (e.g. –1 for the lepton number of a positron and +1 for its charge) ensure that the conservation laws apply to any event in which an antiparticle is involved. (See *annihilation.*)

**antinode:** the point on a *stationary wave* where amplitude is a maximum. Antinodes form at those points where the component waves always arrive in phase. The formation of antinodes is an example of *constructive interference.*

**Archimedes' principle** states that a body that is wholly or partially immersed in a fluid is acted on by an upward force equal to the weight of fluid displaced. The upward force is called an *upthrust.* The resultant force on the body is the difference between the upthrust and the body's weight. This difference is zero for a floating body, i.e. upthrust and weight are equal and opposite.

A hot air balloon rises when the upthrust on it is greater than its weight. In order to reach a greater depth, a diver may attach lead weights to his suit so that his weight will be greater than the upthrust on him.

The first part of the diagram below shows a stone suspended in air from a newton balance. The weight of the stone in air, $W_{air}$, is recorded. The second part of the diagram shows the same stone suspended from the same newton balance but immersed in water. The weight of the stone wholly immersed in water, $W_{water}$, is recorded.

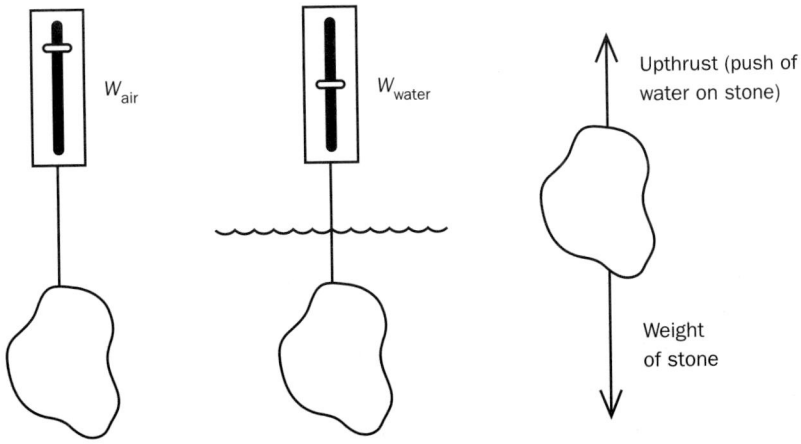

The water pushes up on the stone with a force equal to the weight of water whose place has been taken up by the stone. This is shown in the free-body force diagram.

$$\text{upthrust on stone} = W_{\text{air}} - W_{\text{water}} = \text{weight of water displaced}$$

It is easy to calculate the masses of the stone and of the displaced water in kilograms from their weights in newtons. The volume of the displaced water can be calculated from its mass and the known density of water. This equals the volume of the stone.

Once both the mass of the stone and its volume are known, its density can be calculated.

The same stone could now be used to measure the *density* of any liquid other than water from a measurement of the upthrust on the stone when wholly immersed in the new liquid.

The origin of the upthrust on a body lies in the *pressure* exerted on it. Pressure in a fluid increases with depth; hence, if we consider the stone in the diagram, the upward pressure on the lower surface of the stone will be greater than the downward pressure on the upper surface. The consequence is a net upward force on the stone, which is the upthrust.

**astigmatism:** a defect of vision caused by deformation of the *eye*, with the result that vertical and horizontal lines are focused at different distances. (See *defects of vision.*)

**astronomical unit** (AU) is a unit of distance used in astronomy. It is equal to the distance between the Earth and the Sun averaged over one year. 1 AU = 149 597 870 km. (See *light year, parsec.*)

**astronomy** is the study of the universe as a whole. The main divisions are *astrophysics* (the study of stars) and cosmology (the study of galaxies and the structure of the universe). (See also *star, Hertzsprung–Russell diagram, end states of stars, galaxies* and *telescopes.*)

**astrophysics** is about different kinds of stars and the varied processes that are going on inside them. The life of a star starts from an enormous cloud of hydrogen (with small amounts of other elements). The particles that make up this cloud are widely separated and attract one another gravitationally. As the particles 'fall' towards their common centre of gravity, their gravitational potential energy decreases and is transformed to kinetic energy. Collisions between the particles result in a sharing of this energy and a randomising of the particles' motion. The result is a hot, dense cloud of hydrogen. The centre of the cloud gets hotter and hotter at a rate depending on the mass of hydrogen in the cloud. The mass of the Sun, $1.99 \times 10^{30}$ kg, is known with some accuracy. The masses of about 200 stars (members of double star systems) have been measured directly and the rest of our knowledge is built on generalisations from this basic data. Even so, it is known that stellar masses range from about $10^{28}$ kg to about $10^{32}$ kg. Below this range, the temperature inside a star is never high enough for *nuclear reactions* to start. At best, a low-mass star may release so much gravitational energy that, for a short while, it glows. These stars are known as brown dwarfs, but they have never been observed with any certainty. (The term 'brown' is curious — brown is not a spectral colour.) Above the high end of the mass range, the nuclear reactions would be too violent for any star to remain in a stable condition. Stars within the allowed range are called main sequence stars. (See *star* and *Hertzsprung–Russell diagram.*)

Most of the energy released from main sequence stars derives from the so-called pp chain of reactions (where pp stands for proton–proton). This reaction chain is summarised in three equations:

$$
\begin{aligned}
{}^{1}_{1}\mathrm{p}^{+} + {}^{1}_{1}\mathrm{p}^{+} &\rightarrow {}^{2}_{1}\mathrm{H}^{+} + {}^{0}_{1}\mathrm{e}^{+} + \nu_e \\
{}^{2}_{1}\mathrm{H}^{+} + {}^{1}_{1}\mathrm{p}^{+} &\rightarrow {}^{3}_{2}\mathrm{He}^{2+} + \gamma \\
{}^{3}_{2}\mathrm{He}^{2+} + {}^{3}_{2}\mathrm{He}^{2+} &\rightarrow {}^{4}_{2}\mathrm{He}^{2+} + {}^{1}_{1}\mathrm{p}^{+} + \gamma
\end{aligned}
$$

This set of reactions can get started only if two protons approach one another with enough kinetic energy to overcome the repulsion between their positive charges. This happens once the core temperature reaches about $10^7$ K. To increase the power output, two more conditions must hold:

1 the core temperature must be well above $10^7$ K
2 there must be a high proton density in the core

High-mass stars have higher core temperatures and higher core densities than low-mass stars: they 'burn' faster, they are brighter and their lifetimes are shorter. Hence, the mass of a star correlates with luminosity, and as we move up the main sequence to the brighter stars on the Hertzsprung–Russell diagram, stellar mass increases.

Most stellar energy comes from the burning of hydrogen. Once the hydrogen begins to become scarce, a new set of reactions involving the helium nuclei starts up. What happens next depends on the mass of the star.

A main sequence star can burn for a set life span. The later stages in the life of a star are described in *end states of stars*. The measurement of the distances of nearby stars is described under *parallax (stellar)*. The observed properties of stars are described under *star*.

**atmospheric pressure** usually means the *pressure* of the atmosphere at ground level. There are the large, the local and the microscopic points of view to consider. From the large point of view, air is seen as a compressible fluid with mass — a little more than 1 kg for each cubic metre. It is held on the Earth's surface by the Earth's gravity. Pressure decreases with height because the higher you go, the less atmosphere there is above to create the pressure to compress the atmosphere below.

At a local level, air pressure varies a little from day to day but is uniform enough at any given moment and over a large enough area not to have to pinpoint the place where it is measured. Its magnitude is found by balancing the thrust exerted by the air on an exposed surface against a spring of some sort or a column of mercury. (See *mercury barometer*.)

At the microscopic level, air is seen as a seething mass of countless molecules whose combined reflections on any surface they contact account for the thrust that measures the pressure.

**atomic mass unit:** an obsolete unit of mass equal to one sixteenth of the mass of an atom of oxygen-16, the commonest *isotope* of oxygen. It has been replaced by the *unified atomic mass unit*.

**atomic number,** $Z$, is the number of protons in a nucleus. An alternative name is *proton number*. It is numerically equal to the number of *extra-nuclear electrons* in the non-ionised atom and indirectly governs the chemical properties of an element. The atomic number defines the element an atom belongs to. *Isotopes* of the same element have the same chemical properties except to the extent to which these properties depend on atomic mass. (See *N–Z curve for stable nuclei.*)

**atomic theory of matter:** the theory that matter is made up of particles, called atoms, instead of being infinitely divisible into ever smaller pieces. Although atomic theories have been discussed for more than two thousand years, the modern theory started with the discovery of the laws of chemical combination early in the nineteenth century. It is now universally accepted and the stress has been on understanding atomic and nuclear structure.

The word 'atom' is derived from Greek and refers to something which cannot be cut or divided. Today we know that there are physical processes by which an atom can be split.

**attenuation** is the weakening of a beam of particles (or of electromagnetic radiation) by any material placed in its path. It may be due to scattering or to absorption processes. Either way, the degree of the attenuation is given by an attenuation coefficient.

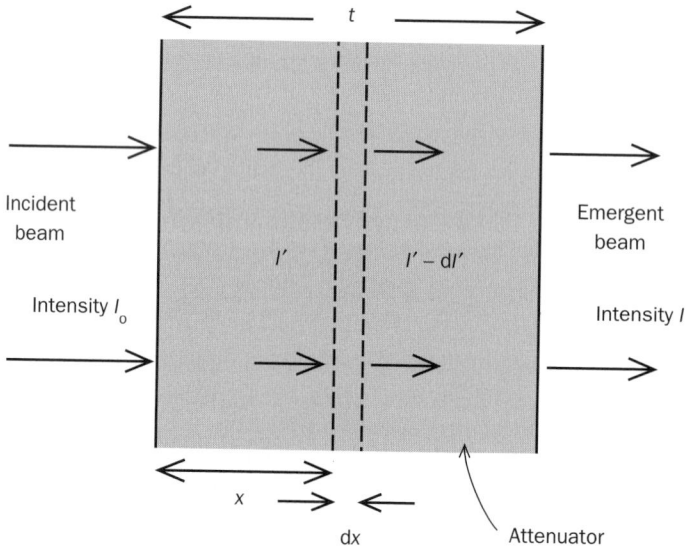


The diagram shows a beam of radiation or particles, incident at the surface of a sheet of material of thickness $t$. A thin section of thickness d$x$ is shown a distance $x$ from the incident surface. The incident intensity $I_0$ is the energy carried to the incident surface per square metre per second. $I$ is the intensity of the emergent beam and $I'$ is the intermediate intensity. Alternatively, $I$ could represent the number of particles crossing unit area per unit time.

If d$x$ is small, then

$$dI' = -\mu I' dx$$

where $\mu$, defined by this equation, is the linear attenuation coefficient for the material exposed to this particular beam. The equation can be integrated over the full thickness of the specimen to give an exponential law:

$$I = I_0 \, e^{-\mu t}$$

The half-thickness $x_{1/2}$ of a material is the thickness of that material which will absorb half of the radiation passing through it. The half-thickness and linear attenuation coefficient are related in the same way that the *half-life* and decay constant are related, namely

$$x_{1/2} = \frac{\ln 2}{\mu}$$

*X-rays* are often identified by the working voltage of the tube from which they come. For X-rays up to about 100 kV, attenuation is primarily a consequence of the *photoelectric effect*. The efficiency with which a material absorbs X-rays by this mechanism increases in proportion to $Z^3$ where $Z$ is the atomic number. This is why bones show up so well on X-ray photographs. At around a million volts, *Compton scattering* takes over and this mechanism is independent of atomic number. This is why mega-voltage therapy is used to destroy offending tissue.

For *alpha radiation*, absorption in solids is too immediate for the exponential law to be of much interest. It works well for beta and gamma radiation. There is the complicating problem with *beta radiation* that the electrons produce X-rays when suddenly stopped in hard matter. These X-rays, known as bremsstrahlung, cause a severe deviation from the exponential decay law, as recorded by a *GM tube*, when a large fraction of the beta particles is lost from the beam.

A low attenuation coefficient corresponds to high penetrating power and vice versa.

**Avogadro constant** is the number of carbon atoms in 0.012 kg of carbon-12. It equals, by definition, the number of elementary entities in a mole. It is denoted by either $L$ or $N_A$, and its magnitude is approximately $6.022 \times 10^{23}\,\text{mol}^{-1}$.

**A–Z Online**

Log on to A–Z Online to search the database of terms, print revision lists and much more. Go to **www.philipallan.co.uk/a-zonline** to get started.

# B

**back e.m.f.** is an alternative name for *induced e.m.f.*, which stresses the directional element of the induced e.m.f.

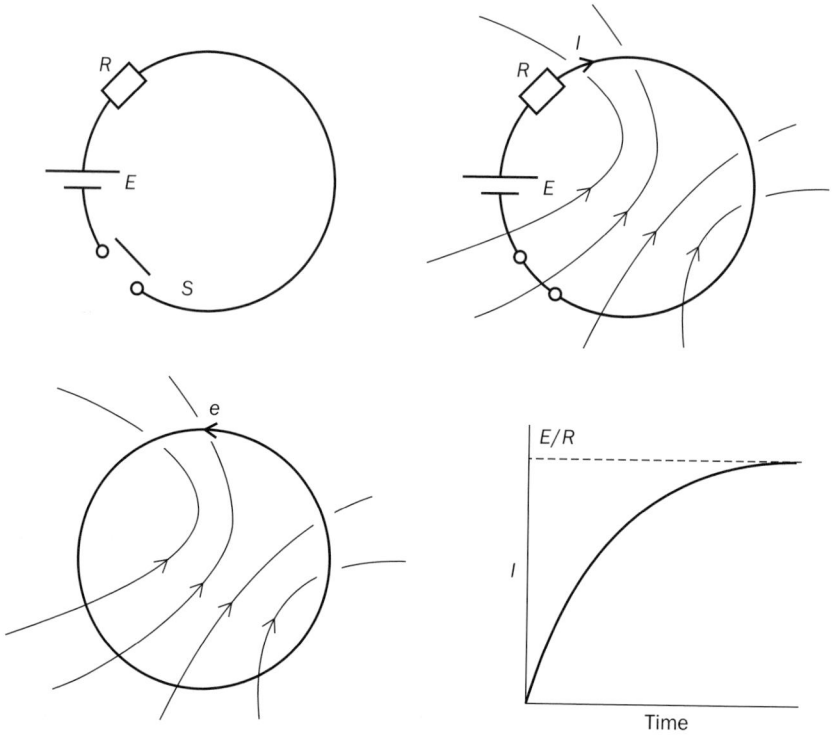


Consider the above set of related diagrams. The first diagram shows a cell of e.m.f. $E$ in series with a resistor of resistance $R$ and an open switch S. The second diagram shows the situation some time after the switch has been closed. There is a steady current $I$ in the circuit and this has an associated magnetic field passing through the circuit. The third diagram shows the growing magnetic field and the induced e.m.f. $e$ immediately after the switch S is closed. This induced e.m.f. arises because the circuit is in a changing magnetic field.

How can we determine the direction of the induced e.m.f.? Start by considering what would happen if $e$ were in the opposite direction to that shown, so that it would add on to $E$. The total e.m.f. in the circuit would then become greater than $E$, and this would cause the current to be greater than $I$. As the current increases, so will $e$, and thus the current will grow exponentially; but this would offend against the law of conservation of energy and cannot be considered as a feasible outcome. Hence we can deduce that the third diagram shows correctly the direction of the induced e.m.f., which must oppose the supply voltage. For this reason it is called a 'back' e.m.f.

Notice that the effect of the back e.m.f. is to slow down the growth of the current to its final value. From the graph it can be seen that initially the current is zero but growing rapidly. This gives a large back e.m.f. opposing $E$. As the current increases, its rate of increase decreases so that the back e.m.f. also decreases. The actual curve followed by the graph depends on the resistance $R$ and on the inductance $L$ of the circuit loop. Inductance in an electric circuit behaves likes mass in a mechanical situation. (See *electromagnetic induction (laws of).*)

**background radiation** is the recorded count rate in the absence of any radiation sources which are about to be monitored. It is the count rate linked to the environment, and its principal sources are: (a) atmospheric radon gas, (b) rocks and building materials, and (c) cosmic radiation. The strengths of these sources depend on the immediate environment. The strength of cosmic radiation is roughly one particle per square centimetre per second, but this depends on altitude.

The measured count rate near a radioactive source exceeds the true count rate by the background radiation count rate. To ignore the background radiation count rate would be to introduce a *systematic error* into the experiment. It is good practice to measure the background radiation count rate several times during an experiment and then to take an average.

**bandwidth:** the range of frequencies used for a given purpose, e.g. for broadcasting a radio or TV channel.

**bar:** a unit of pressure equal to $10^5$ Pa or 0.1 MPa. *Atmospheric pressure* rises and falls by a few per cent on either side of 1000 mbar. Meteorologists use the millibar because it can easily be converted into pascals (1 mbar = 100 Pa) and used in analytical equations with SI units, whereas pressures in units of the standard atmosphere are more awkward. (See *standard pressure.*)

**barium meal** is used, for example, when the alimentary canal of a patient needs to be examined. Alimentary canal tissue is so similar to other nearby tissues in its absorption of X-rays that it does not show up clearly in a usual X-ray image — there is too little contrast. To overcome this problem, the patient swallows fluid containing barium sulfate. Because barium is a good absorber of X-rays, this renders the alimentary canal opaque so that its structure (including any blockages or other defects) will show up with high contrast in the X-ray image. (See *contrast medium.*)

**barometer:** see *mercury barometer.*

**baryons** are *hadrons* made up of three *quarks* to give integral or zero charge, baryon number 1 or –1 and spin ½. Masses are rarely much higher than 1 GeV/$c^2$. The proton and neutron masses are 0.938 GeV/$c^2$ and 0.939 GeV/$c^2$, respectively. Although there are lots of possible baryons that could be formed, given that there are 12 different quarks and antiquarks, all baryons other than *protons* and *neutrons* are short-lived.

Protons and neutrons are stable within the *nucleus.* The neutron is unstable outside the nucleus: it decays, with *half-life* about a quarter of an hour, into a proton, an *electron* and an antineutrino. Other baryons decay with half-lives of around $10^{-10}$ s if the strong interaction is responsible for the decay, or with a half-life of around $10^{-24}$ s if the weak interaction is responsible for the decay. (See *Feynman diagrams* for the beta decays of protons and neutrons.)

Protons have charge $+e$ and the quark mix uud; neutrons have charge zero and the quark mix udd. Protons and neutrons are long-lived partly because the u and d quarks are themselves stable. Beta decay occurs when the weak interaction prompts a d quark to change into a u quark within a neutron, or (less likely) a u quark to change into a d quark within a proton.

The main properties of eight important baryons are summarised in the following table. The quantum numbers of the corresponding antiparticles are not shown, but they have the same magnitudes with opposite signs. Particles are built from quarks, and their antiparticles are built from the corresponding antiquarks.

| **Name** | **Quantum numbers** | | | **Quark** content |
|---|---|---|---|---|
| | Q | B | S | |
| proton | +1 | 1 | 0 | uud |
| neutron | 0 | 1 | 0 | udd |
| lambda | 0 | 1 | –1 | uds |
| sigma plus | +1 | 1 | –1 | uus |
| sigma minus | –1 | 1 | –1 | dds |
| sigma zero | 0 | 1 | –1 | uds |
| xi minus | –1 | 1 | –2 | dss |
| xi zero | 0 | 1 | –2 | uss |

**base quantity:** one of the seven physical quantities corresponding to the seven *base units* in *SI*. They are length, mass, time, electric current, temperature difference, amount of substance and luminous intensity.

**base unit:** one of the seven base units of *SI* whose magnitudes are defined without reference to other units (although they may refer to one another). They are as follows:

- metre, unit of length, symbol m: the distance travelled by light in vacuum during a time interval of 1/299 792 458 of a second
- kilogram, unit of mass, symbol kg: the mass of the International Prototype Kilogram held at Sèvres in France
- second, unit of time, symbol s: the duration of 9 192 631 770 periods of the radiation corresponding to the transition between the two hyperfine levels of the ground state of the caesium-133 atom
- ampere, unit of electric current, symbol A: the constant current which, by flowing in two parallel and infinitely long straight conductors of negligible cross-section held one metre apart in vacuum, sets up a force on these conductors equal to $2\times10^{-7}$ newtons per metre of length
- kelvin, unit of thermodynamic temperature difference, symbol K: the thermodynamic temperature difference between absolute thermodynamic zero and the triple point of water divided by 273.16

- mole, unit of amount of substance, symbol mol: the amount of substance which contains as many elementary entities as there are atoms of carbon in 0.012 kg of carbon-12
- candela, unit of luminous intensity, symbol cd: the luminous intensity in a given direction of a source which emits monochromatic radiation of frequency $540 \times 10^{12}$ Hz and whose radiant intensity in that direction is 1/683 watt per steradian

These seven units are the complete set. You are unlikely to need the candela at A-level. These definitions form an internationally agreed basis for measurement; however, they are always subject to review and new definitions may be authorised by the General Conference on Weights and Measures (CGPM, from its French initials) which meets every 4–6 years.

(See *base quantity, prefixes used with SI units, metre, kilogram, second, ampere, kelvin, mole, candela.*)

**beams** are long bars of rigid material used for bridging gaps. A beam is possibly the simplest example of a *structure*. The exaggerated sagging of the beam in the diagram highlights that, when in place, the lower half of a beam is in tension whilst the upper half is in compression. The tension along the lower half of the beam can only be withstood by a material which is strong, and the deflection will be small only for a material with a high Young modulus. This is why steel is favoured for beams. Where concrete is used, the beam is reinforced with steel rods along its lower half. Concrete beams are even stronger if tensioned steel rods are used to pre-stress the concrete. A low value for the bending implies high stiffness. (See *composite materials, rigidity, strength, cantilever.*)

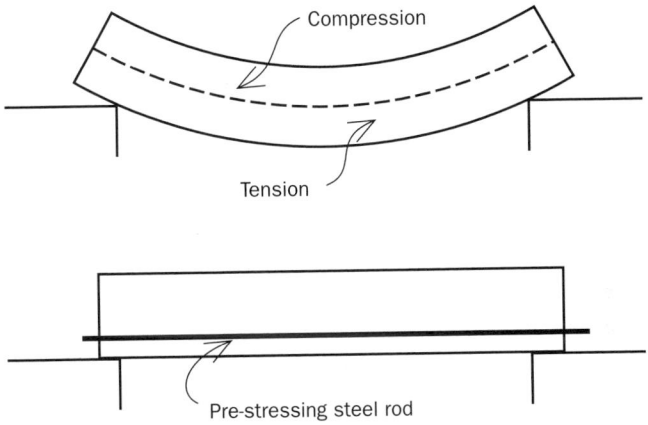


**beats** occur when two sound waves of similar frequencies superimpose. As the waves move in and out of phase with each other, they interfere first constructively and then destructively. The ear hears a single note whose loudness varies regularly at the beat frequency, which equals the difference between the frequencies of the two waves. (See *constructive interference, destructive interference.*)

**becquerel:** the SI unit of *activity*; the symbol used is Bq. A radioactive source of activity (strength) 1 Bq has an activity of one disintegration per second. Note that this is not the same as the hertz, which is the unit of *frequency*. (See *fundamental law of radioactive decay.*)

**beta decay** is the spontaneous emission of a beta particle from a nucleus. Beta decay is accompanied by *neutrino* emission and the release of energy. If the beta particle is negatively charged, it is an electron and an antineutrino is expelled from the nucleus at the same time. If the beta particle is positively charged, it is a positron and a neutrino is expelled at the same time.

The general equation for $\beta^-$ decay is

$$^{A}_{Z}X \rightarrow {}^{A}_{Z+1}Y + {}^{0}_{-1}e + \bar{\nu} + \text{energy}$$

where X is the parent nuclide, Y is the daughter nuclide and $\bar{\nu}$ represents an antineutrino. The mass of the antineutrino, if it has any, is too small to measure and the energy released comes from the mass excess of X compared with [Y+e].

If there were no antineutrinos, all beta particles from a pure source would have the same energy — as is the case with alpha particles. But beta particles are known to have a spread of energies up to a maximum value decided by the mass difference between the two sides of the decay expression (see *beta radiation*).The neutrino was 'invented' to allow for this spread of energies while retaining the conservation of energy law. Later still, when it was recognised that electrons and neutrinos are both *leptons* and that lepton number must be conserved in the decay process, the neutrino was relabelled as an antineutrino. The origin of beta decay is the decay, within the nucleus, of a neutron into a proton with the emission of an electron and an antineutrino (See *Feynman diagrams*).

If a beta particle is positively charged, it is a positron, in which case a neutrino is expelled at the same time. For $\beta^+$ or positron decay, the decay equation is written as

$$^{A}_{Z}X \rightarrow {}^{A}_{Z-1}Y + {}^{0}_{+1}e + \nu + \text{energy}$$

where $\nu$ represents a neutrino.

$\beta^+$ decay is a rare event, mostly because any nuclei that are likely to decay this way are much more likely to decay by electron-capture. See also *beta radiation*, *N–Z curve for stable nuclei*, *fundamental interactions* and *proton decay and neutron decay.*

**beta particle:** an *electron* or a *positron* emitted from the nucleus of an atom during radioactive decay. A flux of beta particles is called *beta radiation.*

**beta radiation** consists primarily of electrons emitted from radioactive nuclei, but the term also covers streams of positrons (positively charged antielectrons). The properties of a beam of *beta particles* seem not to be quite the same as those of a beam of electrons in a cathode ray tube, for instance. This is because electrons in a cathode ray or fine beam tube are accelerated through a few thousand volts, whereas electrons expelled from a nucleus during *beta decay* have about a thousand times as much energy. Beta particles are deflected by magnetic fields, but a much stronger field is needed to give even a modest deflection than with the lower speed electron beam. Beta particles penetrate a thin aluminium sheet whereas a low speed electron beam would do no more than warm its surface. The high penetrating power makes beta radiation a severe health hazard to any animal exposed to even a modest dose. Deep body damage is possible.

Alpha particles emitted from any one radioactive nuclide all have much the same energy and consequently the same range in air (see diagram below). But the diagram shows how beta particles are emitted with a range of energies from zero (improbable) to a maximum value (also improbable). The reason is that in beta decay a second particle, the antineutrino, is emitted from the nucleus and the available energy is shared between the two particles.

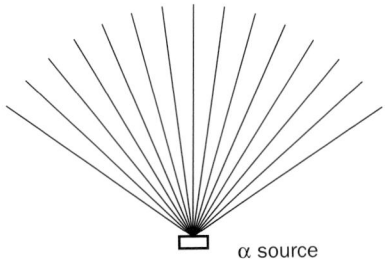


Range in air of alpha particles from a pure alpha emitter

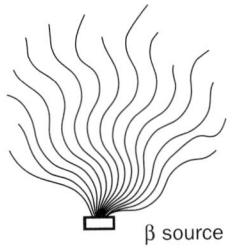


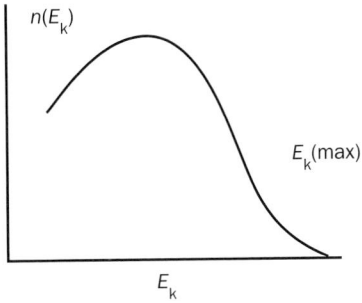


Number of beta particles with energy $E_k$, $n(E_k)$, against energy when emitted $E_k$

Beta radiation can be detected and monitored efficiently with a *GM tube* attached to a scaler.

**B-field:** a three-dimensional space in which the magnitude of the resultant *magnetic field strength B* at any point is mostly non-zero. The zero values of *B* are found at so-called *neutral points*.

**Big Bang theory:** the major theory that attempts to explain the history of the universe. The universe is believed to have emerged from a single point approximately 13.7 billion years ago and been expanding outwards ever since. There are three major pieces of supporting evidence:

- observations of the expansion of the universe, as summarised by *Hubble's law*
- the existence and near uniformity of the *cosmic microwave background (CMB) radiation*
- the relative proportions of the elements in the early universe, as observed in young galaxies (mostly hydrogen, some helium, and tiny amounts of lithium and beryllium)

This theory unites observations on the scale of the entire universe with observations of the properties of fundamental particles — a remarkable achievement.

Since the time of the Big Bang, the universe has been expanding and cooling. It has gone through different 'eras' as different particles have condensed out of the initial hot 'soup' of *quarks* and *leptons*. Quarks combined to form hadrons; then helium nuclei formed, followed by atoms as electrons combined with nuclei. At this stage, after about $3 \times 10^5$

years, the universe became transparent to electromagnetic radiation, and the CMB has existed since this time.

**binding energy** is the energy which would be released were a heavy nucleus to be formed spontaneously from its constituent particles. A simple example is offered by the alpha particle. The masses of the relevant particles are listed below in kilograms and as multiples of the *unified atomic mass unit* u.

proton mass $= 1.672\,623 \times 10^{-27}$ kg $= 1.007\,276$ u

neutron mass $= 1.674\,928 \times 10^{-27}$ kg $= 1.008\,665$ u

alpha particle $= 6.64\,446 \times 10^{-27}$ kg $= 4.0015$ u

The total mass of two protons and two neutrons is $6.695\,103 \times 10^{-27}$ kg or 4.031 883 u.

The *mass defect* for the alpha particle is thus $5.066 \times 10^{-29}$ kg or 0.0305 u.

This 'lost mass' has energy-equivalent ($\Delta m.c^2$) equal to $4.553 \times 10^{-12}$ J or 28.4 MeV, and this is the binding energy of the alpha particle.

The term 'binding energy' can be confusing and may lead you to think that it refers to energy stored in a nucleus. In fact, it is the energy lost by a nucleus upon its formation from separate, isolated nucleons. Hence, the binding energy of a nucleus is the work which would have to be done to separate it into its constituent particles. The *binding energy per nucleon* for the alpha particle is 7.10 MeV per nucleon.

**binding energy per nucleon** for an atomic nucleus equals the *binding energy* for the nucleus divided by the number of *nucleons*. The graph below shows in broad terms how binding energy per nucleon varies with atomic number *Z*.

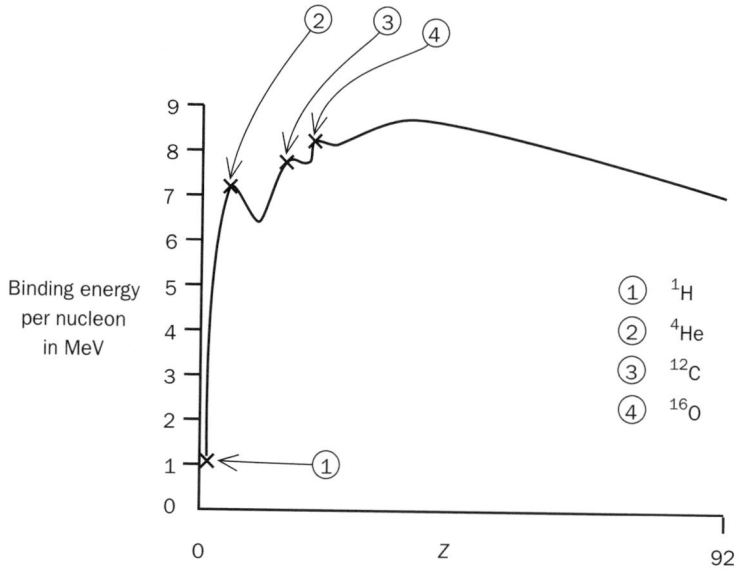


The smoothed out graph peaks near iron-56. Since binding energy is energy released on formation, not stored energy, it is clear that light nuclei can release energy by fusing (going to a state of higher atomic number and higher binding energy) while heavy nuclei can release energy by breaking up (fission).

Some specifications and textbooks present this graph the other way up, emphasising the low energy state represented by nuclides in the central region of the chart.

**biofuels** are materials such as wood which store solar energy recently harnessed by living matter. The term biofuels should not be extended to include *fossil fuels*. Peat is a fossil fuel; wood is a biofuel. Secondary biofuels are produced by the processing of crops such as maize and sugarcane to produce biodiesel, biogas and other fuels. (See *energy sources*.)

**black body radiation** and total radiation mean the same thing. (See *total radiation curve*.)

**black hole:** the end state of a main sequence star whose mass exceeds about $20M_{Sun}$. The gravitational field near the surface of a black hole is so strong that nothing, not even light, can escape. However, beyond this distance, there is nothing unusual about the *gravitational field strength* of a black hole — it obeys *Newton's law of universal gravitation*, so that its strength is proportional to the mass of the black hole and decreases as the inverse square of the distance. It is incorrect to imagine that the gravitational field of a black hole somehow reaches out more powerfully into space than the field of the star from which it formed.

It is believed that many galaxies, including our own (the Milky Way), have a supermassive black hole at their centres. A supermassive black hole has a mass in excess of $10^5$ solar masses. There is no reliable theory of how these form — it may be that they represent old black holes which have gradually drawn in matter over billions of years; they may have formed from single giant stars; or they may have been formed during the Big Bang. (See *end states of stars*.)

**Boltzmann constant** $k$ equals the ratio $R/L$ where $R$ is the gas constant per mole and $L$ is the Avogadro constant. Since $L$ equals the number of molecules in a mole, $k$ represents the gas constant per molecule of gas and its unit is $\mathrm{J\,K^{-1}}$. The value of the Boltzmann constant is $1.38 \times 10^{-23}\,\mathrm{J\,K^{-1}}$.

Note that the phrase 'gas constant per molecule' means the increase in the gas constant for a specimen of gas, per molecule added to the specimen. It does not mean the gas constant for an isolated molecule.

The formal definition of the Boltzmann constant is rooted in thermodynamics and outside the scope of this book. An important result is, however, the relationship between absolute temperature and molecular kinetic energy.

For a monatomic gas:

$$\tfrac{1}{2} m \langle c^2 \rangle = \tfrac{3}{2} kT$$

where $m$ is the molecular mass and $\langle c^2 \rangle$ is the mean square speed of the molecules. This result is used to import the temperature variable into kinetic theory. (See *kinetic theory of gases*.)

**Boyle's law** (1660) states that the pressure of a fixed mass of gas at constant temperature and in an equilibrium state is inversely proportional to its volume. The law can be stated algebraically as follows:

$$\text{provided that } m \text{ and } T \text{ are constant, } p \propto \frac{1}{V} \text{ or } p_1V_1 = p_2V_2 = \text{constant}$$

Although the law is easily derived from the *ideal gas equation*, it is an empirical law and was discovered by experiment. An account of a student experiment to verify the law should include a diagram, a list of the measurements and an explanation of how the law would be checked.

**Experiment to verify Boyle's law**

**Apparatus**

Set up apparatus similar to that shown in the diagram. There is a container, in which a fixed mass of gas is trapped, immersed in a vessel filled with water whose temperature can be checked. There is a scale from which the volume of the gas can be read. There is a means of changing the pressure of the gas and a pressure gauge to measure its new value. If the pressure gauge measures gauge pressure, then the atmospheric pressure at the time of the experiment must be measured separately.

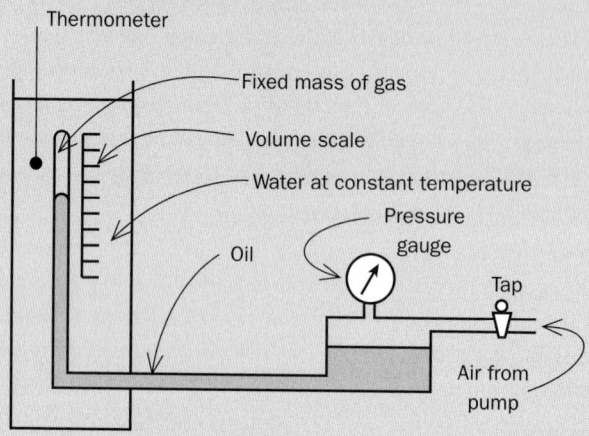


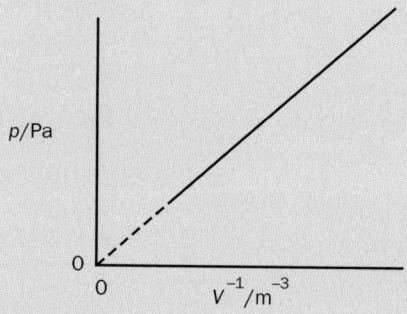


**Measurements**

Once the temperature of the gas in the container has settled down, the initial volume should be read from the volume scale and the initial pressure should be read from the pressure gauge. Using the foot-pump, the pressure should be increased in about six equal stages up to a maximum value. At each stage, the air temperature is given time to settle at its initial value and the volume and pressure values are noted. If the pressure gauge reads the gauge pressure, then the local value for atmospheric pressure should be added to all the pressure gauge values.

**Conclusion**

A graph is drawn of pressure against 1/volume. If the graph is a straight line passing through the origin, then it verifies Boyle's law at this one temperature and for the range of pressures used in the experiment.

(See *ideal gas equation, Charles' law, pressure law.*)

**breaking stress** is the tensile *stress* at which a material fractures. It is a measure of the strength of the material. Alternative terms are *strength* (which may relate to the force or the tensile stress) and *ultimate tensile stress.*

**brittleness** is the quality present in some materials (particularly glasses and *ceramics*) of breaking without warning. Brittleness implies an absence of any form of *plastic deformation* or flow to warn of an impending break up. (See also *stress–strain curves.*)

**Brownian motion** is the random and erratic motion of small particles suspended in a fluid. The suspension may be cigarette smoke in air or pollen particles in water. A particle must be small enough to move about when fewer atoms hit it on one side than on the opposite side but large enough to be visible.

The microscope objective collects light over a large angle. In this system the microscope acts more like an image intensifier than a magnifier. It brightens the spots of light and spreads them out, but the particles themselves remain invisible. If the magnification is too great, the depth of field will be too shallow and particles will be seen coming in and out of focus instead of moving around at random.

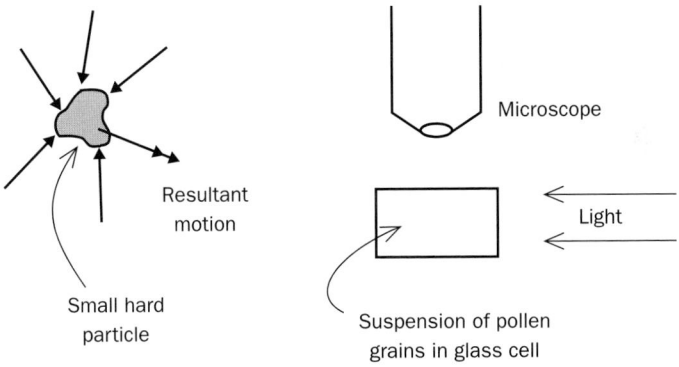


During the nineteenth century Brownian motion was little more than a novelty. Robert Brown, the Scottish botanist who first investigated the phenomenon, did not offer an explanation for it. Others argued that it demonstrated the *atomic theory of matter.* It became a significant phenomenon early in the twentieth century when, in 1905, Einstein showed how measurements of the gross movements of particles after numerous collisions could lead directly to an independent calculation of the *Avogadro constant.*

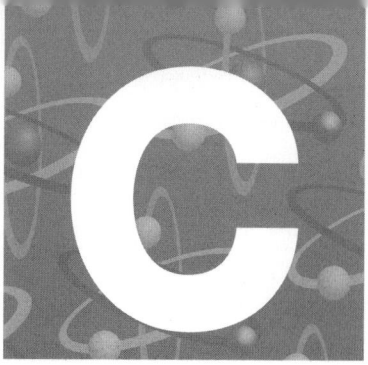

**calibration** is the procedure for marking out and interpreting the numerical scale on an instrument. An example would be converting the voltage scale on a digital voltmeter to a temperature scale to match the temperatures indicated by a particular *thermocouple*. Each number of the completed scale must be multiplied by a unit (e.g. kelvin) and possibly by a multiplier (e.g. $10^3$). (See *measurement*.)

**candela:** a *base unit* in *SI*. It is the SI unit of luminous intensity and has the symbol cd.

**cantilever:** a *beam* which is supported at one end but free at the other. The weight of the cantilever causes it to bend so that the upper surface is in tension and the lower surface is in compression.

**capacitance,** denoted by $C$, is the ratio of electric charge $Q$ on a conductor to its electric potential $V$, assuming that the electric potential of the conductor is zero when the charge is zero. Capacitance is defined by the word equation

$$\text{capacitance} = \frac{\text{charge stored}}{\text{potential difference}}$$

$$C = \frac{Q}{V}$$

The same word equation defines the SI unit of capacitance, the farad, F:

$$\text{farad} = \frac{\text{coulomb}}{\text{volt}}$$

This definition applies to an isolated conductor. It does not apply to a charged insulator; an insulator cannot have a potential because charge cannot flow across the insulator to equalise the potential.

The usual situation is to build a capacitor from conductors placed close together. They are close enough for lines of force that begin on the positively charged conductor to all end on the negatively charged conductor. Capacitance equals the charge stored on one of the conductors divided by the potential difference across the two conductors:

$$\text{capacitance} = \frac{\text{charge stored on one plate}}{\text{potential difference between plates}}$$

(See *energy stored in a capacitor, parallel plate capacitor.*)

**capacitive reactance** is the ratio of peak voltage to peak current for a capacitor. This is given by the equation

$$I_0 = \omega C V_0$$

Compare this with Ohm's law:

$$V = IR \qquad V_0 = \left(\frac{1}{\omega C}\right) I_0$$

In Ohm's law, the resistance $R$ holds the balance between current and voltage. For the capacitor, $1/(\omega C)$ holds the balance between peak voltage and peak current, but these two quantities are not in phase — the current peaks before the voltage. The term $1/(\omega C)$ is called the reactance of the capacitor. The symbol for capacitive reactance is $X_C$ and the SI unit for reactance is the ohm.

(See *frequency, phase, reactance, capacitors in AC circuits, inductive reactance, resonance in AC circuits.*)

**capacitor:** a device for storing *electric charge*. The *capacitance* of a capacitor is defined by the following word equation which can also be used to define the unit of capacitance, the *farad*.

$$\text{capacitance} = \frac{\text{charge stored}}{\text{potential difference}}$$

$$C = \frac{Q}{V}$$

$$\text{farad} = \frac{\text{coulomb}}{\text{volt}}$$

A capacitor usually has two plates which are insulated from one another, and two terminals (one attached to each plate). The potential difference $V$ is then the voltage between the terminals. Should there be one terminal only, as would be the case with the capacitance of an isolated metal spoon, then the relevant potential difference would be the voltage between the spoon and an earthed terminal somewhere.

A capacitor is generally marked with its capacitance and also with a voltage that indicates the maximum potential difference which can safely be applied across it without causing permanent damage. Curiously, capacitance is usually quoted in $\mu$F or pF, rarely in mF or nF. An *electrolytic capacitor* is marked to indicate its polarity, since it must be connected correctly to a supply. (See *parallel plate capacitor.*)

**capacitor, electrolytic:** see *electrolytic capacitor.*

**capacitor size** increases with capacitance and peak voltage (with peak charge stored). (See *electrolytic capacitor.*)

**capacitors in AC circuits** follow the same rule as capacitors in DC circuits. Charge stored is proportional to voltage: $Q = CV$. If $C$ is constant and $V$ alternates, then $Q$ will alternate in phase with $V$.

However, the current in the circuit equals the rate of increase of the charge stored on the capacitor; it is the gradient of the charge–time graph.

The diagram on the next page shows a capacitor in series with an AC supply, followed by graphs of voltage, charge and current against time. Note the use of the subscript $_0$ to indicate a peak value.

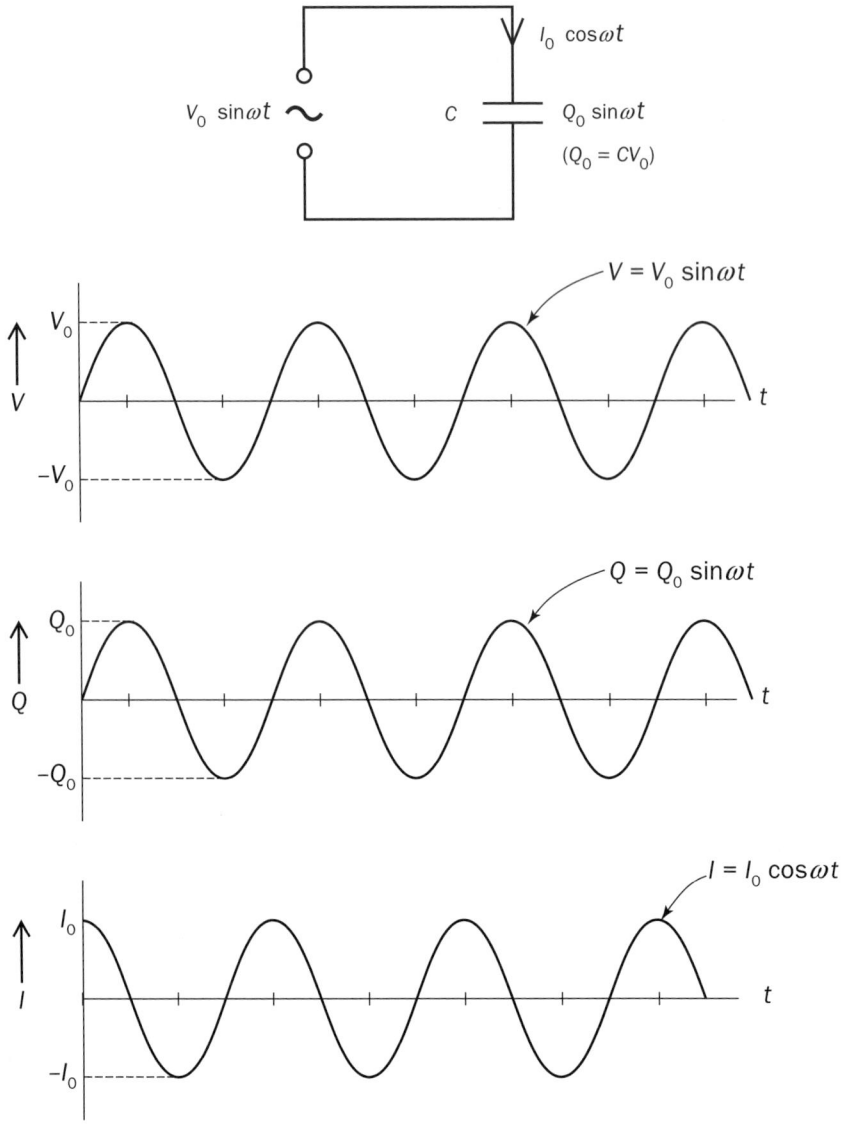


(See *r.m.s., resonance in AC circuits.*)

**capacitors in parallel** are connected side-by-side as shown in the following diagram. A single capacitance $C$ will be equivalent to the parallel set if the charge $Q$ that it stores for the same potential difference $V$ equals the sum of the charges stored on the individual capacitors in the set. For equivalence, the following must hold:

$$Q = Q_1 + Q_2 + Q_3$$

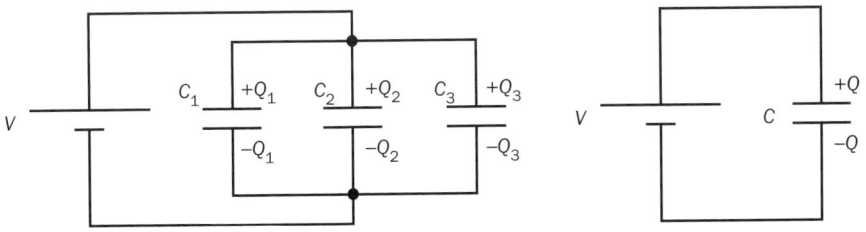


Remembering that capacitance is defined by the equation $Q = CV$, we have:

$$CV = C_1V + C_2V + C_3V$$

$$C = C_1 + C_2 + C_3$$

Thus, the effective capacitance of two or more capacitors in parallel is the sum of their capacitances. (See *capacitors in series, energy stored in a capacitor.*)

**capacitors in series** are capacitors joined end-to-end as shown in the diagram below. The equivalent single capacitor, shown isolated on the right, must store the same charge when the voltage across it is the same as the voltage across the series set, that is,

$$V = V_1 + V_2 + V_3$$

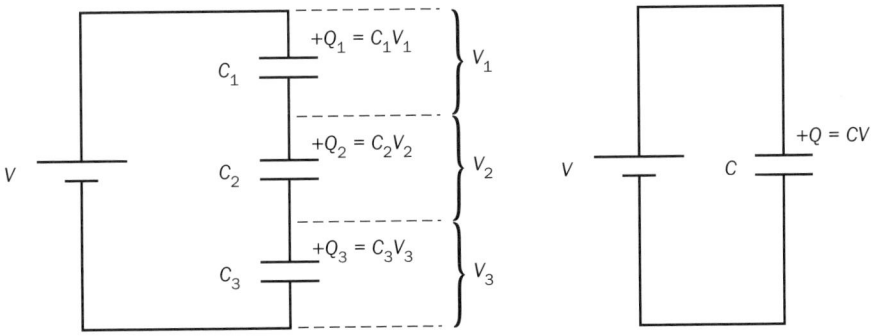


The same charge $Q$ must be stored on each of the capacitors in the series set, or else the adjacent positive and negative charges could not cancel out on discharge. The isolated capacitor must also carry charge $Q$ if it is to be equivalent to the series set. Remembering that capacitance is defined by the equation $Q = CV$, we therefore have:

$$V = V_1 + V_2 + V_3$$

$$\frac{Q}{C} = \frac{Q}{C_1} + \frac{Q}{C_2} + \frac{Q}{C_3}$$

$$\frac{1}{C} = \frac{1}{C_1} + \frac{1}{C_2} + \frac{1}{C_3}$$

One consequence of this relationship is that the equivalent capacitance $C$ of a series set is always smaller than the smallest capacitance in the set. (See *capacitors in parallel, energy stored in a capacitor.*)

**Cassegrain arrangement:** a design for reflecting telescopes which uses a concave mirror to gather light and a convex mirror to reflect it to the eyepiece. (See *telescopes.*)

**Celsius temperature scale** is defined from the *absolute temperature scale* via the relationship

$$\theta / {}^\circ\mathrm{C} = T / \mathrm{K} - 273.15$$

It is another way of choosing the numbers for the absolute temperature scale. Since the ice point is zero degrees Celsius and the steam point one hundred degrees Celsius, it is an example of a *centigrade temperature scale.*

**centigrade temperature scale** is any temperature scale which has its *ice point* at 0°C and its *steam point* at 100°C. There is no limit to the number of possible centigrade scales because there are numerous ways of defining how temperatures other than the ice and steam point are to be measured. For example, a *mercury-in-glass thermometer* and an alcohol-in-glass thermometer, each calibrated at 0°C and 100°C, may give different readings at an intermediate temperature because mercury and alcohol show different patterns of expansion between the two *fixed points.* The *Celsius temperature scale* uses the *absolute temperature scale* to define temperatures between 0°C and 100°C.

**centre of gravity** is the point through which the weight of a rigid body acts. No matter how much the body tumbles or turns, it is a fixed point relative to the body.

In a diagram showing the forces acting on a body, the body's weight is usually represented by a vertical arrow passing through the centre of gravity.

If a rigid body is imagined to consist of innumerable tiny masses, the centre of gravity is the point about which the sum of the moments of the weights of all these tiny masses is zero. It is the point about which the body will balance.

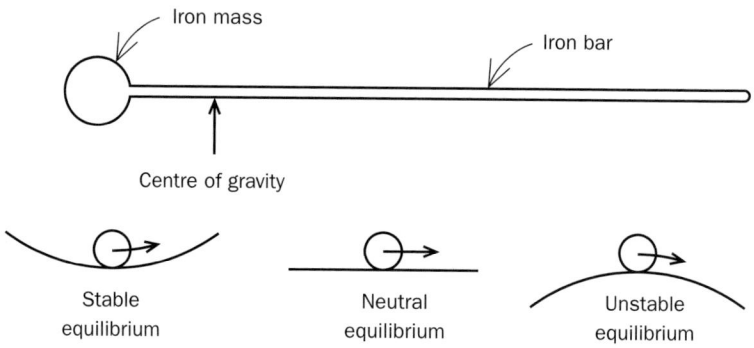


A rigid body resting on a surface is in stable equilibrium if any small rotation raises the centre of gravity. It is in unstable equilibrium if such a rotation lowers the centre of gravity. It is in neutral equilibrium if such a rotation neither raises nor lowers the centre of gravity. The three cases are illustrated in the diagram above.

The distinction between the centre of gravity of a rigid body and its *centre of mass* is not important at A-level. These centres coincide, i.e. they are at the same point, in a uniform gravitational field.

**centre of mass** of a rigid body is the point through which any resultant force must act if it is to accelerate the body without causing it to rotate. A terrestrial body would have to be very large for the centre of mass and the *centre of gravity* to be in two different places.

**centrifugal force** is the force which forms a 'Newton's third law pair' with the *centripetal force* applied to a body undergoing circular motion. Since the centripetal force acts on the body undergoing circular motion, the centrifugal force must act on some other body. For a satellite orbiting the Earth, for instance, the centripetal force is its weight (the gravitational pull of the Earth) holding it in its circular orbit. The centrifugal force is the gravitational force exerted by the satellite on the Earth; this force acts radially outwards from the Earth towards the satellite. The topic is usually avoided in A-level physics because the term 'centrifugal force' has a confusing history. (See *Newton's third law of motion.*)

**centripetal acceleration** is the *acceleration* of a body which travels along a circular path at constant speed. Its direction is towards the centre of the circle. (See *circular motion, centripetal force.*)

**centripetal force** is a force which acts at right angles to a body's path and so constrains the body to follow a circular path about the point towards which the centripetal force acts. For the body to continue round the circle it must be moving at just the right *speed* for that radius. For a body of mass $m$ moving at speed $v$ round a circle of radius $r$,

$$\text{centripetal force} = \frac{mv^2}{r}$$

Notice that this equation does not tell us what *kind* of force is acting. It may be a gravitational force, an electrical force, the force on a charge moving through a magnetic field, or the tension in a length of string. The word 'centripetal' is an adjective describing the direction of the force, which is towards the centre of the circle.

**Worked example**

**An Earth satellite**

The free-body force diagram below shows that only one force acts on the satellite, namely its weight. So the weight is the resultant force and, in this instance, the centripetal force too. But weight is the only force acting on the body; it is the only entry on the diagram. Do not write resultant force or centripetal force on the diagram; these terms describe what forces do, but they are not part of the list of forces acting on the body. Remember also that the weight gets smaller with increasing distance from the Earth's centre.

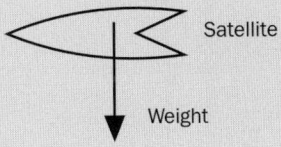


If $G$ is the gravitational constant, $M$ the mass of the Earth, $R$ the radius of the Earth, $m$ the mass of the satellite, $v$ the velocity of the satellite and $h$ its height above the Earth's surface, then

$$\frac{mv^2}{(R+h)} = G\frac{mM}{(R+h)^2}$$

This equation is not saying that the gravitational force equals the centripetal force — that would imply that there are two equal forces. It says that the gravitational force *is* the centripetal force.

**cepheid variable:** a *star* whose *luminosity* (i.e. total radiant output power) varies cyclically with a constant period. Observations of cepheids can be used to determine the distances to other galaxies, as follows.

It happens that the period of one full cycle (typically anywhere between a few hours and a few months) is related to the average luminosity. The longer the period, the greater is the cepheid's luminosity. It follows that if the period of a cepheid is measured with a clock, then the average luminosity $L$ of that cepheid can be calculated. Hence cepheids can be regarded as 'standard candles' in space. (In fact, cepheids are divided into types I and II, and the types have different period–luminosity relationships.)

The intensity $I$ of the light from the star (radiant energy per square metre arriving at the Earth's surface) can be measured with a telescope. Once both $I$ and $L$ are known for the same cepheid, the distance $D$ of the cepheid can be calculated from the relation $I = L/(4\pi D^2)$. Since this distance $D$ is much the same as the distance away of the galaxy in which the cepheid is located, the distance of any galaxy that contains a cepheid can be calculated.

**ceramics** are those substances which, in the solid state, have a characteristic set of properties: they are generally poor electrical and thermal conductors, they are mechanically brittle, and they have high melting points.

These properties are related to the underlying structure of ceramics. Chemically, they are often oxides, nitrides or carbides. The crystalline structure of a ceramic is held together by strong covalent and ionic bonds. This bonding makes it difficult for atoms or ions to slide past one another (unlike in metals) so that little plastic deformation is possible; hence the characteristic brittleness of ceramics.

*Glasses* are sometimes considered to be ceramics, but note that these materials do not have the ordered, crystalline structure generally associated with ceramics.

**chain reaction:** a repetitive process in which a reaction product at one stage (a neutron in this example) is a reactant for the next stage. The diagram illustrates schematically the chain reaction for $^{235}U$ in a *thermal fission reactor.*

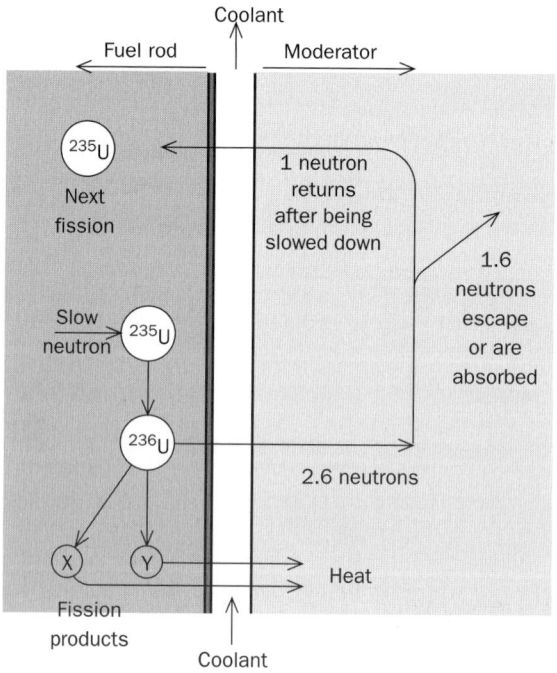

A slow neutron in the fuel rod is absorbed by a uranium-235 nucleus. The uranium-236 nucleus so formed is unstable and divides spontaneously into two *fission* fragments, labelled X and Y, and two or three fast neutrons. The average number of neutrons per fission reaction is 2.6.

The total rest mass of the fission products is less than the rest mass of the uranium nucleus, and the mass difference appears as the kinetic energy of the fission fragments. Most of this energy is linked to the X and Y nuclei and appears as heat in the fuel rods. This heat is carried off by the coolant to power the steam turbines. The fast neutrons escape as far as the moderator where they slow down, and enough of them enter a fuel rod to sustain the fission process. Fast neutrons have a low probability of being absorbed by uranium-235. Slow neutrons are sometimes called thermal neutrons because their average kinetic energy $E_k$ matches the reactor temperature, with

$$E_k = 3/2\, kT$$

**charge carrier:** a charged particle whose movement constitutes electric current. Charge carriers in metals are primarily electrons. In *semiconductors*, they are electrons or holes. Electrons and holes occur in equal numbers in intrinsic semiconductors. There is an excess of electrons in *n*-type semiconductors and an excess of holes in *p*-type semiconductors. It is this asymmetry which makes the *p–n* junction diode possible.

Charge carriers in vacuum include electrons, alpha and beta radiation, and ions.

**charge-coupled device** (CCD) is a rectangular array of light sensitive pixels which forms the image detection sensor in camcorders and some telescopes. For telescopes, the number and distribution of the pixels matches the pixels on a PC monitor.

The diagram shows one CCD pixel. It consists of three tiny metal flags labelled a, b and c. One row of pixels corresponds to one row or horizontal line on the PC monitor. Three 'wires' connect all the 'a' pixels together, all the 'b' pixels together and all the 'c' pixels together. The metal flags are mounted on a very thin layer of silicon dioxide which, in turn, covers a thin but stiff sheet of *p*-type semiconductor.

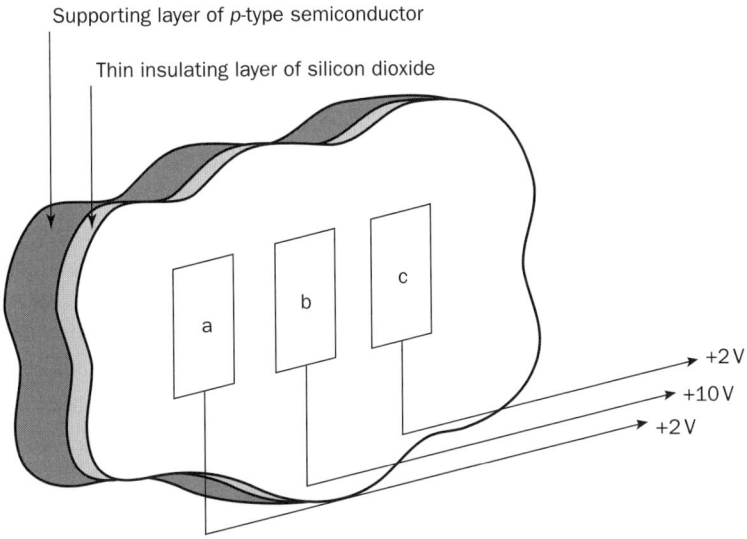

During the detection phase, the 'a' and 'c' wires are held at +2 V while the 'b' wire is held at +10 V. The thin sheet of *p*-type semiconductor faces the incoming light, and an image of part of the sky is formed by the telescope on this thin sheet. About 70% of the photons that light up the image create electron–hole pairs within the semiconductor, and the electrons from these pairs congregate below the 'b' set of metal flags, which are held at the higher positive potential of +10 V. The magnitudes of the charges stored in the pixels form an accurate record of the light intensity distribution falling on the pixels.

To collect the picture for display on a monitor or for storage in memory, the light is blocked off and the potentials of the 'a', 'b' and 'c' sets of metal flags change in sequence in the manner shown in the diagram. The 'c' set changes to +10 V, with the 'a' and 'b' sets both at +2 V; the individual charges stored in the semiconductor below the 'b' flags step to the right. Next, the 'a' set switches to +10 V with the 'b' and 'c' sets both at +2 V. The charges step to the right again. All these charge concentrations are swept in sequence to collectors where the charge amplitudes are measured and stored. With one collector for each row, a picture is soon built up.

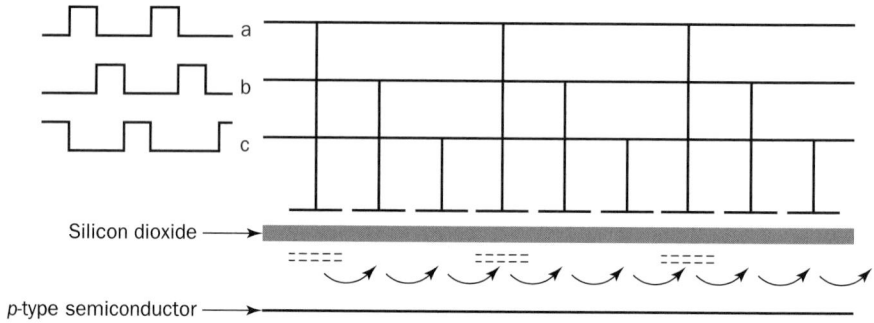


The advantage of a CCD detector is the 70% photon-detection efficiency compared with less than 5% for photography. Much fainter star systems can be observed and examined. Photographs still have the advantage that their grain size can be much smaller than the pixel size. Where resolution is of the essence, long-exposure photographic recording still wins.

**charge-to-mass ratio** is the electric charge of a charged particle in coulombs divided by its mass in kilograms. It is little more than a useful number to give insights, and perhaps this is why it rarely has a symbol of its own and is mostly written out as a ratio. It is called 'specific charge' where the word 'specific' has the meaning 'per unit mass'.

Charge-to-mass ratio gives an indication of how much a particle will be deflected as it moves through an electric or magnetic field. The greater the charge the greater will be the force on the particle, and the smaller the mass the greater will be the deflection produced by this force. Specific charge for the *electron* is about 2000 times that of the *proton* and about 8000 times that of an *alpha particle*. The higher value for electrons explains why *beta radiation* is so strongly deflected by magnetic fields and why alpha radiation is so weakly deflected.

The ratio $e/m_e$ for the electron works out at about $1.76 \times 10^{11}\,\mathrm{C\,kg^{-1}}$. This high value suggests that electrical forces dominate over gravitational ones. One way of thinking about the oil drops used by Millikan to measure the electron charge is as an artificial way of reducing the specific charge by increasing the mass without changing the charge. The charged oil drops used in the *Millikan's oil drop experiment* had so low a specific charge that the electrical force on a drop was of the same order of magnitude as the gravitational force.

**Charles' law** (1787) states that the volume of a fixed mass of gas at constant pressure is proportional to its absolute temperature. It is named after the French scientist Jacques Charles. The law can be stated in the algebraic form

$$V \propto T \quad or \quad \frac{V_1}{T_1} = \frac{V_2}{T_2} = \text{constant}$$

Although Charles' law is easily derived from the *ideal gas equation*, it is an empirical law and was discovered by experiment. The history of its discovery is complicated by the history of temperature scales. Statements of the law based on the Celsius scale are awkward. An account of a student experiment to verify the law should include a diagram, a list of measurements and an explanation of how you would check the law.

**Experiment to verify Charles' law**

**Apparatus**

Set up apparatus similar to that shown in the diagram. A fixed mass of dry air is trapped in narrow glass tube, a capillary tube, and sealed at the open end by a pellet of concentrated sulfuric acid. The acid keeps the air dry. A scale alongside the tube gives the length of the air column and this can be used as a volume measurement. The thermometer attached along the side of the tube gives the temperature of the air. The tube is immersed in water and the water is heated with an electric heating element and kept stirred.

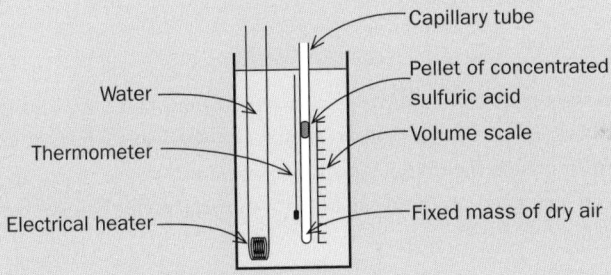


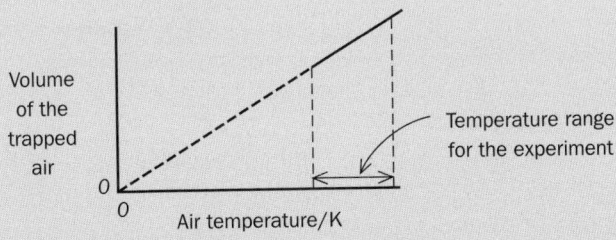


**Measurements**

When the apparatus has settled down at room temperature, the gas volume and the gas temperature are recorded. The heater is switched on for a while and then switched off.

The apparatus is given time to settle down at the new temperature. The new temperature and the new volume are recorded. This procedure is repeated in stages up to about 90°C. Temperatures in degrees Celsius are converted to the absolute scale by adding 273 to each temperature value.

**Conclusion**

A graph is drawn of volume (in the arbitrary unit of volume per unit length of glass tube) against absolute temperature. If the graph is a straight line passing through the origin, then it verifies Charles' law for the value of the ambient atmospheric pressure and for the range of temperatures used in the experiment.

(See *ideal gas equation, Boyle's law, pressure law.*)

**chromatic aberration** is the failure of a glass lens to bring all the colours in a parallel beam of white light to the same focus. The refractive index of glass for light at the blue end of the spectrum is marginally greater than the refractive index for light at the red end. Hence the *focal lengths* are slightly different and white images are weakly coloured at the edges. This gives an advantage to reflecting telescopes when larger aperture size, leading to greater light-collecting power and higher resolution, is what an astronomer is looking for. Various techniques are available to reduce chromatic aberration. For example, a lens may be constructed from two separate lenses that have opposite chromatic aberrations.

**circular motion** is the motion of a body which follows a circular path at constant speed.

In the diagram below the speed of the body is constant, but its direction changes continuously, so the velocity is not constant. Since its velocity is changing, the body must be accelerating. This acceleration is directed from the body towards the centre of the circle; it is called *centripetal acceleration*. For a body moving round a circle of radius $r$ at constant speed $v$,

$$\text{centripetal acceleration} = \frac{v^2}{r}$$

Acceleration implies the presence of a force — this is the centripetal force and is just strong enough to hold the body in its circular path. Note that at A-level we only deal with the steady state situation for which the above equation applies; we do not worry about the complex forces which had acted on the body to get it moving along the circular path at just the right speed.

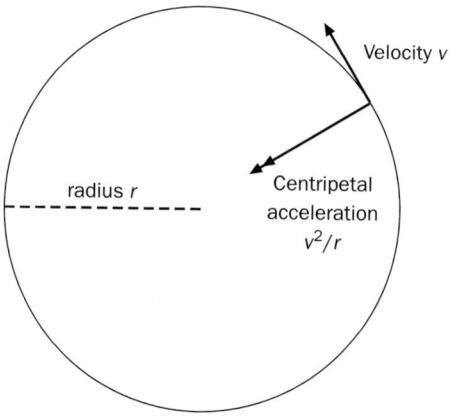

The direction of the centripetal force can be worked out from energy considerations. The speed of the mass is constant and its kinetic energy is constant, so the centripetal force does no work and must be at right angles to the motion. The centripetal force direction must be in the plane of the circle, otherwise the mass would move out of this plane. These two ideas together put the direction of the centripetal force parallel to the radius, towards the centre of the circle.

**coaxial cable:** a cable in which a solid central carrier is surrounded by an insulating dielectric material and an outer tubular conductor. A high-frequency signal travelling down the cable will be screened from external electric fields.

**coherence** implies a permanent phase match between the waves emitted by two separate sources. The rise and fall of one wave perfectly echoes the rise and fall of the other. Coherence is a necessary condition for the two waves to interfere in any way. Should the two waves overlap at some point further from one source than the other, then the two waves may arrive at the point in phase, out of phase, or with some intermediate phase difference. This is what makes *interference* possible. The waves will interfere constructively if in phase, enhancing one another. They will interfere destructively if out of phase, cancelling one another. If the phase difference is somewhere between these two extreme cases, then enhancement will be partial.

Two light beams can be coherent only if they come from the same source. Light from one electric lamp is altogether different from light from another, apparently identical, lamp. Together, light from the two lamps will brighten a room but there will be no interference pattern; the two beams of light are not coherent.

**collision:** a situation in which *linear momentum* is transferred from one body to another. Contact is not essential — for example, repelling magnets can collide and separate without touching.

**colour** is a notional quality associated with *quarks*. Any one of the twelve kinds of quark can take on one of three values or 'colours'. It is a way of allowing three quarks to occupy similar states without violating the Pauli exclusion principle.

**companding** is a way of reducing the distortion of an *analogue signal* during transmission. High-amplitude components in a signal are more subject to distortion and *noise* during transmission than are low-amplitude components. The upper halves of the higher-voltage components of the analogue signal are reduced by, say, 70% of their original size before transmission. The lower-voltage components are left alone. This part of the process is called compression. The transmitted signal picks up less noise and suffers less distortion than would happen without this compression. The compression is reversed by a corresponding expansion of the larger-voltage components after signal reception. The complete process, compression before transmission and expansion after transmission is called companding (compressing and expanding). The process carries the additional advantage of spreading the lower-amplitude values across a larger number of digital values, thereby reducing somewhat the error introduced when the signal is quantised. (See *analogue-to-digital conversion.*)

**component** of a vector is the resolved part of the vector in a particular direction. The component of a vector quantity such as force or velocity is found by the process of *resolution of vectors.*

Problems in mechanics can often be simplified by finding a component of a vector quantity. For example, if a block is sliding down a smooth *inclined plane*, its acceleration is equal to the component of the gravitational acceleration $g$ that is directed downwards parallel to the plane.

**composite materials** are built up from two or more simpler materials to provide a structured material with enhanced or modified properties. The structure can be ordered, as in plywood, or random, as in concrete (which is a composite of cement and an aggregate such as sand). The strength of a concrete *beam* can be further enhanced by including steel rods within the beam to produce *reinforced concrete*. If the steel rods are held under tension while the concrete is setting and later released, the product is called pre-stressed concrete. A pre-stressed concrete beam must be loaded heavily enough to overcome the internal stress from the steel rod before it can begin to bend and crack under the influence of even higher loads. In a similar manner, strong but light composite materials can be built up by compounding innumerable short thin fibres of glass or carbon within a polymer matrix. Bone is a natural composite material consisting of the rubbery protein collagen and the brittle mineral calcium phosphate.

**compressibility** is defined by the following word equation:

$$\text{compressibility} = -\frac{\text{increase in volume}}{\text{increase in pressure} \times \text{original volume}}$$

The SI unit is pascal$^{-1}$. An increase in pressure compresses the specimen. A decrease in volume is a negative change, so the negative sign in front of the definition keeps the compressibility positive. Gases have much larger compressibilities than solids or liquids.

**compressive stress** is force per unit area acting on the ends of a material in bar form to push the ends towards one another. It is the opposite of *tensile stress*. It is particularly relevant to materials in the lower parts of a heavy structure which carry the weight of everything above. Bricks used for the tall arches of railway viaducts have to be very strong under compression. They are called engineering bricks.

**Compton scattering** is the principal mechanism by which high-energy *X-rays* lose energy when they interact with matter. It is best to think in terms of an X-ray *photon*, with an energy of many keV. The photon interacts with an atomic electron, giving up part of its energy to the electron, which recoils. A new photon emerges that has less energy than the original photon and which travels in a different direction (because momentum must be conserved).

**conductance:** the reciprocal of the *resistance* of a component in a circuit. Its symbol is $G$ and its unit is siemens (S). Since resistance = voltage/current, we have

$$\text{conductance} = \frac{\text{current}}{\text{voltage}} \qquad G = \frac{I}{V}$$

$$\text{siemens} = \frac{\text{ampere}}{\text{volt}} \qquad 1\ \text{S} = 1\ \text{AV}^{-1} = 1\ \Omega^{-1}$$

Since conductance is the reciprocal of resistance, it follows that the conductances of components in parallel add up: $G = G_1 + G_2 + G_3 + \ldots$.

**conductivity** is the reciprocal of *resistivity*. Its symbol is $\sigma$ and its unit is siemens per metre (S m$^{-1}$).

$$\sigma = \frac{1}{\rho}$$

For a wire of length $l$ and cross-sectional area $A$, the conductance is given by $G = \sigma A/l$.

**conductors and insulators** have contrasting electrical properties. Conductors are materials in which there are innumerable electrons detached from atoms and forming what is known as an 'electron gas'. Should the conducting material be immersed in an electric field, the electrons will move to new positions within the conductor so as to eliminate the electric field inside the conductor.

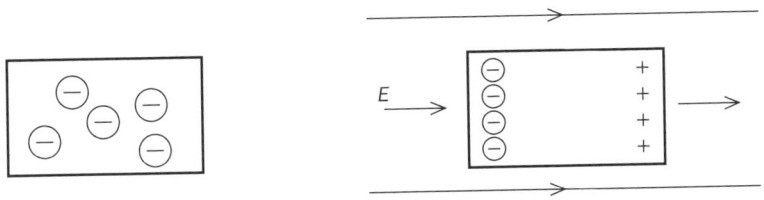


No applied field; electrons randomly distributed

Electric field present; charge in conductor polarises

A battery connected across the ends of a conductor sets up an electric field within the conductor which polarises the charge. This removes electrons from the positive end of the conductor and feeds them into the negative end at the same rate. The effect is to sustain the electric field in the conductor by sustaining the flow of electrons. The strength of the electric field depends on the length of the conductor and the potential difference between its ends.

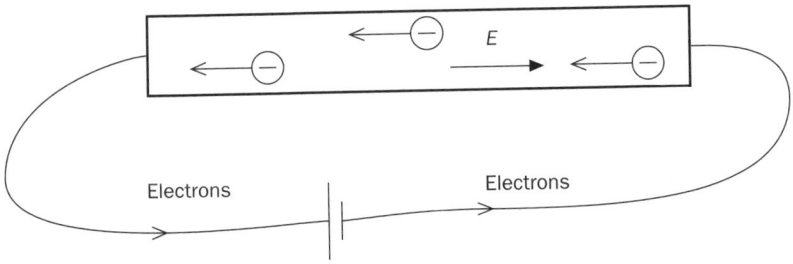


Insulators hold no detached electric charge, i.e. no free electrons. The effect of the electric field is to distort the atoms and molecules into electric dipoles which line up with the electric field and reduce its overall magnitude without eliminating it altogether. This polarisation of the insulating material plays an essential part in the action of dielectric materials in capacitors.

Semiconductors are materials with *resistivity* which is intermediate between that of a good conductor and a good insulator. (See *parallel plate capacitor, relative permittivity, semiconductor.*)

**conservation laws (nuclear)** are the laws which control the pathway of an event involving *subatomic particles.* They include conservation of mass–energy, momentum, angular momentum and charge. They also include another set of conservation laws not encountered in the ordinary course of events.

*Leptons* are not necessarily conserved — they come and go — but lepton number is conserved by virtue of the antiparticles having negative lepton numbers attached to them. For example, in *beta decay*, an electron and an electron antineutrino appear simultaneously. Their lepton numbers (1 and –1) cancel so that the overall lepton number is conserved. The concept is further complicated by having a separate lepton number for each of the three generations.

*Baryon* number is conserved, but there is a difficulty with mesons. Mesons are built from a quark and an antiquark, so they can annihilate. The difficulty is avoided by giving *hadrons* a baryon number 1, antihadrons a baryon number –1, and mesons a baryon number 0.

**conservation of energy** means that the sum total of energy in the universe is a constant, although it can change its form and be transferred from one body to another. The first law of thermodynamics is a precise statement of the same principle applied to a finite 'system', not to the universe as a whole.

When the law of conservation of energy is applied to mechanical energy in mechanical systems it is only an approximate law, since mechanical energy may be transformed into (say) thermal energy and 'lost' from the system. (See *first law of thermodynamics*.)

**conservation of linear momentum** is a principle which states that the total *linear momentum* of a system of interacting bodies in any specified direction is constant provided no external force acts on the system in that direction.

This principle is a consequence of *Newton's third law of motion* and always holds true exactly; it is never just an approximation. It seems to be an approximation in 'real life' because it is impossible to create a set of interacting bodies on which there are no external forces.

To illustrate the law of conservation of linear momentum, you would set up some sort of friction-free collision and measure the total momentum in one direction before and after the collision. (Reflection at a wall or from one end of a linear air track will NOT do. Reflection at a wall involves transferring momentum to the Earth, and you cannot measure the gain in momentum by the Earth during the collision.)

**Experiment to illustrate the law of conservation of linear momentum**

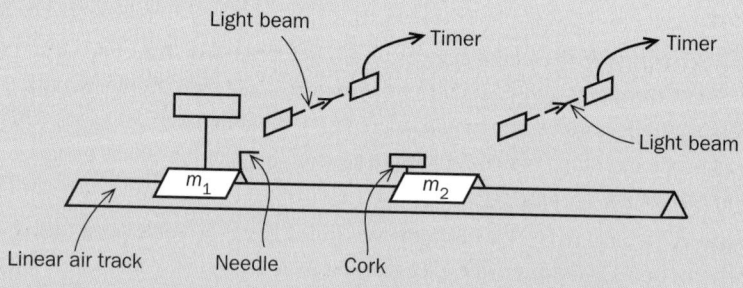


**Apparatus**

The apparatus is shown in the diagram. Place both trolleys on a linear air track or friction-compensated runway. (Always label the runway in a diagram as friction compensated when this is the case.) One trolley carries a 10.0 cm-long card mounted at the same height as the two laser beams. Light detectors, which are operated by the laser beams, are attached to digital timers. The timers record the time intervals during which the laser beams are cut by the card on the left-hand trolley. The needle and cork ensure that the trolleys stick together after the collision.

**Measurements**

Measure the masses $m_1$ and $m_2$ of two trolleys by weighing them on a digital balance. Use a ruler to check the length of the 10.0 cm card. Give the trolley with the card a push so that it approaches the second, still stationary, trolley at constant speed. It will collide with the second trolley, stick to it because of the pin and cork arrangement, and then travel on with reduced constant speed. Record the values of the time intervals $t_1$ and $t_2$ measured by the digital timers. Measure several different pairs of values for $t_1$ and $t_2$. Make sure that the collision occurs in between the two time measurements.

**Conclusion**

The approach speed of the single trolley will be $[0.100/t_1]\,\mathrm{m\,s^{-1}}$ where $t_1$ is the time recorded by the first digital timer. The speed of the two trolleys stuck together is $[0.100/t_2]\,\mathrm{m\,s^{-1}}$ where $t_2$ is the time recorded by the second digital timer.

According to the law of conservation of linear momentum,

$$m_1 \times (0.100/t_1) = (m_1 + m_2)(0.100/t_2)$$

Check that this equation balances for each pair of time values. Each successful check is an illustration of the law.

**constructive interference** means that two or more waves meeting at a point enhance one another at all times. For two sound waves to interfere constructively at a point, they must be in phase with one another when they meet at that point and in phase at all times. This can happen only if they are of the same frequency.

Light waves, too, must be in phase where they meet, but their having the same frequency will not ensure that this is the case — light waves also need to be coherent. The rise and fall of wave displacement for one wave must keep in step with that of the second wave. In practice, this means that the light waves must come from the same source. (See *coherence, destructive interference, interference, principle of superposition.*)

**continuous spectrum:** a spectrum like that shown in the *total radiation curve* for an incandescent solid, in which radiation of all wavelengths is present. This is distinct from a line spectrum in which only certain narrowly defined wavelengths are present. (See *absorption spectrum.*)

**contrast medium** is a substance used in the making of X-ray images to increase the contrast between, for example, tissues of similar densities. An example is barium sulfate, a good absorber of *X-rays*, as used in a *barium meal.*

**control rods** are long, rigid containers filled with a material, such as boron, which is a good absorber of neutrons. They are lowered into holes drilled in the *moderator* of a nuclear power plant, where they control the neutron flux and, as a consequence, the rate of power generation. (See also *thermal fission reactor.*)

**convection** is a circulatory motion within a fluid mass brought about by temperature gradients. The driving force is the replacement of warmer and less dense material lower down by cooler and more dense material flowing from higher up. The cool, dense fluid falls, pushing the warmer fluid upwards. This motion redistributes internal energy. There are no convection currents in weightless circumstances.

The lower layer of the atmosphere (troposphere) is 15 km or so deep and is hotter at the bottom than the top. Convection currents associated with these temperature differences account for much of our wind and weather. The temperature gradient in the next layer up (stratosphere) is the other way round, so here there are no convection currents.

**coolant** is the fluid which circulates around the control rods in a nuclear power plant and which transfers the energy released by the fission processes to the steam boilers of the turbines. (See *thermal fission reactor.*)

**cooling:** see *Newton's law of cooling.*

**cooling by working** is a mechanism by which a gas can transfer energy to its surroundings. It is a consequence of the *first law of thermodynamics* which can be written and extended as follows:

$$\Delta U = \Delta Q + \Delta W = \Delta Q - p\Delta V$$

If the gas is expanding, $\Delta V$ is positive and $\Delta W$ (the work done on the gas) is negative. With $\Delta Q$ equal to zero, $\Delta U$ will be negative, so internal energy falls and the temperature of the gas goes down.

In kinetic theory terms, the gas expands by pushing against the atmosphere. Molecular momentum, and kinetic energy with it, are transferred to the atmosphere. The average molecular kinetic energy of the expanding gas diminishes, so its internal energy goes down and hence also its temperature.

**coplanar forces** are three or more forces whose lines of action all lie in the same plane. This means that they can be represented by drawing arrows (vectors) on a sheet of paper.

**cosmic microwave background (CMB) radiation:** the weak background radiation which can be observed in every direction in the universe. It is a relic of the early, hot phase of the universe following the Big Bang. Its average temperature is about 2.7 K. Slight variations in the temperature of the radiation are believed to explain the formation of galaxies and stars — if the CMB were precisely uniform, there would have been no non-uniformities which could have led to matter and energy clumping together to form the structures we see today in the universe. (See *Big Bang theory.*)

**cosmological principle:** the assumption that, at any given instant in time, the universe looks the same in all directions from any position in the universe. In other words, the universe is both homogenous and isotropic. It follows that the Earth is not a special place in the universe. The principle implies that we would make similar observations of the universe from any other point in it.

The cosmological principle is useful because it allows cosmologists to rule out many different possible cosmologies (models of the universe). However, the principle itself is an assertion rather than a statement of proven fact. There is some evidence that, contrary to the principle, distant galaxies may be rather different from our own.

All this is not to say that our view of the universe remains the same with the progress of time; the universe is not static and an expanding universe implies a falling density.

**coulomb:** the SI unit of *electric charge*. It is a *derived unit* defined in terms of two *base units*, the *ampere* and the *second*. Electric charge is defined by the word equation

electric charge = current × time

and the coulomb is defined by the same word equation with the units replacing the physical quantities:

coulomb = ampere × second

The symbol for the coulomb is C.

As is always the case with units, *the* coulomb is different from *a* coulomb. *The* coulomb is the unit of electric charge defined above. *A* coulomb is an amount of electric charge — the charge per second flowing past a point in a wire in which a current of one *ampere* is flowing.

**coulombmeter:** an instrument which measures *electric charge* in coulombs. The charge $Q$ to be measured is allowed to flow on to a *capacitor* of known *capacitance* $C$. The potential difference $V$ across the capacitor is then measured and the value of the charge calculated using the capacitor equation $Q = CV$.

**Coulomb's law** states that the force $F$ between two point charges $Q_1$ and $Q_2$ a distance $r$ apart in vacuum is given by

$$F = \frac{1}{4\pi\varepsilon_0} \cdot \frac{Q_1 Q_2}{r^2}$$

where $\varepsilon_0$ is the *permittivity of free space*. The value of $\varepsilon_0$ is defined as $1/(\mu_0 c^2)$ where $\mu_0$, the permeability of vacuum, is defined to be $4\pi \times 10^{-7}\,\mathrm{H\,m^{-1}}$. The value of $c$, the speed of light, is $299\,792\,458\,\mathrm{m\,s^{-1}}$ exactly. This sets the value of $\varepsilon_0$ at $8.854\,187\,817 \times 10^{-12}\,\mathrm{F\,m^{-1}}$. The importance of these definitions as far as Coulomb's law is concerned is to make all experiments unnecessary except insofar as they would verify the *inverse square law* relationship.

Coulomb's law can be compared with *Newton's law of universal gravitation*. Both are inverse square laws, and both depend on the product of values of a certain property of each body involved. An important distinction is that the Coulomb force between charges can be either positive or negative (repulsive or attractive) because charge can have either sign, whereas the gravitational force between masses is always attractive because mass can never be negative.

**count rate** is the number of counts per second recorded by a detector near a radioactive source. It depends on the strength, the distance and the direction of the source as well as on the size and geometry of the detector. Provided neither the source nor the detector are moved, count rate is proportional to activity.

The activity of, for example, an alpha source is the number of disintegrations per second. Many of the alpha particles produced will be absorbed within the source itself. Of those that do leave, only a fraction will be going towards the detector. Therefore the detector detects only some of the alpha particles which reach it. This is why count rate is proportional to, but not equal to, activity.

The unit of count rate is counts per second. In practice, measured count rates should be corrected for the effects of *background radiation*.

**couple** is the name given to a pair of equal and opposite forces whose lines of action are parallel but separated.

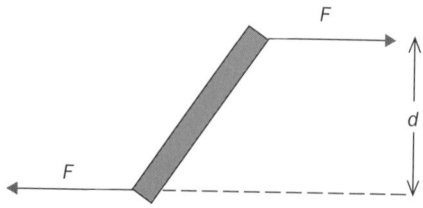


The diagram above shows two equal and opposite forces $F$ acting along parallel lines a perpendicular distance $d$ apart. These two forces form a couple and the moment of the couple is $(F \times d)$ N m. In words:

moment of couple = one force × perpendicular distance between the forces

The moment of a couple is a vector quantity (a *pseudo-vector*, in fact, but this does not matter at A-level) and the SI unit is the newton metre (N m). This unit should not be confused with the joule; the metre in the definition of the joule runs parallel to the associated force. (See *torque*.)

**covalent bond:** a form of attachment between the atoms of a molecule in which neighbouring atoms share electrons. The bond is much stronger than the ionic bond and this strength has two consequences. Firstly, molecules of substances such as hydrogen or methane are stable and self-contained: they remain in the gaseous state at low temperatures. The second point is that when a solid is formed containing this kind of bond (as with diamond) the material is exceptionally hard and has a high melting point. (See *ionic bond*, *metallic bond*.)

**creep** is the slow change of shape of a body under the action of a small but continuous stress acting over a long period of time. An example is the permanent sag that develops slowly along an unsupported metal pipe. The origin of the stress is the pipe's own weight. Creep occurs in glasses, polymers and metals, although the atomic mechanisms may differ.

**critical angle** is the angle of incidence within a refracting material that marks the onset of *total internal reflection*.

**critical temperature** is the temperature (different for each gas) above which it is impossible to liquefy the gas no matter how great the compression applied.

**cross-linking** is the tying together of polymeric chains by atomic bonds along their lengths. Where the binding is by an *ionic bond* or a *covalent bond*, it is very strong and makes the polymeric material tough and rigid; this is the case with *thermosetting polymers*. Where cross-linking is primarily via weak *Van der Waals' bonds*, the material is generally more flexible, like *thermoplastic polymers*. An early example of induced cross-linking is the bonding of *rubber* molecules using sulfur to make a rigid material called *vulcanised rubber* suitable for car tyres or tobacco pipe stems. The rigidity of battery cases contrasts with the flexible rubber used for car tyres and underlines the importance of controlling the density of cross-linking.

**crumple zones** are safety features of modern car designs. Typically, the front and rear areas of the car are designed so that in case of an impact with another vehicle or solid object, the crumple zone crumples up and absorbs much of the energy of the impact. The crumple zone is made of materials which are relatively easily deformed, while the occupants of the car are inside a 'safety cage' made of more rigid materials that can protect them from the impact. Before the impact, the car has *kinetic energy*. During the impact, *work* is done in deforming the crumple zone rather than in deforming the safety cage and its occupants.

The operation of the crumple zone can also be understood in terms of *momentum*. The car has momentum while it is moving. This must be reduced to zero when the car stops. In a sudden impact, the car's momentum is reduced to zero in a very short time, so the force on it must be high. This follows from the relationship between force and momentum as given by *Newton's second law of motion* (force = rate of change of momentum). The crumple zone ensures that the car's momentum gets reduced to zero over a longer interval of time, so that the rate of change of momentum (and hence the force) is reduced. (See also *air bags*.)

**crystal defects** are interruptions to the ordered structure of a crystalline solid. There are three types: defects may occur at a point (*point defects*), extend along a line (*edge dislocations*) or spread across an area (*grain boundaries*).

**crystalline solids** are solids in which an orderly arrangement of atoms extends over so large a volume that the properties of individual crystals decide the properties of the whole. Most salts are ionically bonded solids of this type. These solids have cleavage planes and often display physical properties (thermal expansivity or refractive index) that vary according to the direction from which the crystal is viewed. (See *ionic bond*, *crystal defects*, *slip*.)

Most *metals* are also crystalline. In this case the material is held together by *metallic bonds* arising from the presence of 'free' electrons.

**CT scanner:** an X-ray machine used to produce images of slices through a patient or other subject (such as an engineered object). CT stands for 'computed tomography' and tomography means imaging in sections.

The subject of the scan is positioned horizontally. The X-ray tube rotates in a plane around the subject, with a detector moving around directly opposite. This provides a series of images which are stored in a computer. Images from further series of exposures are combined with these to produce a digital map of the subject. Images of any slice through the subject can then be constructed by the computer and displayed on a screen. (See *X-rays*.)

**current–voltage characteristics** are graphs which show how the current in a circuit component varies with the voltage across it. The three graphs in the diagram on the next page are for a metal wire at constant temperature, a semiconducting diode and a filament lamp. The scales are order-of-magnitude values only. Note the change of scale on the graph for the diode: the reverse (negative) current has units of $\mu$A while the forward current is in mA.

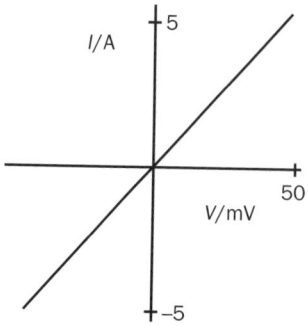


Metal wire at constant temperature

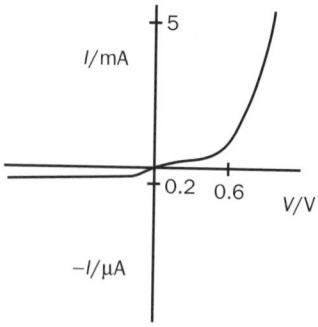


Semiconductor diode

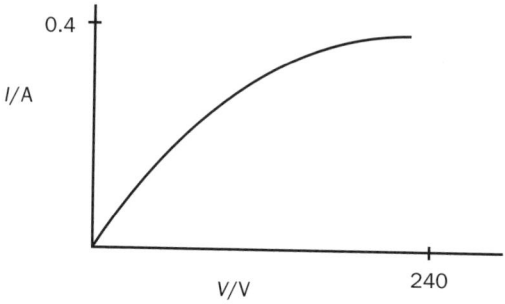


Filament lamp

**cyclotron:** see *particle accelerators.*

**Do you need revision help and advice?**

Go to pages 277–306 for a range of revision appendices that include plenty of exam advice and tips.

# D



**damped harmonic motion** is a *simple harmonic motion* in which *amplitude* diminishes with time as a consequence of a small damping force impeding the motion. A typical example is a *simple pendulum* oscillating in air. The *drag* on the pendulum bob is proportional to the speed of the bob, so when the bob is stationary, the drag force is zero. Because the speed rises and falls periodically, so does the drag force.

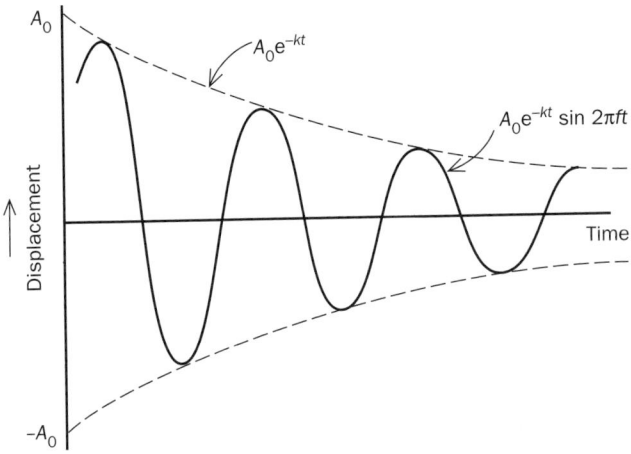


The diagram shows how the displacement of a lightly damped pendulum bob changes with time. The periodic nature of the motion and the independence of period and amplitude are both clear. But when the peak displacements are joined with a smooth curve, we see the extra factor introduced by light damping — an exponential decay of the amplitude.

See *exponential decay* for a discussion of this widespread phenomenon in physics. Here it is enough to note that the work done per cycle by the pendulum bob against the air resistance is a fixed proportion of the energy stored in the motion at the beginning of the cycle. The energy lost to the air resistance is like a negative interest rate and this explains why the decay is exponential. (See also *resonance, forced oscillations.*)

**data logging** is the electronic gathering of experimental data. Electronic sensors are used to make measurements, and the values are recorded in the memory of a datalogger for later manipulation by computer.

Electronic data recording has advantages: large amounts of data can be recorded in a short time or over a protracted period; sensors can be placed where a human experimenter might not to able access easily; some aspects of human error can be eliminated.

However, it is important to realise that data logging is not a method for obtaining perfect results. As with any measuring technique, the sensors used will have their limitations. A temperature sensor may be badly calibrated, for example, and its scale may be non-linear. A light gate is triggered by an object passing through the light beam, but the beam itself has a finite width and it is difficult to know at what point the beam is 'broken'.

When using electronic sensors and data loggers, you should always consider whether their use introduces significant errors into the experiment, and whether you might be able to reduce these errors.

**de Broglie wavelength** is the wavelength associated with a moving particle and is calculated from the relation

$$\lambda = \frac{b}{mv} = \frac{b}{\sqrt{(2meV)}}\left[= \frac{bc}{eV}\right]$$

where $\lambda$ is the de Broglie wavelength, $b$ is the Planck constant, $m$ is the particle mass, $v$ is the speed of the particle, $e$ is the particle's charge and $V$ is the potential difference through which the particle has been accelerated.

The bracketed expression covers the relativistic case. Typical wavelengths for electrons are: $3.9 \times 10^{-11}$ m at 1 keV, $6.2 \times 10^{-15}$ m at about 200 MeV, and $6.2 \times 10^{-17}$ m at about 20 GeV. The longer wavelengths are useful for examining crystal and molecular structures. The 200 MeV region is used for studying *nuclear radius* and nucleon diameter. The 20 GeV electrons are used for what is called 'deep inelastic scattering'. These high energy electrons have wavelengths much smaller than the proton diameter and are used to probe inside the proton. Using even higher voltages, quarks are shown to be less than $10^{-18}$ m in size. (See *electron diffraction, particle accelerators.*)

**decay constant,** $\lambda$, is the probability per second that an individual nucleus will decay. It equals $0.693/t_{1/2}$ where $t_{1/2}$ is the *half-life* of the nuclide the nucleus belongs to. (See *randomness and radioactive decay, fundamental law of radioactive decay.*)

**decay rate:** a term sometimes used instead of *activity.* It means the same thing.

**decibel:** a unit of loudness of sound, symbol dB or dBA, related to the intensity of the sound. (See *loudness.*)

**defects of vision:** any fault in the *eye* which causes the formation of an imperfect image. The imperfect image can often be improved using appropriate spectacle lenses.

In *myopia* or short-sightedness, rays parallel to the axis of the eye are focused in front of the retina. A diverging lens can be used to bring the rays to a focus on the retina.

In *hypermetropia* or long-sightedness, rays parallel to the axis of the eye are focused behind the retina. A converging lens can be used to bring the rays to a focus on the retina.

(See also *astigmatism.*)

**definition:** the meaning of a term or concept stated in a precise verbal or algebraic form that uses only words or symbols whose meanings are already known.

The equation $F = BIl$, for example, can be used as a definition of magnetic field strength $B$, because force $F$, electric current $I$ and length $l$ are all defined and measured independently of this equation. Any formal study of a subject must begin with a few concepts which cannot be defined. The meanings of these concepts are learned by living with them. Straightness, for instance, cannot be defined unambiguously, but we all know what the word means. (See *base quantity, derived quantity.*)



**density** is the mass per unit volume of a material. The symbol for density is $\rho$ and the SI unit for density is kilogram per metre cubed ($kg\,m^{-3}$). The word equation definition is:

$$\text{density} = \frac{\text{mass}}{\text{volume}}$$

$$\text{or, in symbol form, } \rho = \frac{m}{V}$$

The densities of most liquids and solids lie within the range $500\,kg\,m^{-3}$ to $10\,000\,kg\,m^{-3}$, that is, from about half the density of water to about ten times the density of water. The densities of gases at normal pressure are about a thousand times smaller than the densities of the corresponding liquids.

**derived quantity:** any physical quantity which is not a *base quantity* in SI. Where possible a word equation should be used to define the magnitude of a derived quantity. The same word equation can be used to define the corresponding unit. For example, capacitance ($C$) and its unit the farad (F) are defined as follows:

$$\text{capacitance} = \frac{\text{charge stored}}{\text{potential difference}}$$

$$\text{farad} = \frac{\text{coulomb}}{\text{volt}}$$

The newly defined quantity, capacitance, is on the left-hand side of the equation. For the definition to be valid, all the terms on the right-hand side of the equation must be previously defined. Their units are known from their definitions. So the units can be written out on the right-hand side of the units equation and the unit on the left-hand side then named. (See *definition.*)

**derived unit:** a unit in *SI* for any *derived quantity*, that is, any SI unit which is not a *base unit.*

The use of word equations to define derived units should ensure that all SI units are products or quotients of SI base units (e.g. $m\,s^{-2}$ for acceleration). Even so, many commonly used derived units have names of their own. The kilogram metre second$^{-2}$ ($kg\,m\,s^{-2}$) is the unit for force, but it is usually called the newton (N). Most such units you need to know are given in the following table.

| Physical quantity | Name of unit | Symbol | Other units | SI base units |
|---|---|---|---|---|
| activity | becquerel | Bq | | $s^{-1}$ |
| capacitance | farad | F | $C\,V^{-1}$ | $kg^{-1}\,m^{-2}\,s^{4}\,A^{2}$ |
| electric charge | coulomb | C | | $A\,s$ |
| electric conductance | siemens | S | $A\,V^{-1}$ | $kg^{-1}\,m^{-2}\,s^{3}\,A^{2}$ |

*(Continued)*

| Physical quantity | Name of unit | Symbol | Other units | SI base units |
|---|---|---|---|---|
| electric potential | volt | V | $WA^{-1}JC^{-1}$ | $kg\,m^2s^{-3}A^{-1}$ |
| electric resistance | ohm | W | $VA^{-1}$ | $kg\,m^2s^{-3}A^{-2}$ |
| energy, work | joule | J | Nm | $kg\,m^2s^{-2}$ |
| force | newton | N | | $kg\,m\,s^{-2}$ |
| frequency | hertz | Hz | | $s^{-1}$ |
| inductance | henry | H | $WbA^{-1}$ | $kg\,m^2s^{-2}A^{-1}$ |
| magnetic flux | weber | Wb | Vs | $kg\,m^2s^{-2}A^{-1}$ |
| magnetic flux density | tesla | T | $Wb\,m^{-1}$ | $kg\,s^{-2}A^{-1}$ |
| power, radiant flux | watt | W | $Js^{-1}$ | $kg\,m^2s^{-3}$ |
| pressure, stress | pascal | Pa | $Nm^{-2}$ | $kg\,m^{-1}s^{-2}$ |

**destructive interference** means that two or more waves meeting at a point oppose one another at all times and have zero resultant. Two sound waves will interfere destructively at a point where they meet if they are out of phase with one another at all times. For this to happen their frequencies must be the same.

For light beams to interfere destructively, two conditions must hold. First, the beams must be coherent if any kind of *interference* is to occur; *coherence* means that there is a perfect match of phase along the two light beams and, for this to happen, both light beams must come from the same source. Second, for the interference to be destructive, the two light beams must be out of phase when they meet. Destructive interference is the mutual cancellation of two beams. It is altogether different from no interference. Two candles give twice the brightness of one wherever their light coincides; the two beams of light neither cancel nor enhance. Light from two different candles is not coherent and will not interfere.

If two light beams are known to be coherent, the *principle of superposition* is employed to find the resultant disturbance at any point where they meet. The principle states how the mathematical functions which represent the two beams are to be added together to find their resultant. (See *constructive interference.*)

**diffraction** is the spreading of a beam of waves outside the boundaries set by straight line motion.

The extent to which diffraction occurs depends on the scale of the apparatus compared with the wavelengths involved. A typical Young's two slits arrangement is about a metre long, i.e. approximately two million times the wavelength of light. The slits themselves are about a thousand wavelengths across. Diffraction effects are observable on this scale, but only with care. The wavelengths of sound range from a few millimetres to a few metres. On a human scale of things, diffraction of sound is very marked. The diffraction of sound through a doorway is more like the diffraction of light through a *diffraction grating* slit. The diffraction grating slit is typically thinner than the wavelength of light; diffraction is extreme and the *principle of superposition* is needed to decide which directions the light will take.

Curiously, diffraction is not an issue with sound largely because its effect is so dominant — sound goes everywhere. With light, on the other hand, diffraction effects are barely noticeable but impose a limit on the power of optical instruments to magnify without loss of detail. In optical instruments, diffraction is a vital consideration. (See *diffraction at a single slit.*)



**diffraction at a single slit** can be observed with the experimental arrangement shown in the diagram. The slit is illuminated by a parallel beam of *monochromatic light* (from a laser), and the section of beam which passes through the slit sets up the characteristic intensity pattern shown.

The angular positions $\theta_n$ of the successive minima on the screen are given by the equation

$$d \sin \theta_n = n\lambda$$

where $d$ is the width of the slit, $\lambda$ is the wavelength of the monochromatic light, and $\theta_n$ is the angular displacement of the $n$th minimum. Between the two first-order minima is one broad zeroth-order maximum. This central band is twice as wide as each of the other bands.

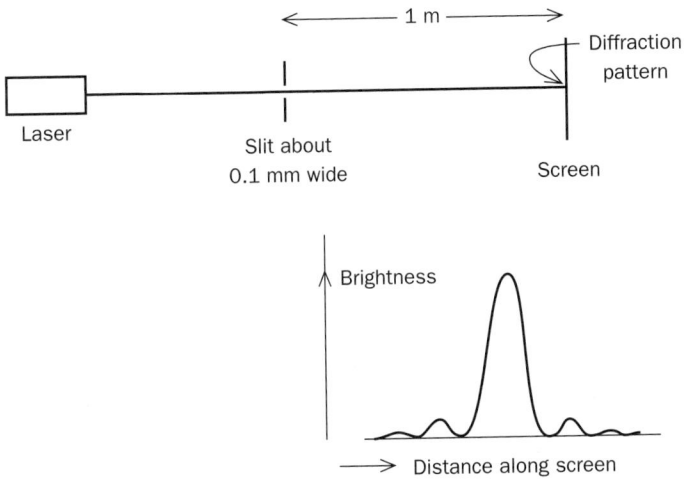


For small angles less than about 5°, $\sin\theta = \theta$ provided that $\theta$ is measured in radians. For example, $\sin 4.5°$ is 0.07846 and 4.5° converts to 0.07854 radians. So, provided the angles involved are not more than a few degrees, the equation for $\theta_n$ becomes $\theta_n = n\lambda/d$ and the minima will be equally spread about the principal axis.

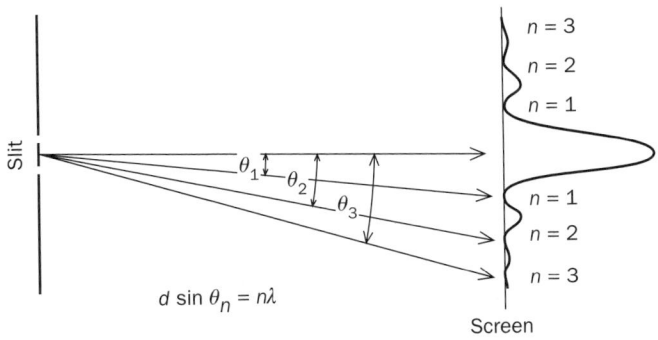

Although the minima are evenly spread in terms of angular displacement, the amplitudes of the illuminated bands between them fall away very fast. You will need a dark room and good equipment to see more than two or three bands on each side of the maximum.

**diffraction at a small circular hole** in an opaque sheet generates, on a screen, a pattern of bright and dark rings about a bright spot, as shown in the diagram below.

The radius of the $n$th dark ring and the radius of the first dark ring are given by the following equations:

$$\sin\theta_n = \frac{122n\lambda}{d} = \frac{r_n}{d} \text{ and } \sin\theta_0 = \frac{122\lambda}{d} = \frac{r_1}{d}$$

where $d$ is the diameter of the hole in the screen, $D$ is the distance of the screen from the hole, $\lambda$ is the wavelength of the light used, $r_n$ is the radius of the $n$th dark ring, and $\theta_n$ is the angle subtended at the centre of the hole by $r_n$. The $r_n/D$ and $r_1/D$ factors are correct for small angles only.

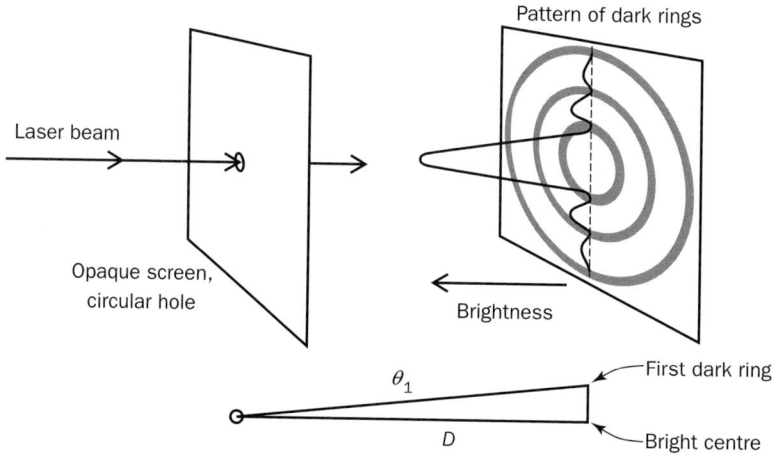


Imagine what happens as the hole gets bigger. The diameter $d$ increases and $\theta_n$ diminishes. Eventually, the diffraction pattern is swamped by the light flooding through the large hole. This is no good. But if there is a lens in the hole focusing all the light on to one spot, then we are back to seeing the diffraction pattern. This is what happens in the *eye* and in *telescopes*. In these cases the distance $D$ is the *focal length* of the lens involved and $d$ is the diameter of the lens ($d$ is the pupil diameter for the eye or the objective lens diameter for the optical telescope). For a radio telescope, the wavelength $\lambda$ is very large, and $d$ has to be very large too — it is the diameter of the radio telescope dish.

A similar diffraction pattern of light and dark rings is seen if a laser beam is shone through a glass sheet over which opaque particles of roughly equal size have been scattered; lycopodium powder is often used. If the wavelength is known and $\theta_1$ is measured, then $d$ can be calculated. In other words, the preferential scattering of light by diffraction into particular angles gives information about particle size. (See *electron diffraction*.)

**diffraction grating:** a sheet of glass, about 4 cm square, with thousands of equidistant parallel lines etched on one side. Typically, the distance between the centres of two adjacent lines is two or three times the *wavelength* of light.

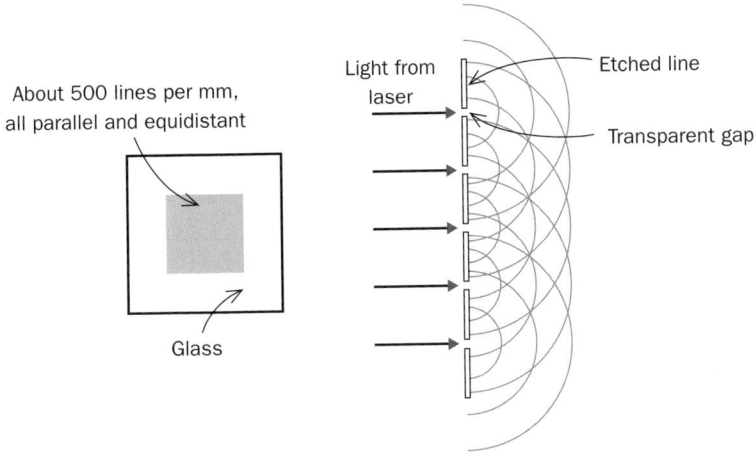


The diagram above shows a plan and a magnified section of a diffraction grating illuminated normally by a parallel beam of *monochromatic light* from a laser. The etching is shown as solid (opaque) lines and the transparent parts as gaps. The gaps are narrow and each one is effectively a source of circular waves.

Consider an arbitrary point on the screen. It will receive a ray of light from each illuminated slit. If these rays happen to interfere constructively with each other, then this point on the screen will be brightly illuminated. It is, however, much more likely that destructive interference occurs, leading to the position on the screen being dark. This is why the bright maxima are well separated.

The next diagram (overleaf) shows how to understand this phenomenon in terms of *wavefronts* emerging from the slits. These circular waves set up new wavefronts and send out beams of light in new directions. The top left picture shows the so-called zeroth-order beam or zeroth-order spectrum. The top right picture shows the formation of the first-order spectrum together with its associated equation. The bottom two pictures show the second-order and $n$th-order beams.

In general, if $\lambda$ is the wavelength of the light transmitted by the grating, $d$ is the distance between the centres of adjacent slits and $\theta_n$ is the angle between the $n$th-order beam and the zeroth-order beam, then

$$d \sin \theta_n = n\lambda$$

Alternatively, since $d = 1/N$ where $N$ is the number of lines per metre of grating, we have

$$\sin \theta_n = Nn\lambda$$

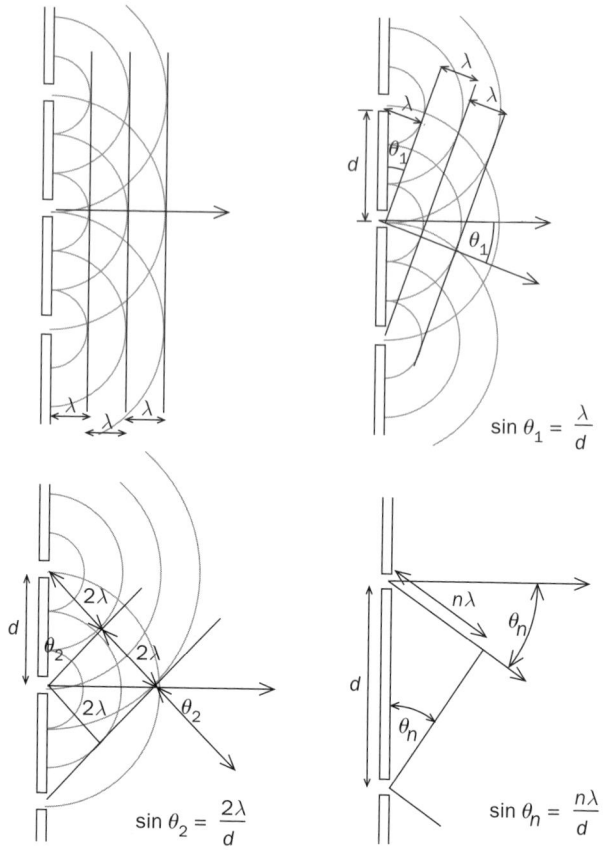


These equations can be applied either to find the angles of the several orders of spectrum for a monochromatic beam or to find the dispersion in the first-order beam, say, for white light.

**Worked examples**

**1 A diffraction grating has 400 000 lines per metre and it is illuminated normally by light of wavelength 600 nm from a laser. Calculate the number of orders of spectrum formed and the angles to the principal axis at which they leave the grating.**

We need to find $n$ for $\theta_n$ equal to 90°.

Since sin 90° equals 1, $n = 1/(N\lambda) = 1/[(400\,000\,\text{m}^{-1}) \times (600 \times 10^{-9}\,\text{m})]$.

This gives the value of $n$ as 1/0.24, or 4.2 to two significant figures. Since $n$ must be an integer, this means that there will be a spectrum for $n = 4$ but not for $n = 5$. If the zeroth order is included, then five orders of spectrum are formed.

The angle of the first-order spectrum is found as follows:

$$\sin\theta_1 = Nn\lambda = \left(400000\text{m}^{-1}\right) \times 1 \times \left(600 \times 10^{-9}\text{m}\right) = 0.24$$

$$\theta_1 = \sin^{-1} 0.24 = 13.9°$$

The other angles are found in a similar manner:

$\theta_2 = \sin^{-1} 0.48 = 20°$

$\theta_3 = \sin^{-1} 0.72 = 46°$

$\theta_3 = \sin^{-1} 0.96 = 74°$ (to 2.s.f.)

**2 The wavelengths of visible light range from 400 nm for deep violet to 700 nm for the far red. Find the dispersion in the first-order spectrum of white light formed by a diffraction grating with 500 000 lines per metre.**

Following the procedure used in the last example:

$\theta_{\text{deep violet}} = \sin^{-1} 0.200 = 11.5$

$\theta_{\text{farred}} = \sin^{-1} 0.350 = 20.5$ (to 3.s.f.)

so the dispersion is 9.0°.



**digital signal:** a signal that is made up of bits. Each bit has two possible values labelled 1 or 0, HIGH or LOW, ON or OFF, ACTIVE or INACTIVE. Examples of a one-bit digital signal include the red indicator lights on an electric iron and on a car dashboard. Flashing car direction indicators are a one-bit signal, either ACTIVE or INACTIVE. Two such one-bit signals make a two-bit signal which can be coded to identify up to four different states (e.g. straight ahead, turn left, turn right, watch it). Binary numbers are used to identify the different possible states. A two-bit signal might be 00, 01, 10, or 11. A four-bit signal (called a nibble) can label up to 16 states, and an eight-bit signal (called a byte) can label up to 256 possible states (i.e. 0 to 255 put into binary numbers).

In digital electronics, a byte usually takes the form of eight square voltage pulses, transmitted in sequence. Each pulse has one of two possible magnitudes and each pulse lasts for the same time interval. If the magnitudes are labelled 1 or 0, then the digital signal in the diagram reads 10110011 (i.e. 128+32+16+2+1 = 179).

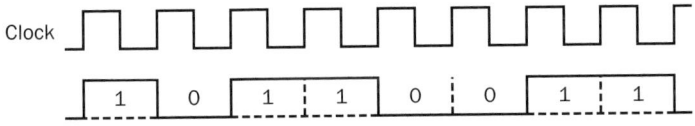


A digital signal that carries information is usually the output signal from an analogue-to-digital converter. The digital output is a coded record of the amplitude of the analogue voltage input. Encoding an analogue signal in digital form has many advantages — a digital signal:

- can be cleaned of any noise it is exposed to during transmission
- can be stored in computer memory
- can take part in a computer-controlled process
- can be kept in step with a clock in a digital circuit

(See *analogue-to-digital conversion.*)

**digital transmission systems** transmit a voltage signal in the form of a succession of square pulses. Each pulse has one of two possible amplitudes, often labelled HIGH or LOW. The usual process is for eight successive bits to represent in binary form the magnitude of an analogue amplitude at the moment of *sampling*. It follows that the bit transmission frequency must be much higher than the sampling frequency unless there is some kind of multiplexing. The principal advantage of digital transmission systems is the efficiency with which *noise* can be removed from the transmitted signals. One disadvantage is the extra expense of the additional electronic activity; another is the poor resolution in a *digital signal* for small changes of amplitude, which leads to a larger relative error at low amplitudes.

**digital-to-analogue conversion** is the reverse of *analogue-to-digital conversion*. It is sometimes referred to as 'decoding'. The output may suffer from the information loss associated with the *quantisation* effect at the analogue-to-digital conversion stage.

**diode:** an electrical component which conducts current in one direction but not the other. Early diodes consisted of two electrodes (hence the word diode) fitted into a glass bulb which was evacuated or, later, filled with inert gas. One electrode, the cathode, was heated to dull red heat and thereby empowered to release electrons by *thermionic emission*. The second electrode, the anode, was not heated. A small positive potential difference would enable electrons to flow from the cathode to the anode but not the other way round.

Most modern diodes are solid state devices built up from semiconducting materials. (See *light-emitting diodes*.)

**dioptre:** the unit of power of a lens; 1 dioptre = $1\,\mathrm{m}^{-1}$. (See *lens equation*.)

**direct current** is any electric current that flows past a point in one direction only. The magnitude of the current may vary but its direction is constant. Direct current is to be contrasted with *alternating current*, whose direction changes with time. (See *electric charge and electric current*.)

**dislocation:** see *edge dislocations*.

**dispersion of light** is the separation of a beam of light into its component wavelengths or colours. This is possible because the speed of light in a substance such as glass varies slightly with wavelength. The dispersion of white light by glass is clearly demonstrated by the formation of a spectrum using a glass prism. This is shown in the diagram below. (It is much easier in practice, however, to produce a spectrum of white light using a *diffraction grating*.)

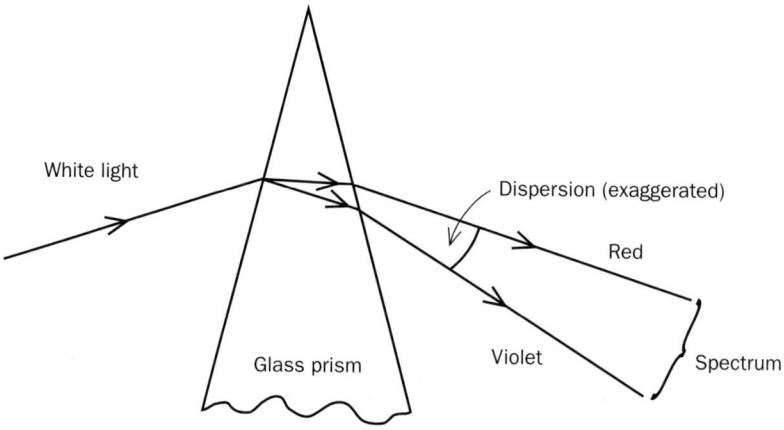


(See *electromagnetic spectrum*.)

**dispersion of sound** means the change in the speed of sound with frequency. It is zero for audible frequencies (speech and music would both fail over modest distances if, say, higher frequencies travelled more quickly than lower frequencies) but is measurable at much higher frequencies. There is some slight dispersion of sound in humid air; this is linked to the absorptive action of the water vapour present. (See *sound waves.*)

**displacement** defines the *position* of one point with reference to another point. It is a *vector quantity.* Its magnitude is the straight line distance between the two points. Its direction is the angle between the straight line joining the two points and a reference direction. The SI unit for displacement is the metre, symbol m.



The second part of the following diagram underlines the difference between 'distance travelled' and 'change of displacement'. Suppose a dog walks from a point A to a point B along a curved path of length $d$. The distance travelled is $d$ metres; but the change of displacement, $\Delta s$ metres, is the vector difference between the initial displacement $s_A$ and the final displacement $s_B$. The change of displacement depends only on the start and finish points; it is independent of the path followed by the dog. It is a vector difference

$$\Delta s = s_B - s_A$$

Had the dog returned to its starting position, the points A and B would coincide and the change of displacement would have been zero. Hence, the average velocity would have been zero. However, the average speed could be anything from very slow to as fast as a dog can run.

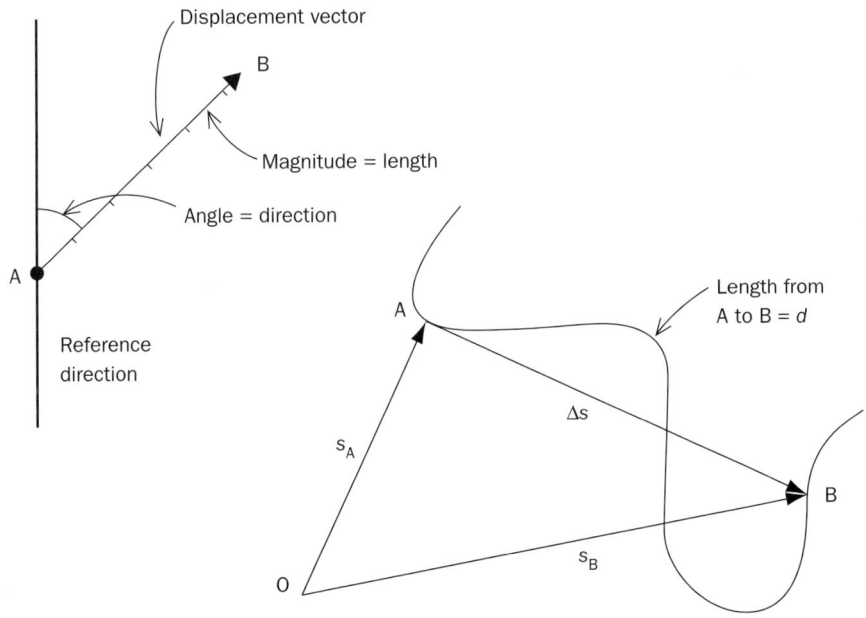


**displacement–time graph:** a graph which shows how the *displacement* of an object varies with time (usually with time on the $x$-axis and displacement on the $y$-axis). The displacement axis of a displacement–time graph gives the magnitudes for displacement but says nothing about direction other than forwards or backwards, up or down. Consequently, these graphs describe motion in one direction only. They can be used for either *straight line motion* or one *component* of a more complex path of travel.

For straight line motion, the gradient of the tangent at a point on a displacement–time graph is the *velocity* at the instant corresponding to that point. (For anything other than straight line motion, the gradient of the tangent is the component of the velocity in the same direction as the displacement.) If displacement decreases with time, the velocity is negative (see the examples below).

The diagram shows a displacement–time graph, along with the corresponding *velocity–time graph* and acceleration–time graph, for a glider on a horizontal linear air-track bouncing backwards and forwards elastically between reflectors which are 1.20 m apart. The glider covers this distance in approximately 1.5 s so that its speed is about $0.8\,\mathrm{m\,s^{-1}}$. Notice that a small adjustment for the zero speed at the moment of bounce has to be included. The displacement increases and decreases uniformly, the velocity is constant but changes direction, and the acceleration is zero except at the moment of bounce. The details of the bouncing action are not exact.

The steady velocity is slightly higher than $0.8\,\mathrm{m\,s^{-1}}$ or slightly lower than $-0.8\,\mathrm{m\,s^{-1}}$. The gradients of the straight parts of the displacement–time graph equal the steady velocity values, and the area of each loop in the velocity–time graph will equal 1.2 m. The direction of acceleration is known, but its peak magnitude is not — this is why there is no scale on the acceleration–time graph. (See also *velocity–time graph*.)

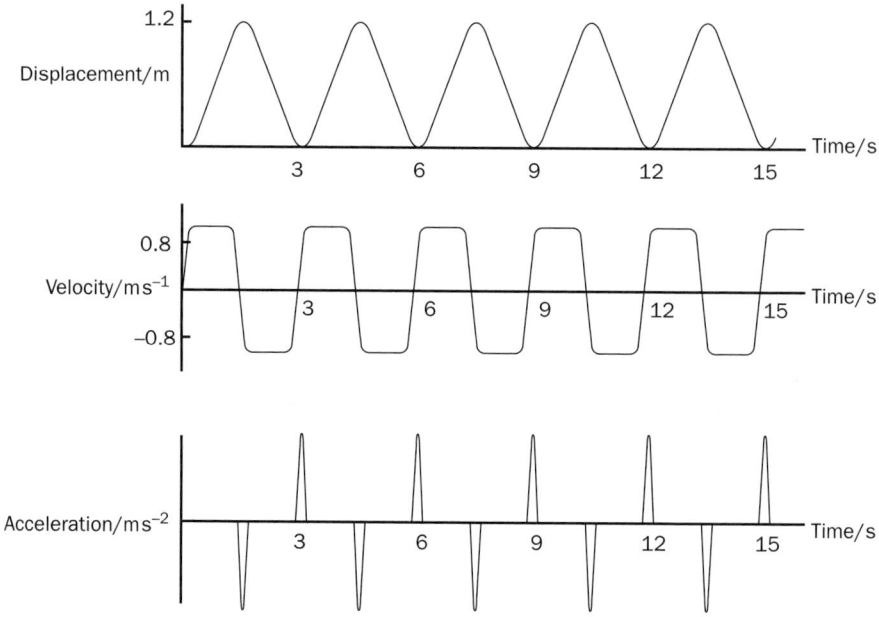


**Worked example**

A student inclines a linear air-track at a small angle to the horizontal and releases a glider from a point located 1.8 m from an elastic reflector at the lower end. The times at which the glider passes particular points on the track are noted from the starting time until the glider returns to its starting position. A displacement–time graph is drawn up and used to sketch velocity–time and acceleration–time graphs.

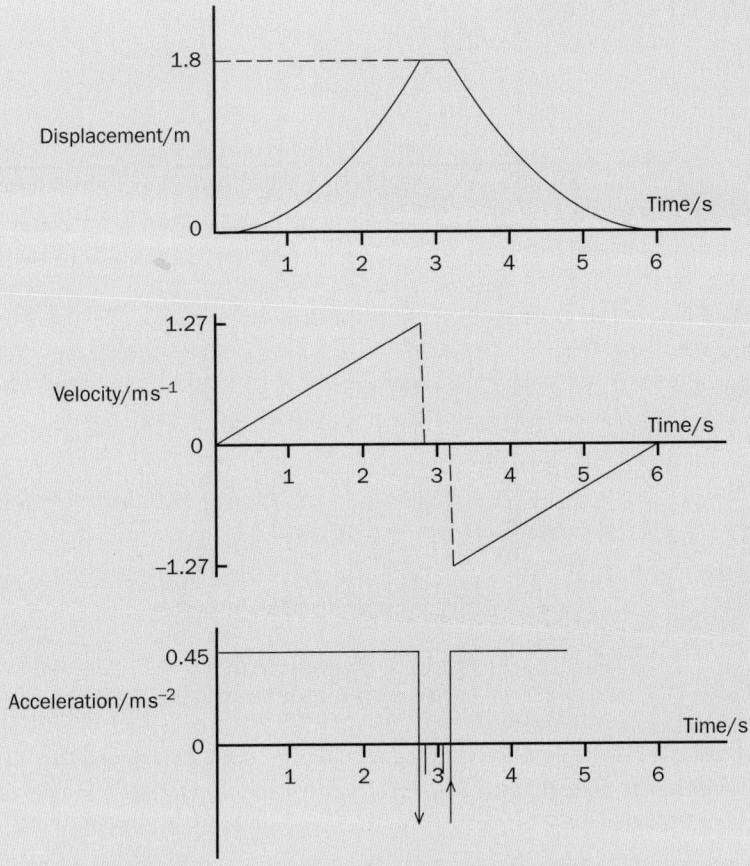


Notice that the final displacement is zero. The velocity suddenly changes direction at the reflection. The acceleration is constant throughout the motion except during the bounce when it goes through two negative peaks separated by a zero period. (The value of the bounce time interval was set to keep the time axis tidy.)

**distance** tells us how far along a line one point is from another. The line may be straight or curved. Distance is a *scalar quantity*. The SI unit for distance is the metre, symbol m.

Mechanics is mostly concerned with either *distance travelled*, which is another scalar quantity, or with *displacement*, a vector quantity. Distance is involved more with topics such as the inverse square law, attenuation and diffraction patterns.

**distance–time graph:** a graph which shows how distance travelled along a line varies with time. (It should be called a distance-travelled–time graph, but never is.) The gradient of the tangent to a point on a distance–time graph is the *speed* of the object at that instant. The diagram on the next page illustrates three important cases: zero speed, constant speed, and constant rate of increase of speed.

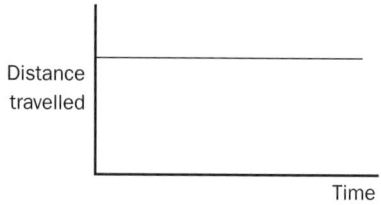


*A stationary object, the gradient is zero*

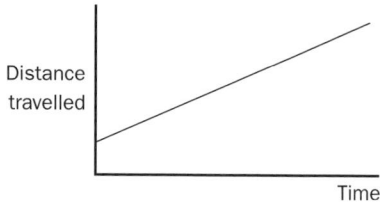


*A body travelling at constant speed, the gradient is constant*

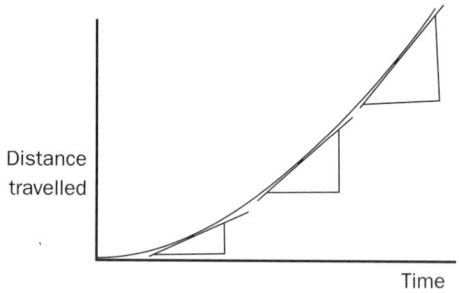


*Equal increases in speed (and in gradient) in equal times*

Remember that the *s* in the equations of motion stands for *displacement* and that, mostly, you will be concerned with *displacement–time graphs*. Distance travelled can only increase or stay constant; displacement can increase or decrease and even go negative.

**distance travelled** is not simply a *distance*. Walk four paces forwards, two backwards and six forwards. The distance from start to finish is eight paces. But the distance travelled is twelve paces.

Distance travelled is measured along the travel path. Only the magnitude is recorded. The line may be curved or straight and the direction is irrelevant. The SI unit of distance travelled is the metre, symbol m. It is a *scalar quantity*.

*Speed* is defined as distance travelled per unit time. Since distance travelled can only increase, speed must always be positive. (See also *displacement*, *velocity*.)

**Doppler effect:** the change in *frequency* (and of *wavelength*) of any wave motion when the source of the waves or the observer, or both, are in motion. Consider a source of sound waves of frequency 100 Hz, moving away from an observer. In one second, it emits 100 waves. The first wave reaches the observer at a certain time; however, the 100th wave arrives more than one second later because it has had to travel a greater distance than the first wave. Hence the observer receives fewer than 100 waves in 1 s and interprets this as a reduced frequency — the *pitch* of the sound is lower.

In analysing the Doppler effect, it is important to appreciate that the waves travel at a speed which is unaffected by the speed of motion of the source. Sound waves, for example, travel through the air at $330\,\mathrm{m\,s^{-1}}$ even if they have been emitted from a source moving at $100\,\mathrm{m\,s^{-1}}$. Light waves from a moving source still travel through space at speed *c*. Wave speed is determined by the medium through which the waves are propagating, not by the speed of the source.

With sound, the immediate observation is a change of pitch. The relevant equation for sound in still air is

$$\frac{f_o}{f_s} = \frac{v \pm v_0}{v \mp v_s}$$

where $f_o$ is the observed frequency, $f_s$ is the source frequency (i.e. the frequency of oscillation of the loudspeaker or whatever), $v$ is speed of sound in still air, and $v_o$ and $v_s$ are the speeds of the observer and the source relative to the air. The upper signs on the right-hand side are for motion towards, and the lower signs are for motion apart. The relationship is more complicated if there is an attempt to allow for wind speed.

With light or any other electromagnetic wave, it is usual to measure wavelength rather than frequency. The Doppler effect (called a Doppler shift) is then expressed as a wavelength change. The relevant equation is

$$\frac{\Delta\lambda}{\lambda} = \pm \frac{v}{c}$$

If the source is moving towards the observer, the – sign is used. The wavelength shortens and the colour shift would be towards the blue. If the source is moving away from the observer, the + sign is used. The wavelength increases and the colour shift would be towards the red.

The main application of the Doppler effect in *astronomy* is to measure line-of-sight velocities. Line-of-sight velocity added vectorially to sideways velocity gives actual velocity, allowing relative motions within our galaxy to be examined. On the larger scale, the *red shift* of light from other galaxies indicates that line-of-sight velocities of other galaxies are always away from the galaxy that contains the solar system. (See *Hubble's law.*)

For an application in medicine, see *Doppler ultrasound.*

**Doppler ultrasound** is the use of *ultrasound* in medicine (and elsewhere) to measure the speed of a moving surface. The surface may be part of a patient's heart, the heart of a foetus, or blood cells carried along in the blood stream. To measure the speed of blood cells, ultrasound waves are directed into a blood vessel. Waves reflected from the cells have a Doppler shift in frequency which can be used to determine the speed and direction of movement of the blood cells. This can give information about blockages in arteries and veins or defects in the action of the heart.

**drag** is the frictional force which opposes the motion of an object through a fluid. If the object is a sphere and its speed equals the *terminal speed*, provided that the flow is streamlined the magnitude of the drag is given by *Stokes' law.* Drag is dramatically increased by the onset of turbulence, and considerable attention is paid to this matter in vehicle design. (See also *aeroplanes.*)

**drift speed** is the average speed of progress of *charge carriers* through a conductor when current is flowing in the conductor. If $I$ is the current in a conductor of uniform cross-section $A$ that has carrier density $n$ with each charge carrier having charge $q$ and moving with drift speed $v$, then

$$I = nAvq$$

If we put $I = 5\,\text{A}$, $n = 1 \times 10^{29}$, $A = 1 \times 10^{-6}\,\text{m}^2$ and $q = 1.6 \times 10^{-19}\,\text{C}$, then $v$ works out at about $0.3\,\text{mm}\,\text{s}^{-1}$. Typical drift speed values in conductors range from about $0.01\,\text{mm}\,\text{s}^{-1}$ up to about $100\,\text{mm}\,\text{s}^{-1}$. Drift speeds are much higher in semiconductors because the carrier density $n$ is much smaller.

**ductility** is the capacity of a metal especially, and of other substances occasionally, to be drawn out into a thin wire.

**dynamo** is another word for *generator*. It is often taken to refer to a generator which supplies direct current via a commutator.

**Are you studying other subjects?**

The *A–Z Handbooks (digital editions)* are available in 14 different subjects. Browse the range and order other handbooks at **www.philipallan.co.uk/a-zonline**.

**ear:** the organ of hearing. The functions of the three main parts of the human ear are collection (the outer ear), amplification (the middle ear) and detection (the inner ear).

The ear reports two sensations to the brain, *pitch* and *loudness*. Pitch is a response to the dominant frequency in the sound. Loudness is a response to the intensity (i.e. the sound energy carried into the ear per square metre per second). The minimum intensity to which the ear can respond varies, but the notional minimum level $I_0$ is defined as $10^{-12}\,\mathrm{W\,m^{-2}}$. The loudness $L$ in *decibels* of a sound of intensity $I$ is defined by the formula

$$L = 10\log_{10}\left[\frac{I}{I_0}\right]$$

$L$ is around 50 dB in ordinary conversation; 80 dB is getting too noisy, and 100 dB is about the level of loud thunder. Around 120 dB is painful and 140 dB causes irreversible damage. Anything above 90 dB is damaging in the long term (loud music, pneumatic drills etc.)

**ECG waveform:** an ECG is an electrocardiogram, a chart produced by a machine called an electrocardiograph. This provides a non-invasive method for examining the electrical activity of the heart by gathering data from electrodes placed on the patient's skin. Expert analysis of the chart can provide a diagnosis of a fault in the heart's functioning.

**eddy currents** are induced currents in metallic supporting parts of electrical machinery such as motors or transformers. These metal parts either rotate at speed in a magnetic field or stand in a rapidly changing magnetic field. The *induced e.m.f.s* set up in the conductor drive current loops, known as eddy currents, through the metal. These current loops will, unless they are diminished by good design, represent a serious energy loss. In the case of transformer cores, eddy current loss is reduced by constructing the cores from thin, insulated steel sheets ('laminae') that are insulated from one another.

**edge dislocations** are *crystal defects* which extend along a line. They are found within a crystal where one plane suddenly ends and the planes on either side bend over the edge to close up the space left. This is a source of considerable weakness in a single crystal. Most metals are assemblies of thousands of tiny crystals called grains whose surfaces are called *grain boundaries*. Because dislocations cannot cross grain boundaries, a tight grain structure inhibits the flow of edge dislocations in the presence of stress and adds to the strength of the material as a whole.

**efficiency (machines):** the ratio of the useful work done by a *machine* (such as a pulley system) on a load (such as a weight) to the work done on the machine by the effort force. It is usually expressed as a percentage:

$$\text{efficiency} = \frac{\text{work done on load}}{\text{work done by effort force}} \times 100\%$$

If a machine has an efficiency of 80%, the implication is that about a fifth of any work done by the effort applied to the system is expended working against *friction*.

**efficiency (thermal power station)** is the ratio of the electrical energy leaving the thermal power station to the internal energy released when the primary fuel burns. The main losses are:

- energy released in the furnaces which is not carried to the turbines by the steam
- inefficiency in the conversion of energy carried in the steam into electrical power
- power losses during transmission of the electrical power

**Einstein's photoelectric equation:** see *photoelectric effect*.

**elastic collision:** a *collision* in which *kinetic energy* is conserved. If a collision obeys a different constraint, such as the two bodies sticking together on contact, then the collision cannot be elastic. The law of *conservation of linear momentum* is always obeyed.

**elastic limit:** the maximum stress which can be applied to an elastic specimen without causing a permanent change in the dimensions of the specimen. (See *stress–strain curves*.)

**elastic strain energy** is the energy stored in a material under stress. If the stress is tensile in nature, then the energy stored equals $\frac{1}{2}Fx$ where $F$ is the *tensile force* applied to the specimen and $x$ is the extension of the specimen, provided that the extension is proportional to the force, i.e. that the material obeys *Hooke's law*. (See *force–extension curves*.)

**elasticity** is the ability of a material to recover its original shape or size once a deforming stress has been removed. (See *stress–strain curves, plasticity*.)

**electric charge** is a fundamental property of matter. Amount of electric charge is defined by the word equation

$$\text{electric charge} = \text{electric current} \times \text{time}$$

The same word equation defines the SI unit of electric charge, the *coulomb*:

$$\text{coulomb} = \text{ampere} \times \text{second}$$

(See *coulomb, Coulomb's law, electric field strength*.)

**electric charge and electric current** are related physical quantities; electric current is the rate of flow of electric charge. Initially electric charge was studied in the static condition, distributed across the surface of a charged body. When different objects were charged by friction it was eventually established that there were two kinds of charge, now labelled positive and negative, and that like charges repel while unlike charges attract. At a later stage it was discovered that matter itself is electrical; atoms consist of negative electrons in their outer regions shielding positive nuclei at their centres.

An analysis of the forces between charged bodies led to the concepts of *electric field, electric field strength* and *electric potential*. Experiments with charged bodies led to the distinction between *conductors and insulators* and to the concept of *capacitance*.

Later still, simple electric cells were discovered. Experiments involving the rapid and repetitive charging and discharging of conductors established that electric current is flow of electric charge. The discovery of the *first law of thermodynamics* and energy conservation led to the definition of the *volt*, a stronger interpretation of electric potential, and the analysis of energy transformations in electric circuits. The final steps were the discovery of the *electromagnetic spectrum* and then the laws of relativity.

Electric current equals charge transferred per second. This idea is summarised mathematically in the equation

$$I = \frac{\Delta Q}{\Delta t} \text{ or } \Delta Q = I\Delta t$$

For a current in a uniform wire, this equation becomes

$$I = nAvq$$

where $I$ is the current, $n$ is the number of *charge carriers* per unit volume of wire, $A$ is the cross-sectional area of the wire, $v$ is the average speed of the charge carriers (called *drift speed*) and $q$ is the charge on the carriers.

For a beam of electrons, this equation becomes

$$I = nev$$

where $e$ is the *electronic charge* and $n$ is now the number of electrons per unit length of beam. Both equations follow immediately from the definition of current as the rate of flow of charge.

**electric circuit:** a complete loop of conducting material which includes a current source and a current detector. In his historic experiments, Galvani brought together by accident a simple battery (a moist iron nail piercing a copper sheet), a completed circuit (a frog's leg in contact with the copper sheet and the iron nail) and a detector (the nervous twitching action of the frog's leg).

For simple circuits, it is enough to be familiar with two equations, *Ohm's law* and the power equation. Both equations can be applied either to individual components or to the circuit as a whole. These equations for a single component are written as:

$$V = IR$$

$$\text{volt} = \text{ampere} \times \text{ohm}$$

$$P = IV = I^2R = v^2/R$$

$$\text{watt} = \text{volt} \times \text{ampere}$$

where $V$ is the *potential difference* across a component of resistance $R$, $I$ is the current flowing in the component and $P$ is the power dissipated in the component. Although it is general practice to assume that Ohm's law applies unless we are told otherwise, its strict application assumes that the temperature of the resistor is somehow held constant. Ohm's law applied to a complete circuit made up of a current source and resistors leads to a longer statement of Ohm's law. The circuit e.m.f. $E$ equals the sum of the potential differences $V$ taken round the circuit:

$$E = V_1 + V_2 + V_3 + \ldots$$
$$= I_1R_1 + I_2R_2 + I_3R_3 + \ldots$$

This equation is fundamentally an energy statement. $E$ is the energy in joules provided by the power supply to each coulomb of charge that loops the circuit. This energy is dissipated in the circuit components, including the power supply itself; each potential difference $V$

across a component is the energy per coulomb and in joules dissipated in that component. Any energy dissipation within the voltage source is looked after by the concept of *internal resistance*. Internal resistance accounts for any difference between e.m.f. $E$ and terminal potential difference $V$.

If $R$ represents the equivalent resistance of a complete circuit, we may write:

$$E = IR$$

Then, multiplying both sides by current $I$, we have:

$$EI = I^2R = P$$

It is helpful to read this equation through as a word equation:

(energy per coulomb) × (coulombs per second) = (energy per second) = power $P$

The longer form of the equation for a series circuit will be:

$$EI = V_1I + V_2I + V_3I + .... = P$$

$$\text{or } P = EI = I^2R_1 + I^2R_2 + I^2R_3 + ....$$

Complex electric circuits are analysed algebraically by applying *Kirchhoff's first law* to the junctions in the circuit and *Kirchhoff's second law* to the smallest number of circuit loops which, taken together, include every component in the complete circuit.

(See *ampere, coulomb, e.m.f., volt.*)

**electric circuit calculations** are numerical exercises which involve the application of Ohm's law, or other circuit principles, to the calculation of an unknown circuit component or quantity. The relevant ideas are the following.

- Ohm's law: $E = IR$ applies to a full circuit
  $V = IR$ applies to any component
- electrical power: $P = IV = I^2R = V^2/R$
- series resistors formula: $R = R_1 + R_2 + R_3 + \ldots$
- parallel resistors formula:

$$\frac{1}{R} = \frac{1}{R_1} + \frac{1}{R_2} + \frac{1}{R_3} + \ldots$$

- Kirchhoff's first law: $I = I_1 + I_2 + I_3 + \ldots$
- Kirchhoff's second law: $EI = I_1V_1 + I_2V_2 + I_3V_3 + \ldots$ for any complete loop in the circuit.

Skill with using these laws comes with practice. Notice that Kirchhoff's first law and the parallel resistors formula apply whenever a circuit divides. (See *Ohm's law, electrical power, Kirchhoff's first law, Kirchhoff's second law, resistors in parallel, resistors in series.*)

**electric field:** a region in which a force would act on an electric charge. The strength $E$ of an electric field is defined by the word equation

$$\text{electric field strength} = \frac{\text{force}}{\text{charge}}$$

$$E = \frac{F}{Q}$$

This definition of *electric field strength* also defines its SI unit as the newton per coulomb ($N C^{-1}$). An alternative SI unit for electric field strength is volt per metre ($V m^{-1}$). Since electric field strength and force are both vectors, it is assumed that the charge involved is positive. Also, the charge must be of infinitesimal size if it is not to distort the electric field whose strength it is being used to measure. The formal definition becomes:

> 'The electric field strength at a point is given, in magnitude and direction, by the force per unit charge acting on a very small positive charge placed at the point.'



We can deduce an equation for the case of two point electric charges. The force $F$ applied to a charge $Q_2$ by a charge $Q_1$ a distance $r$ away is given by *Coulomb's law*:

$$F = \frac{1}{4\pi\varepsilon_0} \cdot \frac{Q_1 Q_2}{r^2}$$

But

$$F = E Q_2$$

So the electric field strength $E$ a distance $r$ from a positive charge $Q$ is given by the equation

$$E = \frac{1}{4\pi\varepsilon_0} \cdot \frac{Q}{r^2}$$

and this equation leads directly (though the derivation is omitted) to an expression for the electric potential $V$ a distance $r$ from a positive charge $Q$:

$$V = \frac{1}{4\pi\varepsilon_0} \cdot \frac{Q}{r}$$

The electric potential $V$ at a point a distance $r$ from a positive charge $Q$ is the work done per unit charge bringing a very small positive charge from infinite distance to the point. This definition is a special case of the general definition for electric potential difference:

> 'The electric potential difference $V$ between two points equals the work done per unit charge bringing a very small positive charge from one point to the other.'

We can now write down a word equation for potential difference:

$$\text{potential difference} = \frac{\text{work done}}{\text{charge}}$$

The same equation defines the unit for potential difference:

$$\text{volt} = \frac{\text{joule}}{\text{coulomb}}$$

**electric field strength**, $E$ at a point is given, in magnitude and direction, by the force per unit charge acting on a very small positive charge placed at the point. The word equation definition is:

$$\text{electric field strength} = \frac{\text{force}}{\text{charge}}$$

$$E = \frac{F}{Q}$$

The SI unit of electric field strength is newton per coulomb ($N C^{-1}$) or volt per metre ($V m^{-1}$). Electric field strength near an isolated positive point charge $Q$ follows an inverse square law and is as follows:

$$E = \frac{1}{4\pi\varepsilon_0} \cdot \frac{Q}{r^2}$$

(See *electric field.*)

**electric motor:** a machine which transforms electrical energy into rotational mechanical energy by exploiting the force on a current-carrying conductor in a magnetic field.

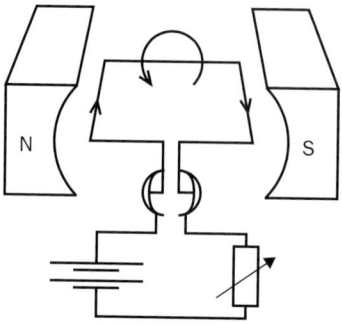


The diagram displays in simplified form the principle of the DC electric motor. The current is fed to the coil through a split ring commutator which ensures that the left-hand half of the coil always receives current and the right-hand half of the coil always returns it. A soft iron cylinder (not shown) between the curved poles of the magnet creates a radial field. This ensures that the plane of the coil is parallel to the magnetic field direction except when its inertia carries it through the vertical position. An application of *Fleming's left hand rule* to this situation shows that the force on the left-hand half of the coil is always downwards and that the force on the right-hand half of the coil is always upwards. The coil is forced by the current and the magnetic field to rotate in an anti-clockwise sense and this can be used to drive machinery and do work.

(See also *generator.*)

**electric potential,** $V$, at a point a distance $r$ from a positive charge $Q$ is the work done per unit charge bringing a very small positive charge from infinite distance to the point.

A little mathematics shows that

$$V = \frac{1}{4\pi\varepsilon_0} \cdot \frac{Q}{r}$$

If $r$ is infinitely large, $V$ goes to zero.

Electric potential is a special case of electric *potential difference*, which is defined as follows:

> 'The electric potential difference $V$ between two points equals the work done per unit charge bringing a very small positive charge from one point to the other.'

We can now write down a word equation for potential difference:

$$\text{potential difference} = \frac{\text{work done}}{\text{charge}}$$

The same equation defines the unit for potential difference, the volt:

$$\text{volt} = \frac{\text{joule}}{\text{coulomb}}$$

The force $F$ on positive charge $Q$ at a point where the electric field strength is $E$ is given by

$$F = EQ$$

and the work done moving this charge a distance $\mathrm{d}x$ against the direction of the electric field strength $E$ is:

$$\mathrm{d}W = F\mathrm{d}x = -EQ\mathrm{d}x$$

The negative sign is present because $E$ and $\mathrm{d}x$ are in opposite directions.

But $\mathrm{d}W = Q\mathrm{d}V$, where $\mathrm{d}V$ is the difference in potential between the two points. (This is how $\mathrm{d}V$ is defined.) These two expressions for $\mathrm{d}W$ can be equated to give

$$Q\mathrm{d}V = -EQ\mathrm{d}x$$

or:

$$E = -\frac{\mathrm{d}V}{\mathrm{d}x}$$

This important result states that electric field strength equals the potential gradient at a point and explains why a possible SI unit for electric field strength is volt per metre ($\mathrm{V\,m^{-1}}$).

This analysis can be extended to give an expression for the rate of energy dissipation when current flows in a resistor. The diagram below shows a conductor of resistance $R$ carrying current $I$ in response to a potential difference $V$.

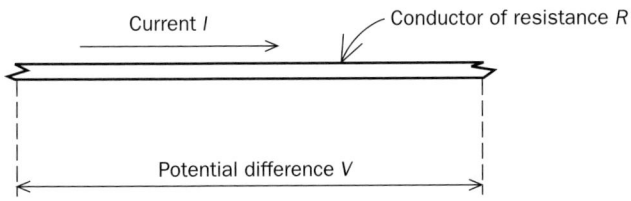


The energy expended by the current source in driving charge $Q$ through resistance $R$ across the potential difference $V$ is $W$, where

$$W = QV$$

But

$$Q = It$$

where $t$ is the time for which the current flows. So we now have

$$W = IVt = I^2Rt$$

and the rate of energy expenditure, the power $P$, is then

$$P = IV = I^2R$$

In terms of units, we have:

$$\text{joule} = \text{ampere} \times \text{volt} \times \text{second}$$

and

$$\text{watt} = \text{ampere} \times \text{volt}$$

(See *newton, joule, watt, ampere, coulomb, volt.*)

**electrical power** is either the rate of supply of electrical energy (= e.m.f. × current) or the rate of dissipation of electrical energy (= potential difference × current). The SI unit for electrical power is the *watt*, for which we now have two possible word equations:

$$\text{watt} = \frac{\text{joule}}{\text{second}} \qquad \text{W} = \text{Js}^{-1}$$

$$\text{watt} = \text{volt} \times \text{ampere} \qquad \text{W} = \text{VA}$$

**electrolytic capacitor:** large *capacitance* (in excess of 1.0μF) is almost always achieved with electrolytic capacitors. The dielectric between the plates is a polarised electrolyte which, because it can be made very thin, gives large capacitance in a small volume. There are two disadvantages, however, with electrolytic types. First, the capacitor has a positive and a negative plate and cannot withstand an alternating voltage. Secondly, electrolytic capacitors are slow-acting and can only be used with modest frequencies (a few kHz). Their stability is never perfect but this tends not to matter in typical applications such as smoothing circuits.

Other capacitors with mica or paper dielectrics can work at much higher frequencies and with alternating voltages, but their capacitance values are much smaller.

**electromagnetic induction** is the setting up of an electromotive force (e.m.f.) in a conductor by a change of *magnetic flux linkage*. Two typical situations, illustrated in the diagram below, are a magnet being passed through a coil and a conductor moving at right angles to a magnetic field. They represent two general cases: a fixed conductor in a changing magnetic field and a moving conductor in a fixed magnetic field. It is the change of magnetic flux linking the conductor (or, more crudely, the cutting of magnetic field lines by the conductor) which can be thought of as the cause of the induced e.m.f.. In neither case need the conductor be part of a complete circuit. If the circuit is incomplete, there will be no current but the e.m.f. is unaffected (this is the same situation as a battery in a circuit with the switch left open).

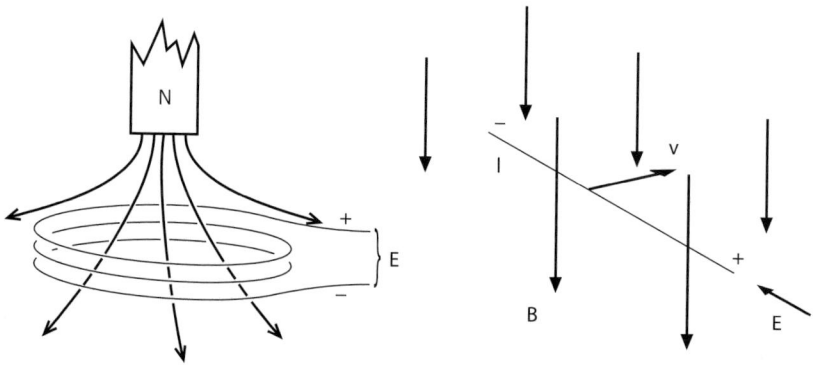


With a coil, let $\phi$ represent the instantaneous flux threading the coil and let $N$ represent the number of turns in the coil. The number of *flux linkages* for the coil is $N\phi$.

If $N\phi$ is changing, then the induced e.m.f. $E$ equals the rate of change of flux linkages:

$$E = -\frac{\mathrm{d}}{\mathrm{d}t}(N\phi) = -NA\frac{\mathrm{d}B}{\mathrm{d}t}$$

where $N$ is constant and $\phi$ equals $BA$, with $B$ being the average value across the coil of the magnetic field strength. The negative sign indicates that if $\phi$ is increasing, then any current driven by $E$ would create flux that is opposite in direction to $\phi$, thereby decreasing the rate of change of flux; on the other hand, if $\phi$ were decreasing, then any current driven by $E$ would create flux in the same direction as $\phi$.

***Faraday's law*** of electromagnetic induction states that induced e.m.f. is proportional to the rate of change of flux. It might seem that we have missed out a constant of proportionality in the equation for $E$; in fact, there is a constant of proportionality but, because of the way electrical units are defined, it equals 1 and has no unit.

Another way of looking at the situation is to observe that for each complete turn in the coil there is an induced e.m.f. $E'$, where

$$E' = -\frac{\mathrm{d}}{\mathrm{d}t}(\phi) = -A\frac{\mathrm{d}B}{\mathrm{d}t}$$

Since there are $N$ turns in series, the total e.m.f. is

$$E = N \times E' = -N\frac{\mathrm{d}}{\mathrm{d}t}(\phi) = -NA\frac{\mathrm{d}B}{\mathrm{d}t}$$

In the case of a single wire of length $l$ cutting across a magnetic field of uniform magnetic field strength $B$, the rate of change of flux is decided by the velocity $v$ of the wire:

$$E = -\frac{\mathrm{d}}{\mathrm{d}t}(N\phi) = -B\frac{\mathrm{d}A}{\mathrm{d}t} = -Bl\frac{\mathrm{d}x}{\mathrm{d}t} = -Blv$$

The significance of the minus sign here is that any current created by the induced e.m.f. would have direction such that the force set up on it by the magnetic field would oppose $v$. The agent responsible for moving the wire would do work on the wire by keeping it moving.

Another way of looking at the minus sign is to recognise that the magnetic flux $\phi$ could well originate with a current $I$ in the coil itself. Since $\phi$ would then be proportional to $I$, the equation for the induced e.m.f. could be written in the form

$$E = -\text{constant} \times \frac{\mathrm{d}I}{\mathrm{d}t} = -L\frac{\mathrm{d}I}{\mathrm{d}t}$$

If the current $I$ 'tries' to grow, the induced e.m.f. $E$ and the current $I$ will be in opposite directions and the growth of current will be inhibited. If the current $I$ 'tries' to get smaller, the induced e.m.f. will be in the same direction as the current and a fall in the value of $I$ will be inhibited. The constant $L$ is called the *self-inductance* of the coil.

The direction of the induced e.m.f. can be worked out also from *Fleming's right hand rule.*

There is no way of discovering that electromagnetic induction happens except by experiment. But once it is known that it happens, the law of conservation of energy must apply. The laws of electromagnetic induction can then be derived analytically.

Where the induced e.m.f. drives an induced current, electrical energy is transformed into heat energy. In the case where the e.m.f. comes from a change of magnetic flux linkages in a coil, energy stored in a magnetic field is transformed first into electrical energy and then into heat energy. Where the e.m.f. derives from the motion of a conducting wire across a magnetic field, energy transferred by mechanical work is transformed first into electrical energy and then into heat energy.

(See *electromagnetic induction (laws of).*)

**electromagnetic induction (laws of):** there are two laws — a law named after Faraday which gives the magnitude of an induced e.m.f. and a law named after Lenz which gives its direction.

You need to remember that the number of flux linkages equals $N\phi$ where $N$ is the number of turns and $\phi$ is the magnetic flux threading a circuit. For uniform magnetic fields, $\phi$ equals $BA$ where $B$ is the magnetic field strength and $A$ the cross-sectional area of the coil imagined to be at right angles to $B$.

Faraday's law:

> 'The magnitude of the e.m.f. induced in a conductor equals the rate of change of flux linkage or the rate at which the conductor cuts a magnetic flux.'

Lenz's law:

> 'The direction of the e.m.f. induced in a conductor is such that it opposes the change producing it.'

(The word 'equals' instead of 'proportional to' in Faraday's law comes about because of the way in which flux and flux linkage are defined, but this need not worry you. 'Conductor' is used instead of 'circuit' because an e.m.f. will be induced in a conductor if the circumstances are right, whether or not it is part of a circuit. For the same reason, there is no reference in the laws to induced current.)

An easier way to work out the direction of the induced e.m.f. is given by Fleming's right hand rule. (See *electromagnetic induction, Fleming's right hand rule, flux linkage.*)

**electromagnetic spectrum:** the range of electromagnetic waves listed in order of increasing wavelength or frequency. The main segments of the electromagnetic spectrum are: gamma radiation, X-rays, UV (ultraviolet), visible, IR (infrared), microwaves, radio waves. Each of these segments is described in more detail under its own heading. The main points are listed in the table opposite.

## The electromagnetic spectrum

| Wavelength | Frequency | Photon energy | Name | Origin | Detection | Properties | Uses |
|---|---|---|---|---|---|---|---|
| 1 fm to 1 nm | 0.3 YHz to 0.3 EHz | 1.2 GeV to 1.2 keV | Gamma radiation | Nuclear decay | Scintillation counter<br>GM tube (poor)<br>Photographic film | High penetration<br>Very high photon energy<br>Damaging | Medical diagnosis<br>Tracing underground pipes |
| 1 pm to 10 nm | 0.3 ZHz to 30 PHz | 1.2 MeV to 120 eV | X-rays | Inner shell excitation<br>X-ray tube | GM tube<br>Photographic film | High penetration of low-$Z$ materials | Diagnosis (low energy)<br>Therapy (high energy)<br>Crystallography |
| 1 nm to 400 nm | 0.3 EHz to 0.75 PHz | 1.2 keV to 3.1 eV | UV (ultraviolet) | Inner shell excitation<br>Mercury vapour lamps<br>Carbon arcs | Photocells<br>Photographic film<br>Solid-state detectors<br>Fluorescence | Damages living cells<br>Absorbed in stratosphere<br>Chemically destructive | Sterilising food etc.<br>Investigating atomic structure<br>Invisible labelling |
| 400 nm to 700 nm | 0.75 PHz to 0.43 PHz | 3.1 eV to 1.8 eV | Visible | Outer shell excitation<br>Hot bodies | Eyes<br>Photocells<br>Photographic film | Selective absorption by coloured surface<br>Chemically active | Vision<br>Photosynthesis<br>Communication |
| 700 nm to 1 mm | 0.43 PHz to 0.30 THz | 1.8 eV to 1.2 meV | IR (infrared) | Molecular excitation<br>Hot bodies | Thermopiles<br>Photography<br>Photocells for near-IR | Penetrates fog and mist<br>Emitted by dark surfaces | Satellite reconnaissance<br>Molecular structure<br>IR control for TV etc. |
| 1 mm to 10 cm | 0.30 THz to 3.0 GHz | 1.2 meV to 12 μeV | Microwaves | Klystron or magnetron valves | Tuned cavities<br>Point contact diodes | Focuses into beam<br>Absorbed by water<br>Reflected by metals | Microwave cooking<br>Communication<br>Satellite reconnaissance |
| > 10 cm | < 3.0 GHz | < 12 μeV | Radio waves | Electrons accelerated in metals (aerials) | Receiving aerials attached to tuning circuits | Reflected by ionosphere<br>Strongly diffracted | Communication and navigation systems<br>Radioastronomy |

Observe that some segments overlap, in particular gamma radiation and X-rays. This is because these segments are named according to their mode of origin and not their wavelength. Gamma radiation is considered to arise from radioactive decay and other nuclear processes, while X-rays arise from the deceleration of electrons. The energy ranges of these processes overlap.

Notice also that this table is not linear. The top of the X-ray energy band, 1.2 MeV, appears to be halfway between the bottom of the gamma radiation band at 1.2 keV and the top of the gamma radiation band at 1.2 GeV. In fact, the scale is logarithmic and 1.2 MeV is a thousandth part of 1.2 GeV. This logarithmic scale can be very misleading; the energy carried by radio waves is minuscule compared with the energy carried by gamma radiation.

(See *gamma radiation, X-rays, UV, visible spectrum, IR, microwaves, radio waves, photon.*)

**electromagnetic waves** are a flow of energy in the form of linked oscillating electric and magnetic fields. The energy is carried in discrete units known as *photons*. Each photon has energy $hf$, where $h$ is the Planck constant and $f$ is the frequency of the electromagnetic oscillation. Electromagnetic waves are classified into different groups which are named according to the mode of origin. (See *electromagnetic spectrum.*)

**electromotive force:** see *e.m.f.*

**electron:** an elementary particle of rest mass $9.109\,389 \times 10^{-31}$ kg which carries a negative electric charge of $1.602\,177 \times 10^{-19}$ C. (See *leptons.*)

**electron beams** usually consist of *electrons* released from a hot cathode by *thermionic emission*, all moving through vacuum with the same acceleration from cathode to anode. The speed with which the electrons arrive at the anode is calculated by equating the mechanical kinetic energy gained and the electrical potential energy lost:

$$eV = \tfrac{1}{2} m_e v^2$$

where $e$ is the electron charge, $V$ is the potential difference responsible for the acceleration of the electron, $m_e$ is the electron mass and $v$ is the final speed of the electron. $V$ is numerically equal to the energy of the electron in electron volts:

$$1 \text{ electron volt } (1 \text{ eV}) = 1 \times (1.602 \times 10^{-19} \text{ C}) \times (1 \text{ volt}) = 1.602 \times 10^{-19} \text{ J}$$

The electron volt may seem an odd unit of energy, but it is very useful in atomic and nuclear physics.

The energy equation is often used in the alternative form

$$v = \sqrt{\frac{2eV}{m}}$$

Electron beams with all the electrons moving at this same constant speed can be produced by arranging for the electrons to pass through a hole in the anode. This is the principle of the *electron gun*. Often, there are two cylindrical anodes held at slightly different voltages which both accelerate the electrons and focus them into a narrow beam. Electron beams can be deflected by electric or magnetic fields. An electron which is moving through an electric field and parallel to the lines of force will be accelerated; this is how electron beams get their energy. A magnetic field which is parallel to the direction of electron motion has no effect.

The diagram below shows three other common situations. Electrons, all with speed $v$, moving through a uniform electric field at right angles to the direction of motion retain their forward speed $v$ but accelerate against the direction of the field (against because of their negative charge). In a similar way to a football kicked sideways over a cliff, the electrons follow a parabolic path. The parabola is tightened by either reducing the speed $v$ or increasing the electric field strength.

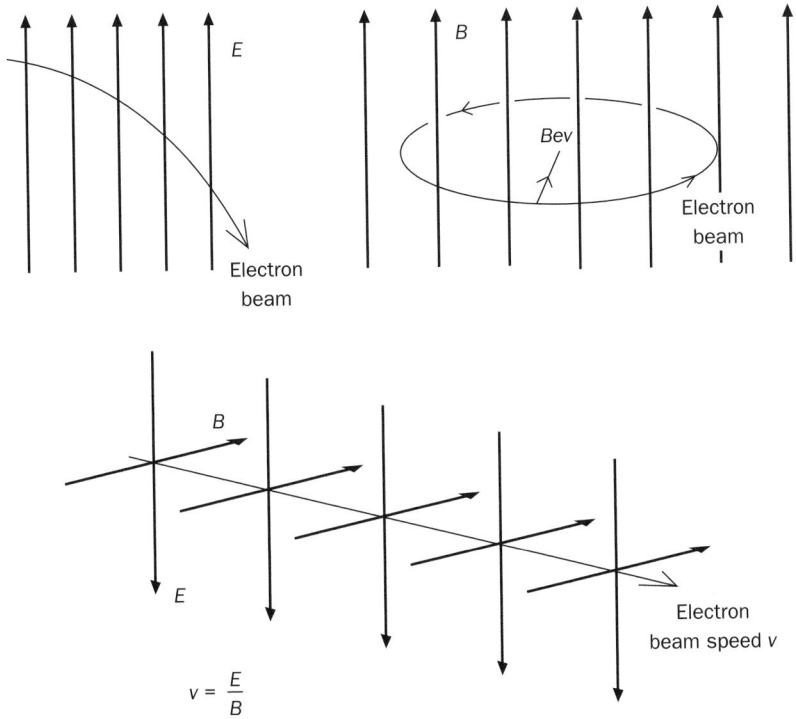


Electrons moving with constant speed $v$ at right angles to a magnetic field of strength $B$ are subjected to a force of magnitude $Bev$ directed at right angles both to the path of the electron and to the magnetic field. The actual direction satisfies *Fleming's left hand rule* — but remember that the current direction is opposite to the direction in which the electrons are moving. As the electron beam swings round, the direction of the deflecting force swings round too. The deflecting force is a centripetal force and the electrons follow a circular path. We may write

$$Bev = \frac{mv^2}{r} \quad or \quad r = \frac{mv}{Be}$$

The third important case is shown in the third part of the diagram; an electron beam with all the electrons moving at constant speed $v$ at right angles to a magnetic field of strength $B$ and an electric field of strength $E$, with $B$ and $E$ themselves at right angles. The magnitudes and direction can be arranged for the two deflections to just cancel and for the electrons to continue along their straight line paths. For this to happen, the speed of the electrons must be just right:

$$Bev = eE \quad or \quad v = \frac{E}{B}$$

This may seem like a non-event. In fact, if the electrons enter the crossed fields at all sorts of speeds and directions, only those electrons with the right speed and the right direction will get through. The arrangement is called a velocity selector. The principle of the velocity selector can be extended for use with any charged particle, especially protons and ions.

**electron capture** means the capture by an atom's nucleus of an electron from the atom's K-shell (hence the alternative name 'K-capture'). The K-shell is the shell nearest to the nucleus and contains the most tightly bound electrons. Electron capture is an alternative to $\beta^+$ decay and is much more common. An example is the decay of beryllium-7 into lithium-7:

$$^{7}_{4}\text{Be} + ^{0}_{-1}\text{e} \rightarrow ^{7}_{3}\text{Li} + ^{0}_{0}\nu$$

The neutrino and the electron have the same lepton numbers; lepton number is conserved. The captured electron combines with a proton in the nucleus to form a neutron:

$$^{1}_{1}\text{p} + ^{0}_{-1}\text{e} \rightarrow ^{1}_{0}\text{n} + ^{0}_{0}\nu$$

**electron diffraction** is illustrated by passing a narrow beam of electrons through thin gold foil. A detecting screen beyond the gold foil shows that the electrons, when they arrive, form a pattern of rings centred on the spot towards which the electrons were directed. The ring pattern is much the same as a diffraction pattern set up by a laser passing through a small circular hole. The relevant wavelength for the electron is the *de Broglie wavelength* $\lambda$ for the electron and is given by the formula

$$\lambda = \frac{b}{m_e v}$$

where $b$ is the Planck constant, $m_e$ is electron mass and $v$ is the speed of the electron.

If the electron wavelength is calculated and the radius of the diffraction rings measured, then a typical dimension can be calculated for the diffracting object. For low-energy electrons (about 100 V), information is collected about atomic size and crystal structure. Energies of up to 100 MeV are used to examine nuclear size, and electrons with energies of around 100 GeV are used to penetrate the proton and gain a modest amount of information about proton structure and quark diameter (less than $10^{-18}$ m). Protons and other subatomic particles can be used in a similar way. (See *diffraction at a small circular hole.*)

**electron gun:** see *particle accelerators.*

**electron volt:** the energy transferred to a free electron when it crosses a potential difference of 1 volt. Using the relation $W = QV$ we find that

$$1\text{eV} = \left(1.602 \times 10^{-19}\ \text{C}\right) \times (1\text{V}) = 1.602 \times 10^{-19}\ \text{J}$$

It is a useful energy unit when discussing events at the atomic level.

**electronic charge** is the charge carried by an electron. It is equal to the elementary charge (the charge of a proton) but opposite in sign. It is written:

$$e = -1.602\,176\,487 \times 10^{-19}\ \text{coulombs}$$

It is useful to memorise the value of $e$ as $1.60 \times 10^{-19}$ C.

**electrostatics** is the study of electric fields, charged matter and their interactions.

**elementary particles** (sometimes described as 'fundamental particles') are those *subatomic particles* which are thought not to have parts and which form the building blocks for other subatomic particles. They are too small to examine for any possible structure. Many of them are unstable and quickly decay into other elementary particles. There are two sets of elementary particles, *leptons* and *quarks*, and their typical diameter is smaller than $10^{-18}$ m.

Examples of elementary particles are electrons and neutrinos. Protons and neutrons are subatomic particles, but they are not elementary because each is made up of three quarks. *Exchange particles* are virtual particles which can only exist for a short time-span during an interaction. (See *fundamental interactions, Feynman diagrams.*)

**e.m.f.** (electromotive force) is the energy transformed into electrical energy per coulomb of charge flowing in a circuit. The symbol used is $E$ and the SI unit is the volt (V).

There is a real and vital difference between e.m.f. and *potential difference.* In loose terms, e.m.f. is the energy supply which makes current flow, and potential difference is the energy dissipated (often as heat) when current flows. A definition for electrical potential difference which would match the above definition of e.m.f. is:

> 'The potential difference between two points is the electrical energy transformed per coulomb of charge flowing between the two points.'

An understanding of the difference between e.m.f. and potential difference is fundamental to an understanding of *Kirchhoff's second law.*

Note that the presence of the word 'force' in 'electromotive force' should not mislead you into thinking that e.m.f. is a force; it is a voltage, that is, an amount of energy transformed per coulomb of charge. It is perfectly acceptable to use the term 'e.m.f.' as a noun in its own right, rather than the full but cumbersome 'electromotive force'.

**emission spectrum:** the electromagnetic radiation emitted by a hot body spread out to show how intensity varies with wavelength. It may be continuous, as in the *total radiation curve*, or discrete, as in the line spectrum of an element such as hydrogen or a band spectrum from a compound such as water. Line spectra have wavelengths ranging from the X-ray region to the IR, according to which electrons in particular atoms are excited. (See *absorption spectrum.*)

**end states of stars:** there are three end states — *white dwarfs, neutron stars* and *black holes.* Red giants and supernovae are intermediate stages. The end state of an individual *main sequence star* depends on its mass, which is usually expressed relative to the mass of the Sun, $M_{Sun}$.

***1 Red giants and white dwarfs.*** If the mass of a main sequence star is less than eight solar masses ($8M_{Sun}$), then, once the core hydrogen is largely used up, the hydrogen in the outer shell starts to fuse and the radiation pressure set up causes the radius of the outer shell of the star to increase a hundred-fold and the surface area ten thousand-fold. The rate of energy release by fusion will increase a thousand-fold, but the surface area increases ten times as much, so the surface brightness diminishes. The surface is cooler and the radius much larger, hence the term red giant.

After about $10^9$ years in the red giant state, the helium in the core suddenly starts to fuse. The whole process is completed in a matter of seconds. The sudden outburst of energy throws the shell away from the core. The core, robbed of any energy releasing process, shrinks into a high density state in which further collapse is prevented by pressure generated in the electron gas and known as 'electron degeneracy pressure'. The high temperature causes the star to look white, and the small radius (typically, the mass of the Sun in the volume of the Earth) explains the description 'dwarf'. The white dwarf cools down over about $10^9$ years and becomes a black dwarf. All this can happen only if the mass of the star remnant is less than $1.4M_{Sun}$ or if the main sequence mass is less than $8M_{Sun}$.

***2 Supernovae and neutron stars.*** Once the core hydrogen of a larger star is mostly gone, the core contracts and cools. If the total mass of the star is greater than about $8M_{Sun}$, then the mass of the core is likely to exceed $1.4M_{Sun}$ (known as the Chandrasekhar limit). In these circumstances, nuclei suddenly break up into a neutron–proton–electron mix. The protons released combine with electrons to give a neutron core which collapses in the absence of electromagnetic repulsion. Contraction is catastrophic; an enormous amount of gravitational energy is released through the shell, and this energy flow (a shock wave) prompts the immediate fusion of much of the shell material. For a short while (about a year), there is a spectacular release of radiant energy known as a supernova. The core is left behind as a neutron star whose mass is typically a few solar masses, with a radius equal to about ten kilometres. The density is enormous. The small radius implies a much reduced moment of inertia and a high spin speed (in radians per ms). This in turn explains the high repetition rate of the bursts of radio waves from pulsars, which are thought to be neutron stars.

***3 Black holes.*** These form if the remnant from a supernova has mass greater than about $2.5M_{Sun}$. This happens if the original total mass of the star exceeded about $20M_{Sun}$. The neutron core contracts into a radius about three or four times smaller still (i.e. a radius of a few kilometres instead of ten kilometres). The gravitational field near the surface is so strong that not even light can escape, hence the name 'black holes'. Efforts to detect black holes concentrate on either the possible influence on a nearby object if the black hole is part of a binary system, or on the deflection of a beam of light from an object far behind the black hole.

Another definition of a black hole is a star whose density is so great that the escape velocity exceeds the speed of light. The escape velocity $v$ for a star (or planet) of mass $M$ is $(2GM/R)^{1/2}$, so the radius of a black hole of mass equal to the sun's mass $M_{Sun}$ is $M_{Sun}$ $(2G/c^2)$; this is called the Schwarzschild radius. For the Sun, it comes out at 2.95 km; for the Earth, it is about 9 mm. (See *Hertzsprung–Russell diagram*, *star*.)

**energy** is the conserved quantity referred to in the *first law of thermodynamics*. It is a scalar quantity. The SI unit of energy is the joule (J). The usual symbol is $W$, but there are other symbols such as $E_k$ for kinetic energy.

The energy concept is now a fundamental part of our thinking. Energy is an intangible quantity. It cannot be seen or observed directly. An amount of energy is always calculated from other quantities which can be observed and measured. Almost all physical processes can be analysed as energy transfer or energy conversion processes. For example, a metal block may be heated using an electrical heater. The energy supplied electrically is calculated as voltage × current × time. The increase in internal energy of the block is calculated as mass × specific heat capacity × temperature rise. These two quantities are equal (energy is conserved) provided no energy is lost to or gained from the surroundings. (See also *work*, *internal energy*.)

**energy level:** a number of joules of *energy* which can be acquired and stored by an *extra-nuclear electron*, initially in the ground state, without the atom's hold on the electron becoming unstable. The energy levels of an atom are usually represented as a series of horizontal lines against a vertical energy scale; in this case the horizontal axis has no significance.

An atom which absorbs energy and stores it by transferring an electron to an energy level above the ground state is said to be in an 'excited' state. An atom which absorbs so much energy that an electron is ejected from the atom is said to be in an ionised state. Ionised atoms carry net positive charge; excited atoms do not.

The word 'state' has to be used carefully. It means the set of physical quantities such as energy, angular momentum and spin which together define the condition of an electron within an atom. The minimum set of values is called the ground state. Other states, the excited states, are defined with reference to the ground state.

If an atom transfers spontaneously from an excited state with energy $E_1$ to a lower state of energy $E_2$, the energy $E_1 - E_2$ is released in the form of a *photon* of frequency $f$, where $E_1 - E_2 = hf$. By measuring the energy changes corresponding to all the spectral lines emitted by an atom, it is possible to map the energy levels.



**energy–separation curve:** a graph which shows how the energy stored in the bond between two atoms varies with their separation. The diagram shows a typical example. The part of the curve where the bond energy is negative corresponds to the stable states; energy is needed to separate the atoms from one another.

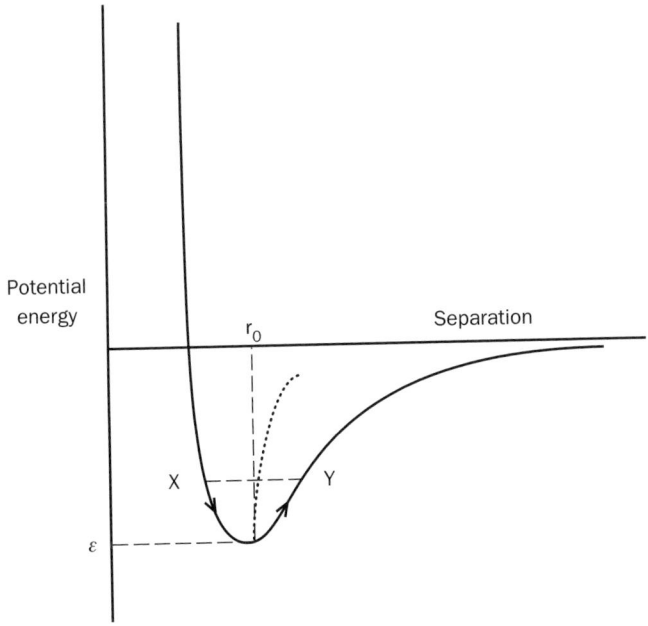


At absolute zero, $r_0$ is the separation of the centres of the two atoms. It is approximately equal to the atomic diameter and can be anything from about 0.1 nm to 0.5 nm. Above absolute zero, the atomic pair has more than this minimum amount of energy, and the extra energy allows the atomic pair to oscillate between a minimum separation at X and a maximum separation at Y. The average separation lies halfway between X and Y. This allows us to construct the dotted line which creeps upwards and outwards, indicating that the average separation of atoms increases as they gain energy (i.e. as the temperature rises). This is one of the reasons why solids expand on heating.

The steepness of the dotted line is inversely related to the linear expansivity of the material. A deep potential well implies low linear expansivity, high specific latent heats, high melting and boiling points, high *Young modulus* and high *strength*.

**energy sources** can be divided into primary and secondary types.

Primary energy sources are sources of energy in their natural state; they are either finite or renewable. Finite energy sources include fossil fuels and nuclear fuels. Renewables include solar energy, hydroelectricity, wind power and *biofuels*. The term *biofuels* is of recent origin and should not be extended to include *fossil fuels*. Peat is a fossil fuel; wood is a biofuel.

Secondary energy sources such as electricity or petrol are produced from primary fuels.

(See also *finite energy sources, fissile materials, renewable energy sources, thermal power station, thermal fission reactor.*)

**energy stored in a capacitor** of capacitance $C$ and with a potential difference $V$ across its plates is $\frac{1}{2}CV^2$. To derive this result, we look at the graph of potential difference $V$ (*ordinate*) against charge $Q$ (*abscissa*). The following diagram of the capacitor shows the negative plate earthed to ensure that it remains at a zero reference potential.

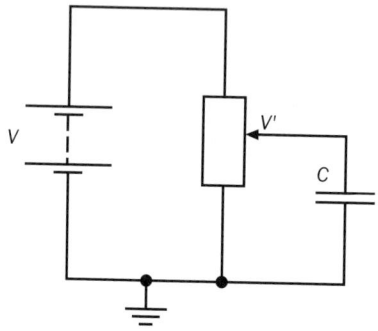


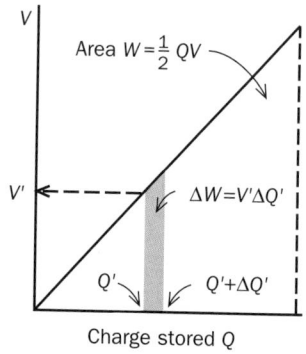


At some point in the charging process, the potential difference across the capacitor will be $V'$ and the charge stored will be $Q'$. Imagine a small extra charge $+\Delta Q'$ added to the positive plate. An equal but opposite small negative charge will be drawn from Earth to the earthed plate to keep it at Earth potential. The work expended in bringing the charge $+\Delta Q'$ to the positive plate is $+V'\Delta Q'$ and this equals the area of the shaded strip of width $\Delta Q'$ and (approximate) height $V'$. It follows that the work $W$ expended in bringing the whole charge $+Q$ to the positive plate is the sum of the areas of countless thin strips, i.e. the area between the potential-charge line and the charge axis. Therefore the energy $W$ stored in a charged capacitor is $\frac{1}{2}QV$.

$$Q = CV \quad \text{and} \quad W = \frac{1}{2}QV = \frac{1}{2}CV^2 = \frac{Q^2}{2C}$$

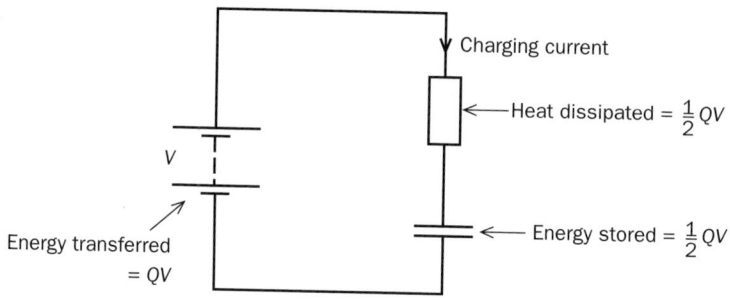


The symbol $W$ in the previous paragraph represents the energy stored in the charged capacitor. The energy transferred from the battery during the charging process is different.

The simplest way to charge a capacitor is to connect it across a battery, through a resistor to control the current. The situation is illustrated in the diagram above. The charge $Q$ which ends up on the capacitor leaves the battery at potential $V$ relative to earth and carries electrical energy $QV$ from the battery. Only half of this energy is stored in the capacitor. The other half is expended in the resistor by the charging current. From the battery's 'point of view', the energy stored in the capacitor is literally only half of the story.



**Worked example**

**Calculate the energy stored in the 4 μF capacitor in the circuit below once the charging process is complete.**

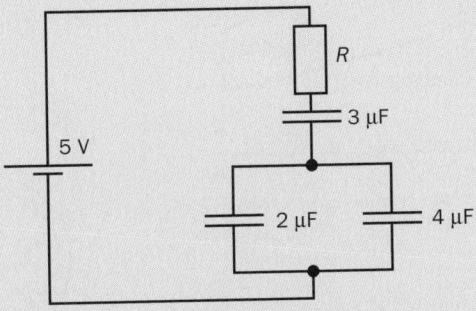


To calculate the energy stored in a known capacitance, the voltage across it must be known. To find this we find the charge on the 3 μF capacitor, but first we need to know the equivalent capacitance of the whole arrangement. The 2 μF in parallel with the 4 μF are equivalent to 6 μF (see capacitors in parallel). The equivalent capacitance for 6 μF in series with 3 μF is calculated as follows:

$$\frac{1}{C} = \frac{1}{C_1} + \frac{1}{C_2} = \frac{1}{3} + \frac{1}{6} = \frac{1}{2}$$

$$C = 2\mu\text{F}$$

The charge carried by this equivalent capacitance is found from the relationship $Q = CV$. With $V$ equal to 5 V, the charge is 10 μC. This equals the charge on the 3 μF capacitor. The voltage across the 3 μF capacitor is found from $V = Q/C$. It equals 3.33 V. The voltage across the 4 μF capacitor must be 1.67 V and the energy stored is 5.6 μJ.

**energy transfer** is either the transfer of energy from one body to another or the displacement of energy within a body. The transfer of energy in an ordered form is called *work*. The transfer of energy in the disordered form is called *heating*. (See *heating and working*.)

**engine cycle:** the full cycle of actions undergone by a repetitive engine such as a steam engine or a car engine. A cyclical engine is in exactly the same condition at the end of a cycle as it was in when the cycle began. Input and output can be precisely balanced.

The equation for the efficiency of a *heat engine*, $\eta = [T_1 - T_2]/T_1$, imposes an upper limit to the efficiency of any engine which transforms heat into mechanical energy, whether or not it is cyclical. It applies, for instance, to a thermocouple delivering current to a micro-motor or to the human body drawing mechanical energy from its food supply. The derivation of the equation hinges on the first and second laws of *thermodynamics*.

Consider two engine cycles, the four-stroke petrol cycle and the Diesel engine cycle. The main difference between these is the ignition phase which is triggered by a spark in the four-stroke petrol engine but is spontaneous in the Diesel engine. This is because the Diesel engine works at a significantly higher temperature and pressure. The two engine cycles are illustrated in the diagram. Such diagrams are, for historical reasons, called indicator diagrams. The area enclosed by the loop in an indicator diagram equals the work done by the engine per cycle.

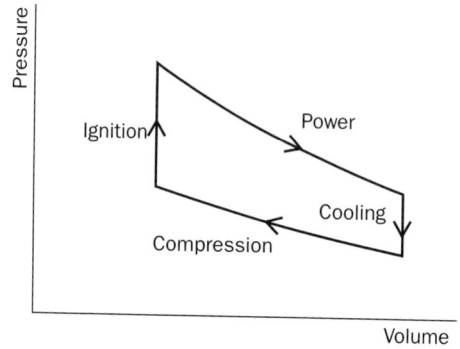


*Four-stroke petrol engine cycle*

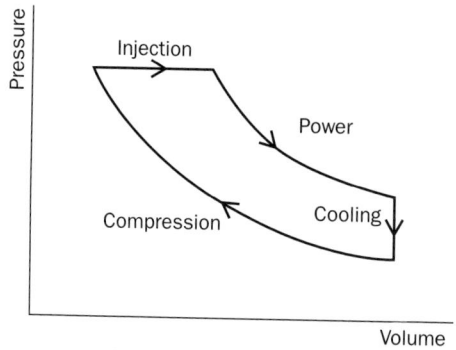


*Diesel engine cycle*

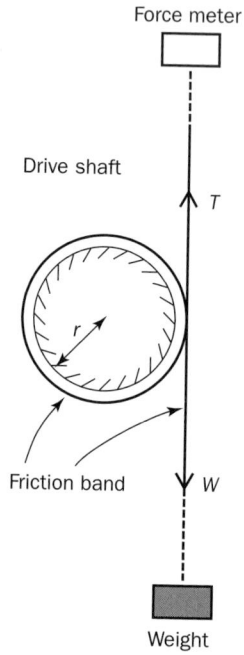


The theoretical upper limit to the efficiency of the four-stroke engine is about 60%, but in practice it is about 30%. The Diesel engine runs at a slightly higher temperature, there is a higher theoretical efficiency, and the efficiency in practice is nearer 40%. These efficiencies can be checked by running the engine against a frictional torque applied to the drive shaft by a large mass of known weight supported by a friction band. The friction band runs once round the shaft and the difference in tensions ($T - W$) multiplied by the radius of the shaft is the output *torque*. The output energy, equal to the output torque multiplied by the *angle* turned in *radians*, can be compared with the energy provided by the fuel.

**equation of state:** an equation relating thermodynamic properties (such as temperature, volume and pressure) of a system; an example is the *ideal gas equation*.

**equations of motion** are the five equations which describe uniformly accelerated motion along a straight line. There are five variables involved:

$s$ displacement in metres ($s$ must be zero at time $t = 0$)
$t$ time in seconds
$u$ initial velocity (i.e. velocity at time $t = 0$) in metres per second ($\mathrm{m\,s^{-1}}$)
$v$ final velocity (i.e. velocity at time $t$) in metres per second ($\mathrm{m\,s^{-1}}$)
$a$ acceleration (which must be constant or zero) in metres per second squared ($\mathrm{m\,s^{-2}}$)

From the symbols for these five quantities, the equations are sometimes dubbed the 'suvat equations'.



Since $s$ is displacement, not distance or distance travelled, the straight line has positive and negative directions. The positive direction for displacement sets the positive direction for velocity and for acceleration. The initial and final velocities and the acceleration, like displacement, may have positive or negative values. This underlines their vector nature. Only $t$ is a scalar. Negative values of $t$ imply times earlier than $t = 0$.

The equations of motion are:

$$s = \frac{u+v}{2}t \quad (a \text{ missing})$$

$$v = u + at \quad (s \text{ missing})$$

$$s = ut + \frac{1}{2}at^2 \quad (v \text{ missing})$$

$$s = vt - \frac{1}{2}at^2 \quad (u \text{ missing})$$

$$v^2 = u^2 + 2as \quad (t \text{ missing})$$

Notice that each of the five variables is missing from one of the equations. The first equation follows from the definition of average *velocity*. The second equation is from the definition of uniform *acceleration*. The last three equations can be derived algebraically from the first two — the third by eliminating $v$, the fourth by eliminating $u$ and the fifth by eliminating $t$.

It is instructive to see how the first four equations can be read out from a velocity–time graph.

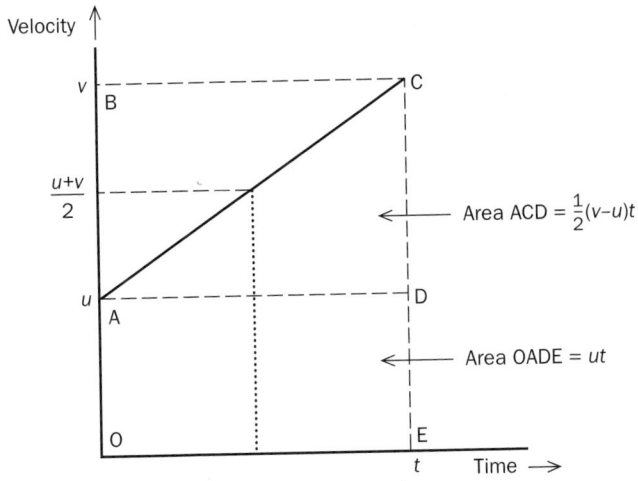


For the first equation, displacement $s$ at time $t$ equals the area OACDE and this equals half of $(u+v)$ multiplied by OE (i.e. multiplied by $t$), so we have $s = [(v+u)/2] \times t$.

For the second equation, notice that acceleration $a$ is the gradient of the graph, and $a$ equals CD/$t$, so CD equals $at$. But also CD = $v - u$, hence the second equation, $v - u = at$.

For the third equation, displacement $s$ equals the area OACDE. But area OACDE equals area OADE (which is $ut$) plus the area ACD. The area ACD equals ½ AD times CD, where AD is $t$ and CD is $at$. Therefore area ACD = $\frac{1}{2}at^2$, whence $s = ut + \frac{1}{2}at^2$

For the fourth equation, displacement equals area OBCE minus area ABC, i.e. $s = vt - \frac{1}{2}at^2$.

**Worked example**

**A student with a stopwatch drops a stick into a well and hears the plop 3.2 seconds later. Calculate the depth of the well and the final velocity of the stick. State two reasons why your answer for the depth of the well is an overestimate.**

Data: $t = 3.2\,\text{s}$, $u = 0\,\text{ms}^{-1}$, $a = 9.8\,\text{ms}^{-2}$; find $s$ and then $v$.

$$\begin{aligned} s &= ut + \tfrac{1}{2}at^2 \\ &= 0 + 0.5 \times \left(9.8\,\text{ms}^{-2}\right) \times \left(3.2\,\text{s}\right)^2 = 50.18\ \text{m} \\ &= 50\ \text{m to 2 s.f.} \\ v^2 &= u^2 + 2as \\ &= 0 + 2 \times \left(9.8\ \text{ms}^{-2}\right) \times 50.18\ \text{m} = 983.4\ \text{m}^2\text{s}^{-2} \\ v &= \sqrt{\left(983.4\ \text{m}^2\text{s}^{-2}\right)} = 31.36\ \text{ms}^{-1} \\ &= 31\ \text{ms}^{-1}\left(\text{to 2 s.f.}\right) \end{aligned}$$

Notice that the calculations are worked through with as many significant figures as appear during the calculation, but the extra significant figures are removed from the answers.

If there were no air resistance, $t$ would be smaller; if eyes were used in place of ears, $t$ would also be smaller (by about 0.15 second) because light travels much faster than sound. The exaggerated fall time gives an exaggerated depth.

The equations of motion are derived from the definitions of average velocity and uniform acceleration. Each equation contains four variables, and you will always need data for three of them. Often, part of the data is given in a hidden form, from which you have to extract the relevant data. One way of doing this might be to derive a uniform acceleration value from a mass and a force given; another is to find, say, a final velocity value by employing the relationship potential energy lost equals kinetic energy gained. Alternatively, a word like 'dropped' implies both that the initial velocity is zero and that the acceleration is that of *free fall* (as in the worked example above).

**equilibrium:** see *forces in equilibrium*.

**equipotential lines** are lines drawn that join points of equal potential in an electric or gravitational field. They are always at right angles to the field lines. No work is done (no energy is transferred) in moving a charge or mass along an equipotential line. (See *radial electric field*.)

**error** is the difference between the result of a measurement and the true value. An error cannot be found unless the true value is known. Where the true value is not known, the relevant concept to deal with is *uncertainty*. Some people use the term 'probable error' instead of 'uncertainty'. Errors can be stated in absolute terms, e.g. 4 mm, or as a percentage of the true value, e.g. –5%. Notice that the symbol ± is used with uncertainties but not with errors. Either an error is positive or it is negative.

Notice that the term error does not imply that the person involved in making the measurements has made a mistake. (See also *random error, systematic error, precision, sensitivity.*)



**escape speed** is the vertical speed with which an object must leave the Earth's surface (or the surface of some other planet or star) to escape from the gravitational field. For this to happen, the object must have more kinetic energy than the potential energy it would lose were it to fall to Earth from an infinite distance away.

The gravitational potential near the Earth's surface is $-GM/r$ where $G$ is the universal gravitational constant ($6.67\times 10^{-11}\,\mathrm{N\,m^2\,kg^{-2}}$), $M$ is the Earth's mass ($5.98\times 10^{24}\,\mathrm{kg}$) and $r$ is the Earth's radius ($6.37\times 10^{6}\,\mathrm{m}$). The potential energy of an object of mass $m$ at the Earth's surface is $-GMm/r$, and for the object to escape from the Earth's gravitational field its total energy within the field must be positive, that is:

$$\frac{1}{2}mv^2 - \frac{GMm}{r} > 0$$

$$v > \sqrt{\left(\frac{2GM}{r}\right)}$$

$$v > \sqrt{\left(\frac{2\times(6.67\times10^{-11}\ \mathrm{N\,m^2\,kg^{-2}})\times(5.98\times10^{24}\ \mathrm{kg})}{(6.37\times10^{6}\ \mathrm{m})}\right)}$$

$$v = 11.2\times10^{3}\ \mathrm{m\,s^{-1}}\ (\text{to 3 s.f.})$$

Hence an object thrown vertically from the surface of the Earth with a speed of $11.2\,\mathrm{km\,s^{-1}}$ or greater will escape from the Earth's gravitational field. (It will gradually slow down as it rises, but its initial speed is great enough for it to escape.)

Note that escape speed is sometimes erroneously known as 'escape velocity'; but it is not a vector quantity.

(See *gravitational potential (radial fields).*)

**evaporation and cooling** are processes which occur together. The average kinetic energy of the molecules in a liquid mass depends only on its temperature. However, there is a spread of energy values among the molecules, and molecules which are both near the surface and moving faster than average can escape from the liquid mass — this is evaporation. The molecules involved in evaporation take away from the liquid more than their share of molecular kinetic energy. The average kinetic energy of the remaining molecules is therefore smaller than before and the temperature goes down.

**event horizon:** see *Schwarzschild radius.*

**exchange particles** are formed momentarily when *subatomic particles* react through the *fundamental interactions*. They exist momentarily during the interaction and their existence is essential to whatever process is going on. Their existence is made possible by the Heisenberg *uncertainty principle* which asserts that a particle of mass–energy $\Delta E$ can exist spontaneously for time $\Delta t$ provided that $\Delta E\cdot\Delta t \le h/(2\pi)$ where $h$ is the ***Planck's constant***. The higher the mass–energy of an exchange particle, the shorter the lifetime.

Exchange particles come in four sets, one set for each fundamental interaction, and they are collectively called gauge bosons. Bosons are particles with integer spin; they are not subject to the Pauli exclusion principle. Gauge bosons are called virtual particles in recognition of their dependence on Heisenberg's uncertainty principle.

*Photons* are associated with the electromagnetic interaction acting alone or with the electroweak interaction. They are formed when charged particles either collide with one another or are deflected in a strong electric or magnetic field. Examples range from radio waves emitted from aerials, through visible photons released when excited atoms return to a lower energy state, to high-energy X-ray photons associated with charged matter racing into a black hole from a nearby star.

Three exchange particles are associated with the weak interaction, namely the $W^-$, $W^+$ and $Z^0$ bosons. Their masses are roughly a hundred times the proton mass and their lifetimes are about $10^{-25}$ s. This does not seem very long, but it is long enough for reactions that take place at the scale of a quark. Following this short lifetime, exchange particles decay into leptons and neutrinos. W particles, which come about when neutrons decay into protons or vice versa, themselves decay into the beta particles and neutrinos apparent in beta decay. (See *Feynman diagrams.*) The electroweak interaction comes about when electromagnetic forces are operating at the same time as the weak interaction.

Gluons are the exchange particles responsible for the operation of the strong interaction. There are eight kinds in all. (See *hadrons.*)

***General relativity*** predicts the existence of gravity waves when two large masses interact gravitationally. Gravitons, which have yet to be observed, are introduced as part of an attempt to reconcile general relativity with the fundamental interactions.

**excitation** is the process by which an atom receives energy and moves from the ground or non-excited state to a higher *energy level* or, as it is also called, an excited state.

**explosion:** a situation in which bodies that are initially close together move apart when energy is supplied to the system. If the bodies are initially stationary, their linear momentum and kinetic energy are both zero. After the explosion, the bodies have gained kinetic energy but their total linear momentum is still zero (because of the law of *conservation of linear momentum*).

In the laboratory, an explosion may be created by arranging for two trolleys to separate when a spring between them is released. The linear momentum of each trolley is the same in magnitude but opposite in direction.

**exponential decay** happens when the rate of decay of a quantity is a constant fraction of the present value of the quantity. Imagine you have £100 in a failing bank which reduces your balance by 15% at the end of each year. You will have £85 after one year, £72 after two years, then £61, £52, £44 and so on.

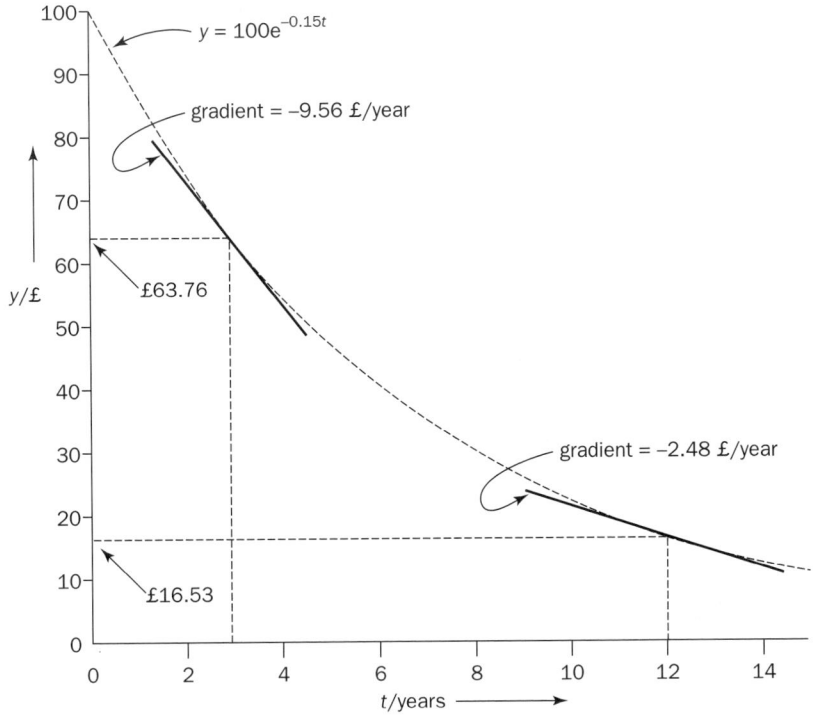


If the negative interest rate, still 15% per annum, is subtracted continuously instead of annually, then the balance would be more difficult to work out. If $y$ represents the balance, then it would decay with time according to the following formula:

$$y = 100\,e^{-0.15t}$$

where the number e is called the exponential constant; it is 2.71828 to six significant figures. A graph of balance $y$ against time $t$ in years is shown above. It represents exponential decay with a halving time of 4.62 years and covers a little more than three half lives.

This graph is called an exponential decay curve. Its most important property is illustrated by evaluating the gradients of the tangents to the curve at two points chosen more or less arbitrarily. When $t$ is 3 years, $y$ is 63.76 and the gradient is –9.56. When $t$ is 12 years, $y$ is 16.53 and the gradient is –2.48. In both cases we have

$$\text{gradient} = -0.15y$$

In other words, the rate of decrease of $y$, $dy/dt$, is proportional to $y$: $dy/dt \propto y$.

A quantity decays exponentially if the instantaneous decay rate equals a constant times the value of the quantity at that instant.

The following examples of exponential decay all follow a graph of the same shape as the curve in the diagram on the next page, but the axes would be labelled differently.

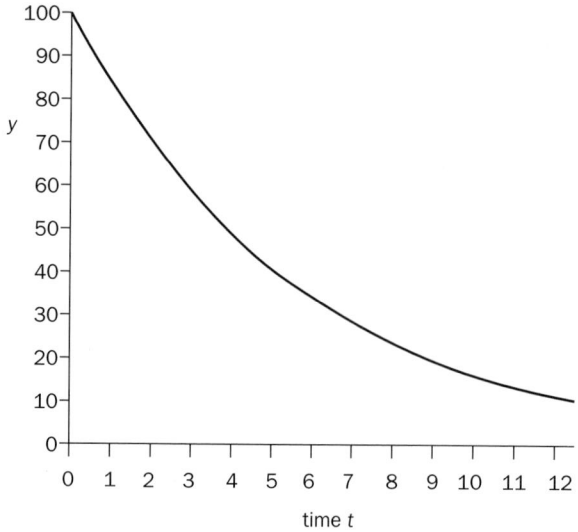


***1 Damped harmonic motion.*** If the $y$-axis represents the peak value at an instant $t$ of the amplitude $x_0$ associated with an object undergoing *simple harmonic motion* and if this peak amplitude diminishes at a rate proportional to the existing value of the peak amplitude, then

$$\frac{dx_0}{dt} = -kx_0$$

where $k$ is a constant. This leads us to the exponential decay of peak amplitude:

$$(x_0)_t = x_0 e^{-kt}$$

and the full equation for the displacement of an object undergoing damped harmonic motion becomes:

$$x = x_0 e^{-kt} \sin \omega t$$

***2 Capacitor discharging through a resistor.*** If the $y$-axis represents the charge $Q$ stored in a capacitor $C$ and discharging through a resistance $R$, then the rate of discharge $dQ/dt$ is proportional to the current $I$ in the resistor. But the current is proportional to the voltage $V$ across the capacitor, and this voltage is proportional to the charge on the capacitor. This leads us to

$$\frac{dQ}{dt} = I = \frac{V}{R} = -\frac{Q}{RC} = -\frac{1}{RC}Q$$

The charge stored in the capacitor diminishes exponentially with time and the rate at which it diminishes is inversely proportional to the product $RC$.

***3 Radioactive decay.*** If the $y$-axis represents the number $N$ of radioactive nuclei in a sample still not decayed after time $t$, and if the number of nuclei decaying per second is proportional to $N$, then

$$\frac{dN}{dt} = -\text{constant} \times N = -\lambda N$$

$$N = N_0 e^{-\lambda t}$$

The first equation is the *fundamental law of radioactive decay*; the second is the *exponential law of radioactive decay.*

All three examples follow the same mathematical pattern — they all lead to a graph of the same shape and end up with an exponential decay law.



**exponential law of radioactive decay** states that if $N$ represents the number of undecayed atoms of a particular *nuclide* present in a sample at time $t$ and $N_0$ represents the number of undecayed atoms that were present at time $t = 0$, then

$$N = N_0 e^{-\lambda t}$$

The *decay constant* $\lambda$ is defined in the *fundamental law of radioactive decay*:

> 'The decay constant $\lambda$ for a radioactive isotope is the ratio of the rate of decay for a large and pure sample of the isotope to the number of undecayed nuclei in the sample.'

The decay constant is shown below to be related to the *half-life* $t_{1/2}$ as follows:

$$t_{\frac{1}{2}} = \frac{\ln 2}{\lambda} = \frac{0.693}{\lambda}$$

The exponential law derives from the fundamental law of radioactive decay but with the random character of the decay smoothed away. Imagine a sample of $N$ nuclei, none of which has yet decayed. Provided that $N$ is a very large number, the number $\Delta N$ which will decay in the next $\Delta t$ seconds is proportional both to the number $N$ of nuclei available for decay and the length of the time interval $\Delta t$, that is,

$$\Delta N = -\lambda N \Delta t$$

where $\lambda$ is a proportionality constant called the decay constant. Its unit is second$^{-1}$. This equation is called the fundamental law of radioactive decay. The negative sign is present because $\Delta N$ represents a reduction in the value of $N$. Both $\Delta N$ and $\Delta t$ are finite quantities.

If $N$ were a continuous variable instead of always being a whole number, the fundamental law of radioactive decay could be written in the modified form:

$$\frac{dN}{dt} = \lambda N$$

This equation can be integrated between time zero and time $t$ to give the exponential law of radioactive decay:

$$N = N_0 e^{-\lambda t}$$

The exponential decay curve is shown in the diagram on page 94. The half-life, i.e. the time interval over which half the specimen decays, is the same for all points along the curve.

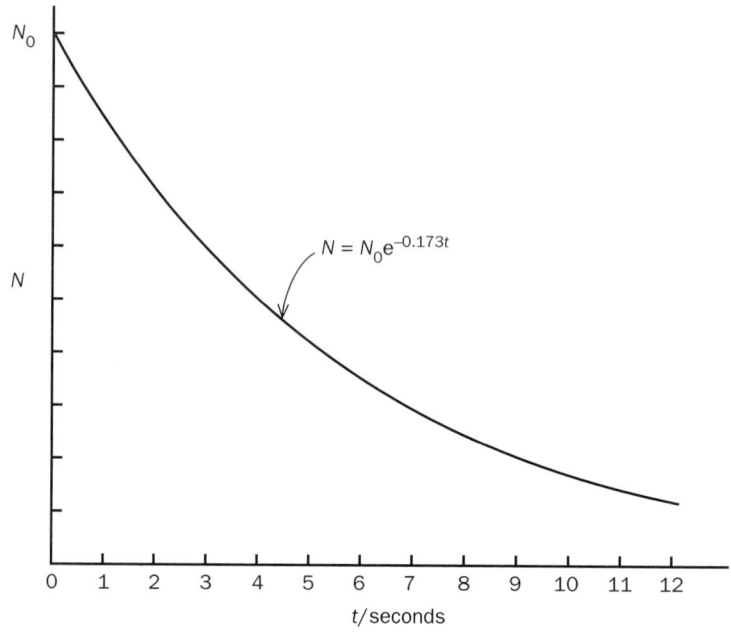


The curve is smooth and mathematical. A magnified section of the graph would contrast the erratic nature of the actual decay with the regularity of the exponential decay curve.

The half-life $t_{1/2}$ of a radioactive nuclide is the value of $t$ for which $N$ equals one half of $N_0$. In equation form, this is:

$$\frac{N}{N_0} = \frac{1}{2} = e^{-\lambda t_{1/2}}$$
$$2 = e^{\lambda t_{1/2}}$$
$$\ln 2 = \lambda t_{1/2}$$
$$0.693 = \lambda t_{1/2}$$
$$t_{1/2} = \frac{0.693}{\lambda}$$

The only way the theoretical curve can be drawn in practice is by measuring the half-life and using it to calculate successive values of $N$. But half-life is another mathematical abstraction. We get around this by defining half-life as follows:

> 'The half-life of a radioactive nuclide is the average time taken for half the nuclei in a sample of the nuclide to decay.'

By insisting that half-life is the average value of the measurements, there is no theoretical limit to its accuracy. This bridges the gap between $\Delta N/\Delta t$ and $dN/dt$.

The activity $A$ of a sample and the detected count rate $C$ follow the same pattern and hence are given by similar mathematical expressions:

$$A = A_0e^{-\lambda t}$$
$$C = C_0e^{-\lambda t}$$

**Worked examples**

1 **The count rate from an irradiated indium foil falls from 8000 counts per minute to 500 counts per minute in 220 minutes. Find the half-life of the decaying isotope.**

The fractional drop in the count rate in 220 minutes is:

$$\frac{500}{8000} = \frac{1}{16} = \left(\frac{1}{2}\right)^4$$

Since 220 minutes is 4 half-lives, the half-life is 55 minutes.

2 **The half-life of $^{226}$Ra is 1620 years. Calculate: (a) the disintegration constant; (b) how long it takes for 60% of a given sample to decay; and (c) the activity of 1 g of pure $^{226}$Ra. (Avogadro constant L = $6.02 \times 10^{23}$ mol$^{-1}$.)**

(a) One year is $31.6 \times 10^6$ seconds:

$$\lambda = \frac{0.693}{t_{1/2}} = \frac{0.693}{(1620 \times 31.6 \times 10^6 \text{ seconds})} = 1.35 \times 10^{-11} s^{-1}$$

(b) When 60% of the radon has decayed, 40% is left, so

$$\frac{N}{N_0} = 0.40 = e^{-\lambda t}$$

$$\ln 0.40 = -0.916 = -\lambda t$$

$$t = \frac{0.196}{(1.35 \times 10^{-11} s^{-1})} = 6.79 \times 10^{10} s$$

$$= 2.1 \times 10^3 \text{ years (to 2 s.f.)}$$

(c) $N_0$ for 1 g of pure radon is $(6.02 \times 10^{23})/226$. We write:

$$\text{activity of 1g of radon} = \frac{dN}{dt} = -\lambda N_0$$

$$= (1.35 \times 10^{-11} s^{-1})\left(\frac{6.02 \times 10^{23}}{226}\right)$$

$$= 3.6 \times 10^{10} \text{Bq} \quad \text{(to 2 s.f.)}$$

**extra-nuclear electrons:** electrons with orbits that take up a large fraction of the atom's volume and whose number equals the number of protons in the nucleus. This is the *atomic number Z*. The extra-nuclear electrons decide the chemical properties of an atom and most of the physical properties of the materials of which they form a part. Note that there are no electrons inside the nucleus. A negative beta particle is an electron emitted by the nucleus in the process of *beta decay*, but the electron itself did not exist inside the nucleus before the decay occurred.

**eye:** the organ of sight. The main parts of the human eye are shown in the diagram. The image of a distant object is focused on the retina mostly by the curved transparent surface at the front of the eye, the cornea. The lens acts as a fine adjustment for this focusing power; its *focal length* is controlled by the ciliary muscles. The lens grows stiffer with age and there comes a time when it is no longer supple enough to bring the focal plane of an object at reading distance from behind the eye onto the retina; the subject becomes long-sighted and needs glasses. Others need glasses from birth, either because the curvature of the cornea is a little high for the eye's length (short-sighted) or a little too low (long-sighted). Short sight is corrected with a diverging lens to push the image back; long sight is corrected with a converging lens to bring the image forward. (See *defects of vision*.)

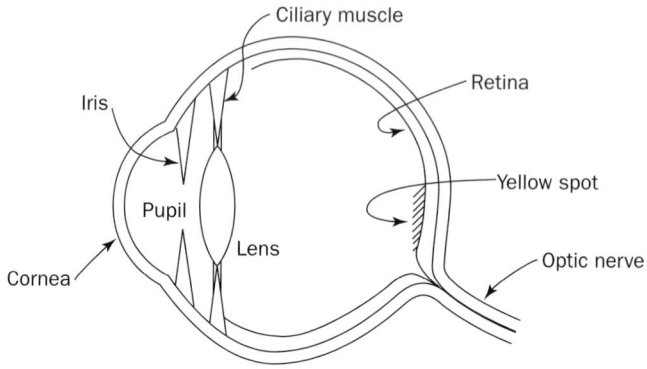


The iris (the coloured part of the eye) controls the size of the hole at its centre, the pupil. The pupil acts as a *diffraction* element and ensures that the image of a bright point object, e.g. a star, forms an image on the retina a few microns across (one micron = $10^{-6}$ m). There is no merit in the light-sensing cells of the retina being any smaller than the image, so this fixes the optimum and actual size of the rods and cones, and limits the detail the eye can resolve. The eye can accommodate an enormous range of intensities and the contraction of the pupil plays no more than a marginal role. The key mechanism involves contractions within the rods and cones.

The cells which are sensitive to light or dark, the rods, are spread across the whole area of the retina. The number of rods in the retina is in the order of $10^9$ and, to avoid having an equal number of nerve cells running down the optic nerve, the first stages in image processing take place within the retinal complex. The colour-sensitive cells, the cones, are mostly confined to a small patch (the yellow spot) on the retina and opposite the pupil. Our sense of colour across the whole field of view is mostly down to memory. Rods are much more sensitive in low light levels than cones.

If light intensity is low, the rods are more active than the cones. Colour is difficult to discern, but any movement is still quite noticeable.

It is interesting how different theories of light are used to explain different functions of the eye. Image formation on the retina and the design of spectacles fall within the area of geometrical optics. To understand the resolving power of the eye, i.e. its ability to distinguish fine detail, we have to appeal to the wave theory of light. Finally, the act of light detection is a chemical process and we need to think of a light beam as a stream of individual photons.

**farad:** the SI unit of electrical *capacitance*, symbol F.

$$\text{farad} = \frac{\text{coulomb}}{\text{volt}}$$

$$1\text{F} = 1\text{CV}^{-1}$$

**Faraday's law:** see *electromagnetic induction (laws of).*

**fatigue** is the failure of a metal component, its *fracture* under the influence of excessive working. It begins with the initiation of a crack, which then propagates through the material under the influence of a fluctuating or alternating *stress.* Provided that the stress reversals are frequent enough and continue for long enough, fatigue occurs at stress levels below the *yield point.*

**feedback** in an electronic system occurs when part of the output signal is fed back to the input. In negative feedback, the signal that is fed back is out of phase with the input, thereby reducing the input; this reduces the gain and gives greater stability and less distortion. In positive feedback, the signal that is fed back is in phase with the input; this increases gain and can lead to instability and oscillations.

**ferrites** are ferromagnetic, polycrystalline ceramic materials in which grain size is smaller than domain size. This allows for high permeability and low *hysteresis* loss coupled with short magnetic reversal times. Ferrite cores work at high frequency. (See *ferromagnetism, polycrystalline solids, ceramics.*)

**ferromagnetism** is the powerful magnetic behaviour associated with substances such as iron below their Curie temperatures. The origin of ferromagnetism is the capacity of the molecules of some solids to collect together in small magnetic domains. The material is in the unmagnetised state when the domains are randomly orientated and in the magnetised state when magnetic domains are aligned.

Ferromagnetic materials include iron, cobalt and nickel, together with some of their compounds; other examples are certain *ferrites* and the rare earth elements gadolinium and dysprosium.

**Feynman diagrams** display events which involve *subatomic particles.* Simplified diagrams show the ingoing particles at the bottom and the outgoing particles at the top. The exchange particles are represented by dashed lines. These diagrams are not trajectories or space–time diagrams. The diagrams prepare the ground for the application of conservation laws to the interaction. The first diagram is particularly important; it contrasts $\beta^-$ decay with $\beta^+$ decay. Both cases involve the decay of a massive but short-lived exchange particle. The relevant conservation laws here are those for baryon number ($B$), lepton number ($L$) and charge ($Q$).

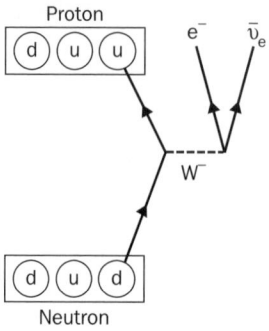


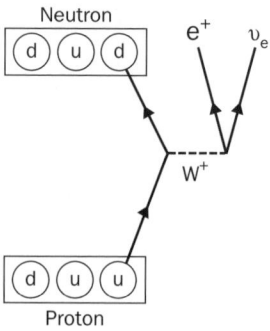


| | | |
|---|---|---|
| (B) | $(+1) = (+1)+0+0$ | $(+1) = (+1)+0+0$ |
| (L) | $0 = 0+(+1)+(-1)$ | $0 = 0+(-1)+(+1)$ |
| (Q) | $(-\frac{1}{3}+\frac{2}{3}-\frac{1}{3}) = (-\frac{1}{3}+\frac{2}{3}+\frac{2}{3})+(-1)+0$ | $(-\frac{1}{3}+\frac{2}{3}+\frac{2}{3}) = (-\frac{1}{3}+\frac{2}{3}-\frac{1}{3})+(+1)+0$ |
| | *Beta minus decay* | *Beta plus decay* |

The second diagram shows examples of weak, strong and electromagnetic interactions. All obey conservation laws. The exchange particles belong to the type of interaction.

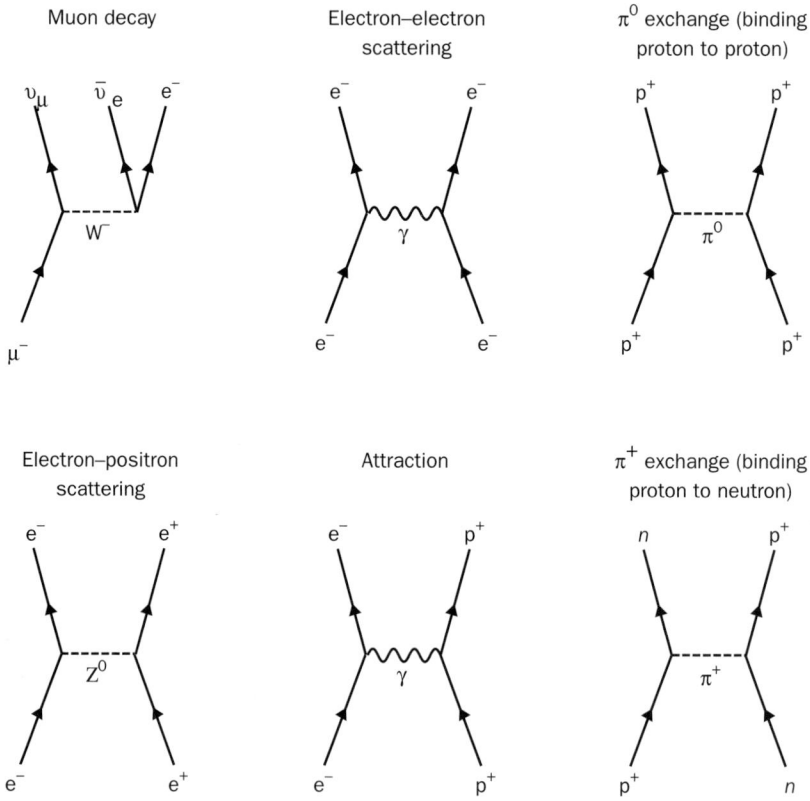


The weak interactions (they must be weak interactions if neutrinos are involved) are muon decay and electron/positron scattering. The electromagnetic interactions show repulsion between two electrons and attraction between an electron and a proton. The strong interactions show the attractions between two protons and between a proton and a neutron. The latter involves a positively charged gauge boson, the $\pi^+$ meson.

**field** is a three-dimensional space which can be mapped with the values of a physical variable. A temperature distribution constitutes a field, as do the velocity vectors along the streamlines of a flowing fluid. The fields which matter in A-level physics are gravitational, electrical and magnetic fields. Each of these quantities is linked to a force field and to a potential (energy) field (though magnetic potentials are complex affairs and are omitted). The *force–separation curve* and the *energy–separation curve* are representations of the force and energy fields between the atoms of a solid. (See *field lines (electric), field lines (magnetic).*)



**field lines (electric)** are a visual presentation of *electric field strength* within a space, indicating both the magnitude and the direction of the field. To give the magnitude and direction of the electric field strength $E$ at any point in the field, the lines must be set up in a particular way. They have the following features:

- the direction of a line at a point is the same as the direction of the electric field vector at that point
- lines begin at a positive charge and end on a negative charge
- the concentration of the lines (the number passing normally through unit area at a point) equals the electric field strength
- the lines cannot cross (if they did, the electric field strength would have two directions at the point where they crossed)
- the lines repel one another
- the lines are in a state of tension

The number of lines leaving unit charge is fixed at a value which ensures that the concentration equals electric field strength. The electric field strength $E$ a distance $r$ from a charge $Q$ is given by the equation

$$E = \frac{1}{4\pi\varepsilon_0} \cdot \frac{Q}{r^2}$$

This electric field strength is uniform in value across a sphere of surface area $4\pi r^2$. If $N$ is the number of lines leaving charge $Q$, then

$$E = \frac{N}{4\pi r^2} = \frac{1}{4\pi\varepsilon_0} \cdot \frac{Q}{r^2}$$

or

$$N = \frac{Q}{\varepsilon_0}$$

The number of lines of force leaving positive charge is $1/\varepsilon_0$ lines per coulomb of charge. (See *radial electric field, uniform electric field.*)

**field lines (magnetic)** illustrate the shape of a magnetic field; they show where the field is strong, where it is weak and what direction it takes. To do this, lines of force must have a number of characteristics:

- their direction is from a north-seeking pole to a south-seeking pole
- their density at a point equals the *magnetic field strength* at that point

- they are in a state of tension
- they repel one another

The diagrams below show how to use lines of magnetic force to describe some familiar magnetic fields. Notice that both the conductor lines and field lines are broken where they pass behind one another. If these gaps are omitted, the diagrams become ambiguous and worthless, so always include them in your diagrams.

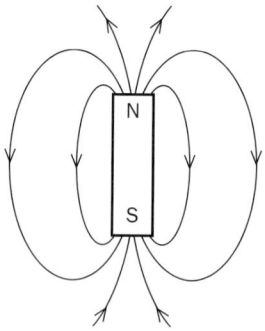


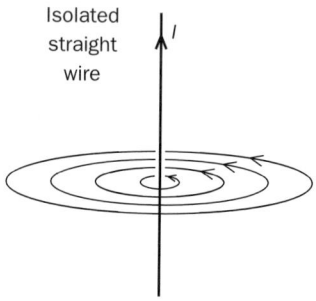


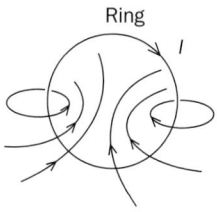


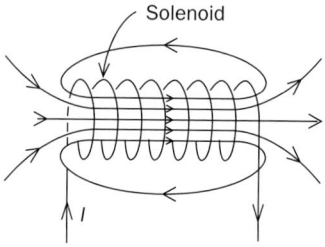


**finite energy sources** are *primary energy sources* such as coal, oil or gas which can be exhausted. (See *energy sources, renewable energy sources.*)

**first law of thermodynamics:** the first law states that any increase $\Delta U$ in the internal energy of a system is the sum of the heat $\Delta Q$ flowing into the system and the work $\Delta W$ done on the system:

$$\Delta U = \Delta Q + \Delta W$$

Internal energy correlates with temperature. Heat is energy flow driven by a temperature gradient and work is ordered *energy transfer.*

A number of points can be made.

- Energy is defined as the physical quantity whose conservation is governed by this law. Consequently, the first law of thermodynamics is a formal statement of the law of *conservation of energy.* It is an assertion and cannot be tested by experiment. Part of the reason for this is the way in which $\Delta U$ is defined (but we cannot follow this matter any further at this level).
- The law hints that there is some fundamental difference between energy $\Delta Q$ and energy $\Delta W$. This is indeed the case. $\Delta Q$ is energy associated with molecular motion and is wholly random and disordered. $\Delta W$ is energy associated with something directed, like a force or a voltage difference; it is an ordered property. The second

law of thermodynamics teaches us that only a fraction of the disordered energy could ever be recovered from the system in a manner which does useful work. But the ordered energy, if it is stored in an ordered fashion, can all be converted to useful work.

- There can never be a physical situation in which the three quantities, $\Delta U$, $\Delta Q$ and $\Delta W$, can be measured separately. The first law of thermodynamics cannot be checked by experiment.

When tackling a question on the first law, remember that a positive or negative value for $\Delta U$ is indicated by a rise or fall of system temperature or by a change of state (melting, freezing etc.). If neither effect is present, then $\Delta U$ is zero, the system is possibly in a thermal equilibrium state (certainly in a steady state), and $\Delta Q$ must equal $-\Delta W$. Three possibilities are nicely exemplified by an electric lamp immediately after it has been switched on. The electric power source does work on the filament: $\Delta W = IV\Delta t$. At the instant of switching on, the filament is at the same temperature as the surroundings and $\Delta Q$ must be zero. It follows that $\Delta U$ equals $\Delta W$ and the temperature of the filament begins to rise. While the filament temperature is rising, $\Delta Q$ is growing in a negative sense (energy radiated from the filament) and there is a corresponding fall in $\Delta U$, the energy which stays behind to raise the filament temperature. Eventually a steady state is reached: $\Delta U$ is zero, and $\Delta Q$ is $-\Delta W$. The radiant energy leaving per second equals the work done per second on the filament by the electrical power source.

**fissile materials** are minerals which contain a proportion of those nuclides such as uranium-235 or plutonium-241 which can release energy in a controlled nuclear *fission* process. That these materials are also radioactive is incidental. The usefulness of uranium in a nuclear reactor hinges on what happens when it is irradiated with neutrons, not on its very slow radioactive decay. (See *energy sources, thermal fission reactor.*)

**fission** means splitting. The word is used in physics to describe the splitting of a nucleus into two nuclei of roughly equal size and with the emission of much energy. The following is an example of a fission reaction:

$$^{235}_{92}\mathrm{U} + ^{1}_{0}\mathrm{n} \rightarrow ^{236}_{92}\mathrm{U} \rightarrow ^{140}_{54}\mathrm{Xe} + ^{94}_{38}\mathrm{Sr} + 2^{1}_{0}\mathrm{n} + \gamma \quad + 200\ \mathrm{MeV}$$

**fixed point:** a temperature at which some recognisable physical event happens. One important example is the *triple point*. Another is the *steam point*: the temperature at which pure water and steam would be in thermal equilibrium at standard atmospheric pressure.

**flavour of quarks:** see *quarks*.

**Fleming's left hand rule** gives the direction of the force on a current-carrying conductor in a magnetic field. The first two fingers and the thumb of the left hand are held at right angles to one another. The rules states that if the first finger points in the direction of the magnetic field while the second finger points in the direction of the current in a conductor immersed in the magnetic field, then the thumb will be pointing in the direction of the force on the conductor, as in the diagram on the next page.

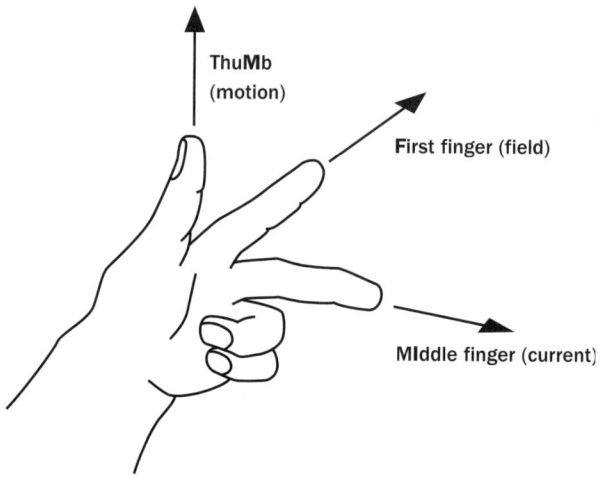


*Fleming's left hand rule*

The force is a *vector quantity.* Fleming's left hand rule gives its direction. The magnitude of the force is given by the equation

$$F = BIl \sin\theta$$

where $F$ is the force on a conductor of length $l$ carrying current $I$ at an angle $\theta$ to a uniform magnetic field of strength $B$. Notice that $Il \sin \theta$ is the *component* of the current element in a direction at right angles to $B$. If $\theta$ is a right angle, the equation reduces to the familiar form $F = BIl$. (See *motor effect, force on current, force on a moving charge.*)

**Fleming's right hand rule** gives the direction of the *induced e.m.f.* in a conductor. The first two fingers and the thumb of the right hand are held at right angles to one another. The rules states that if the first finger points in the direction of the magnetic field and the thumb points in the direction of the motion of the conductor, then the second finger will be pointing in the direction of the induced e.m.f. (or of the induced current, if one flows), as shown in the diagram below. (See *electromagnetic induction, electromagnetic induction (laws of).*)

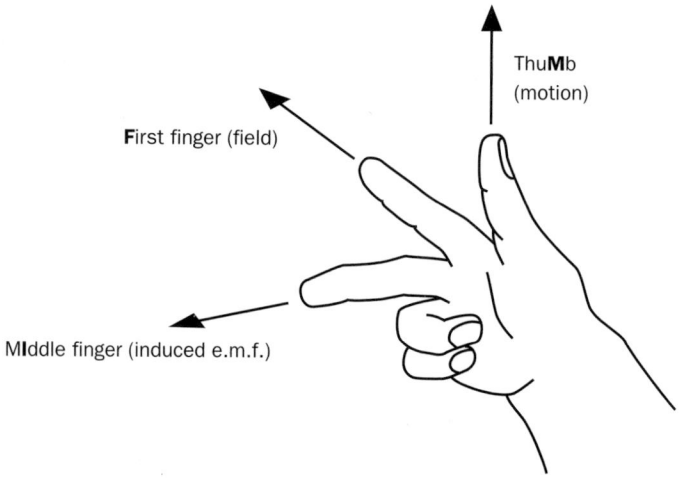


*Fleming's right hand rule*

**flexibility** is the capacity of a material to bend easily without breaking and to revert when the bending stress is removed. The flexibility of a given object is a function of its shape and of the material it is made from. For this reason, flexibility is not defined on a scale of values. If two materials are formed into the same shape, the more flexible material will have the lower value of *Young modulus* to allow it to bend, and a higher tensile strength to stop it from cracking.

**flotation (law of):** this states that the weight of a floating body equals the weight of fluid displaced. (See *Archimedes' principle.*)

**fluid matter** is matter that is in the liquid or the gaseous state but not in the solid state. Fluids are so called because they can flow; they have no shape of their own. In *solids* the molecules are attached to one another in a rigid structure; forces are transmitted along these structures without being deflected sideways. In fluids the molecules are free to move around; push a liquid surface inwards and the liquid mass further down will move out of the way. An immediate consequence of this is that we use forces when working with solids, and pressures with fluids — solids transmit forces; fluids transmit pressures. (See also *gases, liquids.*)

**flux linkage** is the product of the flux $\phi$ passing through a coil and the number of turns in the coil. Picture magnetic flux of density $B$ passing at right angles through a coil of cross-sectional area $A$. The flux through the coil is $\phi = AB$. If there are $N$ turns in the coil, the flux is effectively passing through $N$ loops and so the total linkage is $N\phi$. (See *electromagnetic induction, electromagnetic induction (laws of).*

**focal length** is the distance of the focal point from a lens or spherical mirror. The focal point is the point through which incident light, perpendicular to the plane of the lens or mirror, is directed by the action of the lens or mirror. A lens has two focal points which are at equal distances from the lens and on opposite sides. Concave lenses and convex mirrors have virtual focal lengths, that is, the light is deflected away from the focus and doesn't actually pass through it. You are unlikely to be required to study these, despite driving mirrors being convex and short-sighted people wearing concave spectacles. The diagram illustrates a convex lens (left) and a concave mirror (right). (See *lens equation.*)

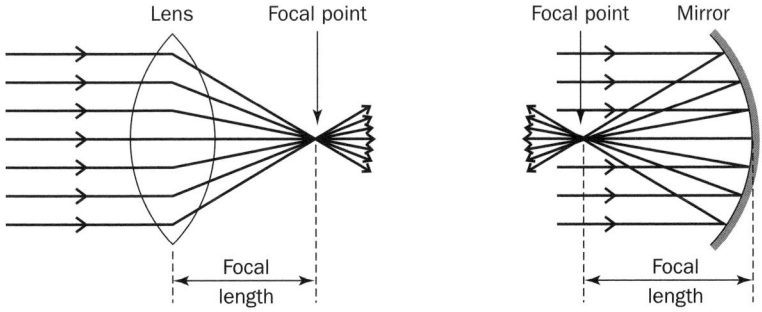


**force,** in classical Newtonian physics, is a *localised vector* quantity associated with rate of change of momentum — either change of magnitude or change of direction. The SI unit is the newton (N) and the symbol is $F$. The second of *Newton's laws of motion* defines force in magnitude and in direction. The same law, by implication, defines the newton.

Word equation definitions of force (for constant mass) and the newton are:

$$\text{force} = \text{rate of change of momentum} = \text{mass} \times \text{acceleration}$$

$$\text{newton} = \text{kilogram} \times \text{metre per second squared} \left(\text{kg ms}^{-2}\right)$$

Forces do not exist in the abstract. They arise when two bodies interact. A force is the push or pull of body A on body B. We learn from *Newton's third law of motion* that forces always occur in pairs (that is, body B will also push or pull body A — giving two pushes or two pulls).

There are four underlying interactions which give rise to forces between bodies. The forces we most commonly experience are gravitational or electromagnetic in origin, but for nuclear particle physics they may come from the strong or weak nuclear interactions.

Contact forces are mostly electromagnetic in origin. The idea of a contact force is introduced in order to facilitate analysis without comment on the origin of the force.

(See also *free-body force diagram, force: a localised vector.*)

**force: a localised vector** is an expression which reminds us that force is a vector with three characteristics: magnitude, direction and line of action. Forces act along lines and through points. Kick a football through the *centre of mass* and the football will just fly off; kick it through a point to one side of the centre of mass and it will fly off a little slower than before and it will be spinning. All your work on turning forces underlines the importance of line of action.

**force–extension curves** are graphs which show how the extension of a material in the form of a wire or a thread varies with the load placed upon it. The information represented by a force–extension graph is in many ways better shown on a stress–strain graph. In particular, the magnitudes on the two axes of a stress–strain graph depend only on the material and are independent of the size of the specimen. A useful property of the force–extension graph relates to the area between the curve and the extension axis. The area of the shaded strip on the force–extension graph shown in the diagram equals the average force $F'$ for the strip multiplied by the increase in extension, XY. But this product is the force–distance product for this small additional extension (the work done increasing the extension). What is true of the narrow strip is true of the whole area OAB which is no more than a set of many thin parallel strips. So the work done stretching the wire, i.e. the elastic potential energy stored in the wire, equals the area OAB, which is equal to ½ $F\Delta x$ where $F$ is the applied force and $\Delta x$ is the final extension. For this particular graph, the elastic potential energy stored is ½ × 60 N × 4.8 mm = 0.144 J. (See also *stress–strain curves.*)

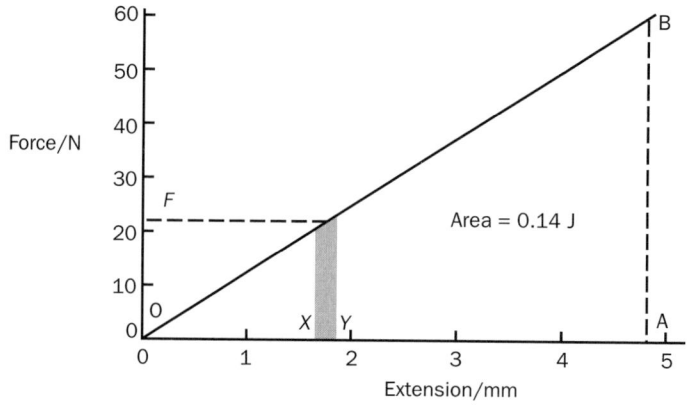

**force on a moving charge:** a phrase which relates to the force on a free charge, usually an electron, moving through a magnetic field at an angle to the field. The force on an electron in an electric field equals $Ee$ whether or not the electron is moving.

The force $F$ on charge $q$ moving through a uniform magnetic field of strength $B$ with velocity $v$ along a path at right angles to the field direction is given by the formula

$$F = Bqv$$

The direction of the force is given by *Fleming's left hand rule.* Remember when applying the rule that the current direction is opposite to the direction of motion for negative charge.



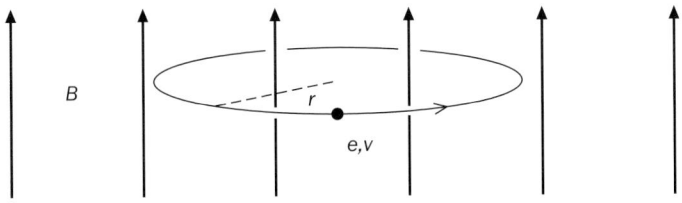


The diagram illustrates an important special case. A beam of electrons, all travelling with speed $v$ at right angles to an extensive uniform magnetic field of strength $B$ is pulled by the force $F$ into a circular path of radius $r$. The centripetal force equals $Bev$.

$$Bev = \frac{mv^2}{r}$$

$$r = \frac{mv}{Be}$$

(See also *electron beams.*)

**force on current:** see *motor effect, Fleming's left hand rule.*

**force–separation curve:** a graph which shows how the force between two atoms varies with the distance between them. A typical example is shown in the diagram on the next page. The force curve is the resultant of two other curves — a short-range but very strong repulsive force and a longer-range attractive force. The repulsion wins at small separations; the attraction is dominant when the atoms are further apart. The equilibrium distance between the atoms is when the two forces are equal and opposite. At this point, where the separation is $r_0$, the curve is approximately straight and this explains why materials obey *Hooke's law.* The gradient at separation $r_0$ is proportional to the *Young modulus* for the material, and the depth of the deepest part of the curve is proportional to the strength of the material.

The curve has been drawn with repulsion increasing upwards and attraction increasing downwards. Some books prefer it the other way round. As with any force–displacement graph, the area between the curve and the separation axis represents work done. In this instance the energy is calculated from infinite distance inwards, and starts off at zero for infinite distance. The work done is increasingly negative until the point $r_0$ is reached ($r_0$ marks the minimum for the *energy–separation curve*), and then it begins to rise again.

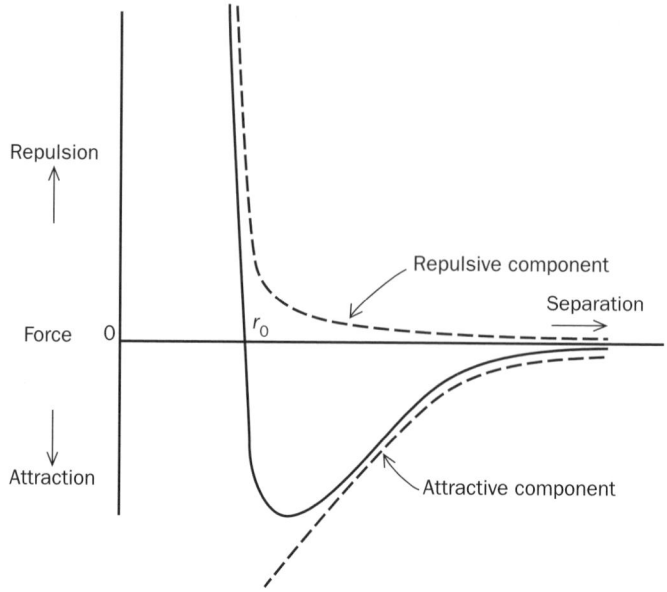


**forced oscillations** are the oscillations of a damped system acted on by a periodic driving force. Were the system not damped, the oscillations would soon go wildly out of control. If the system is damped, an equilibrium situation will be reached when, per cycle, the energy transferred to the system from the driver equals the energy transferred from the system through the damping mechanism. The amplitude of this equilibrium state for a given driver amplitude depends on the frequency of the driver. It is a maximum when the driver frequency is the same as the natural frequency $f_0$ of the undamped system. This is called *resonance*.

The link between resonance and physical damage is connected to this maximum amplitude in an obvious manner: the vibrating system is subject to maximum distortion. Less obvious, but just as important, is the fact that the rate of energy flow from the driver through the system into the damping mechanism is also at its maximum value. This is the principle behind tuning circuits, musical instrument design and many other engineering applications.

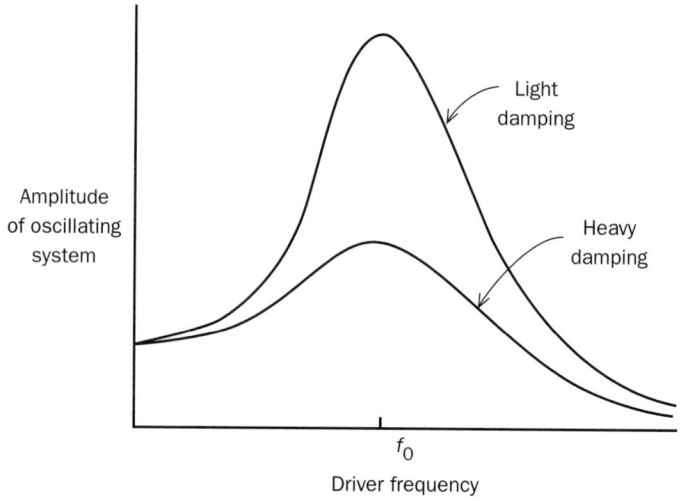

**forces in equilibrium** are forces which cancel one another out in two respects: they provide no net force and no net couple. It is important to note that the forces considered here must all be acting on the same object.

A stationary object acted upon by several forces in equilibrium will neither move nor turn round. At A-level, examples are always confined to situations in which the forces all operate in the same plane (*coplanar forces*).

The two conditions (no net force, no net couple) for a set of coplanar forces to be in equilibrium can be stated in two ways.

The first way:
1 the sum of the components of all the forces in any one direction is zero
2 the sum of the clockwise moments of the forces about any point in the plane equals the sum of the anticlockwise moments about the same point

The second way:
1 the vectors representing the forces, if placed end to end, trace out a closed polygon (if there are three forces, this becomes the 'triangle of forces' statement)
2 the lines of action of all the forces meet at a point

These ideas are more part of applied mathematics than of physics and would only be tested in a superficial way in a physics examination.

**fossil fuels,** such as coal, oil and gas, are derived from once-living matter. Coal is mostly formed from the remains of terrestrial plants, oil and gas from the remains of aquatic organisms including plankton. These organic remains have altered chemically in conditions of high pressure and high temperature and where oxygen was largely absent.

Peat is mostly described as a fossil fuel but sometimes listed as a biofuel. The trouble is that some peat isn't very old. (Avoid mentioning peat if possible.) (See *energy sources*.)

**fracture** is a breaking of a solid mass by the growth of a small crack. The origin of a fracture in a metal is likely to be *fatigue*. In a ceramic it is likely to be the spreading of a crack through the hard, unyielding material.

**free-body force diagram:** a way of showing the forces which act on a body with a view to determining the resultant force.

Never draw more than one body. Do not draw the ground, water or anything else the body is resting on, just a labelled blob to represent the body on which the forces are acting. (A number of examples are shown in the diagram on page 108.)

Do not draw any forces which the body itself is exerting on other objects; we are only concerned with forces acting on the body, in order to find their combined effect on it.

A resultant force (e.g. net downward force, centripetal force) should not appear on the diagram; only the individual forces such as weight, upthrust or drag should be marked, and each of these must be labelled. If you want to include the direction of a velocity, say, label it clearly and put it separately, well to the side of the diagram and separated from it.

Sometimes you have to draw two forces upwards or downwards, both passing through the centre of mass. Put these side-by-side, close to the correct spot, and label them clearly.

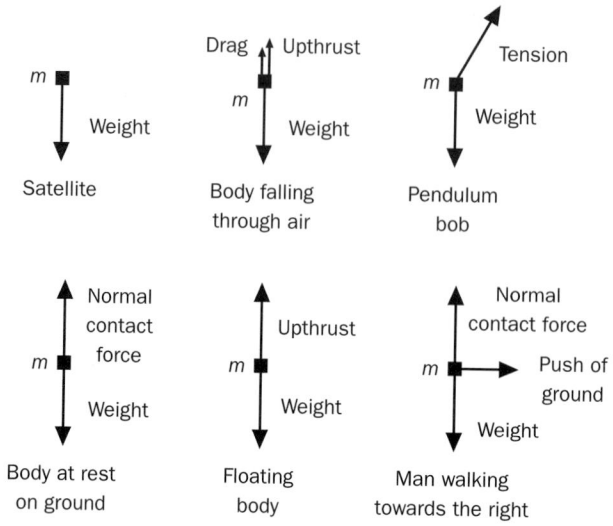


**free fall:** the motion of a body whose weight is the only force acting on it. For example, divers are in free fall from the instant they lose contact with the diving board to the instant when they touch the water. Astronauts orbiting the Earth in a spacecraft at constant speed and height are also in free fall. (See *acceleration of free fall, weightlessness.*)

**frequency** is the number of times per second an event occurs. The symbol for frequency is $f$ and the unit of frequency is 'events per second'. For example, the frequency of cars arriving at traffic lights is in 'cars per second'; for spectators through a turnstile, it is 'spectators per second'.

For *simple harmonic motion* and wave motion the event which matters is a cycle and frequency is the number of cycles per second. The SI unit for frequency in cycles per second is hertz (Hz). (Note that hertz does not mean second$^{-1}$.)

By using the symbol $\omega$ to stand for $2\pi f$, the algebra for simple harmonic motion and alternating current theory can often be simplified. $\omega$ is sometimes called *angular frequency,* sometimes called angular speed, but mostly it is simply called omega. The relationship between $\omega$ and $f$ is set out as follows:

$$\omega = 2\pi f$$

$$\omega \text{ in radians per second} = 2\pi \text{ in radians per cycle} \times f \text{ in cycles per second}$$

$$\frac{\text{radian}}{\text{second}} = \frac{\text{radian}}{\text{cycle}} \times \frac{\text{cycle}}{\text{second}}$$

Frequency measured in cycles per second can be converted into *angular frequency* in radians per second; $2\pi$ radians per cycle is the conversion factor.

Another example of a frequency is *activity* in radioactivity, which is the number of disintegrations per second. The unit for 'disintegrations per second' is the becquerel (Bq). Do not confuse becquerel with hertz, and don't confuse it with second$^{-1}$ either. *Count rate* is a frequency measured in counts per second.

One last point: the $\omega$ used in AC theory is strictly the *angular speed* (in radians per second) of the phasor used on the phasor diagrams. This is why the $\omega$ that stands for $2\pi f$ is sometimes called 'angular speed'. The term $\omega t$ will be a number of radians, so sin $\omega t$, cos $\omega t$ and sin $2\pi ft$, cos $2\pi ft$ make sense.

**frequency division multiplexing** (FDM) is a technique which enables the use of a single telephone wire to carry several sound messages simultaneously and in analogue form. The term FDM is a little forbidding at the first meeting, but it means no more than it says — different frequency ranges in a signal are used to do different jobs. It is about the economic use of resources. A high-frequency carrier wave (several megahertz) has a spread of frequencies, called its *bandwidth*, of perhaps 20 kHz. This bandwidth is split up into half a dozen bands, each of which is wide enough to carry a sound-frequency wave without distortion. To the amplitudes of each of these elements of the bandwidth is added the amplitudes of one of the sound-frequency waves. This addition action feeds the carrier wave with both the amplitude and the frequency of the original sound wave. The carrier wave can then carry several telephone messages at once. A demultiplexer separates the different telephone messages carried on the different frequency bands after reception. The comparatively high frequency range of visible light waves means that the capacity of optical fibres to carry simultaneous telephone messages is proportionately much greater. They carry many thousands of transmissions simultaneously. Time division multiplexing (TDM) is used for the transmission of information in digital form, as in *pulse code modulation* (PCM).

**frequency modulation** (FM) means transmitting information by means of a carrier wave whose amplitude is kept constant but whose frequency is changed in proportion to the amplitude of the information wave (e.g. a radio wave). Since these frequency changes keep pace with the amplitude changes, the frequency of the information wave is transmitted too. See *modulation*.

**friction** is a contact force between two, usually solid, surfaces which acts parallel to the surfaces either to prevent their relative motion, or to oppose it without entirely preventing it. In the latter case some driving force must work against friction; energy will be transferred and the surfaces will warm up.

**fuel rods** are the long metal-clad containers, filled with nuclear fuel, which are inserted into the *moderator* assembly of a nuclear power plant.

**fuels** are usually substances which are burned to release their store of energy. However, nuclear fuels such as uranium are also termed 'fuels', although their stored energy is released by the process of nuclear *fission* (a physical process) rather than by burning (a chemical process).

**full-wave bridge rectifier:** see *rectification, half-wave and full-wave.*

**fundamental interactions:** four fundamental forces account collectively for the properties of the fundamental particles, of the subatomic particles, and of atoms and matter in bulk. They are the strong interaction, the electromagnetic force, the weak interaction and the gravitational force. Their relative magnitudes at a given distance are in the proportions $1 : 1/137 : 10^{-5} : 10^{-39}$.

Electromagnetic and gravitational forces apply to everyday objects, and their actions are usually handled algebraically with inverse square law equations. At the subatomic level all sense of position and timing is lost and we have to think more of events than of processes. Subatomic events are described in *Feynman diagrams*. These diagrams identify the relevant particles before and after the event and identify the responsible interaction by showing the relevant *exchange particle.*

***The gravitational interaction.*** The gravitational interaction is so weak that it might not be expected to operate at all. But there are two points in its favour. First, it operates across large distances which rule out the strong and weak interactions. Second, all lumps of matter of any appreciable size are electrically neutral, and this rules out the electromagnetic interaction. On the large scale, gravitational interaction is the only interaction left. The exchange particle in this case, the graviton, has yet to be detected.

***The electromagnetic interaction.*** The electromagnetic interaction is effective between charged particles, that is, all quarks, some leptons and some subatomic particles. It is more than a hundred times weaker than the strong interaction, but it takes over outside the nucleus and is the principal force accounting for atomic stability and structure, molecular structure, as well as the chemical and mechanical behaviour of matter in bulk. The gravitational force takes over at larger distances because matter in bulk is electrically neutral. The exchange particle, a virtual photon, transmits the interaction between two charged particles.

***The strong interaction.*** Two protons in a nucleus each carry charge $e^+$ and may be as close together as $10^{-15}$ m. Coulomb's law applied to this situation gives a force of repulsion of about 230 N. Unless there were some other force in action within the nucleus, electrostatic repulsion would tear the nucleus apart. The interaction which counters this destructive force was named the strong interaction and is now associated primarily with quarks. This strong interaction is shown by alpha particle scattering to be a short-range force which does not act over distances beyond about $10^{-15}$ m; this is a distance roughly equal to the proton or neutron diameter. This range is far enough to hold a nucleus together but is ineffective at greater distances. The word 'strong' carries a meaning closer to that of a 'strong glue' which holds two pieces of wood together once contact has been made, but is not an attraction that pulls these pieces together from any great distance.

Subatomic particles which are built from quarks and which are consequently affected by the strong interaction are called *hadrons.* Charged hadrons are subject to all four interactions, neutral hadrons to three of them. The strong interaction holds quarks together in triplets to form baryons or in pairs to form mesons. *Nuclear reactions* are the typical events in which the strong interaction operates.

***The weak interaction.*** The weak interaction is best known as the force which operates during *beta decay.* It is a complex force which is treated together with the electromagnetic force as the electroweak interaction. It is about a thousand times weaker than the electromagnetic interaction and operates only within distances of about $10^{-17}$ m. If it was weak in the ordinary sense of the word, it would be swamped. But here the word 'weak' implies a low probability of its coming into play. This probability increases, i.e. the interaction becomes more probable, as the energies of the participating particles increase. Apart from beta decay, it comes into its own at about 100 GeV. The exchange particles for the weak interaction are labelled $W^+$, $W^-$ and $Z^0$ particles.

The weak interaction is the only one of the four interactions to which neutrinos are susceptible, so any event involving a neutrino is controlled by the weak interaction. Energy, mass and charge are interchanged between leptons, quarks and their antiparticles by the electroweak interaction. This is therefore the interaction which controls hadron and quark decay and transformation events. Such events are always in the direction of lower mass, and this explains why most of the mass in the universe is wrapped up in electrons, protons, neutrons and electron neutrinos. Powerful fluxes of electron neutrinos are emitted continuously from the Sun and other stars as a consequence of the hydrogen fusion reaction. (See *exchange particles, Feynman diagrams, conservation laws (nuclear), uncertainty principle.*)

**fundamental law of radioactive decay** states that the activity $\Delta N/\Delta t$ of a radioactive nuclide is proportional to the number $N$ of undecayed atoms of the nuclide in the sample; that is:

$$\frac{\Delta N}{\Delta t} = -\lambda N$$

where $\lambda$ is the *decay constant* for the nuclide and the minus sign indicates that $\Delta N$ is a decrease in the value of $N$. (See *exponential law of radioactive decay.*)

**fusion** means joining together. The word is used in physics to describe the building up of larger nuclei from smaller nuclei with the emission of energy. This is the process by which energy is released from hydrogen and other light elements in stars. (See *binding energy, fission.*)

**Aiming for a grade A*?**

Don't forget to log on to **www.philipallan.co.uk/a-zonline** for advice.

**galaxies:** the concept of a galactic universe properly began with William Herschel. Herschel assumed that the faintness of a star is an indicator of distance. By counting and recording the brightnesses of as many stars as he could see, he showed that stars were distributed over a disc-like region of space. He did not, however, realise that the galaxy he had mapped was just one of many millions of millions of galaxies which make up the universe.

Improved telescopes allowed astronomers to recognise that what appeared to be cloudy patches of light in the night sky were in fact other galaxies, many bigger than our own. A galaxy is now recognised as a group of about $10^{11}$ stars, held together by the gravitational attraction between them and spread across about $10^5$ light years. There are considerable differences in size, shape and stellar distribution. Galaxies are about $10^6$ light years apart (i.e. 10 galactic diameters); the farthest is about $10^{11}$ light years away and there are about $10^{13}$ of them. (See *Hubble's law.*)

**gamma camera:** a device for generating an image of an extended *gamma radiation* source. The essential features are shown in the diagram. The source, typically a radioactive tracer isotope such as $^{99m}Tc$, is attached to a carrier compound which takes it to the organ under test. Gamma radiation which gets through a lead collimator (a tubular device ensuring that only radiation coming from a particular direction is detected) reaches a scintillator crystal of sodium iodide doped with thallium and is absorbed. A proportion of the absorbed energy reappears in the form of visible photons. The different readings from the bank of photomultipliers enables the precise position of the gamma emission event to be calculated. The computer uses the information from tens of thousands of such events to build up an accurate picture of the gamma source, so that an image of the organ can be displayed on a screen.

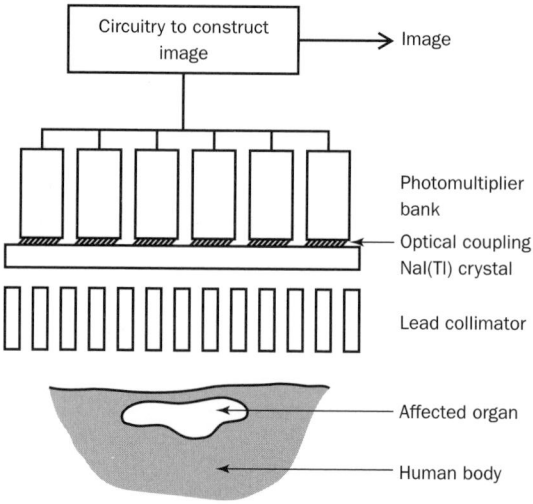

**gamma emission** is the release of high-energy, very-short-wavelength photons (*gamma radiation*) from an excited nucleus. There is no change in the *proton number* or *atomic number* for the nucleus. Gamma emission occurs when a radioactive nuclide emits alpha or beta radiation, although there may be a significant time delay between the two emissions.

**gamma radiation** is very-short-wavelength electromagnetic radiation emitted from nuclei which are in heightened energy states. A nucleus may be in a heightened energy state because it is the radioactive decay product of a parent nucleus; it may have been produced in a fission process, or it may have been struck by a high-energy particle such as a neutron in the shielding of a nuclear reactor. There is no change in the structure of the nucleus when the gamma radiation *photon* is emitted, only a rearrangement and an energy relaxation.

Gamma radiation photon energies are mostly within the range 1.2 keV ($1.9 \times 10^{-16}$ J) to 1.2 GeV ($1.9 \times 10^{-10}$ J). These energy values give wavelengths from about 1 nm ($1 \times 10^{-9}$ m) to about 1 fm ($1 \times 10^{-15}$ m). The corresponding frequency values are from about 0.3 EHz ($0.3 \times 10^{18}$ Hz) up to about 0.3 YHz ($0.3 \times 10^{24}$ Hz). Since there is no known upper energy limit, values given for the wavelengths vary somewhat from one book to the next. One reason for the stress on energies is that photon energies can be measured; wavelengths are rarely measured, and then only if there is a need to verify that particles are photons and not something else. The lower energy end, up to a few MeV (a few per cent of the overall energy range), overlaps with the X-ray segment, but *X-rays* do not come from nuclear relaxation processes.

The properties of gamma radiation are what you would expect of high-energy, short-wavelength particles. Their paths are effectively straight with little evidence of diffraction, and their interaction with matter is largely destructive. The straightness of their paths ensures the applicability of the *inverse square law* to the fall-away of beam intensity with distance from the source. Low-energy gamma radiation is strongly scattered. At higher energies, photoelectric absorption becomes more likely. As photon energy increases still further, *Compton scattering* begins to take over and, finally, *pair production*. Short wavelengths mean that interaction probabilities are low, and this favours deep penetration of matter by gamma radiation before destructive absorption begins. From a biological or medical point of view, this allows deep body damage and so gamma radiation sources should be efficiently shielded and kept far away.

Detection of gamma radiation is largely by photography or scintillation counter. GM tubes are largely transparent to gamma radiation and only a small proportion of an incident beam is detected. Uses of gamma radiation are linked to their high powers of penetrability — leaks in gas and water pipes can be detected deep underground; rock structures can be investigated for depth and continuity; metal components can be examined for internal cracks. Medical uses range from the destruction of cancerous tissue to the exploratory powers of the *gamma camera*. (See also *electromagnetic spectrum, GM tube, radiation detectors.*)

**gases** are fluids in which molecules are spread as far apart as the container will allow. The average molecular kinetic energy is too high for the intermolecular forces to hold the molecules together; shape and volume are decided by the container. (See *ideal gas equation, kinetic theory of gases, solids, liquids.*)

**gauge bosons:** another name for *exchange particles.*

**general gas equation:** see *kinetic theory of gases, ideal gas equation.*

**general relativity** sets out to extend the space–time concepts of *special relativity* to all reference frames, in particular to accelerating reference frames. An important outcome of the theory was the correct quantitative forecast for the deflection of light by the Sun's gravitational field.

**generator:** a device for transforming mechanical energy into electrical energy by means of a coil rotating in a magnetic field.

The principle is shown in the diagram below. A coil constructed from many turns of fine wire is mounted on a spindle in a magnetic field. It is made to rotate on the spindle by a turning force applied to the pulley. The coil rotates in the magnetic field and the e.m.f. induced in the coil is picked up from the two commutator rings. The output voltage is the familiar sine-wave alternating voltage, the frequency of which is decided by the angular speed of the coil. The magnitude is decided by the strength of the magnetic field, the number of turns in the coil, the cross-sectional area of the coil and (again) the angular speed.

The angular speed of the coil governs the output frequency, because output voltage goes through one complete cycle each complete turn of the coil. The angular speed influences the output voltage amplitude, because an increasing angular speed causes the magnetic *flux linkages* to change at a faster rate. Also, if the angular speed is zero, the output voltage is zero. All this should be clear from the equation for the output voltage:

$$V = \omega NAB \sin \omega t = V_0 \sin \omega t = V_0 \sin 2\pi ft$$

where $V$ is the output voltage at time $t$, $N$ is the number of turns, $A$ is the cross-sectional area of the coil and $B$ is the magnetic field strength of the uniform field in which the coil is mounted.

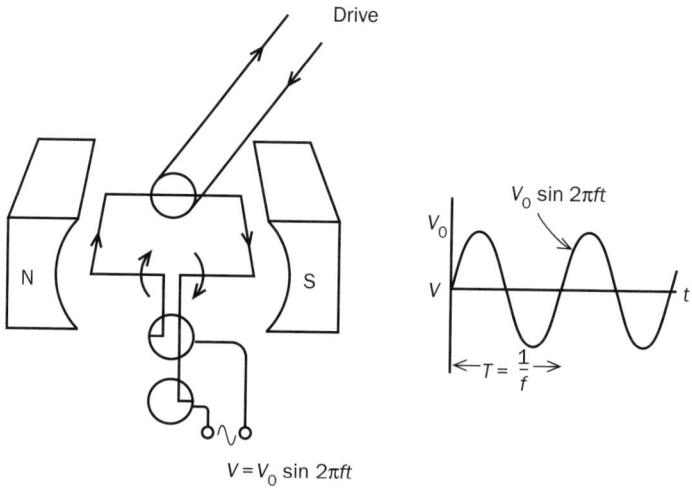


If current is drawn from the output, the generator will be supplying *electrical power*. The direction of the current in the coil, shown on the diagram, is found from *Fleming's right hand rule*. If we now apply *Fleming's left hand rule* to this current, we find that the magnetic field interacts with the rotating coil to give a slowing down turning force. The coil is prevented from slowing down by the mechanical turning force applied to the pulley. In this way, the mechanical work needed to turn the coil is regained as electrical energy in the output circuit. Draw more current and more work must be done on the spindle to keep the generator turning at the right angular speed. (See *electric motor, electromagnetic induction, electromagnetic induction (laws of).*)

**geostationary orbit:** a satellite orbit that has the satellite orbiting the Earth once in 24 hours (or, more correctly, 23 hours and 56 minutes) in a circular path above the equator. The consequence is that the satellite is always at the same point in the sky as seen from the Earth's surface. Another way to describe this is to say that the satellite remains above the same point on the Earth's surface.

Geostationary orbits are above the equator and at a distance of about 6.6 Earth radii from the Earth's centre. Geostationary satellites are used for satellite TV broadcasting and for relaying telecommunications signals.

(A geostationary orbit is a special case of a geosynchronous orbit, which is any orbit with a period of one day. A satellite in a geosynchronous orbit follows the same path across the sky every day, so an observer can be sure that it will return to the same point in the sky at the same time each day.)



**Worked example**

**Calculate the height above the Earth of a geostationary satellite. The radius of the Earth is $6.37 \times 10^6$ m, its mass is $5.98 \times 10^{24}$ kg, and the universal gravitational constant is $G = 6.67 \times 10^{-11}\,\mathrm{N\,m^2\,kg^{-2}}$.**

The period of the satellite will be 24 hours since it circles the Earth in the time that the Earth takes to revolve once.

$$G\frac{mM}{r^2} = \frac{mv^2}{r} = \frac{m}{r} \times \left(\frac{2\pi r}{T}\right)^2$$

$$= \frac{m4\pi^2 r}{T^2}$$

$$r^3 = \frac{GMT^2}{4\pi^2}$$

$$\text{so } r = \sqrt[3]{\left(\frac{GMT^2}{4\pi^2}\right)} = 42.3 \times 10^6\,\mathrm{m}$$

But this is the distance of the satellite from the Earth's centre. The distance above the Earth's surface is therefore $35.9 \times 10^6$ m.

Many numerical problems involving satellites can be worked out by starting with the first line in the worked example above.

(See *Newton's law of universal gravitation.*)

**geothermal energy** is energy drawn directly from hot parts of the Earth's interior which happen to be close enough to the surface to use in this way. Suitable sites are rich enough to encourage optimism, but they are not very widespread.

Geothermal energy may be extracted in different ways. In some places, hot water or steam is drawn directly from underground reservoirs. In others, water is pumped down from the surface so that it passes through hot rocks before returning, heated, to the surface. In some cases, this results in cooling of the underground rocks so that the resource must be regarded as finite. (See *energy sources.*)

**glass fibres** are fibres of glass that are too thin to contain any weakening deformations within their structure and which are, therefore, able to support considerable tensile stresses. They can be used collectively as a thermal insulator or, when set in a bonding matrix, to form a light composite material (popularly called 'fibre glass') of great strength which can be moulded as required. (See *optical fibre systems.*)

**glasses** are those apparently solid substances which when heated slowly soften into a visibly liquid state without an identifiable melting point. The reason for the smooth transition from an apparently brittle solid to a recognisably liquid state is that, at the lower temperature, atoms are attached to one another but not in an orderly and regular crystal form; thus there is no solid-state bonding to break down. The strong forces between the atoms accounts for the brittleness, and the absence of order accounts for the irregularity of the broken surface. (See *solids, liquids.*)

**gluons** are the exchange particles associated with the strong interaction and the strong binding of *quarks* within *hadrons* and of *protons* and *neutrons* within a nucleus. There are eight kinds of gluons, which match the colours (not the flavours) of the individual pairs of quarks that they bind together. (See *fundamental interactions.*)

**GM tube:** see *radiation detectors.*

**graded index fibre:** see *optical fibre systems.*

**gradient** is a measure of steepness. It is defined for a straight line graph as the tangent of the angle between the line and the $x$-axis (abscissa). An example is shown in the diagram below. Notice that the gradient is the ratio of two lengths (two sides of a triangle), each measured against the corresponding axis. Remember always:

- to draw and use as large a triangle as possible
- to evaluate the length of each of the two lines from the corresponding axis
- to give as the unit for the gradient the ratio of the $y$-axis unit to the $x$-axis unit

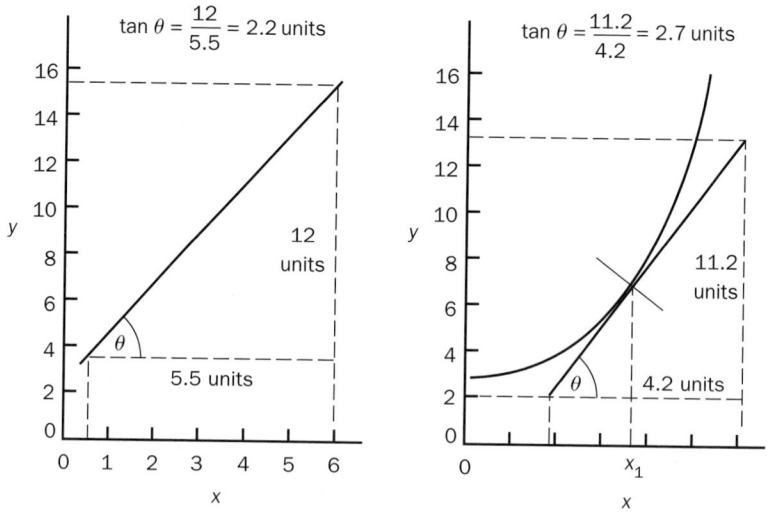


The second graph is not straight but curved. The instantaneous *rate of change* of the $y$ variable with respect to the $x$ variable when the value of the $x$ variable is $x_1$ is the gradient of the tangent to the curve at this value of $x$. The gradient is a property of the tangent.

When drawing a tangent to a curve, it is often helpful to draw a short line through the curve at the point of interest and at right angles to the curve, i.e. draw a short 'normal' to the curve. The tangent can then be drawn at right angles to this normal. The sharper the curve, the better it is to follow this procedure.

Avoid using the word 'slope'; it can mean too many different things.

**grain boundaries** are *crystal defects* which spread across an area. They are the surfaces of small single crystals that make up the structure of a metallic solid. In practice, grains prevent the flow of the material when it is subjected to stress, and the smaller the average grain size the stronger the material becomes. This is because the other forms of dislocation become ineffective.

**graph:** a way of displaying how one physical or mathematical quantity changes in value should another physical or mathematical quantity change in value. The latter quantity is sometimes called the independent variable; it is usually plotted across the page along the $x$-axis (*abscissa*). The other quantity is called the dependent variable and would be plotted up the page along the $y$-axis (*ordinate*).

You should draw graphs as large as possible. A graph is an instrument which shows the relationship between two quantities; a small graph would be an inaccurate instrument. Each centimetre along either axis should correspond to 1, 2 or 5 units; 3 units or 7 units would make it impossible to plot something like 5.3 or 15.7. You will be penalised in an examination for using an awkward scale.

Graphs should have a title. Position the title so that it cannot be confused with the labelling of the $x$-axis.

The axis labels should include any multiple or sub-multiple of the unit so that the numbers on the axis are precisely defined in the label. Sometimes this proves difficult. If a typical $x$ value (e.g. the size of a water droplet) is, say, $1.2 \times 10^{-5}$ m, then label the axis:

water droplet diameter $/10^{-5}$ m

The mark 1.2 along the $x$-axis now means what you want it to mean.

**gravitation** is the mutual attraction between any two masses in the universe. (See *Newton's law of universal gravitation.*)

**gravitational constant** $G$ is the constant in the mathematical expression of *Newton's law of universal gravitation*. Its value is $6.67 \times 10^{-11}\,\mathrm{N\,m^2\,kg^{-2}}$.

It happens that if the distances of the planets from the Sun and the periodic times of travel of the planets round the Sun are measured, Newton's law of universal gravitation will only enable us to calculate the product of the gravitational constant and the Sun's mass; neither is known separately. To find the mass of the Sun, or the mass of any planet with a moon, we must break the deadlock by measuring the gravitational constant $G$ in the laboratory. This was first achieved by Cavendish in 1797. He was able to claim that he had 'weighed the Earth' (found its mass), since the *acceleration of free fall* $g$ is given by

$$g = \frac{GM}{r^2}$$

**gravitational field strength** $g$ at a point in a gravitational field is the force per unit mass acting on a small mass placed at that point in the field. It is a vector quantity and has the unit $\mathrm{N\,kg^{-1}}$. The word equation definition is:

$$\text{gravitational field strength } g = \frac{\text{gravitational force}}{\text{mass}}$$

$$\text{unit for gravitational field strength } g = \frac{\text{newton}}{\text{kilogram}} = \mathrm{N\,kg^{-1}}$$

The difference between gravitational field strength and the *acceleration of free fall* is linked to the difference between gravitational mass and inertial mass. The greater the gravitational mass of an object, the greater the force exerted on it in a gravitational field (i.e. the greater its weight $W = mg$). The greater the inertial mass of an object, the greater the force required to give it an acceleration ($F = ma$). Although we regard gravitational and inertial masses as the same, even giving them same symbol, it is difficult to show that they are actually the same thing.

We can write, using the idea of a gravitational field:

$$F = G\frac{mM}{r^2} = mg \qquad \text{where } g = \frac{GM}{r^2}$$

$g$ is the gravitational field strength a distance $r$ from a point mass $M$, and $m$ is the gravitational mass of the object placed at the relevant point. But we could, instead, follow *Newton's second law of motion* and write:

$$F = mg$$

where $F$ is the force which will act on the object, $m$ is the object's inertial mass and $g$ is the expected acceleration, called the acceleration of free fall, with the unit $\mathrm{m\,s^{-2}}$. One achievement of Einstein's relativity theory was to show that these two treatments are essentially identical. (See *acceleration of free fall.*)

**gravitational potential (radial fields):** the gravitational potential at a point in a radial field is the work done per unit mass against the field in bringing a small mass from infinite distance to the point. Since gravitational fields are attractive and the potential at infinite distance is zero, all points within the field have negative values of potential. Gravitational potential is a scalar quantity with SI unit $\mathrm{J\,kg^{-1}}$. Mostly the symbol used is $V$, but sometimes $V_r$ or $V\{r\}$ is used to emphasise the radial nature of the field. A radial gravitational field is one in which the field strength has the same magnitude at all points at a given distance from the centre.

A few lines of calculus (not in the specifications) are sufficient to show that the gravitational potential a distance $r$ from a point mass is given by:

$$V = -\frac{GM}{r}$$

**gravitational potential (uniform fields):** the gravitational potential at a point in a uniform field is the work done per unit mass bringing a small mass to that point from some reference point where the gravitational potential is arbitrarily zero. Gravitational potential is a scalar quantity with SI unit $\mathrm{J\,kg^{-1}}$. The symbol used is $V$. Gravitational potential enables us to solve many problems by considering energy transformations only. Forces have directions and so are more complicated to work with than potentials, which do not.

Whether or not a field is uniform is a question of scale. The gravitational field near the Earth's surface is uniform over vertical or horizontal distances that are very small compared with the Earth's radius. Go too far horizontally and the direction of the Earth's gravitational field changes, too far vertically and the magnitude changes. The meaning of 'small' depends on how many significant figures are involved. Over a distance of a few kilometres horizontally or vertically, just above the Earth's surface, the gravitational field can be treated as uniform.

The diagram below shows the essential features of a uniform gravitational field. The magnitudes and directions of the gravitational field strength vectors are the same at all points in the field, and the lines of equipotential are parallel to one another, normal to the field lines and equally spaced.

An equipotential surface in a gravitational field is a plane within which a mass can be moved around without exchanging energy with the field. The arbitrary nature of the numerical values of the gravitational potentials does not matter; in uniform fields, it is potential difference that matters.

With a gravitational field strength of $9.8\,\mathrm{N\,kg^{-1}}$, the work done against the gravitational field when moving a mass of 1 kg a distance of 10 m against the direction of the field (i.e. upwards) is $98\,\mathrm{N\,m\,kg^{-1}}$ or $98\,\mathrm{J\,kg^{-1}}$. This is the change in gravitational potential over a 10 m increase in height and it explains where the equipotential values come from. The height at which $V$ is zero is wholly arbitrary.

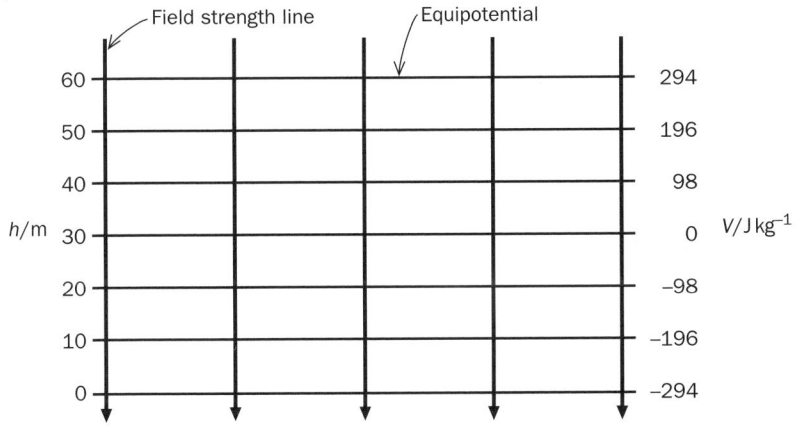


It is well known that change of potential energy equals $mgh$. The term $gh$ is the gravitational potential $V$ with respect to an arbitrary height where $h = 0$, and $m \times gh$ is the work done moving the mass $m$ through the height $h$. For a falling body:

$$mgh = \text{potential energy released} = \text{kinetic energy gained} = \tfrac{1}{2}mv^2$$

There are no uniform gravitational fields in nature. The ideas outlined above are tested to see whether or not you understand the concept of gravitational potential and the usefulness of a scalar quantity in solving problems connected with vector fields.

(See *gravitational potential (radial fields)*.)

**greenhouse effect:** the increase in the Earth's average temperature caused by the presence of its atmosphere. Although the Earth and the Moon are the same distance from the Sun, the Earth's average temperature is about 20°C higher than the Moon's. The temperature of a planet is determined by the balance between incoming and outgoing *radiation*. If the planet is absorbing energy at a greater rate than it is radiating energy, its temperature will rise. When the two rates are equal, the planet has reached a stable equilibrium temperature.

Radiation from the Sun is absorbed by the planet and re-radiated at longer wavelengths. The Earth's temperature is raised compared to that of the Moon because its atmosphere contains greenhouse gases, particularly water vapour and carbon dioxide. These gases transmit ultraviolet and visible radiation, which can therefore reach the Earth's surface; on the other hand, they tend to absorb infrared radiation, which is then radiated outwards from the Earth's surface. As a consequence, the Earth's temperature is elevated to the point at which the outward rate of radiation equals the rate of arrival of radiation from the Sun.

The enhanced greenhouse effect arises from increased levels of greenhouse gases in the atmosphere, mostly carbon dioxide from the burning of fossil fuels. Climate models suggest that this is the cause of the observed rise in the Earth's average temperature that is known as anthropogenic (man-made) global warming.

**A–Z Online**

Log on to A–Z Online to search the database of terms, print revision lists and much more. Go to **www.philipallan.co.uk/a-zonline** to get started.

**hadrons** are subatomic particles which are composed of quarks and hence subject to the strong interaction. Particles which are not hadrons are unaffected by the strong interaction. Hadrons are subdivided into *baryons* (spin ±3/2 or ±1/2) and *mesons* (spin ±1 or 0). Baryon number $B$, which has value 1 for baryons and 0 for mesons, is conserved in all reactions involving hadrons. Another quantum number associated with hadrons is the strangeness quantum number $S$; $S$ takes integral values and is conserved in nuclear reactions controlled by the strong interaction but not in nuclear reactions controlled by the weak interaction. Charge $Q$ is a further quantum number which must be conserved.

To account for the many different kinds of hadrons and their wide range of properties, it has been proposed that hadrons are constructed from a more primitive set of particles called *quarks*. Baryons are formed from three quarks; mesons are formed from two quarks. The quarks are held together by the strong interaction; this ensures that hadron diameter is always round about $10^{-15}$ m, where $10^{-15}$ m is the maximum distance over which the strong interaction can act.

The quarks in a hadron are held together by the *exchange particles* corresponding to the strong interaction; these exchange particles are called gluons. There are eight different kinds of gluons, this large number being needed to accommodate interactions between quarks of different *colour*. (See *quarks, baryons, mesons, gluons, fundamental interactions.*)

**half-life** of a radioactive nuclide equals the average time needed for half the nuclei in a sample of the nuclide to decay. The symbol used is $t_{1/2}$. It is related to the *decay constant* $\lambda$ via the relationship

$$t_{1/2} = \frac{\ln 2}{\lambda} = \frac{0.693}{\lambda}$$

There are two curious points about half-life that are worth remembering. First, it has the largest range of values of any known physical quantity, ranging from tiny fractions of a second to billions of years. Second, there is no known way of changing the half-life of a specimen of a particular nuclide; high temperatures, strong magnetic fields etc. have no effect. (See also *decay constant, randomness and radioactive decay, exponential law of radioactive decay.*)

**Hall effect:** a difference in potential $V_H$ set up in a conductor at right angles to the current flow direction by a magnetic field $B$. The diagram on page 122 shows a thin rectangular conductor with the current $I$ flowing parallel to the long side. A magnetic field of strength $B$ is switched on at right angles to the face of the specimen with the largest area. The force on the current in the magnetic field causes it to be deflected downwards; check this with

*Fleming's left hand rule.* The concentration of charge on the lower edge sets up a voltage which opposes further deflection of the moving charge. Equilibrium is reached when

$$V_H = \frac{BI}{nqt}$$

where $n$ is the number of *charge carriers* per unit volume of conductor, $q$ is the charge per carrier and $t$ is the thickness of the specimen in the direction of the magnetic field.

The Hall effect is significant for a number of reasons. Because $V_H$ is proportional to $B$, it provides a method for determining *magnetic field strength* (flux density). A calibrated *Hall probe* gives an immediate read-out of magnetic field strength. It can also tell us about the material involved because it provides a method of determining the number of charge carriers per unit volume. With semiconductors, the direction of $V_H$ indicates whether the majority carriers are positive holes or negative electrons.

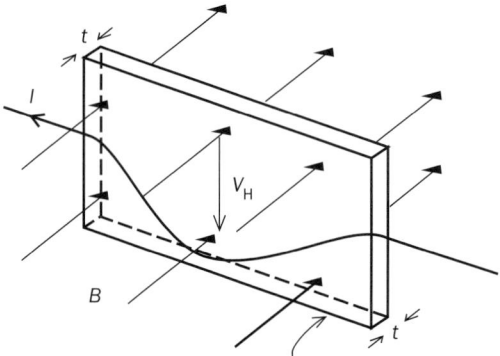


Specimen with $n$ carriers per limit volume
($V_H$ is correct for electrons as carriers)

**Hall probe:** an instrument, based on the *Hall effect*, for measuring *magnetic field strength*. The probe is attached to a calibrated meter to give an immediate read-out. To determine the magnetic field strength at a point, the probe should be placed at the point and rotated until the maximum read-out is obtained. The meter reading gives the magnitude of the magnetic field strength, and its direction will be at right angles to the plane of the probe. (See *Hall effect*.)

**hardness** is a measure of how difficult it is to scratch a material. Scales of hardness are built up either by testing which materials scratch which (squirrels' teeth are harder than steel) or by pressing the surface with a standard force on a hard vertical point and measuring the depth of any depression.

**harmonic:** any sinusoidal note whose frequency is an integer multiple of the fundamental frequency. A vibrating string, for example, may have a fundamental frequency of 120 Hz; this is the first harmonic. The vibration may also have higher-frequency components with frequencies of 240 Hz, 360 Hz etc. These are the second harmonic, third harmonic etc. The number of the harmonic is its multiple of the fundamental frequency.

An alternative term for harmonic is overtone. The numbering of overtones starts with the second harmonic, which is the first overtone. The third harmonic is the second overtone, and so on. (See *stationary wave*.)

**heat** is energy moving down a temperature gradient, that is, from a region of higher temperature to a region of lower temperature. (See *heat capacity, thermal conduction, heat transfer.*)

**heat capacity** is the *heat*, in joules, needed to raise the temperature of a body by one degree kelvin. The SI unit for heat capacity is joules per kelvin, $JK^{-1}$. The symbol used is $C$ (note the upper case form). The word equation definition is:

$$\text{heat capacity} = \frac{\text{heat transferred}}{\text{temperature rise}}$$

$$JK^{-1} = \frac{J}{K}$$

$$C = \frac{\Delta Q}{\Delta \theta}$$

The heat transferred must cause a temperature rise and nothing else. There must be no change of state. Heat capacity is a physical property of a body, not of a material. A bus has a heat capacity. If the body is a homogeneous lump of one material, the heat capacity divided by the mass (the heat capacity per unit mass) is called the *specific heat capacity* of the material. Specific heat capacity is a property of a material, not of a body.

**Worked example**

**A tea urn is equipped with a 3.0 kW heating element. When it is half-filled with water the temperature rises 55 K in 11 minutes. Calculate the heat capacity of the tea urn.**

$$C = \frac{\Delta Q}{\Delta \theta} = \frac{(3.0 \times 10^3 W)(11 \times 60s)}{(55K)} = 36kJ\ K^{-1}\ (\text{to 2 s.f})$$

How far this heat capacity belongs to the urn and how much of it belongs to the water cannot be decided without more information.

**heat engine:** a mechanism which receives *heat* from a hot 'source' and passes some of this heat to a cooler 'sink' while converting the remainder into useful *work*. (See also *heat engine concept.*)

**heat engine concept:** the abstract model of a *heat engine* illustrated in the diagram below. The engine takes in heat $Q_1$ from the hot 'source' whose temperature is $T_1$. It passes heat $Q_2$ to a second body, called the 'sink', at temperature $T_2$. ($T_1$ and $T_2$ are temperatures on the absolute scale.) The engine does work $W$ on its surroundings, where $W = Q_1 - Q_2$.

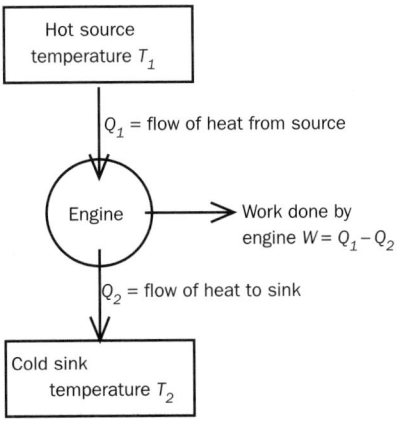

The efficiency of a heat engine is defined as

$$\text{efficiency} = \frac{\text{work done by engine}}{\text{heat taken in from source}}$$

$$\eta = \frac{W}{Q_1}$$

where $\eta$ denotes the efficiency of the engine. This equation is a definition; it applies to any engine no matter how inefficient it may be.

A heat engine which can be run backwards, that is, can be worked upon to absorb heat $Q_2$ from the cold sink and reject heat $Q_1$ into the hot source, is called a reversible heat engine. The *second law of thermodynamics* applied to a reversible heat engine shows that its efficiency sets an upper limit for all heat engines. This efficiency comes out as follows:

$$\eta = \frac{Q_1 - Q_2}{Q_1} = \frac{T_1 - T_2}{T_1} = \frac{W}{Q_1}$$

This equation shows that high efficiency in real heat engines is obtained by ensuring a large temperature difference between source and sink. (See *engine cycle, heat pump, refrigerator.*)

**heat pump:** a *heat engine* that is worked backwards and which thereby removes internal energy $Q_2$ from a cold region and discards heat $Q_1$ to a hotter region, where $Q_1$ equals the sum of $Q_2$ and the thermal equivalent of the work done on the heat engine, i.e. $Q_1 = Q_2 + W$.

Heat pumps are used for domestic heating, and the emphasis is on the heat $Q_1$ discarded into the house, not on the heat $Q_2$ removed from the cold exterior. For this reason, the coefficient of performance for a heat pump is defined differently from the same term used with refrigerators:

$$\text{coefficient of performance} = \frac{\text{heat cliscarded at high temperature}}{\text{work done by engine}}$$

$$= \frac{Q_1}{W} = \frac{Q_1}{Q_1 - Q_2}\left(= \frac{T_1}{T_1 - T_2}\right)$$

If the engine is less than perfect, $W$ is proportionately too large and the part of the expression involving absolute temperatures (the part in the large brackets) no longer holds.
A refrigerator is a heat pump in which the emphasis is on the heat $Q_2$ removed from the low-temperature container. (See also *refrigerator.*)

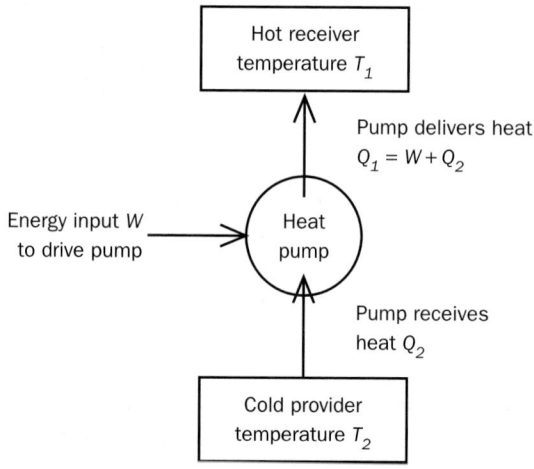

**heat transfer** is the flow of energy away from a body into the surroundings by *thermal conduction*, *convection*, heat radiation or evaporation.

**heating** is the flow of disordered molecular kinetic energy into a body, leading to an increase in the body's internal energy and a rise in its temperature. The two conditions which are necessary for heating to occur are a temperature difference and thermal contact. The warmer of the two bodies heats the cooler body. Thermal contact implies the existence of a pathway for radiation to travel from a hot source like the Sun to a cooler body like the Earth.

**heating and working** are two forms of *energy transfer*. Heating is energy transfer driven by a difference in temperature, whereas working is energy transfer driven by a force of some description.

**Heisenberg uncertainty principle:** see *uncertainty principle*.

**henry** (H) is the SI unit for *self-inductance* and *mutual inductance*.

**Hertzsprung–Russell diagram:** a scatter diagram which relates values of luminosity of a large number of stars to their temperatures. The diagram may be drawn with various quantities on its *x*- and *y*-axes, but the pattern it exhibits is the same.

The diagram below is a plot of absolute magnitude against spectral type. Alternatives to spectral type are temperature $T$ or colour index $M_B - M_V$. If spectral type is spread out evenly, then the temperature scale will be non-linear. The luminosity ratio $L/L_{Sun}$, expressed as a power of ten, can be used instead of absolute magnitude. These different possibilities are shown on the diagram.

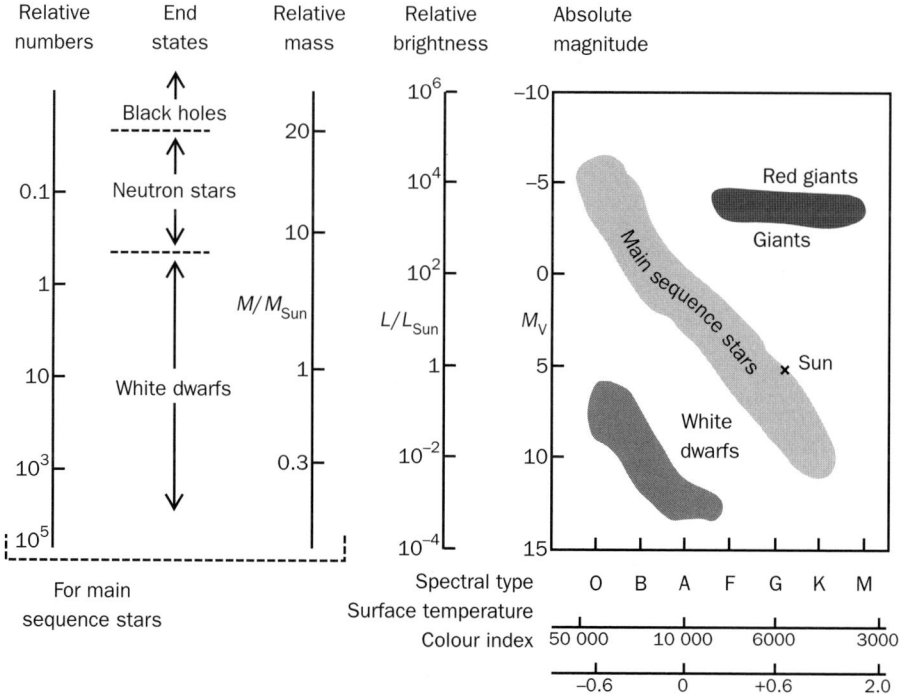


The shaded line from top left to bottom right represents stable stars; it is called the main sequence. Theory shows that luminosity for these stars increases with stellar mass, and the relationship is verified by those stars whose masses are known. The relative mass scale on the left applies to main sequence stars only. To the left of this scale are marked the possible end states. The scale on the extreme left shows the relative numbers of stars of different masses. Notice how small is the proportion of very large stars.

Note that the diagram does not represent the 'life-cycle' of an individual star. The Sun, for example, will remain at a fixed point on the main sequence for billions of years. As it becomes a red giant, it will migrate across the diagram, ending up at a point in the red giants section.

The luminosity $L$ of a distant star can be read from the diagram once the temperature of the star is known from *Wien's law*. The intensity $I$ of the same star can be measured using a telescope with a radiation sensor. The distance $D$ of the star can now be calculated from the relation

$$I = \frac{L}{4\pi D^2}$$

**high-voltage transmission** is a technique for reducing the power loss incurred when *electrical power* is transferred across large distances through power *transmission lines*. The trick is to have a step-up transformer at the input end of the transmission line and a step-down transformer at the output end. Imagine that electrical power is generated at 25 kV and supplied to the consumer at 240 V. The input transformer can step up the voltage from 25 kV to 400 kV. Employing the transformer equation

$$I_P V_P = I_S V_S$$

we see that the current in the transmission lines will be one-sixteenth of the current in the generator output circuit. But power loss in a cable is $I^2R$ where $I$ is the *r.m.s.* current in the cable and $R$ is the resistance of the cable. Reducing the transmission current to one-sixteenth of its former value reduces the power loss in the cable by a factor of 256. In practice the gain is not as dramatic as this, but it is substantial. The voltage at the consumer end will be cut down in stages to ensure similar savings in transmission at the local level.

**Hooke's law** states that *stress* is proportional to *strain*. It applies to elastic substances within the *limit of proportionality*. (See *stress–strain curves*.)

**Hubble's law** states that the speed of recession, $v$, of any one galaxy from another is proportional to their distance apart, $d$. The constant of proportionality $H$ (= $v/d$), known as the Hubble constant, is between 50 and 100 km s$^{-1}$/Mpc. The value of $H$ is found by measuring the speed of recession for those galaxies whose distances are known. The speed of recession is measured using the *Doppler effect*. Galactic distance is measured in a number of ways. If, for example, a *cepheid variable* star is present in the galaxy, its peak brightness can be determined from its period, and its apparent brightness can be measured directly. These two quantities give the distance.

The Hubble constant $H$ can be used to deduce an approximate age for the universe:

$$\text{age of universe} \sim 1/H$$

Note that the units of $H$ must be converted to s$^{-1}$ if this relationship is to be used. Currently accepted values of $H$ give the age of the universe as approximately 13.7 billion years.

Whether or not the remote galaxies will eventually slow down, reverse direction and trigger another Big Bang some long time into the future depends on their speeds and the average density of the universe. At the moment, this average density is not known with sufficient accuracy to foretell the future.

**hypermetropia:** long-sightedness. See *defects of vision*.

**hysteresis** is a term used with elastic and magnetic materials.

In elastic hysteresis, a material is repeatedly subjected to *stress* followed by removal of the stress. The path followed to elastic deformation differs from the path for stress release. Rapid repetition of the stress process results in a heating of the specimen. The elasticity effect is shown especially by *rubber* and other polymers. In elastic hysteresis, the energy linked to the strain corresponding to the stress is released before the strain is wholly removed.

In magnetic hysteresis, a material is subjected to repetitive magnetisation and demagnetisation. In this case, the effect works the other way: the material keeps some of its magnetisation when the magnetising field is switched off.

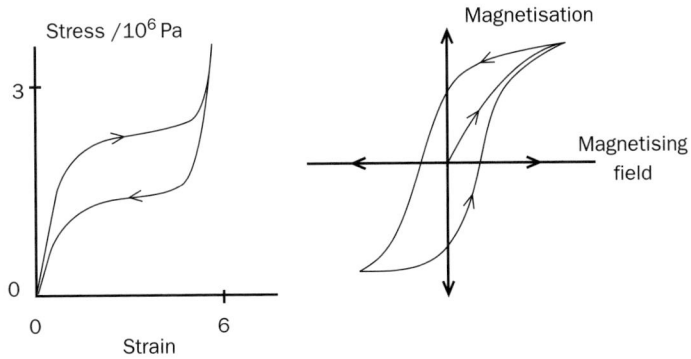


(See *stress–strain curves*.)

**Do you need revision help and advice?**

Go to pages 277–306 for a range of revision appendices that include plenty of exam advice and tips.

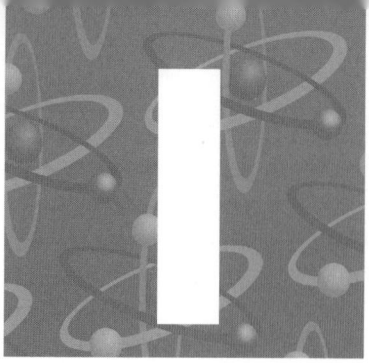

**ice point:** the temperature of a pure ice and water mixture in *thermal equilibrium* at standard atmospheric pressure. It is 273.15 K.

The definition of the *triple point* leaves out the reference to standard atmospheric pressure and adds water vapour to the equilibrium mixture.

**ideal gas equation:** an equation which describes an equilibrium state of an ideal gas and which is usually presented in the form

$$PV = \frac{m}{M}RT = nRT$$

where:

$p$ is gas pressure in pascals (Pa)

$V$ is the volume of gas in cubic metres ($m^3$)

$m$ is the mass of gas in kilograms (kg)

$M$ is the molar mass in kilograms per mole ($kg\,mol^{-1}$)

$n$ is the amount of gas in moles (mol)

$R$ is the molar gas constant whose magnitude is $8.31\,J\,K^{-1}\,mol^{-1}$

$T$ is the gas temperature in kelvins (K)

The ideal gas equation is suggested by experiments with real gases, and many pure gases (such as helium) and mixtures (such as air) obey it to a high degree of accuracy. But an ideal gas remains a concept, not a reality. It is a standard to which the behaviour of real gases can be approximated.

Of the five or six physical variables which appear in the equation, all but one (namely temperature $T$ on the *absolute temperature scale*) are experimental quantities which can be measured for real gases. The constant volume hydrogen thermometer gives values which can be corrected to the absolute scale and given in kelvins.

When the equation is applied to real gases, they must be in an equilibrium state — all the variables must have settled down to their equilibrium values. The equation applies to a gas before and after a change but not during the change. Also, like any other equation we use, it is valid only if we remember to use SI units.

**Worked examples**

**1 The molar mass of air is $0.029\,kg\,mol^{-1}$. Find the density of air at atmospheric pressure (101 kPa) and room temperature (25°C).**

We must use temperatures on the absolute scale:

$$T = 273\,\text{K} + 25\,\text{K} = 298\,\text{K}$$

Density is mass/volume:

$$\text{density} = \frac{m}{V} = \frac{pM}{RT}$$

$$= \frac{(1.01 \times 10^5\,\text{Pa})(0.029\,\text{kg mol}^{-1})}{(8.31\,\text{JK}^{-1}\text{mol}^{-1})(298\,\text{K})}$$

$$= 1.2\,\text{kg m}^{-3}\ (\text{to 2 s.f.})$$

**2 A 250 cm³ volume of air at 100 kPa pressure and exactly 0°C is allowed to settle down in a space of 320 cm³ at 30°C; find the new pressure.**

Since the question refers to a constant mass of gas, we can use a reduced form of ideal gas equation:

$$\frac{p_1V_1}{T_1} = \frac{p_2V_2}{T_2}$$

There are four points which we must remember about this equation:

- the states, before and after, must be equilibrium states
- the mass of gas must be the same for both states
- pressures (or volumes) do not have to be in SI units but must be in the same units
- temperature must always be in kelvins

We then have:

$$p_2 = p_1\frac{V_1T_2}{V_2T_1} = (100\,\text{kPa})\frac{(250\,\text{cm}^3)(303\,\text{K})}{(320\,\text{cm}^3)(273\,\text{K})} = 87\,\text{kPa}\ (\text{to 2 s.f.})$$

(See also *Boyle's Law, Charles' Law, pressure law, absolute temperature scale.*)

**impulse** is the product of an average force and a time interval; it is not a kind of force. When a tennis ball is struck with a racket, the force on the ball changes magnitude rapidly and the impact is all over in a moment. How can we deal with such a situation? At any instant during the collision the force the racket applies to the ball is matched by the reaction force from the ball on the racket. Represent these two forces with symbols $F_{r\to b}$ for the force of the racket on the ball and $F_{b\to r}$ for the reaction force of the ball on the racket.

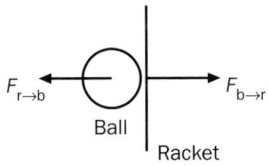


We have, from *Newton's third law of motion*, the relationship

$$F_{r\to b} = -F_{b\to r}$$

If these forces are active for time d$t$ seconds, then

$$F_{r\to b}\mathrm{d}t = -F_{b\to r}\mathrm{d}t$$

But we know from *Newton's second law of motion* that

$$\text{resultant force} \times \mathrm{d}t = \mathrm{d}(mv)$$

It follows that

$$F_{\mathrm{r}\to\mathrm{b}}\mathrm{d}t = \text{momentum transferred to the tennis ball in time } \mathrm{d}t$$
$$= -\text{momentum transferred to the tennis racket in time } \mathrm{d}t$$

If all the small changes in momentum are added up for the whole period of contact, then, using the symbol $\Sigma$ for 'the sum of', we have:

$$\Sigma F_{\mathrm{r}\to\mathrm{b}}\mathrm{d}t = \text{change in momentum of tennis ball during the strike}$$
$$= (\text{average value of force of racket on ball}) \times \text{contact time}$$
$$= \text{impulse of racket on ball}$$

(The second line is, in fact, the definition of average force.)

The word equation definition for impulse is:

$$\text{impulse} = \text{momentum transferred during contact in a collision}$$

and it equals average force × contact time.

Given this, the SI unit for impulse must be the same as the SI unit for momentum, i.e. newton second (N s).

If a graph is drawn of force against time, then impulse equals the area between the curve and the time axis.

A working definition of impulse is the product of average force and contact time. Therefore, for a given impulse, increasing the contact time lowers the average force.

**Worked example**

**A cricket ball of mass 145 g travelling at speed 35 m s$^{-1}$ is caught by a fielder and brought to rest in 0.080 s. Calculate the average force applied to the ball and the distance over which this force acts.**

$$\text{average force} = (\text{momentum change}) \div \text{time}$$
$$= \left(0.145\text{kg} \times 35\text{ms}^{-1}\right) \div (0.080\text{s}) = 63\text{N (to 2 s.f.)}$$
$$\text{distance} = (\text{loss of kinetic energy}) \div (\text{average force})$$
$$= \left(\frac{1}{2} \times 0.145\text{kg} \times \left(35\text{ms}^{-1}\right)^2\right) \div 63\text{N} = 1.4\text{m (to 2 s.f.)}$$

**inclined plane:** a sloping surface with a uniform gradient. An object sliding down a smooth inclined plane shows the same pattern of accelerated motion as an object in *free fall* but with a smaller uniform acceleration. Galileo used an inclined plane to show that an object, once dropped, does not travel at constant speed as it falls. Free fall corresponds to a plane inclined at 90° to the horizontal.

**induced e.m.f.:** an *e.m.f.* generated in a conductor either by a changing magnetic flux around the conductor or by the conductor itself cutting across the magnetic field. (See also *back e.m.f., electromagnetic induction, electromagnetic induction (laws of).*)

**inductance:** see *self-inductance, mutual inductance.*

**inductive reactance** is the ratio of peak voltage $V_0$ to peak current $I_0$ for an inductor. This is given by the equation

$$V_0 = \omega L I_0$$

where $L$ is the *self-inductance* of the inductor and $\omega$ is the *angular frequency* of the voltage across it.

Compare this with *Ohm's law*:

$$V = IR$$

In Ohm's law, the resistance $R$ holds the balance between current and voltage. For the inductor, $\omega L$ holds the balance between peak voltage and peak current, but the quantities are not in phase. The expression $\omega L$ is called the reactance of the inductor. The symbol for inductive reactance is $X_L$ and its SI unit is the ohm ($\Omega$).

(See also *reactance, capacitive reactance, resonance in AC circuits.*)

**inelastic collision:** a collision in which *kinetic energy* is not conserved. *Linear momentum* will be conserved as the law of *conservation of linear momentum* is always obeyed.

**inelastic deformation** is another name for *plastic deformation.*

**infrared radiation:** see *IR.*

**insulators** are materials which contain no *charge carriers* free to move within them. Electrical insulators cannot carry electrical current. Even so, the insulating properties of many materials break down if too high a voltage is applied. Note the contrast with good thermal conductors and poor thermal conductors. (See *conductors and insulators, resistivity.*)

**intensity (stellar):** the radiant power per square metre reaching the Earth's surface from a star. If $D$ is the distance of the star from the Earth and $L$ is its *luminosity*, then $I = L/(4\pi D^2)$. See *star.*

**intensity of radiation is** the rate at which energy is transferred across unit area at right angles to the direction of propagation. Other names for this are radiation flux and irradiance. Its unit is $\mathrm{W\,m^{-2}}$.

**interference** is the formation of a new wave pattern where two or more incident wave patterns overlap. It is a visible phenomenon. Young's fringes can be seen by someone who has no knowledge of physics. The interpretation of an interference pattern, the explanation of how it happens, is convincing evidence of the wave character of the incident beams. Sets of sound waves can also be used to produce audible interference patterns, provided the waves have the same frequency.

Interference is a consequence of the *principle of superposition* and happens provided that certain conditions are met. (See also *constructive interference, destructive interference, coherence, two slits experiment.*)

**internal energy** is the sum total of the kinetic and potential energies of all the individual molecules which make up an object. In an ideal gas there are no intermolecular forces and no intermolecular potential energy, so the internal energy is kinetic only. Internal energy decides the temperature and state of a body; an increase is accompanied either by an increase in temperature or by a change of state (e.g. melting). In practice, *changes* of internal energy are more significant than attempts to evaluate the actual level of internal energy. Internal energy can be increased in either or both of two ways: by working on a body or by heating it. (See *heat capacity, heating and working, first law of thermodynamics.*)

**internal resistance** is the resistance to current flow in an electrical power source. It is a topic which needs to be approached with a little care.

When a cell or power supply causes a current to flow in a circuit, charge carriers (electrons or ions) move within the supply as well as in the external circuit. There is resistance within the supply to the movement of charges, which gives rise to loss of energy within the supply. (This can be demonstrated by short-circuiting a cell with a length of wire — a large current flows and the cell becomes hot.)

To account for this energy loss, we imagine an internal resistance $r$ within the cell. Resistance is defined as the ratio of the potential difference $V$ across a conductor to the current $I$ in the conductor: $R = V/I$. It is not possible to use this equation to define internal resistance, because the voltage drop $V_r$ across the imagined internal resistance $r$ is not accessible. The best we can do is to write down the equation

$$E = I(R + r)$$

where $E$ is the e.m.f. of the cell, $R$ is the external resistance, $r$ is the internal resistance and $I$ is the current in the circuit. We then record a series of measurements of the current $I$ for different values of the external resistance $R$ and draw a graph of $1/I$ against $R$:

$$\frac{1}{I} = \frac{R}{E} + \frac{r}{E}$$

The graph is a straight line of gradient $1/E$ and intercept $r/E$ on the $1/I$ axis.

A clearer idea of the meaning of internal resistance is arrived at by multiplying the equation for internal resistance through by the current $I$, leading to the equation

$$EI = I^2r + I^2R$$

$EI$ is the energy transformed into electrical energy in the power source, $I^2R$ is the work done by the power source on the external circuit, and $I^2r$ is the work done within the power source.

When internal resistance is measured, there appears to be a choice between taking a series of measurements of current and resistance or a series of measurements of current and voltage. In fact, standard resistors are expensive devices which are meant to be operated at low current. But internal resistances are often small, often a fraction of an ohm. In such cases an appreciable current must be drawn from the cell or power source to enable the internal resistance to be calculated with reasonable accuracy. For this reason, it is better to use a rugged, reliable and variable external resistance (whose precise magnitude we do not need to know) in conjunction with a digital voltmeter and a digital ammeter.

In practice, the assumption that the internal resistance of a supply can simply be represented by a single, fixed value $r$ proves rather unsatisfactory. The value of $r$ may change as the current flowing through the supply changes, and it may also change as a cell ages.

**International Practical Temperature scale:** a temperature scale which is used for calibrating thermometers and which is as close as possible, numerically, to the absolute thermodynamic temperature scale (see *absolute temperature scale*). It is defined in two stages:

**Experiment to measure the internal resistance of an electrical power source**

**Apparatus**

A power source, with e.m.f. $E$ and internal resistance $r$, is connected to an external variable resistor of resistance $R$. The current $I$ in the external resistance and the potential difference $V$ across it are measured with a digital ammeter and a digital voltmeter. The circuit is shown in the diagram.

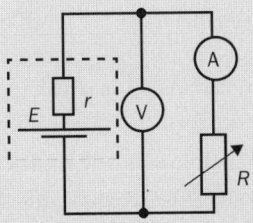


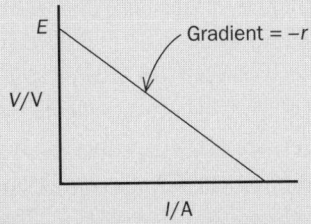


**Measurements**

The potential difference $V$ is read from the digital voltmeter and the current $I$ is read from the digital ammeter for each of six values of the variable resistor. The resistance values should be arranged such that the voltage $V$ should drop from a maximum value almost equal to $E$ to a minimum value about a third lower. A larger drop in voltage would mean drawing a larger current than would be good for the power source.

**Conclusion**

The voltage $V$ equals the e.m.f. $E$ of the power supply less the voltage drop $Ir$ across the internal resistance:

$$V = E - Ir$$

A graph of the voltage $V$ against the current $I$ will be a straight line of gradient $-r$ starting from the point $E$ on the voltage axis. The measurements will cover about the top third of this line; the rest of the line is an extrapolation.

**Comment**

The restricted set of voltage values looks like a fault in the design of the experiment. In fact, this ensures that measurements are taken within the range of current values that the power supply would be called upon to deliver. Also, the internal resistance would probably increase if too large a current were drawn from the supply.

- A large number of *fixed points* are mapped onto particular numbers on the scale. The *triple point* of water, for instance, is mapped onto 273.16 K.
- The specifications for constructing thermometers to measure temperatures between the fixed points are defined (for instance, the design of a thermocouple to measure temperatures between the ice point and the steam point).

**inverse square law:** any law according to which one quantity is inversely proportional to the square of another, that is, $x \propto 1/y^2$. Two important examples are the following.

Radiation such as light spreads out into a uniform medium so that its intensity $I$ decreases as the inverse square of the distance $r$ from the source: $I \propto 1/r^2$. This can be understood as arising from the spreading out of the rays of light in the space around the source.

The *electric field strength* of a point charge and the *gravitational field strength* of a point mass also follow inverse square relationships. This can be understood as arising from the spreading out of the field lines in the space around the charge or mass which gives rise to the field. :

**ionic bond** is a form of attachment between the atoms in a molecule in which electrons from an atom of one element are transferred to the atom of a second element. The two atoms are now oppositely charged. An ordered structure can be built up in which the oppositely charged atoms of the two elements alternate in all three directions to give a crystalline solid.

The ionic bond is not as strong as the *covalent bond* and, since it relies on the electrical attraction between neighbouring atoms, it breaks down in the presence of polar solvents such as water. The weakness of the bond gives us a solid which is not very hard and which either has a low-to-modest melting point or dissociates on heating. The neutralising of the inter-atomic attraction in the presence of water implies a strongly soluble substance. (See *metallic bond*.)

**ionisation** is the process by which an atom receives enough energy to lose at least one electron. An atom also becomes ionised if it gains one or more electrons. (See *energy level*.)

**ionising radiation** is a term which covers any kind of radiation that will ionise a gas put in its path. This includes *alpha radiation*, *beta radiation* and *gamma radiation* in addition to *X-rays*. Note that ionising radiation may consist of particles of matter or photons of electromagnetic radiation.

**IR** (infrared radiation) is that segment of the electromagnetic spectrum which lies between the visible and the microwave regions. It is primarily associated with hot surfaces. Human skin senses it easily but there is little resolution.

IR wavelengths are from 700 nm (0.7 μm) up to about 1 mm. This range is so broad that it is usual to divide it into near IR (0.7 μm to about 3 μm), thermal IR (3 μm to 10 μm) and far IR (to cover the remainder). This division is essential to the study of the Earth by remote sensing techniques, since the different classes of IR relate to different kinds of source and give different types of information. Near IR can be detected with a photocell or photo-diode, but the rest of the spectrum is investigated with a bolometer (a thin strip of blackened platinum creating a kind of *resistance thermometer*), a *thermocouple* or a thermopile (lots of thermocouples in series).

**irradiance:** another name for *intensity of radiation*.

**isothermal change** is a change occurring at constant temperature. A fixed mass of gas obeys *Boyle's law* when undergoing an isothermal change (constant temperature is a requirement if Boyle's law is to apply). It is sometimes convenient to resolve (i.e. separate) changes in the state of a gas into two changes: an *adiabatic change* and an isothermal change.

**isotope:** a nuclide with the same *atomic number* as another nuclide but with a different *mass number*.

**jet engines** create a forward *thrust* on an aeroplane by the explosive discharge of hot burnt fuel through the rear of the engine. The *momentum* of the burnt fuel discharged per second towards the rear equals the increased momentum of the aeroplane in the forward direction. The design of the engine is complicated by the need to access the surrounding air for the oxygen in which the fuel burns. As a consequence, jet engines cannot fly very high. Rockets carry their own supply of oxygen and can operate in space.

**joule:** another name for the newton metre. It is the SI unit for energy and its symbol is J. The *base unit* equivalent of the joule is $kg\,m^2\,s^{-2}$. (See also *work*, *derived unit*, *kilowatt–hour*.)

**K-capture:** see *electron capture.*

**kelvin:** the *SI* unit of temperature difference and one of the seven SI *base units.* The symbol is K. It is defined as the temperature difference between *absolute zero* and the *triple point* of water divided by 273.16. Temperatures measured from absolute zero are expressed in kelvins (K). Temperatures measured from the freezing point of water (273.15 K) are expressed in degrees Celsius (°C). Temperature differences measured on either scale are given in kelvins (K).

**Kelvin scale:** another name for the *absolute temperature scale.* It was Lord Kelvin who showed that the theory of heat engines led to the definition of an absolute thermodynamic scale of temperature which was independent of the properties of any real substance. He showed further that this scale of temperature was identical to the ideal gas scale of temperature. He went on to show how temperatures measured with a constant volume gas thermometer filled with hydrogen could be corrected to temperatures measured on the absolute scale.

**Kepler's laws** are three laws of planetary motion which were discovered empirically by Kepler early in the seventeenth century and shown later in the same century by Sir Isaac Newton to follow from the law of universal gravitation. They are as follows:

1 A planet moves round the Sun along an elliptical path with the Sun at one focus of the ellipse.
2 The straight line joining a planet to the Sun sweeps out equal areas in equal times.
3 The ratio of the square of a planet's orbital period $T$ to the cube of the major diameter $d$ of its orbital path is the same for all planets ($T^2 \propto d^3$).

**kilogram:** a *base unit* in *SI.* It is the SI unit of *mass* and has the symbol kg. It is the mass of the International Prototype Kilogram held at Sèvres in France. Historically, the kilogram was based on the mass of one litre of water, and it is useful to remember this rough equivalence for use in experimental work and in calculations.

**kilowatt–hour:** the energy transferred from a source which delivers energy for one hour at a constant rate of a thousand watts. It is not an accepted SI unit, but is widely used as a practical unit (for example by energy suppliers, who may refer to 1 kWh as a 'Unit'). It has the symbol kWh and equals exactly 3.6 MJ.

$$1\,\text{kWh} = 1\,\text{kW} \times 1\,\text{h} = 1000\,\text{W} \times 3600\,\text{s} = 3.6\,\text{MJ}$$

**kinematic equations:** another name for the *equations of motion.*

**kinetic energy** is the energy possessed by a mass by reason of its motion. It is a *scalar quantity.* The SI unit is the *joule* (J). The symbol used may be the energy symbol $W$, or there may be a subscript 'k' (e.g. $W_k$) to distinguish it from potential energy $W_p$. The symbol $E_k$ is also used. (Some writers use k.e. or even K.E.)

For a mass $m$ travelling at speed $v$:

kinetic energy $= \frac{1}{2}mv^2$

This expression can be deduced from one of the equations of motion. Consider a body of mass $m$, initially at rest (i.e. with $u = 0$) and acted on by a force $F$ over a distance $s$. Starting from $v^2 = u^2 + 2as$, eliminating $u$ and multiplying both sides by $m$ gives $mv^2 = 2mas$. But $mas$ is the *work* done by the force, and this is the energy transferred to the body — its kinetic energy. Hence kinetic energy $= \frac{1}{2}mv^2$.

You need to be familiar with 'work done equals increase in kinetic energy' calculations, with the interplay between *potential energy* and kinetic energy in gravitational fields, and with *simple harmonic motion* (this is straightforward with the *simple pendulum* but more complicated with the *mass–spring system* where potential energy is stored in two forms).

*Thermal energy* is wholly kinetic in gases. It is partly kinetic and partly potential in liquids and solids where inter-atomic distances are small.

**kinetic theory of gases:** an explanation of why gases obey the gas laws, it is based on the idea of a gas as a set of hard particles (this is called the model) which obey *Newton's laws of motion*. The kinetic theory is remarkable because it shows that, starting from a picture of the microscopic nature of matter (as particles which obey Newton's laws of motion), we can deduce an equation which correctly describes the macroscopic (large-scale) behaviour of gases. The theory is developed in stages:

- write out a set of postulates which define the model
- apply Newton's laws of motion to this model and so relate pressure to average kinetic energy
- assume that average *kinetic energy* is proportional to absolute temperature
- confirm that the theory leads to a full statement of the *ideal gas equation*

***Postulates:***

- a gas consists of a large number of identical particles called molecules
- molecular diameter is much smaller than the average distance between the molecules
- molecules obey Newton's laws of motion
- molecular speeds and directions are distributed randomly
- there are no forces between molecules except when they collide
- collisions are elastic and instantaneous

***Applying Newton's laws of motion:*** Imagine $N$ molecules each of mass $m'$ occupying a cube of side $l$ with hard walls. The momentum change at the wall resulting from the reflection of a molecule with speed $v_1$ normal to the wall is $2m'v_1$ (see the diagram on page 138).

$$\begin{aligned}\text{momentum change per second} &= 2m'v_1 \times \text{number of collision per second}\\ &= 2m'v_1 \times \frac{v_1}{2l} = m'v_1^2/l\\ &= \text{force on one wall from one molecule}\end{aligned}$$

Since, for each molecule,

$$u_1^2 + v_1^2 + w_1^2 = c_1^2$$

$$\begin{aligned}\text{the total force on all six walls} &= 2 \times [m'/l] \times [c_1^2 + c_2^2 + c_3^2 \ldots c_N^2]\\ &= [2m'/l] \times [N\langle c^2\rangle]\\ \text{where } \langle c^2\rangle &= [c_1^2 + c_2^2 + c_3^2 \ldots c_N^2]/N\end{aligned}$$

$\langle c^2\rangle$ denotes the average value of molecular speed squared. It is called the *mean square speed*.

We now have:

$$\text{pressure } p \text{ on wall} = \text{total force/area}$$
$$= [2m'/l] \times [N\langle c^2\rangle] \div [6l^2]$$
$$= [Nm'/3V]\langle c^2\rangle = p$$

and since $Nm'/V$ is the gas density $\rho$, we have

$$p = \tfrac{1}{3}\rho\langle c^2\rangle$$

or

$$pV = \tfrac{1}{3}Nm'\langle c^2\rangle$$

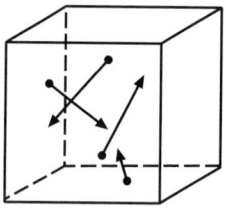

N molecules;
different speeds
different directions

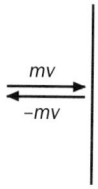


$\Delta(mv) = 2mv$

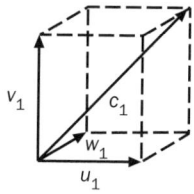


$u_1^2 + v_1^2 + w_1^2 = c_1^2$

***Assumption concerning temperature:*** The next step is to involve temperature by assuming that average molecular kinetic energy is related to temperature in the following manner:

$$\tfrac{1}{2}m'\langle c^2\rangle = \tfrac{3}{2}kT$$

(The strict statement of the assumption is that each of the three components of average molecular kinetic energy is $\tfrac{1}{2}kT$.)

***General gas equation:*** If we put this assumption in our expression for gas pressure, we have:

$$pV = \left(\tfrac{2}{3}N\right)\left(\tfrac{1}{2}m'\langle c^2\rangle\right) = NkT$$

where $k$ is the *Boltzmann constant*, $1.38\times10^{23}\,\mathrm{J\,K^{-1}}$.

Next, note that

$$N = \frac{m}{M}L = nL$$

where $m$ is the mass of the gas in kilograms, $M$ is the molar mass, $L$ is the Avogadro constant ($6.022 \times 10^{23}\,\mathrm{mol^{-1}}$) and $n$ is the number of moles. And if we put

$$R = kL = (1.38 \times 10^{-23}\,\mathrm{J\,K^{-1}})(6.022\times10^{23}\,\mathrm{mol^{-1}}) = 8.31\,\mathrm{J\,K^{-1}\,mol^{-1}}$$

then our equation becomes

$$pV = \frac{m}{M}RT = nRT$$

where $n$ is the number of moles of gas in the sample.

The derivation of this law confirms our confidence in the molecular theory of matter. The next stage would be either to introduce other postulates to account for deviations from the gas laws at high densities and pressures, or to explain other phenomena such as diffusion rates or thermal conductivity. But none of this is in the A-level specifications. (See also *ideal gas equation*.)

**Kirchhoff's first law** states that the total electric current flowing into a junction along all possible roots is zero. An alternative form states that the sum of the currents flowing towards the junction of a number of conductors equals the sum of the currents leaving the junction. Either way, the implication is that *electric charge* is a conserved quantity.

$$I = I_1 + I_2 + I_3 + \ \ldots$$

The law may seem an empty and even pointless statement to someone in the early stages of studying electricity, but it is an essential step in setting up a formal algebra for circuit analysis as performed by, say, computer systems which design complex circuitry. There is a hint of this formalism in the derivations of the rules for combining *resistors in series* and for combining *resistors in parallel*.

**Kirchhoff's second law** states that the net *e.m.f.* in a circuit loop equals the sum of the *potential differences* round the loop. e.m.f.s are sources of electrical energy; potential differences are drains of electrical energy. A 'loop' is any section of a circuit which can be traced continuously, starting at a point and returning to the same point. It does not matter whether there are junctions leading off the loop or connections across the loop. The loop need not include a source of e.m.f.

Kirchhoff's second law is a statement of the law of *conservation of energy* in a form which applies to electric circuits. The net e.m.f. $E$ is the electrical energy provided by the power source per coulomb of charge flowing in the circuit. Each potential difference states how much electrical energy is dissipated, per coulomb of charge flowing, in the element to which the potential difference applies. The law tells us that for any complete loop in a circuit:

$$E = V_1 + V_2 + V_3 + \ldots + V_n$$

**Are you studying other subjects?**

The *A–Z Handbooks (digital editions)* are available in 14 different subjects. Browse the range and order other handbooks at **www.philipallan.co.uk/a-zonline.**

**laminar flow** is an alternative name for *streamline flow.*

**latent heat:** see *specific latent heat.*

**length** is a *base quantity* in SI. It is a property of a line. The length of a line, whether or not it is straight, is measured with a ruler or its equivalent. The SI unit of length is the metre (m). (See also *distance, distance travelled, displacement.*)

Length, *distance* and *displacement* are three closely related concepts. Length is part of our language. If length has a definition, it is the outcome of measuring a length with a ruler. Length is the physical quantity: it is the magnitude that is being measured. It may be the length of a conducting wire, the length of a solenoid or the length of a river. The unit is the metre.

*Distance* is the length of a pathway between two points. Imagine that a string is laid along the pathway, marked at each of the two points and then pulled out straight. The distance between the two points on the pathway is the length of the straightened string between the two marks. Distance and length are both scalar quantities.

*Displacement* is a *vector quantity* which defines the position of a second point relative to a fixed point. No pathway is involved. The magnitude of the displacement is the straight line distance between the two points, and its direction is the angle between this straight line and a reference line; these two lines must start at the first point.

(The position vector in vector work for A-level mathematics is the displacement of a point from the origin of the coordinate system in use.)

**lens equation** is the equation

$$\frac{1}{u} + \frac{1}{v} = \frac{1}{f}$$

where $u$ is the distance of the object (the light source) from the lens, $v$ is the distance of the image from the lens and $f$ is the *focal length* of the lens. Always draw light going from left to right. Object distances to the left and image distances to the right are positive. Object distances to the right (light converging on the lens) and image distances to the left (light diverging from the lens) are negative. Negative distances are called virtual. Focal length $f$ is positive for convex lenses and negative for concave lenses. If any two quantities are given, the third may be calculated. The ratio $v/u$ equals the magnification.

Using the lens equation, we find that if an object is placed 25 cm in front of a convex lens whose focal length is 10 cm, then the image distance works out at +16.7 cm. This example is illustrated in the first ray diagram on page 141. The image is real and could be focused on a screen. Alternatively, if the same object is placed 7 cm in front of the same lens, the image distance works out at −23.3 cm; the image is virtual — it cannot be focused on a screen and can be seen only by looking through the lens. In this second example, illustrated by the second ray diagram, the lens is used as a magnifying glass.

Drawing ray diagrams to scale is an alternative to using the lens equation. The sequence of events is as follows:

- Draw a straight line from side to side across the page. This line is called the principal axis.
- Draw a line at right angles to the principal axis to represent the lens.
- Mark the positions of the two focal points at equal distances from the lens but on opposite sides. Use a suitable scale for the focal length.
- Draw a line at right angles to the principal axis and to the left of the lens to represent the object. Use the same scale for object distance as you did for focal length.
- From any off-axial point on the object line, draw a straight line through the point where the lens line crosses the principal axis.
- Draw a straight line from the same point on the object parallel to the principal axis. From the point where this line crosses the lens line, draw a straight line through the focal point on the right-hand side of the lens.
- These last two lines cross at the image. Draw the image and measure the image distance.

The broken lines in the second diagram indicate a virtual image through which no light has passed.

A lens with short focal length bends the light more than a lens with long focal length. The reciprocal of the focal length $f$, measured in metres, is called the power $P$ of the lens.

$P = \frac{1}{f}$ is measured in dioptres

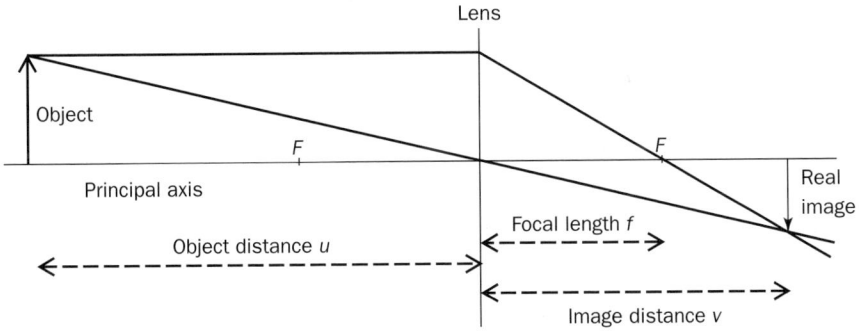


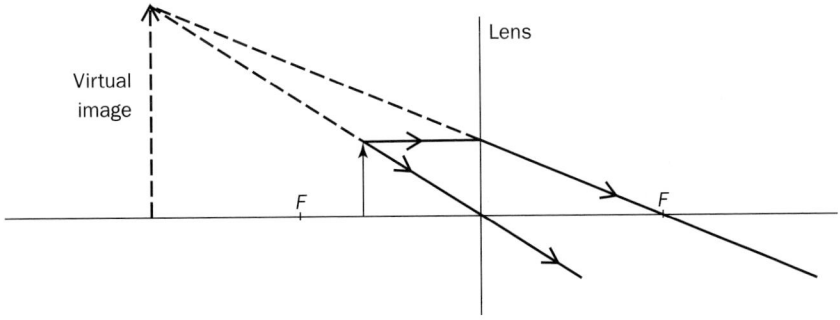


**Lenz's law:** see *electromagnetic induction, electromagnetic induction (laws of).*

**leptons** are those elementary particles that do not respond to the strong interaction. There are 12 of them altogether. Six leptons are shown in the following table; the other six are their antiparticles.

| | Particles of charge –e | | Particles of charge zero | |
|---|---|---|---|---|
| **Generation** | **Particle** | **Rest mass** | **Particle** | **Rest mass** |
| First | electron, e | 0.51 MeV/$c^2$ | electron neutrino, $\upsilon_e$ | 0 |
| Second | muon, μ | 106 MeV/$c^2$ | muon neutrino, $\upsilon_\mu$ | 0 |
| Third | tau, τ | 1784 MeV/$c^2$ | tau neutrino, $\upsilon_\tau$ | 0 |

There are three principal leptons which carry negative charge and mass: the electron ($e^-$), the muon ($\mu^-$) and the tau ($\tau^-$). These, and the corresponding positively charged antiparticles, are subject to gravity, to electromagnetic fields and to the weak interaction. To each of these six elementary particles there corresponds a neutrino or an antineutrino, giving us 12 leptons in all. The six neutrinos and antineutrinos carry no charge, and any mass they might have is too small to measure. They are immune to the electromagnetic interaction and to gravity; they are subject to the weak interaction only. Any nuclear event is controlled by the weak interaction if it in some way involves neutrinos or antineutrinos.

The 12 leptons are separated into three generations. Each generation starts with one of the three negatively charged leptons and includes its antiparticle and the corresponding neutrino and antineutrino.

Why don't we see more of them? The electron is stable but any positrons lucky enough to be around are soon annihilated. The heavier muon (about a tenth of the proton mass) decays after an average lifetime of about 2.2 microseconds into an electron, a neutrino and an antineutrino. The tau particle is not far short of two proton masses and decays in a number of ways to produce muons, electrons or even pi mesons. Muons and π mesons end up as electrons. Only neutrinos in the first generation (e.g. from the Sun) can exist in any numbers, and they are largely inactive. The material universe is mostly protons, neutrons, electrons and neutrinos — we live in a low-energy universe.

Apart from everyday electron behaviour, beta decay processes and positron *annihilation*, lepton interactions are observed only in high-energy collision experiments. A number of conservation laws apply:

- mass–energy
- charge (either $e^-$, $e^+$ or zero)
- spin (all 12 leptons carry spin ½)
- lepton number (conserved separately for each generation: +1 for negative leptons and their neutrinos, –1 for the other six).

The neutrino idea was introduced into physics in order to reconcile beta decay with the concept of mass–energy conservation. The electron neutrino (so-called at the time) was later discovered to be the electron antineutrino.

**lift** is the upward thrust on an *aeroplane* brought about by the downward force exerted by the wings on the air as the aeroplane moves forwards through the air.

**light as a transverse wave motion** accounts for the phenomenon of polarisation. If light were a longitudinal wave motion (like sound), there would be no polarisation effects. (See *polarisation phenomena, transverse waves, longitudinal waves.*)

**light-dependent resistor** (l.d.r. or LDR) is a resistor whose resistance decreases if the ambient light level increases. The current $I$ in a conductor of cross-sectional area $A$ is given by the relationship:

$$I = nAqv$$

where there are $n$ charge carriers per unit volume moving with an average drift velocity $v$, each carrying charge $q$. Thin layers of semiconducting material can be constructed with the special property that the number of charge carriers per unit volume of semiconductor, $n$, increases with ambient light level. (Electrons within the semiconducting material gain energy from the light and this allows them to break free and contribute to the increased conductivity of the material.) There is then more current for a given potential difference across the specimen, so resistance has fallen.

**light-emitting diode** (l.e.d. or LED) is a semiconducting diode which emits light when it is forward biased and carries current. A light emitting diode is made from semiconducting materials which require a forward bias of 2 V or so before forward current will rise appreciably. A proportion of the electrons flowing across the junction into the *p*-type material recombine with an equal number of holes moving the other way. The energy released upon each recombination appears as a single *photon*. The colour of the light emitted depends on the forward voltage at the 'knee' of the current–voltage characteristic.

l.e.d.s are more efficient in their conversion of electrical energy to light than are filament lamps. Modern l.e.d.s have an energy efficiency of above 20% so that, despite the relatively high cost of their production, they are increasingly being used for lighting.

(See *semiconductor diodes*, *current–voltage characteristics*.)

**light gates** are used in *data logging*. A beam of light or infrared radiation travels from a source (usually a light-emitting diode) and falls on a sensor (usually a photodiode or phototransistor). When an opaque object passes into or out of the beam, the current in the detector circuit changes and this can be used to trigger a timer.

Light gates are often used in experiments in which motion is to be recorded and analysed. For example, a trolley may have an 'interrupt card' attached. This card has one or more sections positioned in such a way that they break the beam of the light gate as the trolley passes through. The associated circuitry responds to the change in voltage when the beam is broken and when it is re-made. The timer can be set to start or stop according to the requirements of the experiment.

(See *conservation of linear momentum*.)

**light rays** are the straight lines light is imagined to travel along when approaching a mirror or a refracting surface. Light is real but light rays are imaginary. Light rays are fundamental to the principle of rectilinear propagation — the principle that light travels in straight lines.

Experiments in *ray optics* are often carried out using a ray box. Although this produces a narrow 'ray' of light, it would more correctly be thought of as a narrow beam; a ray has zero width. (See *ray diagram*.)

**light year:** a unit of distance, used in astronomy, that equals the distance travelled by light in a vacuum in one year. Its symbol is ly. $1\,\text{ly} = 9.46 \times 10^{15}$ m. See *astronomical unit*, *parsec*.

**limit of proportionality** is the point on a stress–strain curve at which the line stops being straight. It marks the maximum stress for which *Hooke's law* applies.

By its definition, the limit of proportionality is different from the *elastic limit*, which is the point beyond which plastic deformation occurs. In practice, however, these two points may be close together and they are both difficult to determine experimentally.

(See *stress–strain curves.*)

**linear accelerator:** see *particle accelerators.*

**linear momentum** is defined by the word equation

linear momentum = mass × velocity

It is a *vector quantity* and has the same direction as its velocity vector component. Mass, a *scalar quantity*, acts like a multiplier. The *conservation of linear momentum* is perhaps the most fundamental law of Newtonian mechanics, and the concept of force draws its definition from rate of change of linear momentum. The SI unit for linear momentum, the newton second (N s), comes from the definition of impulse. $1\,\mathrm{N\,s} = 1\,\mathrm{kg\,m\,s^{-1}}$.

(See also *impulse, Newton's laws of motion.*)

**lines of force:** see *field lines (electric)* and *field lines (magnetic).*

**liquid pressure (laws of):** the pressure $p$ in a stationary liquid mass is calculated from the following equation:

$$p = p_0 + h\rho g$$

where $p_0$ is the pressure on the surface, $h$ is the depth below the surface, $\rho$ is the *density* of the liquid and $g$ is the *acceleration of free fall.* (Gases do not obey this simple form of the law; they are compressible, so density increases with depth.)

We are often concerned with the change in pressure $\Delta p$ which arises from a change in depth $\Delta h$. This is simply given by

$$\Delta p = \rho g \Delta h$$

The pressure within a liquid mass:

- acts at every point in the liquid mass, not just at the surfaces
- increases linearly with the depth below the surface
- increases linearly with the density of the liquid
- increases linearly with the gravitational field strength
- is independent of the shape of the container
- acts in any direction at a point
- exerts a normal thrust on any solid surface with which it is in contact

**liquids:** fluids in which every molecule is in contact with its neighbouring molecules but is not attached to any of them. The short-range order which accounts for crystal structure in solids, especially when it continues into the long range, is absent in liquids. Molecules in a liquid are not tied together; they are free to move about within the body of the liquid, but they are not free to separate. As a consequence, a liquid is almost incompressible but has no shape of its own: a liquid takes the shape of its container. Like gases, liquids can transmit pressure but not force. The molecular speeds have a spread of values and this is linked to the process of evaporation. (See *liquid pressure (laws of), pressure, thrust, Archimedes' principle, solids, gases, viscosity, evaporation and cooling.*)

**localised vector:** a vector which has magnitude and direction and which acts through a particular point. One example is force; the weight of an object is a force which acts through the object's centre of gravity. (See *force: a localised vector.*)

**longitudinal waves** are *progressive waves* whose displacements are along the line of energy flow. *Sound waves* are longitudinal waves. (See also *stationary wave, transverse waves.*)

**loudness** is the subjective estimate of sound intensity made by the *ear.* However, experiments with large numbers of people judging the loudnesses of sounds of known intensity support the following relationship between loudness $L$ and intensity $I$:

$$L = 10 \log_{10}\left(\frac{I}{I_0}\right)$$

where $L$ is the loudness of the sound in decibels, $I$ is the sound intensity in $\mathrm{W\,m^{-2}}$ and $I_0$ is the minimum sound intensity which is just audible to a 'standard ear', corresponding to a loudness of 0 dB. An accepted value of $I_0$ is $1 \times 10^{-12}\,\mathrm{W\,m^{-2}}$, and 120 decibels corresponds to a sound which is so loud that it begins to hurt. The intensity value for this level of loudness is $1\,\mathrm{W\,m^{-2}}$. Thus, ears operate across twelve orders of magnitude — an astonishing feat.

The symbol dBA is used for a modified scale which takes into account the response of the human ear to different frequencies. This scale is often used when specifying allowed limits, for example, of noise in public places.

**luminosity** $L$ of a *star* is the total radiant power output in watts. If luminosity and surface temperature are both known, then by using *Stefan's law* the radius of the star can be found via the formula

$$L = A\sigma T^4 = 4\pi r^2 \cdot \sigma T^4$$

**Aiming for a grade A*?**

Don't forget to log on to **www.philipallan.co.uk/a-zonline** for advice.

**machine:** a device which allows a force to be applied at one point in order to move a load at another point. Examples are levers, *inclined planes*, wheel-and-axles, pulley systems, and gears. The force applied by the user is known as the effort; the machine provides the force needed to move the load.

Unless the machine has an efficiency of 100%, the work done by the effort will be greater than the work done on the load. Nevertheless, machines are used because they make it easier for the user to move the load, often because the effort is a smaller force than the load.

Many complex mechanical devices can be regarded as a combination of simple machines. (See *efficiency (machines).*)

**magnet:** a block of permanently magnetised ferromagnetic material, usually with opposite poles at the far ends. (See *ferromagnetism.*)

**magnetic effect of current:** the power of electric current to create a magnetic field in its immediate vicinity. The diagram below shows three cases: a straight wire, a ring and a solenoid. The *right hand grip rule* gives the direction of the magnetic field. For a straight wire, the thumb points along the direction of the current and the fingers follow the direction of the circular magnetic field lines. For the solenoid, the fingers follow the direction of the current and the thumb points along the solenoid towards the north-seeking pole. The direction of the magnetic field near the ring can be worked out from either of these applications.

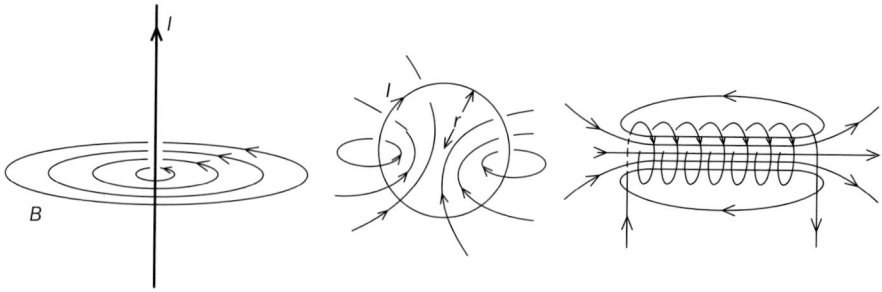


The magnetic field strength $B$ a perpendicular distance $r$ from a long straight conductor carrying current $I$ in vacuum is given by

$$B = \frac{\mu_0 I}{2\pi r}$$

The magnetic field strength $B$ at the centre of a circular ring of radius $r$ with $N$ turns and carrying current $I$ in vacuum is given by

$$B = \frac{\mu_0 NI}{2\pi r}$$

The magnetic field strength $B$ along the centre of a long solenoid with $n$ turns per metre of length and carrying current $I$ in vacuum is given by

$$B = \mu_0 nI$$

In an examination, always draw at least four or five magnetic field lines and remember to leave gaps in the lines and coils as shown in the diagram. If these gaps are absent, the diagrams become ambiguous and you will lose marks.

**magnetic field strength,** $B$, at a point is defined by the equation

$$F = BIl$$

where $F$ is the force on a straight conductor of length $l$ which carries current $I$. The value of $F$ is in newtons, $I$ is in amperes, $l$ is in metres and $B$ is in tesla (T), the SI unit of magnetic field strength. This equation can be used to define $B$ because $F$, $I$ and $l$ can all be measured independently and separately from $B$.

Magnetic field strength is sometimes called magnetic flux density. (See *magnetic effect of current, force on a moving charge, magnetic flux.*)

**magnetic flux,** $\phi$, threading an area is the product of *magnetic field strength* and the *component* $A \sin\theta$ of the area $A$ that is at right angles to the magnetic field. The word equation is:

magnetic flux = magnetic field strength × area × sin $\theta$

$$\phi = B \times A \times \sin\theta$$

where $\theta$ is the angle between the area and the magnetic field direction (see diagram below).

The SI unit for magnetic flux is the weber (Wb):

weber (Wb) = tesla (T) × metres squared ($m^2$)

The definition of magnetic flux should be clear from the following diagram:

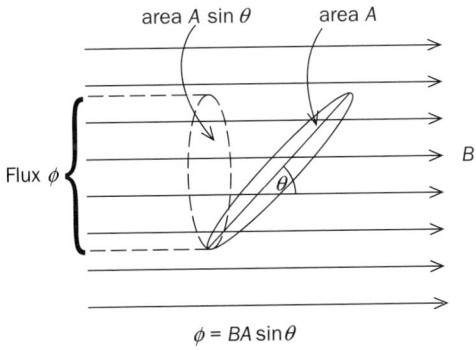


**magnetic flux density,** $B$, is another name for *magnetic field strength*. Lines of magnetic force or flux are used to describe the shape of a magnetic field near a magnet or solenoid.

The density of the *lines of force* increases in proportion to field strength. The number of lines of force can be defined in such a way that magnetic flux density is identical to the magnetic field strength.

**magnetic flux linkage:** see *flux linkage.*

**magnitude:** see *star.*

**main sequence star:** see *Hertzsprung–Russell diagram.*

**malleability** is the extent to which a material can be hammered out into a thin, flat sheet. It is a characteristic feature of metals (hot more than cold) and especially of gold. Formally, it is the ability to undergo *plastic deformation* in response to a compressive load.

**Malus' law:** When light is passed through two polarising filters, the intensity of light emerging from the second filter depends on the angle $\theta$ between the axes of the two filters. If $I_0$ is the intensity of light reaching the second polariser, then, according to Malus' law, the transmitted intensity $I$ is given by

$$I = I_0 \cos^2 \theta$$

The $\cos^2$ term comes about because the transmitted amplitude $A$ is given by $A = A_0 \cos \theta$, and intensity $I \propto A^2$.

**manometer:** a device based on a U-tube for measuring pressure difference. The principle is shown in the diagram below. The pressure difference between the inside of the vessel and the outside is calculated from the equation:

$$p = p_0 + h\rho g$$

where $p$ is the pressure inside the vessel, $p_0$ is the pressure outside the vessel, $h$ is the difference in level between the two surfaces in the U-tube, $\rho$ is the density of the liquid and $g$ is the acceleration of free fall.

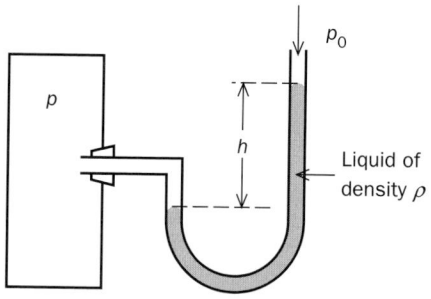


**mass** is so basic a quantity in Newtonian mechanics that it defies definition in terms of simpler concepts. This is why we have to make do with less-than-satisfactory descriptive phrases such as 'mass is the amount of matter in a body'. Mass is a *scalar quantity.* Its unit, a *base unit* in SI, is the kilogram (kg). Mass is measured, in principle, with the chemical balance or its equivalent. It cannot have a negative value.

Mass is distinct from amount of matter measured in *moles.* The number of moles indicates how many identical, countable particles are present. The two concepts are related through the idea of *molar mass.*

For the difference between gravitational mass and inertial mass, see *gravitational field strength.*

**mass defect,** written $\Delta m$, is the difference in mass between a nucleus and the combined masses of its constituent neutrons and protons. $\Delta mc^2$ is the energy that would be needed to pull apart all the neutrons and protons of the nucleus. This energy is called the *binding energy.*

**mass–energy equivalence** is the idea expressed in the equation

$$E = \Delta m.c^2$$

If a body acquires extra kinetic energy $E$, then its mass increases by the amount $\Delta m$ given in this equation. The word 'equivalence' is important. During nuclear fission, mass is not lost; it is dispersed as an equivalent amount of energy. There is no such thing as 'mass–energy conversion'. (See also *binding energy.*)

**mass number,** $A$, is the number of nucleons (neutrons and protons) in a nucleus. An alternative name is nucleon number. The definition can be stated as a simple addition: mass number equals *atomic number Z* plus *neutron number N*, that is,

$$A = Z + N$$

**mass spectrometer:** an instrument in which a beam of positive ions is projected into a plane at right angles to a strong, uniform magnetic field. The ions follow a semi-circular path to a photographic plate or electronic detector which forms an accurate record of the point of arrival. The radius $r$ of the semicircle is measured; the magnetic field strength is known, so the mass of the positive ion can be calculated from the relation $r = mv/Bq$.

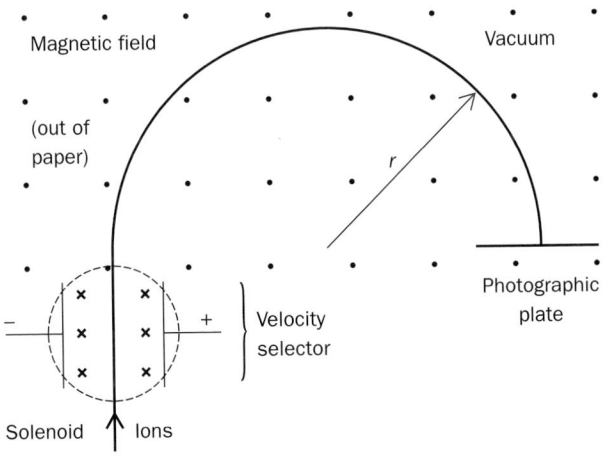


The positive ion speed $v$ is found as follows. The source of positive ions includes a velocity selector which consists of an electric field $E$ and a magnetic field $B'$ at right angles to one another and at right angles to the ion beam. Only those ions whose speeds are $E/B'$ can get through. See *electron beams.*

**mass–spring system:** a helical spring (formed by winding a wire round and round a uniform cylinder) is suspended with a mass attached to its lower end. The usefulness of a helical spring is linked to its main property: its extension is proportional to the load applied. This relationship is called *Hooke's law*. It can be stated in the algebraic form

$$F = kx$$

where $k$ is called the *spring constant*, $F$ is the stretching force and $x$ is the extension. A typical spring in a school laboratory will be stretched by about 5 cm by the weight of a 100 g mass. The weight of a 100 g mass is about one newton and 5 cm is a twentieth of a metre, so the resulting spring constant is in the region of $20\,\mathrm{N\,m^{-1}}$. It can be checked by suspending the spring from a rigid support and measuring carefully the extensions corresponding to different loads. The gradient of the load–extension graph is the spring constant $k$.

**Maxwell's corkscrew rule:** a rule for finding the direction of the magnetic field near a straight wire. Imagine you are driving a right-handed corkscrew in the direction of the current in the wire. The direction in which you turn the handle of the corkscrew is the direction of the circular magnetic lines of force. (Alternatively, imagine turning a pencil in a pencil sharperner.) (See *right hand grip rule*.)

**mean power in a resistive load** is the average power dissipated in the load during one complete cycle by a sinusoidal AC current. The circuit in the diagram on page 151 links an AC power supply $V_0 \sin \omega t$ to a resistor $R$. If $V_0$ is 6 V and $R$ is 15 Ω, then $I_0$ is 0.4 A. The instantaneous AC current is linked to the instantaneous voltage by *Ohm's law*:

$$I = I_0 \sin \omega t = \frac{V_0}{R} \sin \omega t$$

The instantaneous power $P$ equals $IV$, and we can write:

$$P = IV = I_0 V_0 \sin^2 \omega t$$

We can use this equation to deduce the values of two qualities:

- $I_{\text{r.m.s.}}$ – the root-mean-square current. The *steady direct* current that has the same heating effect as the alternating current.
- $V_{\text{r.m.s.}}$ – the root-mean-square voltage. The steady direct voltage that will make $I_{\text{r.m.s.}}$ flow.

It is clear from the lower graph (on page 151) that the average value of $\sin^2 \omega t$ is 0.5 exactly; the graph is symmetrical above and below the 0.5 line. So $<P>$, the mean value of the power supplied to the resistor, is one half of the peak value:

$$<P> = \tfrac{1}{2} I_0 V_0 = \tfrac{1}{2} I_0^2 R = \frac{V_0^{\,2}}{2R}$$

Compare this result with the DC case:

$$P = IV = I^2 R = \frac{V^2}{R}$$

If $P$ equals $<P>$, then $I$ equals $I_{\text{r.m.s.}}$ and $V$ equals $V_{\text{r.m.s.}}$. Comparing the two sets of equations gives

$$I_{\text{r.m.s}}^2 = \tfrac{1}{2} I_0^2 \quad \text{or} \quad I_{\text{r.m.s}} = \frac{I_0}{\sqrt{2}}$$

$$\text{and } V_{\text{r.m.s}}^2 = \tfrac{1}{2} V_0^2 \quad \text{or} \quad V_{\text{r.m.s}} = \frac{V_0}{\sqrt{2}}$$

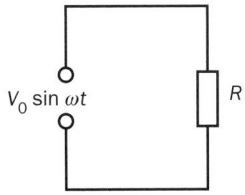


$V_0 + 6\,V,\ R = 15\Omega$

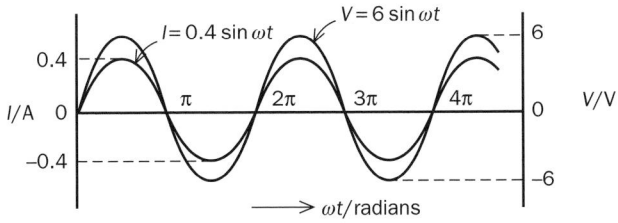


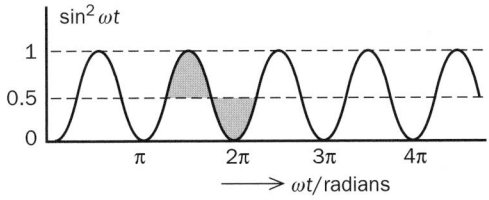


(See also *r.m.s.*)

**mean square speed** $<c^2>$ is defined by the equation

$$<c^2> = [c_1^2 + c_2^2 + c_3^2 \cdots c_N^2] / N$$

where $c_1, c_2, c_3, \ldots, c_N$ are the instantaneous speeds of the $N$ molecules in a gas sample. Mean square speed $<c^2>$ is the average value of molecular speed squared. The mean speed of molecules in a gas sample is zero because for each molecule moving in one direction at a particular speed, there will be another moving in the opposite direction at the same speed.

Although $<c^2>$ is defined by the above equation, it is never calculated using this equation. Once defined, its properties can be determined, and its most important property is the link it provides between gas pressure and temperature. (See *kinetic theory of gases.*)

**measurement** is the process of linking a physical quantity with a magnitude. There are three stages in the complete process: the physical quantity has to be defined, instrumentation must be provided and the unit must be known. An instrument is a device which compares two magnitudes. A ruler compares two lengths, a chemical balance and a box of weights will compare two masses and a galvanometer will compare two voltages. The output of the instrument usually appears on a scale of some sort. This scale can be calibrated in terms of the unit by noting the outputs for a range of standard inputs.

**mercury barometer:** an instrument which measures *atmospheric pressure* by balancing it against the pressure at the base of a column of mercury. The device shown in the diagram below is sometimes called a mercury barometer, sometimes a 'simple barometer'. The pressure of the atmosphere, $p_0$, equals the pressure at the bottom of the mercury column at the same level as the surface of the mercury in the reservoir. Since there is a vacuum (and therefore zero pressure) above the mercury, the pressure at the bottom of the mercury column is $H\rho g$ where $H$ is the vertical distance from the surface of the mercury in the bowl to the top of the mercury meniscus in the tube, $\rho$ is the *density* of mercury and $g$ is the *acceleration of free fall.* We have, then:

$$p_0 = H\rho g$$

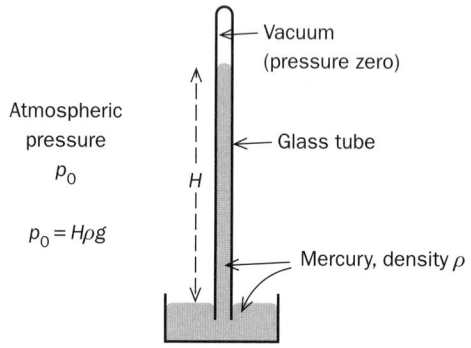


The Fortin barometer is an accurate version of the simple barometer. It has an arrangement for setting the mercury at just the right level in the reservoir and a vernier scale for measuring the height of the mercury column. There is also a thermometer should a temperature correction for the density of mercury be needed.

**mercury-in-glass thermometer:** a well-known liquid-in-glass thermometer in which mercury stored in a glass bulb expands along a uniform capillary in the glass stem as the temperature rises. The mercury always expands to the same point for a given temperature. The stem is usually calibrated to read temperatures between 0°C and 100°C, but the instrument can be constructed to cover other ranges. Mercury thermometers are usually calibrated by marking the glass at the 0°C mark using iced water and at the 100°C mark using steam over boiling water at normal pressure. A scale with a hundred equal divisions is then marked on the stem starting at 0°C and finishing at 100°C. This method of *calibration* assumes that the temperature $\theta$ recorded by the thermometer is related to the mercury column length in the following manner:

$$\theta = \frac{l_\theta - l_0}{l_{100} - l_0} \times 100$$

In formal language, this equation defines temperature on the mercury-in-glass temperature scale.

Care should be taken when using a mercury thermometer to avoid systematic errors. The instrument should be held upright (hold it upside down and watch the temperature rise a degree or so) and dipped in the liquid up to the immersion mark on the thermometer. Solids must be brought into good thermal contact with the thermometer, and gas temperatures can only be measured if the thermometer is given plenty of time to settle. The mercury thermometer cannot be used to measure temperatures of small objects.

**mesons** are made up of a quark and an antiquark with opposite values of the same *colour.* They can have integral or zero charge, baryon number zero and spin 1 or 0. The $\pi$ minus, for instance, is $d\bar{u}$ . Four such $\pi$ mesons or pions can be formed from first-generation quarks and are created frequently in collision experiments. One consequence of the quark–antiquark arrangement is that mesons can annihilate in interactions. Meson number, unlike baryon number, is not necessarily conserved in an interaction event. Mesons decay into leptons (and eventually into electrons and antineutrinos) and photons. The table shows details of those mesons that were discovered in the 1940s. Pi mesons are sometimes called pions and K mesons are sometimes called kaons.

| Name | Quantum numbers | | | Quark content |
|---|---|---|---|---|
| | Q | B | S | |
| $\pi$ meson | | | | |
| neutral | 0 | 0 | 0 | see below* |
| positive | +1 | 0 | 0 | u anti-d |
| negative | –1 | 0 | 0 | d anti-u |
| K meson | | | | |
| neutral | 0 | 0 | +1 | d anti-s |
| positive | +1 | 0 | +1 | u anti-s |
| negative | –1 | 0 | +1 | s anti-u |

* the neutral $\pi$ meson occurs as a mixture of (u anti-u) and (d anti-d) particles.

**metallic bond:** a form of attachment between atoms in which each atom releases one or more electrons to a collective 'electron gas' and the resulting positive ions build up a granular structure, kept stable by these electrons which inhabit the spaces between the atoms. The strength of the bond accounts for the hardness and high melting point of many metals. The presence of mobile electrons accounts for the electrical and thermal conduction properties of such solids.

**metals** are those substances which, in the solid state, have a characteristic set of properties: they are good thermal and electrical conductors, and they are mechanically malleable and ductile.

These properties are related to the underlying structure of metals. Metals consist of a latticework of positive ions held in a stable condition by free electrons. The electrons behave like a gas which inhabits the open spaces within the crystal lattice. The number of electrons is just sufficient for their combined negative charge to cancel the net positive charge of the lattice. The directional quality of the inter-atomic forces is not strong enough to build up and hold together large crystal structures. Because of this, metals consist of numerous small crystals or grains. The sizes of these grains and the forces locking them together decide the particular physical properties. The existence of these tiny grains also accounts for the possibility of beating metals out into thin sheets (*malleability*), the readiness with which they can be drawn out into wire form (*ductility*) and the stability and sharpness of ground edges. In contrast, the strengths of these inter-atomic forces, leaving aside their modest directional qualities, account for the high values of *Young modulus*, *hardness*, great *strength* and high melting point of many metals. (See *metallic bond*.)

**metre:** a *base unit* in *SI*. It is the SI unit of length and has the symbol m. The metre equals the distance travelled in vacuum by light during a time interval of $1/c$ seconds, where $c$ is the *speed of light* in vacuum. The original historical definition of the metre was the length of the Earth's circumference on a great circle through Paris and the poles divided by 40 million. This gives a value of 6366 km for the average radius of the Earth at the equator, compared with the present estimate of 6378 km. The metre is now defined as a given number of wavelengths of krypton-86 in vacuum.

**MeV** is an energy unit. It is an abbreviation for a million electron volts. It is the energy transformed when an electron passes through a potential difference of 1 MV and equals $1.602 \times 10^{-13}$ J.

**MeV/$c^2$** is a mass unit. It is the mass equivalent of 1 MeV. It equals $1.78 \times 10^{-30}$ kg. Proton mass can be written as 940 MeV/$c^2$ and, similarly, electron mass as 0.512 MeV/$c^2$.

**Michelson–Morley experiment** was an attempt to detect the motion of the Earth through the ether which was believed to permeate space. An interferometer produced interference fringes from two beams of light which had travelled at right angles to each other. When the interferometer was rotated through 90°, the fringes were expected to move because of the effect of the ether. But this was not observed; the result can be explained by Einstein's postulate that the speed of light is the same in all directions and is independent of the speed of its source — this is one of the basic postulates of the special theory of relativity. (See *special relativity.*)

**micrometer screw gauge:** an instrument used to measure thicknesses such as the diameter of a wire or the thickness of a metal sheet. Measurements can often be made to within ±0.01 mm.

The object to be measured is placed between the jaws of the gauge and the rotating barrel is then turned so that the jaws close on the specimen. Use of the ratchet mechanism ensures that the correct pressure is applied.

The main scale can be read to the nearest 0.5 mm below the correct reading; the rotating fractional scale gives a reading in hundredths of a millimetre. Adding the two readings together gives the final measurement. (See also *Vernier callipers.*)

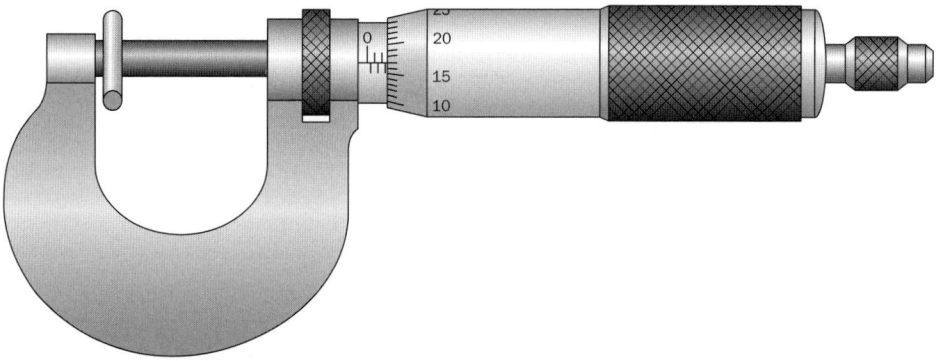


The thickness of the rod measured here is 2.67 mm

**microwaves** are *electromagnetic waves* with wavelengths from about 1 mm to about 10 cm. A typical microwave source is either a low power klystron valve (a few mW) or a high power magnetron valve (up to a few kW). The microwaves are radiated from electrons oscillating in an aerial or within a cavity. The same waveband is used for radar.

Microwave wavelengths are just short enough to allow modest focusing and approximately straight line transmission. This is important in the communication field because it cuts down the power needed to send information from one parabolic transmitter to the next parabolic receiver. (You may see microwave transmitters and receivers on mobile phone masts where they are used to transmit signals over considerable distances between neighbouring masts.) Microwave frequencies are in the range of 3.0 GHz ($3.0 \times 10^9$ Hz) to 300 GHz ($300 \times 10^9$ Hz). These high frequencies result in a high capacity for carrying information and account for the emphasis placed on this waveband by communication engineers. This application is now giving way, in part, to optical fibres with their much higher information capacities.

Much information about the Earth's surface can be collected on microwave frequencies. This explains the emphasis on these wavelengths in the design of the European survey satellite Envisat.

**Millikan's oil drop experiment** was the first tolerably accurate and direct measurement of the charge on an *electron*. The experiment established that *electric charge* is a quantised physical variable with a minimum increase or decrease in value now identified as the charge on one electron $e$.

The apparatus, in broad outline, consisted of two parallel brass plates. The upper plate had a hole in the centre; the plates were mounted exactly horizontally, and the voltage between them could be adjusted to any value from zero to about 6 kV, positive or negative. A microscope was used to watch oil drops from an atomiser falling vertically through the hole. The oil drops were illuminated from the side and charged by friction at the exit of the atomiser.

The first stage of the experiment involved trapping a charged oil drop by adjusting the *electric field* so that the upward force equalled the downward force. The forces on an oil drop are the weight $mg$, the buoyancy (which will be ignored) and the electric force $qV/d$. In these circumstances:

$$mg = qV/d$$

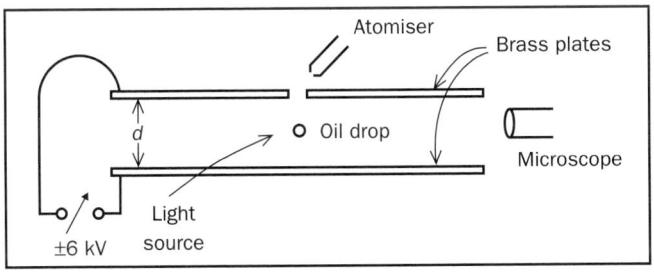


The second part of the experiment involved switching off the electric field and measuring the *terminal speed* of the oil drop. In these circumstances (again, ignoring the buoyancy) the viscous *drag* equals the weight $mg$. The viscous drag force is given by the expression $6\pi a\eta v$ (*Stokes' law*) where $a$ is the radius of the oil drop, $\eta$ the viscosity of air and $v$ the terminal speed of the oil drop. We thus have:

$$mg = 6\pi a\eta v$$

The second diagram (below) shows the *free-body force diagrams* for these two situations.

Knowing the *density* of the oil, it is possible to eliminate the radius of the oil drop from these two equations and thereby derive a single equation with $q$ as the single unknown quantity.

Millikan measured the charges on many oil drops and found that the measured value of $q$ was always a small integral multiple of $-1.59 \times 10^{-19}$ coulombs. He took this to be the charge on one electron. Criticisms have subsequently been made that Millikan was selective in the results he chose to make use of and that he rejected many results which did not fit with his final value for $e$. These can be answered by saying that, as Millikan became more confident in his experimental technique, he learned when it was behaving reliably and when not. His experimental value is close to the currently accepted value of the electron charge.

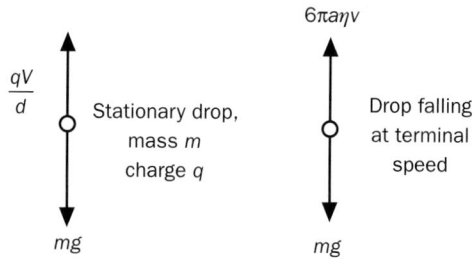


**moderator:** a large mass of graphite or other material which provides the matrix in which the *fuel rods*, the coolant pipes and the *control rods* of a nuclear power plant are supported. The principal function of the moderator is to slow down to thermal energies the fast neutrons emitted in the nuclear *fission* reactions in the control rods so that further fission reactions can proceed.

**modulation** originally meant the combination (in a form of addition process) of an information wave with a carrier wave before transmission. An example would be the mounting of a sound wave signal on a radio-wave carrier of much higher frequency. The opposite procedure, called demodulation, took place after signal reception.

The word modulation now describes any signal modification process which prepares a signal for transmission. (See *amplitude modulation, frequency modulation* and *pulse code modulation.*)

**molar mass:** the mass of one *mole* of substance. It varies from one substance to another according to the mass of the relevant entity whose count identifies the mole. So the molar mass of carbon-12 is 0.012 kg; the molar mass of a large protein might be 200 kg.

**mole:** the SI *base unit* for amount of substance. The symbol is mol. It is the amount of substance that contains as many elementary entities as there are in 0.012 kg of carbon-12. (See *Avogadro constant.*)

**moment of a force** about a point is the product of the force and the perpendicular distance from the point to the line of action of the force. The unit is the N m. Do not confuse this with the definition of the *joule*. Energy is a *scalar quantity* and the distance measured in the definition of the joule is parallel to the direction of the force. In the N m as a unit of moment of a force, the distance and the force are at right angles. Moment of a force is not a scalar quantity; it is a pseudo-vector (but this does not matter at A-level).

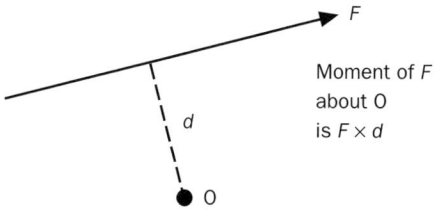


There are two situations to consider. The sum of the moments of several forces acting on a body may all cancel, in which case the body will be in equilibrium (dealt with in the entry *principle of moments*). The alternative is for the sum of the moments to add up to a resultant turning force; this case is dealt with under *torque*.

(See also *principle of moments, couple, forces in equilibrium.*)

**moment of inertia** is defined by the word equation

$$\text{moment of inertia} = \frac{\text{torque}}{\text{angular acceleration}}$$

$$I = \frac{T}{\alpha}$$

The unit of moment of inertia is $\text{kg m}^2$. Moment of inertia plays an analogous part in *rotational motion* to mass in *translational motion*. The moment of inertia of a disc-shaped object of given radius (such as the flywheel in a car engine) about an axis normal to the disc and passing through its centre increases if the mass distribution can be moved towards the edges. A heavy door has a much higher moment of inertia than a light door. It is much harder to get moving and, once started, it is harder to stop again.

*momentum*: see *linear momentum, angular momentum.*

*monochromatic light* is light of a single wavelength, such as that produced by a laser. The word 'monochromatic' means 'single coloured'.

*monomode fibre:* see *optical fibre systems.*

**motor effect:** the force experienced by a current-carrying conductor in a magnetic field. If $B$ is the strength of the (uniform) magnetic field, $l$ is the length of conductor under consideration and $I$ is the current in the conductor, then the force $F$ on the conductor is given by

$$F = BIl \sin\theta$$

where $\theta$ is the angle between the direction of the current and the *magnetic field strength*. The direction of the force is given by *Fleming's left hand rule*. This equation is the basis of the definition of magnetic field strength and is at the heart of the definition of the *ampere*.

**MRI:** an acronym for magnetic resonance imaging. The imaging system is built around the behaviour of atomic nuclei, especially hydrogen, in powerful magnetic fields in excess of 1 tesla. The magnetic resonance image of the human body is built up in stages:

- First, the body is placed parallel to and within a powerful uniform magnetic field, set up by a high and permanent current in a superconducting solenoid. Next, a second coil imposes a second magnetic field, the 'gradient field', in the same direction as the first but which is strong at one end, weak at the other and diminishing uniformly along the body. Each slice of the body has its own magnetic field strength.

- The human body is rich in hydrogen atoms. Most hydrogen nuclei precess about an axis parallel to the strong magnetic field direction, but some precess in the anti-parallel direction. The precession frequency is proportional to the magnetic field strength $B$.
- A brief signal from a radio frequency coil excites the hydrogen atoms within one slice of the human body where the magnetic field is just the right strength for that radio frequency. Many hydrogen atoms within the slice and precessing in the parallel direction flip to the anti-parallel state.
- Once the radio signal has passed, the hydrogen atoms revert to their previous states and release the absorbed energy as a radio signal. The rate at which they relax depends on their local environment, so that hydrogen atoms in different tissues have different relaxation rates. Each point in the plane is scanned in turn and the reception of the full set of signals from any one plane indicates the tissue type present. An image of the slice can be built up.
- The scanner then moves on to the next slice.

**mutual inductance,** $M$, of two circuits equals the *e.m.f.* induced in one of the circuits when the current in the other circuit changes at the rate of one ampere per second. A practical example is a *transformer*: the current in the primary coil changes and this induces an e.m.f. in the secondary coil. The word equation definition is:

$$\text{mutual inductance} = \frac{\text{e.m.f. induced in one circuit}}{\text{change of current per second in the second circuit}}$$

The numerical value of the mutual inductance can be shown to be the same whichever of the two circuits is chosen for the changing current. The SI unit for mutual inductance is the *henry* (H). (See also *self-inductance.*)

**myopia:** short-sightedness. (See *defects of vision.*)

**A–Z Online**

Log on to A–Z Online to search the database of terms, print revision lists and much more. Go to **www.philipallan.co.uk/a-zonline** to get started.

**natural frequency:** the frequency with which an oscillating system vibrates after it has been stimulated to oscillate and then left to oscillate freely. When such a system is stimulated at its natural frequency, *resonance* occurs.

**net force:** another name for the *resultant* force acting on a body — that single force which has the same effect as the combined effect of all the forces acting on the body.

**neutral point:** a point within a magnetic field where the resultant *magnetic field strength* is zero. Neutral points are especially significant when they result from the overlapping of a non-uniform magnetic field (like that near a bar magnet) and a uniform magnetic field (like the horizontal *component* of the Earth's magnetic field on a local scale). They occur at those points where the magnetic field strengths of the two magnetic fields are equal and opposite.

Since neutral points occur where the two magnetic field strengths are equal and opposite, if one field is known then so is the other. For instance, if the current in a vertical wire is known and the distance of the neutral point from the wire is measured, then the strength of the magnetic field set up by the current in the wire at the neutral point can be calculated. The horizontal component of the Earth's magnetic field strength at the point in question is then known.

**neutrino:** an *elementary particle*, a *lepton*, that has zero charge and very little mass. The neutrino released in beta-minus decay is more correctly called an electron antineutrino; that released in beta-plus decay is an electron neutrino.

There are three types (flavours) of neutrino (and antineutrino) associated with each of the three charged leptons. These are the electron neutrino, the muon neutrino and the tau neutrino. Neutrinos are subject to the weak interaction and to gravitation.

The Sun produces vast numbers of neutrinos as a result of the *nuclear reactions* occurring in its interior. Every second, about 65 billion neutrinos pass through each square centimetre of the Earth's surface facing the Sun. However, because of their limited interaction with matter, virtually all these neutrinos pass through the Earth and continue their journey through space.

**neutron:** an elementary particle which carries no electric charge and whose mass is almost the same as that of a proton or a hydrogen atom.

**neutron number** $N$ is the number of neutrons in a nucleus. (See also *atomic number.*)

**neutron star:** the end state of a main sequence star whose mass is between eight and 20 solar masses. The stellar remnant following a supernova explosion has a mass greater than the solar masses but a radius of roughly 10 km. This corresponds to a density of $10^{16}\,\mathrm{kg\,m^{-3}}$

and upwards. This high density is linked to the conversion of core protons and electrons (under the weak interaction) into neutrons, together with the loss of the electron degeneracy pressure which supports white dwarfs. Neutron stars are observed as pulsating radio sources (pulsars) of which several hundred are known. Neutron stars are also identified with binary X-ray sources.

The flashes of radio waves which are the characteristic property of pulsars are attributed to a steady narrow-beam radio emission coupled with a rapid period of rotation. This period, ranging from a few milliseconds to a few seconds, is explained by the conserved angular momentum and the much reduced moment of inertia of the contracting core. For any one star, the period is stable to about one part in $10^{13}$, which matches the stability of atomic clocks. See *end states of stars, fundamental interactions.*

**newton** is a short way of writing kilogram metre per second squared ($\mathrm{kg\,m\,s^{-2}}$). It is the *SI* unit of *force.* The statement 'One newton is that force which is just strong enough to give a one-kilogram mass an acceleration of one metre per second squared in the direction of the force' is true, but it defines a force of *one* newton, not the unit itself, *the* newton. What you should write depends on what you are asked. The word equation definitions of force and the newton are as follows:

force = mass × acceleration

newton = kilogram metre per second squared $\left(\mathrm{kg\,m\,s^{-2}}\right)$

(See also *Newton's second law of motion.*)

**Newton's first law of motion:** 'A body subject to zero resultant force either remains still or moves with constant velocity.'

It is the second part of the law which may be surprising: if an object is moving and there is no resultant force acting on it, it will continue to move at a steady speed in a straight line. Our intuition tends to suggest otherwise — that moving objects automatically come to rest. But this is simply because we rarely experience the motion of bodies moving in the absence of any resultant force.

This law is a kind of baseline. It tells us about the behaviour of a body under zero resultant force. The second law extends this to explain the behaviour of a body under non-zero resultant force. (See *Newton's laws of motion, Newton's second law of motion, Newton's third law of motion.*)

**Newton's law of cooling** states that the rate at which a body cools, $\mathrm{d}T/\mathrm{d}t$, is proportional to the temperature excess of the body above its surroundings. This is not a universal law. It applies provided that (i) the body is in a strong draught, and (ii) the temperature excess is not greater than about 30 K. If there is no strong draught, convection cooling becomes progressively less effective and the cooling rate diminishes unacceptably. If the temperature excess rises much above 30 K, the *radiation loss* is too rapid and this interferes with the law.

We can represent Newton's law as $\mathrm{d}T/\mathrm{d}t \propto T$. Notice that, since the rate of change of temperature is proportional to temperature, the law satisfies the condition for *exponential decay.*

**Newton's law of universal gravitation** states that between any two particles of matter in the universe there is an attractive gravitational force $F$ which is proportional to the product of their masses and inversely proportional to the distance between them.

If $m_1$ and $m_2$ are the masses of the two particles and $r$ is their distance apart, then the gravitational force of attraction, $F$, is given by

$$F = G\frac{m_1 m_2}{r^2}$$

where $G$ is the universal gravitational constant with a value of $6.67 \times 10^{-11}\,\mathrm{N\,m^2\,kg^{-2}}$.

A law that applies only to particles would be of very limited use, but Newton was able to show that, as far as its external gravitational field is concerned, a uniform sphere (such as the Earth, Moon or Sun) behaves as if its whole mass were concentrated at its centre.

**Worked example**

**The masses of the Sun, Moon and Earth are respectively $2.0\times10^{30}$ kg, $6.0 \times 10^{24}$ kg and $7.4\times10^{22}$ kg. The distances of the Sun and the Moon from the Earth are respectively $1.50\times10^{11}$ m and $3.8\times10^{8}$ m. Calculate the magnitude of the gravitational force exerted on the Earth by the Sun and by the Moon and comment on the ratio of these forces.**

$$F_{\text{Sun}} = \left(6.67\times10^{-11}\ \mathrm{Nm^2\,kg^{-2}}\right)\frac{\left(2.0\times10^{30}\ \mathrm{kg}\right)\left(6.0\times10^{24}\ \mathrm{kg}\right)}{\left(1.50\times10^{11}\ \mathrm{m}\right)^2}$$

$$= 3.6\times10^{22}\ \mathrm{N}\ (\text{to 2 s.f.})$$

$$F_{\text{Moon}} = \left(6.67\times10^{-11}\ \mathrm{Nm^2\,kg^{-2}}\right)\frac{\left(7.4\times10^{22}\ \mathrm{kg}\right)\left(6.0\times10^{24}\ \mathrm{kg}\right)}{\left(3.8\times10^{8}\ \mathrm{m}\right)^2}$$

$$= 2.1\times10^{20}\ \mathrm{N}\ (\text{to 2 s.f.})$$

(See also *gravitational constant, gravitational field strength, gravitational potential (radial fields), planetary motion, satellite, escape speed.*)

**Newton's laws of motion** are the fundamental principles of Newtonian mechanics. Newton needed to define the relationship between force and motion before he could use the law of universal gravitation to explain the motion of the planets around the Sun.

You may be asked to describe an experiment to 'illustrate' one of Newton's laws of motion. The wording sounds a little tentative but it has to be — Newton's laws of motion cannot be verified by experiment. The first law is the worst; it is just not possible to create force-free conditions across a large enough region to be interesting. The failure of any experiment to check the second or third laws will always be attributed to *friction*, and the magnitude of the frictional forces is always calculated by assuming that these forces just account for the disparity between experiment and theory. Fundamental ideas never can be checked but they can be illustrated. Newton's laws are justified by the success of the classical mechanics they support.

An experiment which illustrates one of the laws need do no more than provide some data which more or less fits the mathematical statement of the law. The laboratory experience is part of learning what Newton's laws mean.

The three laws are discussed under *Newton's first law of motion*, *Newton's second law of motion* and *Newton's third law of motion*.

**Newton's second law of motion:** 'The magnitude of the resultant force acting on a body is proportional to the rate of change of the body's momentum and the direction of the force is the direction of the momentum change.'

There are two ways to think about this:

- If a body is acted on by a resultant force, its momentum will change (i.e. it will accelerate).
- If a body's momentum is changing (i.e. if it is accelerating), we can deduce that there must be a resultant force acting on it.

Newton's second law tells us how the force and the rate of change of momentum are related.

Note that the formal statement is written in terms of changing momentum, not acceleration. The difference is that momentum is more general — it takes account of situations where the body's mass is changing.

In most situations, you can assume that the mass of the body in question is constant. Then, using calculus notation:

$$\text{resultant force} \propto \frac{\mathrm{d}}{\mathrm{d}t}(mv) \propto m\frac{\mathrm{d}v}{\mathrm{d}t} = \text{constant} \times m \times a$$

where $m$ is mass and $a$ is acceleration. The unit of force is defined by setting the constant equal to unity:

$$\text{unit of force} = \text{unit for}\,(m \times a) = \mathrm{kg\,m\,s^{-2}}$$

Instead of writing $\mathrm{kg\,m\,s^{-2}}$, we write N and call this unit the newton.

The word equation definitions of force and the newton are as follows:

force = mass × acceleration

newton = kilogram metre per second squared ($\mathrm{kg\,m\,s^{-2}}$)

Newton's second law tells us about the direction of the change in momentum produced by a force. Consider a ball thrown horizontally above the Earth's surface. Its initial momentum is horizontal. The only force acting on it is the constant downward force of gravity (supposing we can ignore air resistance). This results in a steady increase in the ball's downward momentum; its horizontal momentum is unaffected and remains constant. A vertical force can only change momentum in a vertical direction. The outcome is that the ball follows a curved path (see *projectiles*).

An account of an experiment to illustrate Newton's second law must include a diagram, a list of apparatus, a list of the measurements (to include how acceleration is found) and how the data is used to establish the conclusion.

**Experiment to illustrate the proportionality of acceleration to applied force for a body of fixed mass**

**Apparatus**

Set up the linear air track arrangement shown in the diagram. The falling mass $M$ provides the force which causes the trolley of mass m to accelerate. The ingenious part of the design of this experiment is that $M$ consists of several known masses which can be detached and then attached to the trolley. This ensures that the total mass of the accelerating system, $M+m$, is constant. The card which is carried by the trolley and which breaks the light beams is 10.0 cm long. The computer can record the time intervals

$\Delta t_A$ and $\Delta t_B$ for which the light beams at A and B are broken by the card. The time interval $t$ between the arrival times of the card at A and B is also recorded.

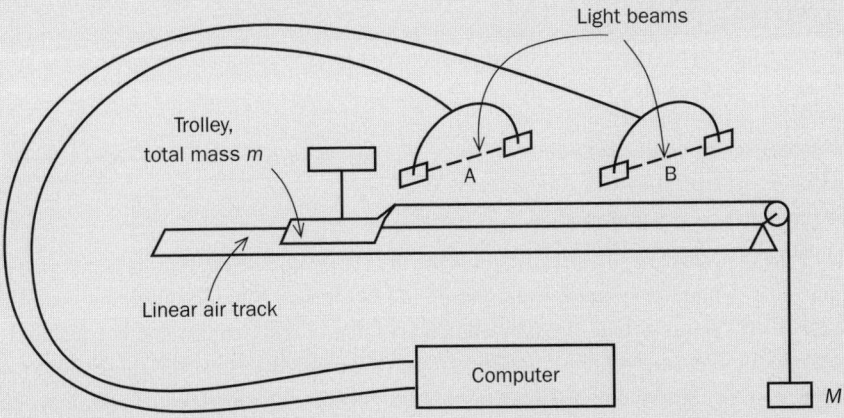


**Measurements**

For each run of the trolley, the computer records its velocity at A [$v_A = (0.100\,\text{m})/\Delta t_A$], its velocity at B [$v_B = (0.100\,\text{m})/\Delta t_B$] and the acceleration [$(v_B - v_A)/t$]. The value of the acceleration $a$ for each value of the mass $M$ is recorded. Remember to keep the total mass $(m+M)$ constant.

**Conclusion**

Draw a graph of the applied force $Mg$ against the acceleration $a$ for constant total mass $(m+M)$. If it is a straight line passing through the origin, the proportionality of force and acceleration for constant mass will have been illustrated.

**Comments**

1 Although the acceleration of the trolley can be measured reliably, the experiment assumes that the force provided by $M$ is proportional to $M$. This is correct according to Newton's second law — but this is the very law we are trying to illustrate. An experiment of this sort can be no more than a learning exercise.

2 You must state precisely what data is recorded by the computer and what calculations it performs to determine the acceleration of the trolley. Otherwise the examiner will think that you are using the computer as a cover-up and give you no marks.

3 There are other ways of applying a variable force, such as using a variable number of elastic strings, all stretched by the same amount.

4 A neat alternative method is to attach a trolley to a ticker tape and pull the tape through the vibrator with a constant force using a newton meter or elastic threads. Since the distance $s$ moved in time $t$ is given by $s = \frac{1}{2}at^2$, and since $s$ and $t$ can be found from the tape, the acceleration $a$ for a given force can be calculated. Repeat the experiment for a range of forces and a range of masses.

(See *newton, momentum, impulse.*)

**Newton's third law of motion:** 'Whenever a force acts on a body an equal but oppositely directed force of the same kind acts on a different body.'

Note the following points:

- forces occur in pairs
- the two forces are of the same kind (e.g. both gravitational or both electrostatic)
- the forces are equal in magnitude
- the forces act in opposite directions
- the forces act along the same line
- the forces act over the same time interval
- the forces act on different bodies

Some of these points are similarities, and some are differences. Note that there are pairs of forces that, while being equal and opposite, do not form a Newton's third law pair. For example, if you sit on a chair, the upward contact force of the chair on you is equal and opposite to the downward pull of gravity on you (your weight). However, these are not a third law pair, because they do not act on different bodies. The force equal and opposite to the contact force of the chair on you is the contact force you exert on the chair. The force equal and opposite to your weight is the gravitational attraction which you exert on the Earth. (We usually picture this upward force acting at the Earth's centre of gravity.)

It can be shown that the law of *conservation of linear momentum* is implicit in Newton's third law of motion. If, when two bodies collide, the forces that each of the two bodies exert on the other are equal and opposite at each and every instant, then their impulses must be equal and opposite at each and every instant. This means that the momentum gained by one body must just equal the momentum lost by the other. The linear momentum of the two bodies treated as an isolated system is unchanged; it is conserved.

The law of conservation of linear momentum is an absolute (i.e. it is always true). It applies to any collision within a system of colliding bodies in the absence of external forces on the system. It is a consequence not of experiment but of principle. In contrast with this, the law of conservation of mechanical energy may or may not apply in a particular collision. (See *impulse*.)

**node:** a point on a *stationary wave* where the amplitude is zero. It is a point where the two component waves arrive out of phase at all times.

**noise** might be a sound which is too loud for comfort or which is undesirable to the listener. Alternatively, it might be an unwanted (voltage) signal superimposed on a clean signal during transmission, detection or amplification and which thereby obscures the value of the clean signal.

**nuclear atom:** the model of the atom introduced by Rutherford (1911) in his analysis of the *alpha particle scattering experiment*. The model proposes that the mass content of an atom is almost wholly confined to a central positively charged nucleus whose diameter is about $10^{-14}$ m. Atomic radius is typically $10^{-10}$ m.

The nucleus itself consists of $Z$ protons and $N$ neutrons. The integer $Z$ is called the proton number or atomic number while the integer $N$ is called the neutron number and their sum

$A$ (= $Z+N$) is called the mass number. Protons and neutrons are both *baryons* and they are collectively called nucleons in their role as nuclear particles. Nuclei with one value for $Z$ but different values for $N$ are called *isotopes*.

The alpha particle scattering experiment established the idea of the nucleus but said nothing about the extra-nuclear electrons. This key development came a year or two later with the publication of Bohr's theory of the hydrogen atom in which the electrons are held in their orbits by a centripetal force provided by the electrostatic attraction between the opposite charges of the electron and the nucleus.

The discrete energy levels occupied by the extra-nuclear electrons lead to the concepts of *excitation* and *ionisation* and to the distinction between emission spectra and absorption spectra. (See *emission spectrum*, *absorption spectrum*, *N–Z curve for stable nuclei*.)

**nuclear fuels:** see *fissile materials*.

**nuclear matter** is the collection of neutrons and protons that makes up a nucleus. The positive charges on the protons should ensure that nuclear matter will blow itself apart. But this is to ignore the influence of the strong interaction, which balances out the electrostatic repulsion between protons in the nucleus. The weak interaction acts within nucleons, not outside them. (See *fundamental interactions*.)

**nuclear power** is invariably provided by controlling a *chain reaction* consisting of numerous neutron-induced *fission* reactions, such that each fission reaction triggers another reaction in sequence. No reliable way has yet been found of employing a *fusion* process to supply power in a controlled manner.

The technology of nuclear power is built around the *fuel rod*, the *moderator* and the *coolant* collected together in the *thermal fission reactor*. Hot, high pressure steam leaves the reactor and is used to turn turbines which then drive generators to produce electricity.

**nuclear radius** can be calculated from the formula

$$R = r_0 A^{1/3}$$

where $A$ is the *mass number* and $r_0$ is approximately equal to $1.2 \times 10^{-15}$ m. This result is confirmed within limits by electron and proton scattering experiments; it is not exact. It implies that nuclear density, at around $10^{17}\,\mathrm{kg\,m^{-3}}$, is much the same for all atoms.

**nuclear reactions:** these occur when the *nucleus* of an atom is struck by a fast nuclear particle or a high-energy photon which is then absorbed. The fast particle or photon, together with the energy it carried, usually renders the transformed compound nucleus unstable. If stability is reached by the emission of a particle which is different from the incident particle, then a *nuclear transformation* will have taken place.

Nuclear reactions are often written out in the following conventional way:

initial nuclide (incident particle, emergent particle) final nuclide

The following nuclear reactions are all of some historical significance.

The first artificial transmutation (Rutherford, 1919) was achieved by bombarding nitrogen with alpha radiation, thus forming some oxygen which was detected spectroscopically:

$$^{14}_{7}\mathrm{N}\,(^{4}_{2}\alpha,\ ^{1}_{1}\mathrm{p})\,^{17}_{8}\mathrm{O}$$

The first transmutation triggered by a particle from an accelerator (Cockcroft and Walton, 1932) was the changing of lithium into helium by bombarding it with protons:

$$^{7}_{3}\mathrm{Li}\left(^{1}_{1}\mathrm{p},\ ^{4}_{2}\alpha\right)^{4}_{2}\mathrm{He}$$

The neutron was discovered (Chadwick, 1932) by bombarding beryllium with alpha particles and transforming it into carbon:

$$^{9}_{4}\mathrm{Be}\left(^{4}_{2}\alpha,\ ^{1}_{0}\mathrm{n}\right)^{12}_{6}\mathrm{C}$$

**nuclear reactor:** see *thermal fission reactor.*

**nuclear transformation:** a change in the structure of a nucleus which may be brought about by the *spontaneous* emission of a nuclear particle (*radioactive decay*) or by bombarding a nucleus with fast nuclear particles which are absorbed and so bring about a change of nuclear structure (*nuclear reactions*).

**nucleon:** either a proton or a neutron; a particle found in the atomic nucleus.

**nucleon number:** an alternative name for *mass number.*

**nucleus:** the dense, central portion of an atom. It is made up of neutrons and protons. It has a density around $10^{12}$ times the average density of the atom and a diameter about ten thousand times smaller than the atomic diameter.

**nuclide:** a *nucleus* for which *mass number A* and *atomic number Z* are specified. A nuclide is represented as $^{A}_{Z}\mathrm{X}$, where X is the chemical symbol of the element concerned.

**Nyquist's theorem** states that the sampling frequency needed to monitor a signal component of frequency $f_m$ must be greater than $2f_m$. This is the theoretical minimum below which the required information cannot be recovered. In practice, the sampling frequency needs to be around $10f_m$ or greater.

***N–Z* curve for stable nuclei** is a chart, not a graph, of *neutron number N* against *proton number Z.* It is also known as a Segrè plot. Each square on the chart represents the *N* and *Z* values of a particular *nuclide.* The diagram is called a chart because the allowed *N* and *Z* values are integers only and it makes no sense to connect them together with lines. Most squares represent nuclei which are too unstable ever to be produced; this is why most of the squares are empty. The three thousand or so known nuclides occupy squares in the curved fan-shaped strip. The strip is curved because the *N* values rise slightly faster than the *Z* values. Only about 10% of the known nuclei are found in nature. The rest are produced artificially in nuclear reactors or particle accelerators. The largest stable nucleus belongs to bismuth, with $Z = 83$ and $N = 126$. The *Z* values for artificially produced nuclei can exceed 110.

The following statements are broadly correct but there are occasional exceptions.

- Stable nuclei are found mostly along the centre of the strip.
- Nuclei above this strip are unstable and are brought back towards the centre through radioactive decay. This will be by beta-negative decay if they are of low *Z* number (one neutron less and one proton more) or by a mixture of alpha decay and beta-negative decay for high *Z* number.
- Unstable nuclei below the stable strip are subject to electron-capture (mostly) and to beta-positive decay (less often). Beta-positive decay was discovered some time after beta-negative decay because most of the nuclei that decay by this means are artificial. Electron capture describes the combination of an inner K-shell electron with a proton

in the nucleus to form a neutron. The electron shells have to readjust and the right number of electrons for this to happen are still present.

The three nuclear decay processes are shown on the chart. (See also *alpha decay, beta decay.*)

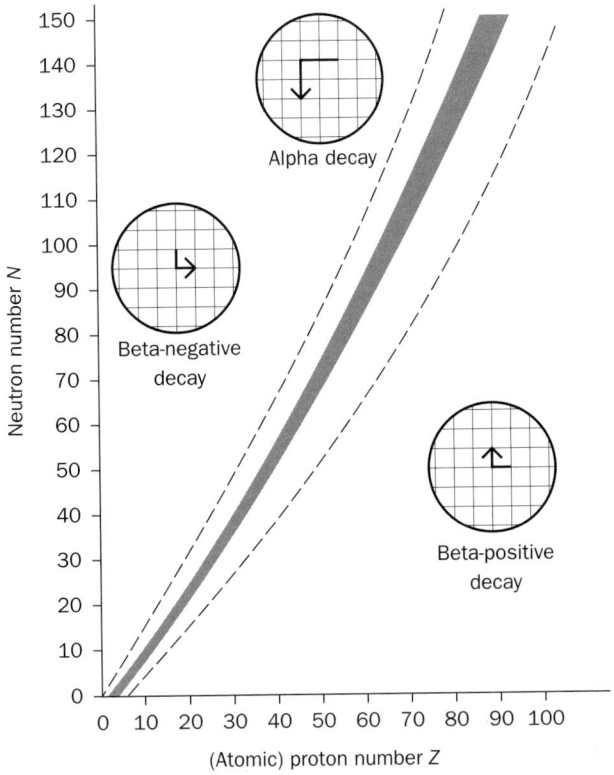


*N–Z curve for stable nuclei*

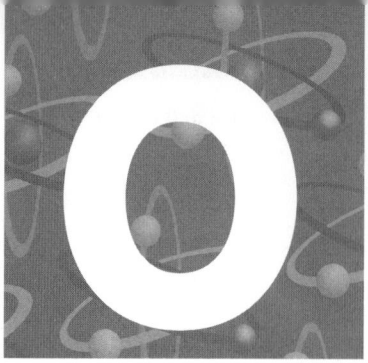

**object position:** the source of light in a *ray diagram*.

**ohm:** the SI unit of *resistance*. The symbol used is Ω. The ohm is defined by the word equations:

$$\text{resistance} = \frac{\text{voltage}}{\text{current}}$$

$$\text{ohm} = \frac{\text{volt}}{\text{ampere}}$$

**Ohm's law** states that for a conductor held at constant temperature, the current $I$ flowing in it is proportional to the potential difference $V$ across its ends. The ratio of potential difference to current is called the resistance $R$ of the conductor. Ohm's law is generally written in the form:

$$\text{potential difference in volts} = \text{current in amperes} \times \text{resistance in ohms}$$

$$V = IR$$

Ohm's law can be written down for a complete circuit. In these circumstances the potential difference becomes the circuit e.m.f. $E$ and Ohm's law is written:

$$E = IR$$

where $R$ is the equivalent resistance of the circuit as a whole. (The logic gets a bit involved. We would really be saying that the e.m.f. is the sum of the voltage drops around the circuit and that Ohm's law enables us to say of each voltage drop that $V = IR$, whence...)

Ohm's law is an odd statement in that it applies to those conductors to which it applies. This does not seem very helpful. However, Ohm's law applies to a large enough set of components for it to be an important starting point in any analysis. The mathematical statement of the law (the equation) has no constant in it. This is because the equation which states Ohm's law is effectively a definition of the ohm.

**ohmic conductors** are ones which obey *Ohm's law*. They are sometimes called linear components. Non-linear components are sometimes described as 'active'; the discriminating behaviour of many electronic circuits usually begins with an active or non-ohmic component such as a transistor. Control and stability are achieved partly by feedback and partly by using non-ohmic conductors.

**oil drop experiment:** see *Millikan's oil drop experiment*.

**oil film experiment:** an experiment in which a small drop of oil, of known diameter, is placed carefully on the surface of clean water in a tray. The water in the tray has been previously dusted with fine powder so that the area over which the oil drop spreads can be seen and measured with a ruler. The oil drop is about half a millimetre in diameter and this can be measured with a millimetre scale and a good magnifying glass. If $d$ is the diameter of the oil drop and $A$ is the area of the oil film on the water, then the diameter of the oil molecule cannot be larger than $t$, where

$$t = \left[\frac{4}{3}\pi\left(\frac{d}{2}\right)^3\right] \div A$$

This method of measuring 'molecular diameter' is no more accurate than an order of magnitude for molecular size. It is not even much good for this because oil molecules are long and thin and end up packed vertically. But it is simple, direct and tells us what sort of magnitudes are involved.

**Olber's paradox** states that if the universe is infinite, eternal and unchanging, and if it is uniformly filled with stars, then the sky will be bright at all times of the day and night. This is because a star will be seen in any direction we care to look, and the whole sky will be as bright as the surface of an average star.

In reality, in a universe with a finite age of $10^{10}$ years, say, only those stars within a radius of $10^{10}$ light years will be visible. The comparatively low density of stars makes the light level tolerable. This resolution of the paradox, that the universe is not infinitely old, is consistent with a *Big Bang theory* but not with a steady state theory of the universe.

**operational amplifier** (op amp) is an electronic device used with external *feedback* to achieve high gain. It is a basic building block of many electronic circuits. An inverting amplifier has a negative gain; that is, the output voltage is a negative multiple of the input voltage. A non-inverting amplifier has a positive gain.

**optical fibre systems** are signalling systems which rely, at some point, on the transmission of light pulses along lengths of narrow *glass fibres*. The fibres are mechanically faultless (otherwise they would already be broken), flexible (because they are so thin) and almost 100% transparent.

Optical fibres are about an eighth of a millimetre across and consist of core and cladding in a protective sheath. Both core and cladding are made of glass, and in older fibres the core diameter is a little more than half the total diameter. The cladding has a lower refractive index than the core; this ensures *total internal reflection* of oblique *light rays*. The change in refractive index can be either stepped (i.e. sudden) or graded (i.e. smoothed out).

A sharp pulse entering one end may arrive at the other end spread out in time. There are two reasons for this time dispersion. First, the light can travel over a small range of zigzag paths at slightly different angles; the steeper the angle, the further the light has to travel. Second, the longer wavelength components travel faster than the shorter wavelength components. Time dispersion places a serious limit on the information-carrying capacity of the fibre, since the pulses of a digital signal will start to overlap after travelling a relatively short distance.

To reduce these limiting effects, graded index fibres were introduced. In these, the refractive index of the core decreases towards the edges so that rays following a longer path spend more time in a faster medium and arrive at the end of the fibre at the same time as those travelling down the centre of the fibre. Most modern fibres, still with a total diameter of about an eighth of a millimetre, have a core diameter of only 5 μm. Since there is now no chance of any zigzagging, the fibres are called monomode fibres. Also, as the light comes from small laser chips whose light output is essentially monochromatic, both sources of time dispersion are much reduced and the information carrying capacity is much improved.

**optoelectronics** is the science and technology of the interconversion of optical (light) and electronic (electrical) signals. Digital and analogue electrical signals are easily manipulated, for example, by a telephone handset. Optical signals are easily transmitted over long distances by *optical fibre systems*. Devices are thus required which can convert back and forth between these two types of signal and this is the domain of optoelectronics.

**ordered and disordered energy** are the two forms of incoming energy referred to in the *first law of thermodynamics*. Ordered energy is like gravitational potential energy, kinetic energy of a single moving mass or energy stored in a stretched spring. It can be transferred from one system to another wholly in the form of useful work. Disordered energy is energy stored in the form of random molecular motion. No more than a fraction of this can be transferred in the form of useful work; the remainder is transferred as disordered energy in a heating action.

**ordinate:** the $x$ coordinate of a point on a graph. (See *abscissa*.)

**overtone:** see *harmonic*.

**Do you need revision help and advice?**

Go to pages 277–306 for a range of revision appendices that include plenty of exam advice and tips.

**packing** describes the three-dimensional pattern taken up by atoms within a crystal. Face-centred cubic and body-centred cubic structures are examples. With close packing the density of the crystal moves towards its maximum value, as in the hexagonal close packed structure of materials such as zinc. The tetragonal structure of diamond is a rare example of high crystal strength coupled with an open packing arrangement.

**pair production** relates to the formation of a particle–antiparticle pair from the energy provided by a single gamma-ray *photon*. The reaction takes place in the vicinity of a particle such as a nucleus, whose recoil helps to conserve energy and momentum in the transformation event. The opposite process, called *annihilation*, occurs at the meeting of a particle with an antiparticle. The energy and momentum are carried off by two gamma-ray photons.

Note that pair production has nothing to do with the formation of electron–hole pairs, which appear in semiconducting materials when an electron is freed from a fixed atom in the lattice by an excitation process and leaves behind a hole. The hole is no more than a vacancy which is mobile in an intrinsic *semiconductor* but static if it is linked to an impurity atom in an extrinsic semiconductor.

**parallax (stellar)** is the angle $\theta$ shown in the diagram; that is, the parallax angle for a star is the maximum angle between the Earth and the Sun as seen from the star. Since the radius of the Earth's orbit round the Sun is known accurately, the distance of the star can be calculated once $\theta$ is known.



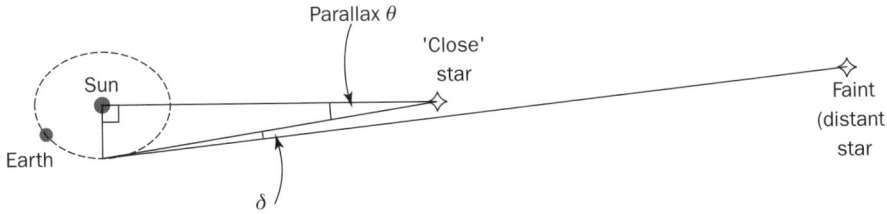


The angle of parallax is found by measuring the angle $\delta$ between the star and a nearby faint star over a period of several months. The actual calculation of the angle of parallax from changes in the value of the angle $\delta$ is complicated, mainly because neither the bright star nor the faint star will be in the plane of the Earth's orbit about the Sun. The calculation is therefore a three-dimensional affair. Measurements for one bright star against several faint stars are taken and averaged. The method assumes that the bright stars are the stars nearest the Earth and that faint stars are much more distant. Should the bright star also be a distant star, the angle $\delta$ will not vary as the months go by.

Useful parallax measurements can be made for no more than about the two thousand or so stars nearest to the solar system, that is, for one star per hundred million stars in this galaxy. And there are about $10^{13}$ galaxies. These relatively few measurements allow the absolute brightnesses of these stars to be determined from their apparent brightnesses. Absolute brightness can then be correlated with surface temperature using *Wien's law*. This is the basis for the *Hertzsprung–Russell diagram*. All other distance measurements used by astronomers hinge one way or another on these first parallax measurements.

Parallax is the basis for the definition of a unit of distance, the *parsec*: an object whose parallax is one second of arc is at a distance of one parsec.

**parallax error** is the random error associated with identifying the position of a point when observing it obliquely (e.g. the reading for a needle above a scale). It is a *random error* and the average of several independent measurements should be close to the correct value. If a parallax error is a consequence of a poor arrangement of the apparatus, it becomes a *systematic error*. Parallax errors should be minimised wherever possible by using mirrors; a mirror is placed just behind the scale against which the needle is read and the user must ensure that the needle and its reflection are aligned when taking a reading.

**parallelogram law:** the law applying to the addition of vectors. Each of the vectors is represented in magnitude and in direction by the sides of a parallelogram. The included diagonal of the parallelogram represents, in magnitude and in direction, the resultant of the two vectors.

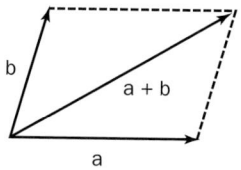


**parallel plate capacitor:** a device for storing electric charge constructed from two parallel conducting plates mounted a short distance apart.

The diagram below shows a parallel plate capacitor with the distance between the plates exaggerated so that the *field lines (electric)* can be shown clearly.

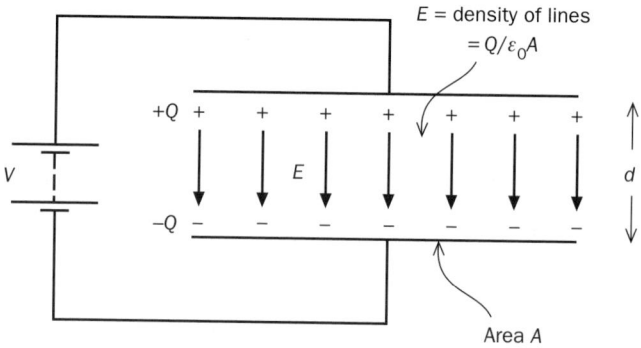


The *capacitance* of the arrangement is defined by the equation:

$$\text{capacitance} = \frac{\text{change stored on one plate}}{\text{potential difference between plates}}$$

All the lines of force go from the positive charge $+Q$ on the upper plate directly to the negative charge $-Q$ on the lower plate. The number of lines of force is $Q/\varepsilon_0$ since there are $1/\varepsilon_0$ lines of electric force per unit charge. The *electric field strength* $E$ is the number of lines of force per unit area. If the area of the plates is $A$, then

$$E = \frac{Q}{A\varepsilon_0}$$

But

$$E = \frac{V}{d} = \frac{Q}{A\varepsilon_0}$$

and since $C=Q/V$, we have

$$C = \frac{\varepsilon_0 A}{d}$$

If the space between the plates is filled with insulating material, the capacitance of the arrangement changes by a numerical factor $\varepsilon_r$ where $\varepsilon_r$ is the *relative permittivity* of the insulating substance. The equation for the capacitance becomes:

$$C = \frac{\varepsilon_r \varepsilon_0 A}{d}$$

How this increase in the capacitance comes about is indicated in the diagram below.

On the left is a capacitor filled with vacuum. Charge $Q$ is stored and the field between the plates is $E$. On the right is an identical capacitor filled with an insulating material. The electric field polarises the insulator. Many of the lines of force which set out from the positive plate end on the polarised charge on the dielectric. A small positive charge carried from B to A would have to fight against a reduced number of lines of force for most of the way. The charge on the plates is the same, but the electric field strength and the potential difference between the plates are both reduced. Since $C = Q/V$, the capacitance must increase. The factor by which it increases is called the relative permittivity of the insulator.

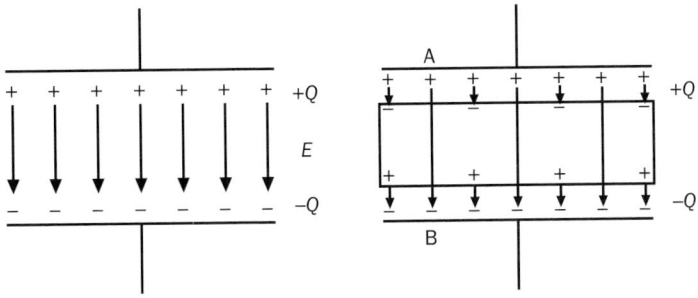

Although we say that a capacitor is a device used for storing charge, it is clear that the two plates of a parallel plate capacitor store zero charge because their charges are equal and opposite. It may be better to think of a capacitor as a device for storing energy in a circuit. (See *energy stored in a capacitor.*)

**parsec:** a unit of distance, used in astronomy, which equals 3.2616 light years or $3.086 \times 10^{16}$ m. Its symbol is pc. A megaparsec (Mpc) is $10^6$ pc or $3.086 \times 10^{22}$ m. (See *star, parallax (stellar).*)

**particle accelerators** provide beams of high-energy particles, especially electrons and protons, for scattering and collision experiments. They are usefully divided into linear accelerators and ring accelerators.

***Electron gun.*** This consists of a heated filament that provides electrons by *thermionic emission*, a negative cathode to give them direction, and two cylindrical anodes at different voltages to focus and accelerate the beam.

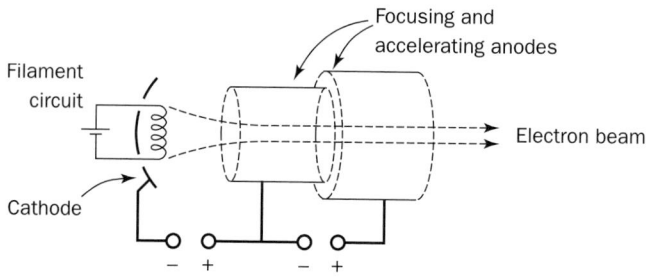


***Linear accelerators.*** These machines are based on the principle that the kinetic energy of a negatively charged particle will increase when it passes from a region of low electrical potential into a region of higher electrical potential. For protons, the voltages will be the other way round.

High-speed electrons from a Van de Graaff generator (with an electron gun within the sphere) are projected through a series of conducting cylinders. The speed of the electron increases as it leaves one cylinder and enters the next provided there is an increase in potential. This is achieved without recourse to enormous voltages by changing the directions of the voltages while a bundle of electrons is within a cylinder. With the changes happening at equal intervals of time, the lengths of the cylinders are progressively increased to accommodate the increasing electron speeds. The final cylinder length is measured in kilometres. The cylinder lengths have to take the relativistic speeds of the electrons into account.

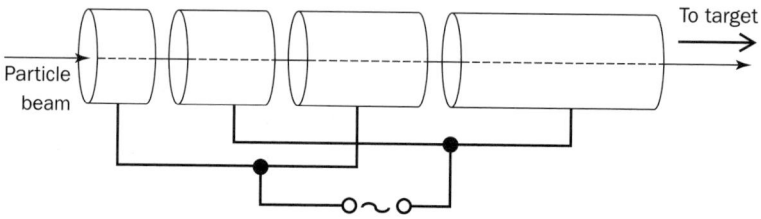

***Ring accelerators.*** A proton moving with speed $v$ at right angles to a magnetic field of strength $B$ follows a circular path of radius $r$, and $r = mv/Be$ (see *force on a moving charge*). This principle is adopted in the cyclotron to accelerate protons or ions to high energies.

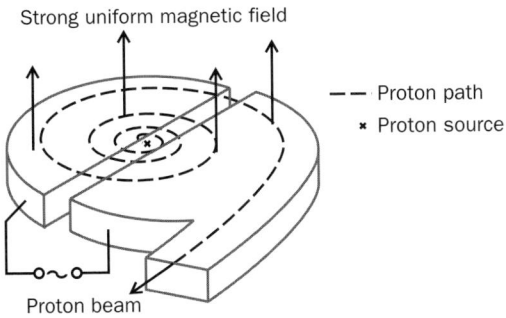


The cyclotron is similar to a linear accelerator in that the proton speed is boosted each time the bunch of protons passes from one D section to the other and that the direction of the voltage between the two D sections changes with a frequency which matches the protons' arrival times. The changing proton speed is accommodated by the increase in the length of its semicircular path. The frequency $f$ of the AC power source which controls the direction of the potential difference between the D sections is as follows:

$$f = \frac{v}{2\pi r} = \frac{Be}{2\pi m}$$

Electrons reach relativistic speeds at too low an energy for the cyclotron to be useful. Synchrocyclotrons are used instead.

**particle interactions** is a phrase that refers to what happens when two or more *elementary particles* collide, mostly at high energies in a *particle accelerator*. In this context, particle decay is treated as an interaction.

The outcome of a collision must satisfy a number of conservation laws and these laws must take account of the creation of new particles and the *annihilation* of incident particles. Apart from conservation of mass–energy, linear momentum and angular momentum, there are nuclear conservation laws characterised by quantum numbers. These include charge $Q$, baryon number $B$ and strangeness $S$. Conservation of charge is nicely illustrated by electron–positron annihilation or by *pair production*. In both cases, the total charge before and after the event adds up to zero. Conservation of baryon number implies that when second- and third-generation baryons decay, they must decay (eventually) into protons or neutrons, thereby conserving baryon number. Mesons consist of quark–antiquark pairs and have baryon number zero. There is therefore no barrier in respect of baryon number to the creation and annihilation of mesons; but charge must be conserved, so either the mesons are neutral or they come and go in positive–negative pairs. Strangeness $S$ is more trouble. It is conserved in events controlled by the strong interaction but not in events controlled by the weak interaction.

Lepton number is another conserved quantity. Remember that lepton number $L$, like baryon number $B$, is a quantum number which may have value +1, –1 or zero. It is not the number of leptons. In the beta decay of neutrons, for example, the lepton numbers of the electron and the antineutrino on the output side are +1 and –1, respectively. The electron and proton have $Q$ values of –1 and +1; the proton and neutron both have baryon number $B$ equal to 1. (See *baryons, hadrons, leptons, mesons, conservation laws (nuclear), proton decay and neutron decay.*)

**particle physics** is the study of *subatomic particles*, including *elementary particles*. We live in a low-energy environment and, mostly, the subatomic particles that matter are the *nucleus*, the *proton*, the *neutron*, the *electron* and the *photon*. Atoms, molecules and solid materials need a low-energy environment, such as we find on the Earth's surface, for their very existence. The inside of a star is a high-energy environment in which atoms cannot exist. Environments of far higher energy are needed for the generation of the more massive elementary particles; it is these environments that are briefly replicated on a small scale by the collisions inside *particle accelerators*.

Protons and neutrons are members of a large group of compound particles known as *hadrons*. Hadrons, which consist of either two quarks (*mesons*) or three quarks (*baryons*), are subject to all four of the *fundamental interactions*. The strong interaction acts only on quarks; for this reason, the strong interaction acts on hadrons but not on *leptons* or *exchange particles*.

Leptons, such as electrons or positrons, are immune to the strong interaction but can and do react with hadrons through the weak interaction.

The photon is an example of a third group of elementary particles known as *exchange particles*. (See *conservation laws (nuclear), Feynman diagrams, particle interactions, radiation detectors.*)

**path difference** is the extra distance one wave motion travels compared to another; the two distances are measured from points where the two waves are in phase and end at the point where the two waves meet. The *phase difference* at the meeting point is calculated as follows:

$$\text{phase difference} = \frac{2\pi}{\lambda} \times \text{path difference}$$

The wavelength value can be omitted if, as is often the case, the path difference is expressed as a multiple of the wavelength.

The diagram opposite shows an example in exaggerated form. Rays emerging from the two slits are in phase with each other.

Path difference is usually the first thing to be calculated when determining or explaining the *interference* pattern formed where two waves meet. (See also *coherence.*)

**penetrating power:** see *attenuation*.

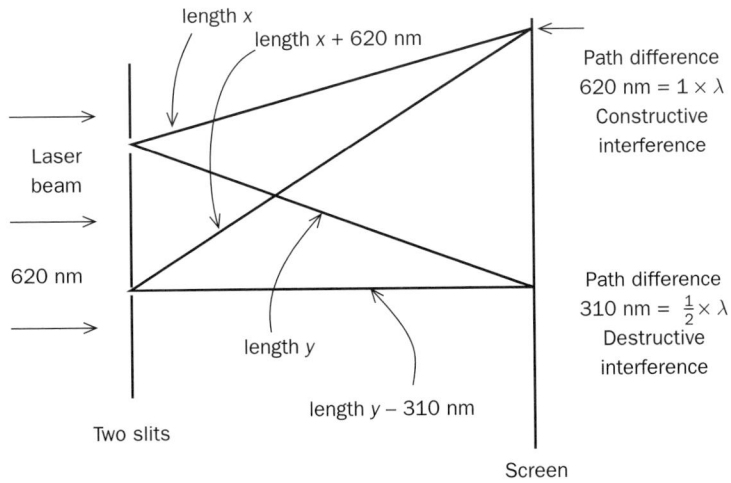


**period** is the time taken for one complete oscillation of a vibrating system. More formally, it is the time interval between successive occasions when a body whose motion is oscillatory moves through the same point in the same direction. The SI unit of period is the second (s), and the symbol used is $T$.

It is general practice to use period when discussing simple mechanical oscillations but to use frequency when dealing with complex mechanical or electrical oscillations. This is because oscillatory systems of the latter types are driven by frequency generators.

**permeability of free space,** $\mu_0$, is a constant which appears in any expression that relates the magnetic field strength $B$ at a point to the current $I$ flowing in a nearby conductor, for example $\mu_0 I/(2\pi r)$ near a straight wire and $\mu_0 nI$ within a solenoid.

The SI unit for $\mu_0$ is henry per metre ($\mathrm{Hm^{-1}}$). The magnitude of $\mu_0$ is defined to be $4\pi \times 10^{-7}\,\mathrm{Hm^{-1}}$ as a step towards the definition of the *ampere*. (See *speed of light*.)

**permittivity of free space** is the constant $\varepsilon_0$ which appears in *Coulomb's law*. The magnitude of $\varepsilon_0$ is set by defining the magnitudes of $\mu_0$, the permeability of free space, and $c$, the speed of light. These definitions put the value of $\varepsilon_0$ at $8.854\,187\,817 \times 10^{-12}\,\mathrm{Fm^{-1}}$. This comes about because electromagnetic theory shows that

$$C = \frac{1}{\sqrt{\mu_0 \varepsilon_0}}$$

**PET scanning** is positron emission tomography. A radioactive tracer which is an emitter of beta-plus radiation (positrons) is injected into a subject. The tracer is a radioactive chemical which will accumulate at a point of interest in the body. As it undergoes radioactive decay, it emits positrons. Each positron annihilates almost immediately with an electron, releasing two gamma photons which travel in opposite directions. These photons are detected and their point of origin is deduced from their times and directions of arrival at the detector surrounding the subject. (See *tracer elements, annihilation*.)

In this way, a computer image can be built up of the site where the tracer has accumulated in the subject. The computer image can be presented in a series of 'slices' through the subject's body (hence the word 'tomography' in the name, which means 'imaging in sections').

**phase** is an angle in *radians*, between 0 and $2\pi$, which indicates a fraction of a cycle completed. (See *phase difference.*)

**phase difference** is an angle in radians, between 0 and $2\pi$, which indicates the extent to which two wave motions of the same frequency are out of step. It is the fraction of a complete cycle, in radians, by which one signal would have to be retarded or advanced to be in phase with another signal of the same frequency.

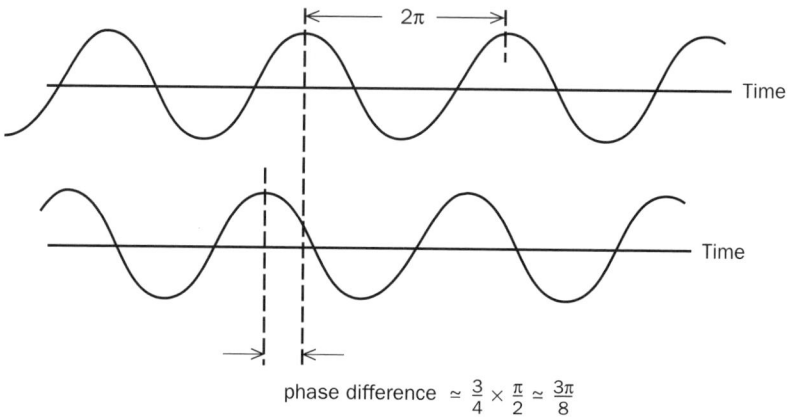


The definition and its meaning are illustrated in the diagram above. The lower signal leads the upper signal by about $3\pi/8$ radians. 'Leading' seems the wrong way round until we remember that, for time, 'later' is on the right. The upper signal peaks about $3\pi/8$ radians later, so it lags the lower signal. The concept is particularly relevant to alternating currents and voltages.

(See *path difference, interference, coherence, wavefront.*)

**photoelectric effect:** the enforced expulsion of *electrons* from a metal surface when the surface is irradiated with electromagnetic radiation of sufficiently high frequency. For most metals, this frequency lies in the ultraviolet. The alkali metals show the effect with visible radiation, which for sodium is in the range we see as green. There are semiconducting materials and metals with special coatings which release photoelectrons for the full span of the visible spectrum and into the near infrared.

A beam of electromagnetic radiation consists of innumerable *photons.* If the beam is monochromatic with frequency $f$, all the photons in the beam have energy $hf$ where $h$ is the *Planck constant*, $6.626 \times 10^{-34}$ J s. If the radiation is incident upon a metal surface, the occasional photon will release all its energy to a single conduction electron. Some of these conduction electrons will escape from the metal and are then called photoelectrons.

In normal circumstances, conduction electrons are free to roam within the metal but cannot escape. To get out, they must pay a sort of 'energy exit fee', called the 'work function'. The work function (symbol $\phi$) differs from metal to metal but is a constant for each particular metal.

If $v$ is the maximum speed acquired by a photoelectron and if $m_e$ is electron mass, then a simple application of the conservation of energy law gives:

$$bf = \phi + \tfrac{1}{2} m_e v^2$$

This is known as Einstein's photoelectric equation. It was published in 1905 and verified experimentally in 1912, following the publication of an accurate value for $m_e$ calculated from a value for $e$ produced by *Millikan's oil drop experiment* and earlier measurements of $e/m_e$. Millikan himself reported a detailed experimental investigation of Einstein's equation using the alkali metals in 1916. The principal features of his apparatus are shown in the diagram below.

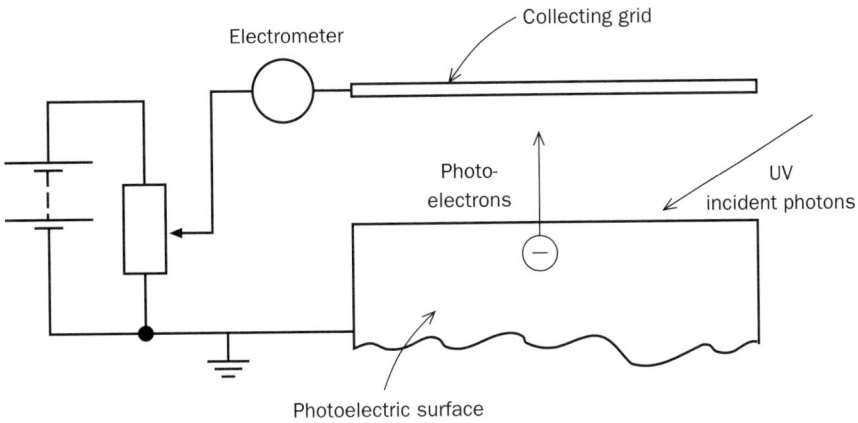


Using monochromatic radiation of frequency $f$, Millikan measured the minimum negative voltage between the collecting electrode and the earthed photoelectric surface for the photoelectric current to become zero. This is called the stopping potential $V_s$. Einstein's equation can then be rewritten as

$$bf = \phi + e \,.\, V_s$$

or

$$V_s = \frac{b}{e} f - \frac{\phi}{e}$$

Results obtained for barium were as follows:

| Stopping potential in volts | Wavelength in mm | Frequency in $10^{15}$ Hz |
|---|---|---|
| 2.40 | 0.254 | 1.18 |
| 1.47 | 0.313 | 0.958 |
| 0.91 | 0.365 | 0.821 |
| 0.57 | 0.405 | 0.740 |

From these, the graph below has been drawn.

The gradient of the line is $4.16 \times 10^{-15}$ volt seconds. It equals $h/e$. The value for the Planck constant comes out at $(4.16 \times 10^{-15}\,\text{V s})(1.60 \times 10^{-19}\,\text{C}) = 6.67 \times 10^{-34}\,\text{J s}$ (to 3 s.f.). The negative intercept is 2.51 V. This equals $\phi/e$. The work function $\phi$ for barium comes out at $4.0 \times 10^{-19}$ J (to 2 s.f.) or 2.5 eV (to 2 s.f.).

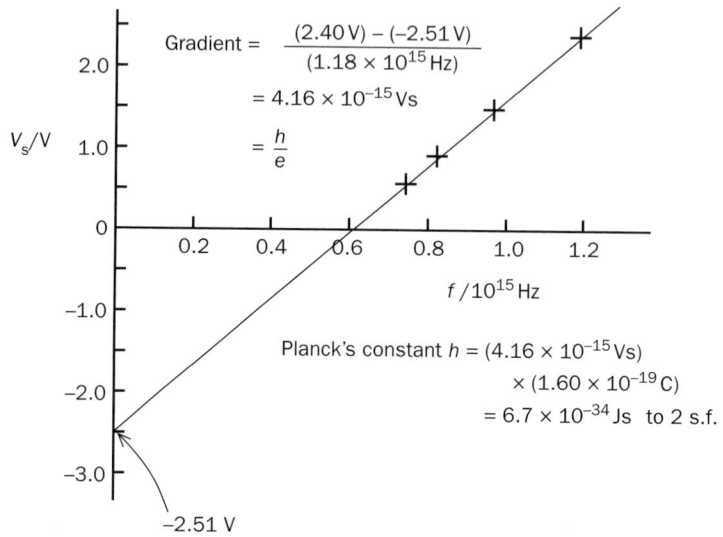


The cut-off frequency equals the work function $\phi$ divided by the Planck constant $h$ and comes out at $0.60 \times 10^{15}$ Hz.

The first graph below illustrates the way photoelectric current varies with the voltage on the collector grid, for different values of illumination. The second graph underlines the proportionality between the photoelectric current and the light intensity for light of fixed frequency above the cut-off frequency and for a fixed collector grid voltage above the stopping potential.

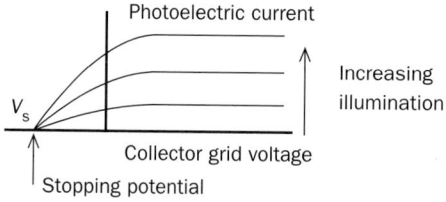


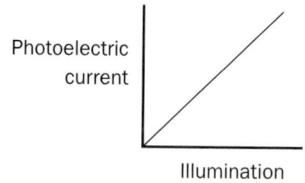


**photon:** a quantum of electromagnetic radiation. Each quantum of frequency $f$ has energy $hf$, where $h$ is the *Planck constant*, $6.626 \times 10^{-34}$ J s. (See also *leptons, wave–particle duality, photoelectric effect.*)

**photovoltaic cells** convert energy from solar radiation directly into electrical energy. The efficiency of such processes is around 10%, and the mechanism involves the release of loosely bound electrons in the vicinity of the interface between two semiconducting layers (one $p$-type, the other $n$-type). The average energy possessed by the electrons generates a voltage of about half a volt between the two metal electrodes on the far sides of the semiconducting layers. The source of the energy for any current flow is the photon energy employed to release the electrons.

**physical quantity:** any physically measurable quantity. Temperature, density and electrical potential are physical quantities; appearance, usefulness and worth are not.

**piezoelectric transducer:** a device used to produce or detect mechanical waves such as sound or ultrasound. It makes use of the fact that certain crystals are distorted when a voltage is applied across them — this is the piezoelectric effect. It also works in the reverse sense: when pressure is applied to the crystal, it deforms slightly and this produces a voltage across the crystal. Some microphones are based on a piezoelectric crystal. Sound waves strike the crystal, causing it to alternately compress and expand. This produces an alternating voltage across the crystal which can then be amplified.

To produce ultrasound waves, a high-frequency alternating voltage is applied to a piezoelectric crystal. This causes the crystal to deform, compressing and expanding with the same frequency as the applied voltage. In this way, mechanical waves can be sent through any object with which the crystal is in good contact.

To detect ultrasound waves, the waves must be directed on to the piezoelectric crystal. This leads to the crystal deforming so that a varying voltage appears across it with the same frequency as the ultrasound waves.

In an ultrasound scan, the probe that is passed over the patient's body contains a single transducer which sends pulses of ultrasound into the patient and then detects the reflected waves. (See *ultrasound*.)

**pitch** is the subjective response of the *ear* to the *frequency* of *sound waves*. The ears can hear frequencies ranging from about 10 Hz to about 15 kHz — around three orders of magnitude. The upper limit comes down with increasing age; young children can hear up to 20 kHz while adults can only manage 12 kHz to 15 kHz. Many older people cannot hear high-pitched bird song.

**Planck constant:** a constant, symbol $h$, which is used in *quantum mechanics* to describe the size of quanta. It is the ratio of the energy $E$ of a photon to the frequency $f$ of its associated electromagnetic radiation:

$$E = hf$$

The value of the Planck constant is approximately $6.62606896 \times 10^{-34}$ J s. You may prefer to think of the units as 'joules per hertz', to emphasise that $h$ relates an energy to a frequency. The factor of $10^{-34}$ ensures that, even for radiation of very high frequency, the photon energy is small (on the human scale).

**planetary motion** is the orbital motion of planets about the Sun. We will assume that the orbits are circular — a reasonable assumption for several of the planets. The first step in a problem is almost always to write down that the gravitational force holding the planet in its orbit is the *centripetal force*. Suppose that $M$ is the mass of the Sun, $m$ is the mass of the planet, $r$ is the radius of the planet's (imaginary) circular orbit, $v$ is the speed of the planet and $T$ is the planet's orbital period; then

$$G\frac{Mm}{r^2} = \frac{mv^2}{r} = \frac{m}{r} \times \frac{2\pi r}{T} = \frac{4\pi^2 mr}{T^2}$$

$$so\ T^2 = \frac{4\pi^2}{GM} \times r^2$$

$$or\ T^2 \propto r^3$$

This is Kepler's third law of planetary motion, which states that the square of the period of a planet's orbit about the Sun is proportional to the cube of its average distance from the Sun.

**plastic deformation** is the change in shape or size of a solid specimen when a stress close to the breaking value is applied. It arises from the flow and change of structure within a material, leading to a drastic increase in strain. Where movement within the material centres around countless dislocations, the plastic deformation appears to be uniform throughout the specimen. Where deformation is primarily due to slippage between crystal planes, it tends to be more localised and the specimen will be closer to breaking.

A material not subject to plastic flow is described as 'brittle'. A material in which the onset of plastic flow occurs at high values of stress is described as 'strong'. A metallic, crystalline material such as copper, which can endure large plastic deformations, allows dislocations to move freely within its volume and will accommodate appreciable *slip*. It will be both malleable and ductile.

(See *edge dislocations, brittleness, strength, malleability, ductility, stress–strain curves.*)

**plasticity** is the ability of a material to retain any change of shape or size once a deforming stress has been removed. It is the opposite of *elasticity*. (See also *stress–strain curves.*)

**point defects** are *crystal defects* which occur at a point. They can be associated with:

- a space where an atom ought to be (vacancy)
- an impurity atom replacing an ordinary atom in a crystal (substitution)
- an impurity atom trapped between two crystal planes (interstitial)

Whatever the source of the trouble, there are strains set up in the neighbouring parts of the crystal and the point defect is a source of weakness.

**polarisation phenomena** are those properties taken on by light and other *electromagnetic waves* when the direction of the transverse wave vector is the same for all parts of the wave. The diagram that follows shows a rectangular sheet of *Polaroid* cut in half after two parallel reference lines have been marked on it. A beam of ordinary light from a lamp is shown passing through the two sheets of Polaroid. If the two reference lines are parallel (so that the two Polaroids are aligned), the light gets through both sheets. If the reference lines are at right angles ('crossed polars'), the light gets through the first sheet but not the second.

The first sheet of Polaroid is called the polariser, and the second sheet is called the analyser; the light between the two sheets is polarised light.

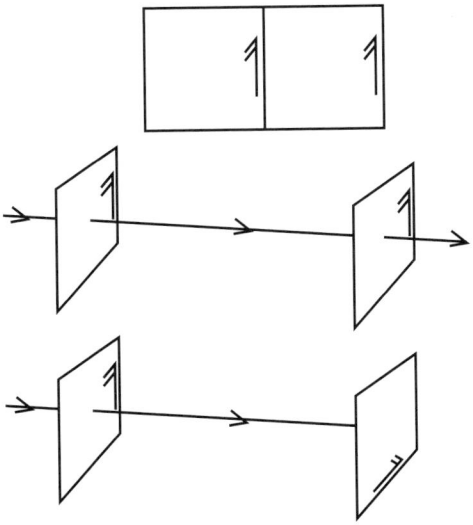

The next diagram shows a glass container filled with a solution of an optically active material such as dextrose and placed in the path of the polarised light. This time, the light should be monochromatic. If the analyser is set for darkness before the container was put in place, then some light will now get through. The light can be absorbed once more by rotating the analyser. Experiment shows that the angle through which the analyser is rotated for darkness is proportional to both the path length in the solution and the solution's concentration. By comparing the rotation angles with solutions of known and unknown concentrations, it is possible to measure quickly the concentration of any optically active solution.

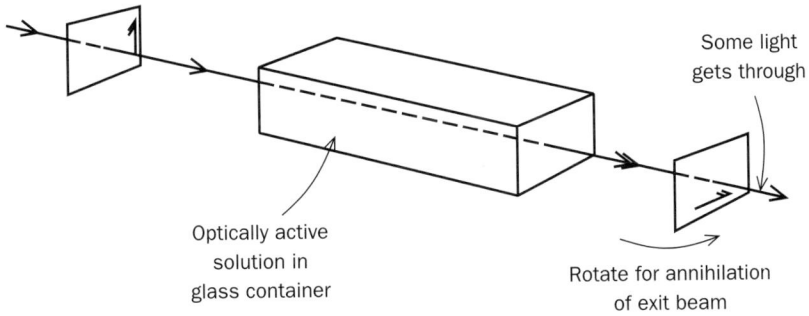


The same set-up can be used for *stress* analysis. A Perspex model is made of a component whose design is incomplete, and the model is placed between the polariser and the analyser. A large number of dark lines will be seen within the Perspex component and these lines will be heavily concentrated in the areas of maximum stress. The design can then be modified by trial and error to ensure that stresses are distributed evenly throughout the component.

**Polaroid** is the brand name (hence the capital P) for a nitrocellulose sheet covered with crystals of quinine iodosulfate. All the crystals are lined up in the same direction so that normal light passing through the sheet comes out plane polarised. There is one particular orientation of the sheet at which polarised light passes through unaffected (except for some modest absorption). Then, starting from this position, as the polaroid is slowly rotated about an axis parallel to the light, the light is increasingly absorbed. The peak absorption position corresponds to one right angle of rotation from the minimum absorption position.

**polycrystalline solids** are crystalline solids in which the individual crystals are tiny compared with the dimensions of the whole, and whose physical properties depend, in large part, on the manner in which the individual crystals are linked together. In metals, the small crystals are known as grains. Annealing (which involves heating to a high temperature followed by slow cooling) encourages a growth in grain size and results in a softer, more pliable metal.

**polymeric solids** are formed from long chains of carbon atoms linked together by strong *covalent bonds*. Each carbon atom in the chain is left with two more bonds that hold more atoms along the length of the chain. The diagram below shows two polymeric molecular structures: polyethylene and polyvinyl chloride. The physical characteristics of the solid depend on the nature of the *cross-linking* bonds which hold the neighbouring long molecular chains together. (See *thermoplastic polymers*, *thermosetting polymers*.)

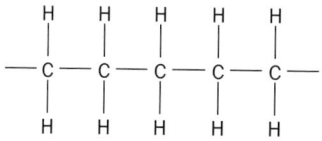


Polyethylene

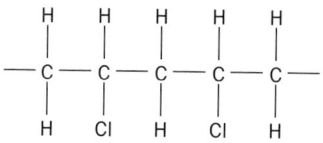


Polyvinyl chloride

**position:** an identifiable point on a line or within an area or space.

**positron:** a elementary antiparticle identical in mass to the *electron* and bearing an equivalent but opposite (positive) charge. This is one of the particles emitted during beta-positive decay.

**positron emission tomography:** see *PET scanning*.

**potential (electric)** at a point equals the work done per coulomb bringing a small positive charge from a point at infinite distance from other charges to the point. It is a *scalar quantity* and the symbol is $V$. The SI unit is the volt (V), which is another name for the joule per coulomb ($JC^{-1}$).

Electric potential is zero at infinite distance, negative near a negative charge, and positive near a positive charge. The electric potential $V$ a distance $r$ from a positive charge $Q$ is calculated from the formula

$$V = \frac{Q}{4\pi\varepsilon_0 r}$$

Electric potential decreases with distance from a positive charge but increases (i.e. gets less negative) with distance from a negative charge.

**potential (gravitational)** at a point equals the work done per kilogram bringing a small mass from a point at infinite distance from other masses to the point. Because gravitational forces are always attractive, gravitational potential is zero at infinite distance and negative elsewhere. You will be familiar with the idea that the gravitational potential energy of a mass increases as it is raised above the surface of the Earth. For many practical purposes, we treat the surface of the Earth as the 'zero' of gravitational potential. However, if we are thinking on an astronomical scale, we have to treat a point at infinite distance away as the 'zero' of gravitational potential. An object on the surface of the Earth is then at a negative potential; as it is raised, its (negative) potential energy increases towards zero.

Gravitational potential is a *scalar quantity*. The symbol used is $V$. The SI unit is the joule per kilogram ($\mathrm{J\,kg^{-1}}$). (See *gravitational potential (radial fields), Newton's law of universal gravitation.*)

**potential difference** (electrical) between two points is the work done per coulomb of charge transferring a small positive charge from one point to the other. It is a *scalar quantity*. The symbol used is $V$. The SI unit is the volt (V), which is another name for the joule per coulomb ($\mathrm{JC^{-1}}$). Definitions can usefully be stated as the word equations

$$\text{potential difference} = \frac{\text{work done}}{\text{change}}$$

$$\text{volt} = \frac{\text{joule}}{\text{coulomb}}$$

**potential divider:** a fixed resistor which may be tapped at any point along its length to enable part of the *potential difference* across the whole resistor to be accessed. In the diagram below, the circuit on the left shows how a potential divider may be used to adjust the voltage across a lamp between zero and any pre-decided value.

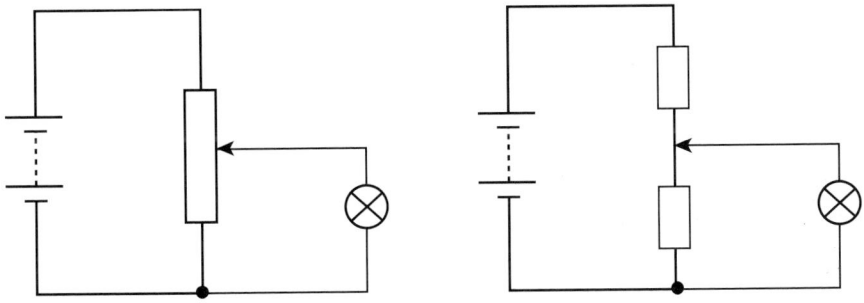

The voltage across the lamp or any other component will vary linearly with the distance moved by the slider, provided that the resistance of the lamp is much larger than the end-to-end resistance of the potential divider.

The potential divider could be replaced by two separate resistors, but this would give a fixed value of the voltage across the lamp. The circuit on the right-hand side of the diagram shows how a potential divider can be constructed from two fixed resistors; in this case, the voltage across the lamp cannot be varied.

**potential energy** is the energy stored in a system by reason of its position or its condition. It is a *scalar quantity*. The SI unit is the joule (J). The symbol used may be the energy symbol $W$ or there may be a subscript 'p' (e.g. $W_p$) to distinguish it from kinetic energy $W_k$. The forms $E_p$ and $E_k$ for potential energy and kinetic energy are also used. A mass $m$ raised a height $h$ above the ground has potential energy $mgh$ joules. Potential energy can also be stored as *elastic strain energy*, as electrical energy in a capacitor and as one component of internal (thermal) energy in solids and liquids.

The expression $mgh$ used for gravitational fields is misleadingly simple. Height $h$ is measured from a level at which potential energy is assumed to be zero — usually the surface of the Earth. In addition, the value of $g$ is assumed to be constant. This is sufficient for many purposes. Precise work requires us to set the potential energy to be zero for a mass which is at infinite distance from the centre of the gravitational field. Because potential energy depends on the mass as well as on the position in the field, we remove the mass dependence by introducing the concept of potential. Potential energy released or stored equals (mass × change of potential). This approach works for electric fields too. (See *gravitational potential (uniform fields), gravitational potential (radial fields).*)

**power** is rate of *energy transfer*. It is a *scalar quantity*. The SI unit of power is the watt (W). The symbol for power is $P$. Power and the watt are defined by the word equations

$$\text{power} = \frac{\text{energy transferred}}{\text{time}}$$

$$\text{watt} = \frac{\text{joule}}{\text{second}}$$

The topic is made more complicated for the A-level student by the variety of ways in which 'energy transferred' has to be calculated. A simple problem in mechanics is solved by multiplying a force by a displacement and dividing by a time (all in SI units, of course):

$$\text{power} = \frac{\text{force} \times \text{displacement}}{\text{time}}$$

But displacement divided by time is velocity (which is usually constant in these circumstances), so power becomes the product of force and velocity. If, for instance, a 200 g mass is falling towards the ground, then at the instant when its speed is $12\,\text{m}\,\text{s}^{-1}$, the gravitational field is working at a rate of:

$$\begin{aligned}\text{power} &= \text{force} \times \text{velocity}\\ &= \left(0.200\,\text{kg} \times 9.8\,\text{ms}^{-2}\right) \times \left(12\,\text{ms}^{-1}\right)\\ &= 23.52\,\text{W}\\ &= 24\,\text{W (to 2 s.f.)}\end{aligned}$$

At the starting point of the fall, the rate of working of the gravitational field is close to zero; the rate increases as the mass falls. One way of looking at this increase of power is to remember that the distance fallen per second increases with speed. So potential energy lost per second increases with speed. Therefore the rate at which gravity works increases with speed, which makes the force × velocity formula more understandable.

Alternatively, a vessel filled with liquid and having a total thermal capacity of $5000\,\text{JK}^{-1}$ will be heated by a power supply of 800 W at a rate of $(800\,\text{W})/(5000\,\text{JK}^{-1})$ or $0.16\,\text{Ks}^{-1}$.

An electrical source transfers power to the external circuit at a rate of $IV$, where $I$ is the current and $V$ is the terminal potential difference:

power = current × voltage

watt = ampere × volt

**power of a lens:** see *lens equation.*

**precision** is a compound of the range of magnitudes that an instrument can measure and the smallest difference in magnitude that an instrument can resolve. The precision of a balance might be, say, ±10 mg up to 200 g.

The problem with precision is to know when, and how far, it is significant. A *micrometer screw gauge* can be read to a precision of ±0.01 mm up to about 3 cm without even trying to divide up the scale divisions by eye. With this kind of precision you can check the roundness of a thick copper wire, but you cannot measure the diameter of a piece of string since the jaws would squash the string.

Most instruments have a precision which goes beyond their reliability. A good voltmeter will be accurate to about ±1% of full-scale deflection, but the scale can be read more closely than this. A good magnifying glass will help read a temperature to ±0.1 K from a *mercury-in-glass thermometer* which is reliable to no more than ±1 K. In both cases, the precision is swamped by *systematic errors* inherent in the instruments.

Precision is sometimes used to mean *uncertainty*, but this is not strictly correct. (See *error, sensitivity, uncertainty.*)

**prefixes used with SI units:** two sets of prefixes are used with SI units — a set of multiples and a set of sub-multiples. They, along with their meanings and abbreviations, are listed in the following table.

| **Multiples** | | | **Sub-multiples** | | |
|---|---|---|---|---|---|
| deca- | $\times 10^{1}$ | da | deci- | $\times 10^{-1}$ | d |
| hecto- | $\times 10^{2}$ | h | centi- | $\times 10^{-2}$ | c |
| kilo- | $\times 10^{3}$ | k | milli- | $\times 10^{-3}$ | m |
| mega- | $\times 10^{6}$ | M | micro- | $\times 10^{-6}$ | μ |
| giga- | $\times 10^{9}$ | G | nano- | $\times 10^{-9}$ | n |
| tera- | $\times 10^{12}$ | T | pico- | $\times 10^{-12}$ | p |
| peta- | $\times 10^{15}$ | P | femto- | $\times 10^{-15}$ | f |
| exa- | $\times 10^{18}$ | E | atto- | $\times 10^{-18}$ | a |
| zetta- | $\times 10^{21}$ | Z | zepto- | $\times 10^{-21}$ | z |
| yotta- | $\times 10^{24}$ | Y | yocto- | $\times 10^{-24}$ | y |

**pressure** and its SI unit, the pascal (Pa), are defined by the word equations

$$\text{pressure} = \frac{\text{thrust}}{\text{area}}$$

$$\text{pascal (Pa)} = \frac{\text{newton (N)}}{\text{metre squared (m}^2\text{)}}$$

Pressure is a non-directional *scalar quantity*. Pressure is concerned with fluids, not solids. This is because pressure arises from collisions between molecules of the fluid and the surfaces with which it is in contact; the molecules of a solid cannot bounce off a surface. A solid can receive and transmit a *thrust*, but it cannot transmit a pressure. (These distinctions are, however, never absolute. Some solids, especially polymers, behave like liquids when they are exposed to long-term forces.) (See *fluid matter, solids, liquid pressure (laws of), Archimedes' principle.*)

**pressure law:** this law states that the pressure of a fixed mass of gas at constant volume increases in proportion to the absolute temperature. It can be stated in the following algebraic form:

provided that $m$ and $V$ are constant, $p \propto T$

$$\text{or } \frac{p_1}{T_1} = \frac{p_2}{T_2} = \text{constant}$$

Although the law is easily derived from the *ideal gas equation*, it is an experimental law and its validation by experiment was largely the work of the Frenchman Gay Lussac (1802). (See *ideal gas equation, Boyle's law, Charles' law.*)

**primary energy sources:** see *energy sources.*

**principle of moments** states that, for a rigid body to be in equilibrium, the sum of the clockwise moments acting on the body must equal the sum of the anticlockwise moments acting on the body.

If this condition on the moments is satisfied, the body will not turn. But another condition must also be satisfied for the body to be in equilibrium: there must be no net force on the body in any one direction. (See *forces in equilibrium, moment of a force.*)

**Worked example**

**The diagram shows a horizontal uniform steel bar AB of length 5 m and mass 76 kg. It rests on two walls. Calculate: (i) the smallest downwards force $F_B$ at end B which is just strong enough to raise a bag of mass 24 kg hanging at the far end A, and (ii) the force that the bar will then exert on the wall nearer to B. B is 1.20 m from the nearer wall.**

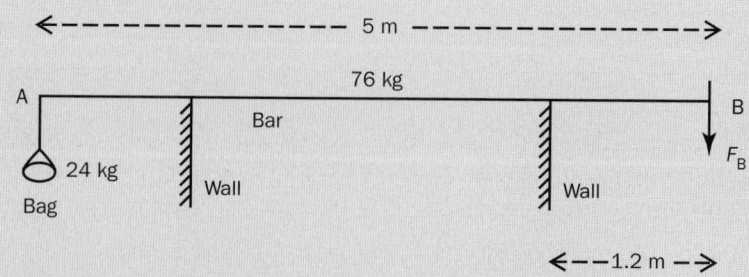

(i) Taking moments about the wall nearer to B, we have:

sum of the clockwise moments = sum of the anticlockwise moments

$$F_B \times (1.20\,\text{m}) = (76\,\text{kg})(9.8\,\text{ms}^{-2})(1.30\,\text{m}) + (24\,\text{kg})(9.8\,\text{ms}^{-2})(3.80\,\text{m})$$
$$= 968.24\,\text{Nm} + 893.76\,\text{Nm} = 1862\,\text{Nm}$$
$$F_B = (1862\,\text{Nm})/(1.20\,\text{m}) = 1.55\,\text{kN}$$

(ii) The downwards force on the wall is the sum of the three downwards forces the wall supports when the bar is about to tip, that is:

$$0.745\,\text{N} + 0.235\,\text{kN} + 1.55\,\text{kN} = 2.53\,\text{kN}$$

**principle of superposition** states that the disturbance at a point where two wave motions meet is the vector sum of the disturbances from each of the two waves at that point. With two sound waves, the disturbances will be *displacements* in two different directions, so the *parallelogram law* operates. With light, the right answers can generally be reached by adding the waves according to their *amplitudes* and their *phase difference* (or their path difference). This sounds all right but leaves difficulties — for example, how is light energy redirected from the dark parts of an interference pattern into the brighter parts? All too soon we are into *quantum mechanics.*

The principle of superposition is a statement of how two waves combine when they meet. Do not confuse it with the conditions for constructive and destructive *interference.*

**progressive and stationary waves:** see *stationary wave* for a contrast between these two phenomena.

**progressive waves** carry energy of oscillation through a medium if they are mechanical waves or through space if they are *electromagnetic waves.* (See *stationary wave, longitudinal waves, transverse waves, sound waves.*)

**projectiles** are objects, usually solid, which are thrown upwards ('projected') from the Earth's surface, mostly at an angle to the vertical, only to come down again. The situation is analysed in the usual way for *two-dimensional motion*, using the *equations of motion.* The horizontal and vertical motions are tackled separately. This is because the only force acting is gravity, which acts vertically downwards. The projectile's acceleration is zero in the horizontal direction and $g$ in the vertical direction.

**Worked example**

**A rubber ball is thrown to the ground at an angle and bounces 2.5 m high. It hits the ground again 4.0 m further on. With what velocity did the ball leave the ground at its first bounce?**

This question requires you to determine the horizontal and vertical components of the ball's velocity at the instant when it first leaves the ground.

First, find the sideways velocity component from the time in the air for the first bounce. We use the fact that at the midpoint of the bounce, the ball's vertical velocity is zero.

Data: $s = 2.5\,\text{m}$, $a = -9.8\,\text{ms}^{-2}$, $v = 0\,\text{ms}^{-1}$. Find $t$.

$$s = vt - \tfrac{1}{2}at^2$$
$$2.5 = 0 - \tfrac{1}{2}\left(-9.8\,\text{ms}^{-2}\right)t^2$$
$$t = \sqrt{(5.0/9.8)} = 0.714\,\text{s}$$

The first bounce lasts for twice this time, i.e. $2 \times 0.714$ seconds.

The horizontal velocity component is displacement/time:

$$(4.0\,\text{m})/\left(2\times 0.714\,\text{s}\right) = 2.8\,\text{ms}^{-1}\,(\text{to 2 s.f.})$$

Now we can calculate the vertical component of the ball's velocity at the instant when it first leaves the ground.

Data: $s = 2.5\,\text{m}$, $a = -9.8\,\text{ms}^{-2}$, $v = 0\,\text{ms}^{-1}$. Find $u$.

$$v^2 = u^2 + 2as$$
$$u^2 = v^2 - 2as = 0 - 2\left(-9.8\,\text{ms}^{-2}\right) \times 2.5\,\text{m} = 49\,\text{m}^2\text{s}^{-2}$$
$$u = 7.0\,\text{ms}^{-1}$$

The ball's initial velocity can now be found by calculating its magnitude (speed) and direction from the horizontal and vertical components:

$$\text{speed}^2 = 7.0^2 + 2.8^2 = 56.84\,\text{m}^2\text{s}^{-2}$$
$$\text{speed} = 7.54\,\text{m}\,\text{s}^{-1}$$

The angle $\theta$ that the velocity vector makes with the horizontal is given by

$$\tan\theta = 7.0 / 2.8 = 2.5$$
$$\theta = \tan^{-1} 2.5 = 68.2°$$

**proton:** an *elementary particle* that has positive charge of the same magnitude as the negative charge on the *electron* but whose mass is almost equal to the mass of a hydrogen atom. A hydrogen atom (hydrogen-1) has a single proton for its nucleus.

**proton decay and neutron decay** are examples of the weak interaction at work. Protons and neutrons are both baryons and their quark structures are (uud) for the proton and (udd) for the neutron. The up quark u has charge $+\tfrac{2}{3}e$; the down quark d has charge $-\tfrac{1}{3}e$. The charge total for the proton is $+e$ while the charge total for the neutron is zero. When a neutron decays into a proton or vice versa, a beta particle is created to keep the charge in balance. But the beta particle is a lepton, so an antineutrino has to be created to conserve lepton number. It helps to tabulate the reactions and the quantum numbers that are conserved.

| | Neutron decay | | | | | | | Proton decay | | | | | | |
|---|---|---|---|---|---|---|---|---|---|---|---|---|---|---|
| | n | → | $p^+$ | + | $\beta^-$ | + | $\nu_e$ | p | → | n | + | $\beta^+$ | + | $\nu_e$ |
| Baryon number *B* | 1 | = | 1 | + | 0 | + | 0 | 1 | = | 1 | + | 0 | + | 0 |
| Charge *Q* | 0 | = | (+1) | + | (–1) | + | 0 | 1 | = | 0 | + | 1 | + | 0 |
| Lepton number *L* | 0 | = | 0 | + | (+1) | + | (–1) | 0 | = | 0 | + | (–1) | + | (+1) |

These decay processes are illustrated in the entry *Feynman diagrams*. Those diagrams underline the fact that the beta particles and antineutrinos are the decay products of the W and Z exchange particles and that the exchange particles momentarily conserve the charge during the reactions.

**proton magnetometer:** a device used to measure weak magnetic fields such as the Earth's field or the fields of weakly magnetised archaeological artefacts. It makes use of the fact that protons (the nuclei of hydrogen atoms) precess about a magnetic field; that is, they spin, and the axis about which they spin is at an angle to the magnetic field and rotates around it like a spinning top.

To measure the strength of the Earth's magnetic field, a sample of a hydrogen-containing substance such as oil is exposed to a strong field inside a solenoid. The protons precess about this field. The current to the solenoid is then switched off so that the applied field falls to zero. The protons now reorient themselves to precess about the Earth's field. As they do so, they emit a weak radio signal whose frequency is proportional to the *magnetic field strength*. This frequency is measured and the field calculated. (This is an example of magnetic resonance, which is the basis of *MRI* scanning.)

**proton number,** *Z*, is another name for *atomic number*, the number of *protons* in the *nucleus*.

**pulse code modulation** (PCM) is the transmission of information in the form of a stream of equal-sized pulses or digital bits. An essential part of the process is *analogue-to-digital conversion* before transmission and *digital-to-analogue conversion* after transmission. Information which is transmitted in the form of digital bits can be cleaned of any noise during reception. This elimination of noise is a major advantage of PCM. Information is tied to the bit stream by a coding process. The bit stream might, for example, be broken up into a sequence of 12-bit groups, each consisting of two start bits, two stop bits and eight bits in the middle which can be coded in 256 different ways.

**p–V diagram:** see *engine cycle*.

**quantisation** is an essential part of any *analogue-to-digital conversion* process. The voltage amplitude of the analogue signal at the input of a converter is a continuous variable. This infinite number of possible input values must now be shared among a fixed number of possible digital values at the output of the converter. It follows that each digital value corresponds to a range of analogue values, and small differences within this range can never be recovered. We say that the analogue values have been quantised. Quantisation always implies a small information loss.

**quantisation of charge** means that electric charge is not a continuously variable quantity. The smallest possible increase or decrease in quantity of electric charge is the *electronic charge* $-e$ (charge on one electron), the value of which was established by *Millikan's oil drop experiment*. Although quarks may have charges which are fractions of $e$, changes in charge always take place in multiples of $e$.

**quantum mechanics** is a term that covers those approaches to theories of fields and the structure of matter which hinge on the idea that the magnitude of a physical variable must be one of a discrete set of values. For example, the magnitude of an electron's angular momentum can only be $nh/(2\pi)$ where $n$ is an integer. A consequence of this is the quantisation of the orbital electron energies in an atom and a detailed explanation of atomic spectra.

**quarks** are the elementary particles from which *hadrons* are constructed. Scattering experiments with 50 000 GeV electrons show that quarks, like electrons, are less than $10^{-18}$ m in diameter — that is, smaller than can be measured. Over 200 heavier particles discovered in cosmic rays or particle accelerators can be shown to be built up from six different kinds of quark and their antiquarks. These heavier particles are unstable and decay eventually into protons, neutrons, electrons and electron antineutrinos. Quarks are subject to all *fundamental interactions*. The strong interaction holds quarks together in a *nucleon*, and holds nucleons together in a nucleus.

That quarks, unlike leptons, are subject to the strong interaction is attributed to a quality possessed by quarks known as *colour*. Colour is a bit like charge but comes in three kinds, not two. The colours are called red, green and blue. The antiparticle quarks have anticolours. Quarks will form stable groupings only if the colours combine to form a neutral set: three quarks of three different colours (making white) form a baryon; three antiquarks with three different anticolours form an antibaryon; or two opposite colours (e.g. red and anti-red) form a meson. The main properties of the six known kinds of quark are listed in the following table.

| Flavour | | Generation | Mass/MeV | Charge/e | Baryon no. | S | C | B | T |
|---|---|---|---|---|---|---|---|---|---|
| d | down | 1 | 5–15 | –1/3 | 1/3 | | | | |
| u | up | 1 | 2–8 | +2/3 | 1/3 | | | | |
| s | strange | 2 | 100–300 | –1/3 | 1/3 | –1 | | | |
| c | charm | 2 | 1000–1600 | +2/3 | 1/3 | | 1 | | |
| b | bottom | 3 | 4100–4500 | –1/3 | 1/3 | | | –1 | |
| t | top | 3 | 180000 | +2/3 | 1/3 | | | | 1 |

Flavour is conserved in strong interactions. The four quantum numbers S, C, B and T take opposite values in the antiparticles and are involved in the conservation of the individual flavours. Flavour is not conserved in processes controlled by the weak interaction (see *proton decay and neutron decay*). Antiquarks have opposite values of charge and baryon number to those listed in the table. All quarks have spin ±½ and these spins combine to give ±3/2 or ±½ for baryons and ±1 or 0 for mesons.

The strong interaction responsible for bonding quarks together in hadrons is associated with eight different *exchange particles* or gauge bosons called gluons. A gluon carries both colour and anticolour; it can bind to another gluon or bind two quarks together. The bonding is so strong that the energy needed to pull a quark out of a nucleon is always sufficient to create a second meson or boson. Quarks cannot be isolated.

A proton consists of two up quarks and one down quark (uud), giving a charge $+e$ and baryon number 1. The antiproton has charge $-e$ and baryon number –1. The neutron (udd) has charge zero and baryon number 1. Mesons consist of a quark and an antiquark, so their baryon number is always 0; but because the flavours are different, the charge may be $+e$, $-e$ or 0.

**quasars** (quasi-stellar objects) are stellar objects which were formerly known as 'quasi-stellar radio sources' because the first quasars were detected by their radio emissions. They share four characteristics: a large *red shift* which implies that their distances are greater than those of remote galaxies; luminosities (as calculated using the inverse square law) in excess of many galaxies; a small size comparable with the solar system; and a varied radiation output which includes visible light, radio waves and X-ray radiation all varying in intensity over a time scale of about a year.

It is generally thought by astronomers that a quasar is a region at the centre of a galaxy; at its heart is a supermassive black hole. As matter is sucked into the region around the black hole, vast amounts of radiation are emitted.

# R

**radial electric field:** the electric field near an isolated point electric charge. The diagram below shows the field lines (solid) and the equipotential lines (dashed) near an isolated positive charge. Notice how the field lines get further apart as the field weakens. Notice, also, how the spacing of the equipotential lines increases if the change in potential from line to line is always the same. (See *field lines (electric), equipotential lines.*)

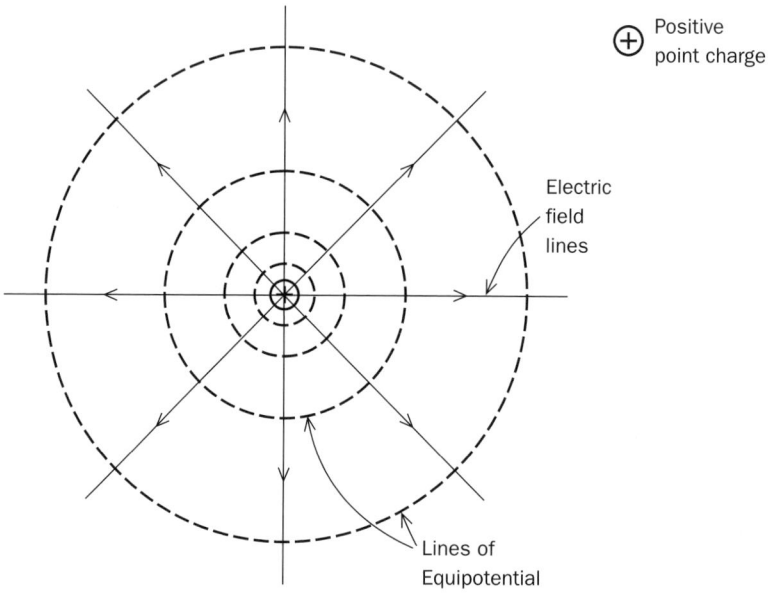


**radial magnetic field:** the magnetic field in the space between the poles of a correctly shaped horseshoe magnet and a soft iron cylinder placed symmetrically between the poles. The magnetic field within the space is everywhere aligned with the direction from the centre of the cylinder.

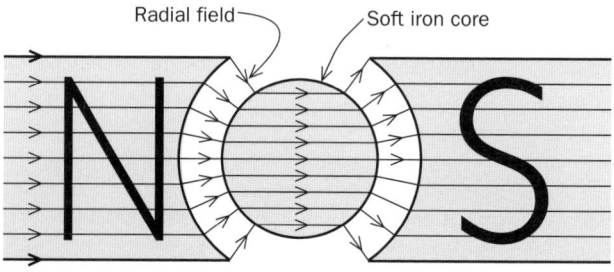

A coil suspended within the radial field is effectively immersed in a magnetic field parallel to the plane of the coil. In these circumstances, if the coil carries current, the *torque* on the coil has a maximum value for that current. (See *electric motor.*)

**radian** is a unit of *angle.* One radian is the angle subtended at the centre of a circle by an arc whose length is equal to one radius. The symbol for radian is 'rad'. Since the length of the circumference of a circle is $2\pi \times$ radius, 360° corresponds to $2\pi$ radians.

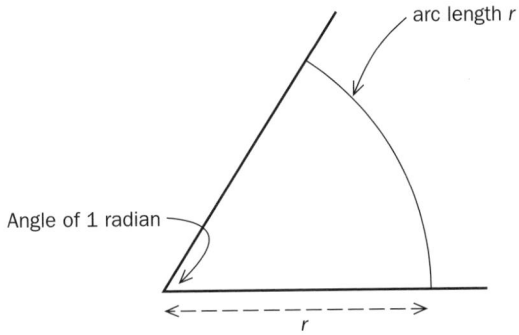


**radiation** is energy travelling through space in the form of *photons.* (See *electromagnetic spectrum.*)

**radiation detectors** are broadly of two kinds: those which are used for *ionising radiations* (mostly alpha, beta and gamma radiation, X-rays and sometimes UV) and those which are used to observe electromagnetic radiation only, from UV down to radio waves.

Ionising radiations are detected with photography, GM tubes, cloud chambers, bubble chambers, ionisation chambers, scintillation counters, *gamma cameras* and solid state detectors. Longer-wave electromagnetic radiation is detected by bolometers, thermopiles and *light-dependent resistors* as well as by photography. For longer wavelengths, aerials are also used.

**radiation dosage** is a measure of the effect on living tissue of exposure to radiation. It involves three related ideas: absorbed dose, quality factor, and the dose equivalent. Absorbed dose is the beam energy absorbed per kilogram of body tissue. The unit, the gray (Gy), is an absorbed dose of $1\,\mathrm{J\,kg^{-1}}$.

Quality factor is a number with no unit. It is defined as a ratio:

$$\text{quality factor} = \frac{\text{absorbed dose using 250 kV X-radiation}}{\text{absorbed dose of radiation having the same effect}}$$

Dose equivalent (also known as effective dose) in sieverts (Sv) equals absorbed dose × quality factor. The total dose equivalent for a patient subjected to different types of radiation is the sum of the individual dose equivalents.

Radiation damage that is certain to happen, such as tissue destruction, is said to be non-stochastic. Damage such as mutation, which may or may not happen, is said to be stochastic. (Stochastic is another word for random.)

**radiation flux:** see *intensity of radiation.*

**radiation loss** is the energy radiated into the surrounding space by a hot object. (See *Stefan's law.*)

**radio waves** are *electromagnetic waves* with wavelengths longer than about ten centimetres. The modest frequencies (MHz or lower) have limited information-carrying capacity, and this has led to 'crowding of the air waves'. Radio waves play an important role in *MRI* scanning.

**radioactive decay** is the *spontaneous* but delayed emission of an alpha or beta particle (positive or negative) from a *nucleus*. The atomic number (proton number) of the nucleus must change. *Gamma emission* is a way of ridding the nucleus of excess energy when it is in an excited state following a radioactive decay event. (See *alpha decay, beta decay.*)

**radioisotopes** are found in nature only if they have long half-lives. Short-lived radioisotopes are mostly prepared by irradiation techniques. Examples include alpha particle bombardment [e.g. $^{121}Sb\ (\alpha,2n)\ ^{123}I$] and neutron bombardment [e.g. $^{130}Te(n,\gamma)^{131}Te\ (\beta^-)\ ^{131}I$]. Where the half-life is shorter than a day or so, radioisotopes are prepared close to the point of use. An example is the preparation of the metastable isotope $^{99m}Tc$ (half-life six hours) which is a decay product of $^{99}Mo$ (half-life almost three days) and is separated from the molybdenum by washing the molybdenum with saline solution. The saline dissolves the pertechnetate ions but not the molybdenate ions.

**random error** is a discrepancy, which comes about by accident, between the true value of a physical quantity and the actual value of the measurement of the physical quantity. A digital clock never stops or starts at exactly the right time; a scale might be read slightly on the low side or slightly on the high side. *Parallax error* is a common example of a random error. There is no way of knowing the size of the random error present in a single measurement since the true value will not be known. But random errors can be reduced by taking the average of several independent measurements. This is possible because a random error is as likely to be positive as negative, to be larger or smaller. (If you study statistics, then you will notice that the different measurements must be normally distributed about the true value unless there is a systematic error.) Random errors, like *systematic errors*, contribute to the *uncertainty* of a measurement.

**random motion** is the motion of an atom in a fluid whose velocity changes randomly in both magnitude and direction as a consequence of repeated collisions. The distance travelled between collisions is also random. A change is random if the new value cannot be determined from previous values. (Compare with *Brownian motion.*)

**randomness and radioactive decay** are two concepts which are linked by the laws of probability. An event is random if the probability of its happening in a given time interval depends on the length of the time interval but is independent of when the time interval begins (i.e. independent of age). This idea can be stated mathematically and applied to radioactive decay.

Let $\lambda$ be the probability per second that a nucleus will decay. Then the probability that a nucleus will decay during a time interval of length $\Delta t$ seconds is $\lambda\Delta t$.

If there are $N$ nuclei waiting to decay at some time $t$, then the expected number $\Delta N$ of nuclei which will decay between times $t$ and $t + \Delta t$ is $N \times \lambda\Delta t$. That is:

$$\Delta N = -N\lambda\Delta t = -\lambda N\Delta t$$

This equation is called the *fundamental law of radioactive decay.* The negative sign tells us that $\Delta N$ is a reduction in the value of $N$. The probability $\lambda$ is defined by the above equation; it is the probability per second that a nucleus will decay, and is called the decay constant, with unit second$^{-1}$. (See *decay constant, exponential law of radioactive decay.*)

**rate of change** of a physical quantity is the increase per unit time in the magnitude of the physical quantity. The increase per unit time of the temperature $T$ shown in the graph can be written as either $\Delta T/\Delta t$ or $dT/dt$. The difference between these two expressions is of some importance and can be understood from the diagram. The diagram is a graph of temperature $T$ against time $t$. The increment in time, $t_B - t_A$, is written as $\Delta t$. The corresponding rise in temperature, $T_B - T_A$, is written as $\Delta T$.

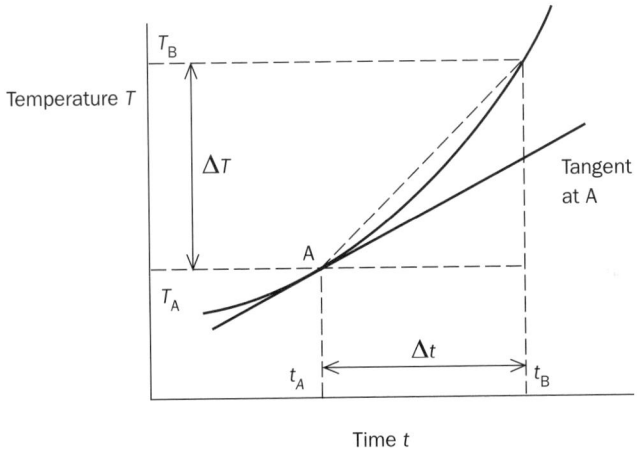


The average rate of change of temperature during the time interval $t_A$ to $t_B$ is written $\Delta T/\Delta t$. The limiting value of this average rate of change as the time interval $\Delta t$ is made progressively smaller until it approaches zero is written $dT/dt$. This is the instantaneous value of the rate of change.

$\Delta t$ implies a small but finite time increment, $dt$ represents an infinitesimal time increment. Rate of change is positive for a growth and negative for a decay. $dT/dt$ at time $t_A$ is the *gradient* of the tangent to the curve at the point A.

The $x$-axis does not have to be a time scale. Using more formal language, the rate of change of a dependent physical variable $y$ with respect to an independent physical variable $x$ is the gradient of the tangent to the graph of $y$ against $x$ at the relevant value of $x$.

**rate of cooling** means rate of fall of temperature. It does not mean rate of loss of heat. It equals the gradient of a temperature against time graph at the relevant instant. (See *Newton's law of cooling.*)

**ray diagram:** a diagram of an optical lens or mirror system which accounts for the formation of the image. A ray diagram illustrates the formation of a real image by showing the rays of light diverging from the *object position*, meeting again at the image position and thereafter diverging away from the image position. For a virtual image, the rays diverge from a point behind the lens or mirror. Rules for constructing a ray diagram involving a lens are given in the entry on the *lens equation*. (See *ray optics.*)

**ray optics** is an analysis of mirrors and lenses based on the idea that light travels in straight lines. It is successful except where the outcome of an optical arrangement hinges on the *wave nature of light*.

**Rayleigh criterion:** see *resolving power*.

**reactance** is the ratio of peak voltage to peak current for a capacitor or for the inductive component of an inductor (how the inductor would behave if it had zero ohmic resistance). Reactance is $1/(\omega C)$ for a capacitor and $\omega L$ for a pure inductor. The SI unit for reactance is the ohm ($\Omega$). Reactance differs from resistance in that the voltage and current for a capacitor or for a pure inductor are not in phase, that is, they peak at different times. (See *capacitive reactance, inductive reactance.*)

**rectification, half-wave and full-wave,** are methods for changing an alternating current into a direct current. Remember that 'alternating' means 'changing direction' and not 'changing magnitude'.

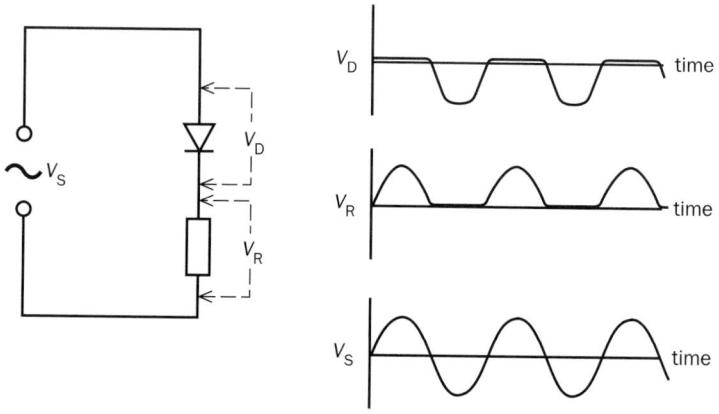


The half-wave rectifier in the circuit above consists of an alternating power supply in series with a diode and resistor. Assuming that the diode has infinite resistance for current in one direction and zero resistance to current in the other direction, the circuit will conduct in alternate half-cycles. The input voltage falls across the diode ($V_D$) in the non-conducting half-cycles and across the resistor ($V_R$) during the conducting half-cycles. The three graphs on the right-hand side of the diagram show how these two voltages add up to the supply voltage ($V_S$).

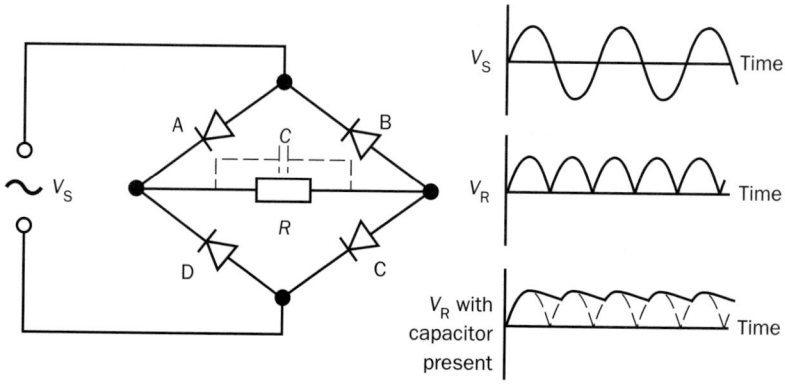

The full-wave rectifying circuit shown in this second diagram employs four diodes in a bridge circuit. Whatever the direction of the voltage from the AC power supply, current flows through the resistor at the centre of the bridge from left to right. It helps to remember that the four diodes should all point towards the left (or all point towards the right, in which case the current in the resistor flows the other way). During positive half-cycles, A and C conduct, so that current flows downwards through A–R–C and back to the supply. During negative half-cycles, D and B conduct. The second graph on the right shows the pulsating but direct voltage $V_R$ across the resistor. This is the output voltage and the resistor represents the load. A large capacitor connected in parallel with the load smoothes the output voltage.

The third graph shows the effect on the output voltage $V_R$ of connecting a capacitor across the load. The capacitor charges up when the input voltage is growing and discharges slowly when the input voltage falls away. After a few cycles the circuit reaches the situation indicated in the graph with a small ripple added to a steady DC voltage. The ripple amplitude increases if more current is drawn for the load resistor.

The two circuit diagrams are drawn on the assumption that the diode is perfect. In practice, diodes need a voltage drop of half a volt or so in the forward direction. If, therefore, four diodes are used to fully rectify a low voltage supply (say 3V at the peak) the output voltage will include a gap between the pulse as shown below.

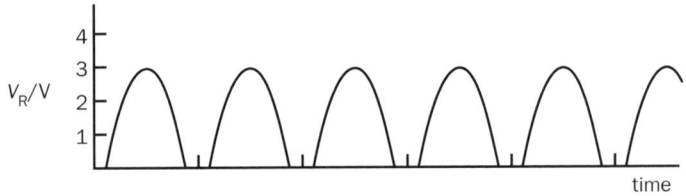


**rectilinear motion:** see *straight line motion.*

**red giant:** the first stage in the decay of a main sequence *star* whose mass is less than about eight solar masses. Although light output during this stage is much higher than during the main sequence stage, the proportionate increase in surface area is even greater. Therefore, less radiation gets emitted per unit surface area, surface temperature falls and the peak wavelength shifts towards the red. See *end states of stars, Wien's law.*

**red shift:** the displacement of spectral lines in the spectra of astronomical objects towards longer wavelengths, and effect which arises from the objects' motion away from an observer on Earth. This is an example of the *Doppler effect.* The greater the recessional velocity of the source of light, the greater the red shift. *Hubble's law* relates the recessional velocity of galaxies to their distances apart.

Any object with a component of its velocity towards the Earth will show the opposite effect, a blue shift of spectral lines towards shorter wavelengths.

**reflection of light:** the change of direction of a light ray at the surface of a medium which ensures that the light ray remains in the one medium. The change of direction obeys two laws known as the laws of reflection.

1 The incident ray, the reflected ray and the normal to the reflecting surface at the point of incidence all lie in the same plane.
2 The angle of incidence equals the angle of reflection.

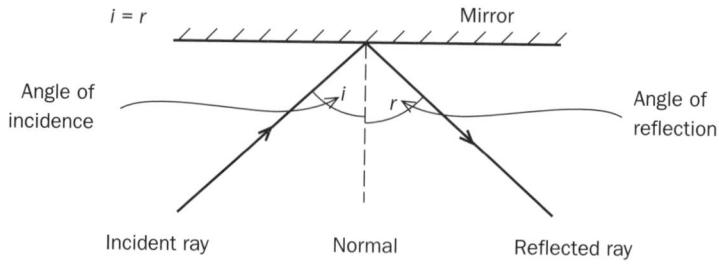


The first law states that reflection is a two-dimensional phenomenon which can be represented by a two-dimensional diagram on a flat piece of paper. The second states the principle to be followed when drawing these diagrams.

**refraction of light** is the bending of light when it passes from one transparent medium into another. The change of direction obeys two laws known as the laws of refraction. These are:

1 The incident ray, the refracted ray and the normal to the refracting surface at the point of incidence all lie in the same plane.

2 The sine of the angle of incidence divided by the sine of the angle of refraction is a constant for two given media.

The diagram illustrates a typical situation.

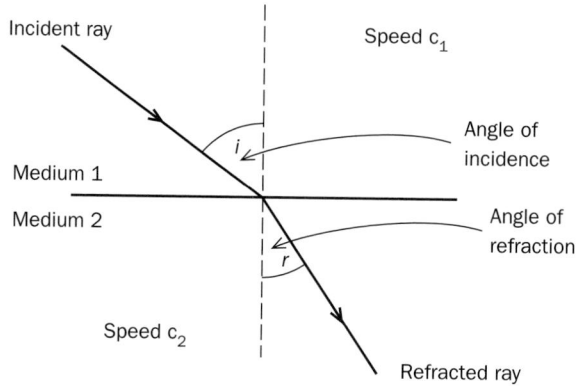


The first law states that refraction is a two-dimensional phenomenon which can be represented by a two-dimensional diagram on a flat piece of paper. The second states the rule which enables us to trace the path of a ray of light from one medium into another. The constant defined by the second law of refraction is called the refractive index, usually written with symbol $n$. With this in mind, the second law can be rewritten in the form

$$\frac{\text{sine of the angle of incidence}}{\text{sine of the angle of refraction}} = \text{refractive index}$$

$$\frac{\sin i}{\sin r} = n$$

This last equation is known as Snell's law; it defines refractive index. But electromagnetic theory gives us another relationship:

$$\text{refractive index} = \frac{\text{speed of light in the incident medium}}{\text{speed of light in the refracting medium}} = \frac{c_1}{c_2}$$

It is usual practice to identify the materials and the direction using subscripts — a subscripted prefix for the material on the incident side and a subscripted suffix for the material on the far side. For example, for light travelling from air to glass:

$$_{\text{air}}n_{\text{glass}} = \frac{\sin\theta_{\text{air}}}{\sin\theta_{\text{glass}}} = \frac{\text{speed of light in air}}{\text{speed of light in glass}} = \frac{c_{\text{air}}}{c_{\text{glass}}} = 1.52$$

1.52 is the refractive index of ordinary glass (called crown glass). Heavier flint glasses have higher refractive indices. For light travelling from glass into air:

$$_{\text{glass}}n_{\text{air}} = \frac{\sin\theta_{\text{glass}}}{\sin\theta_{\text{air}}} = \frac{\text{speed of light in glass}}{\text{speed of light in air}} = \frac{c_{\text{glass}}}{c_{\text{air}}} = \frac{1}{1.52}$$

These statements can be generalised for any two transparent materials:

$$_1n_2 = \frac{\sin\theta_1}{\sin\theta_2} = \frac{c_1}{c_2} = \frac{1}{_2n_1}$$

(See *refraction of light*, *total internal reflection*, *critical angle*.)

**refrigerator:** a device which removes internal energy from a low temperature container and discards it to the surroundings at a higher temperature. It is a *heat engine* worked backwards; work $W$ is done on the refrigerator, internal energy $Q_2$ is removed from the container, and energy $(W + Q_2) = Q_1$ is transferred to the surroundings.

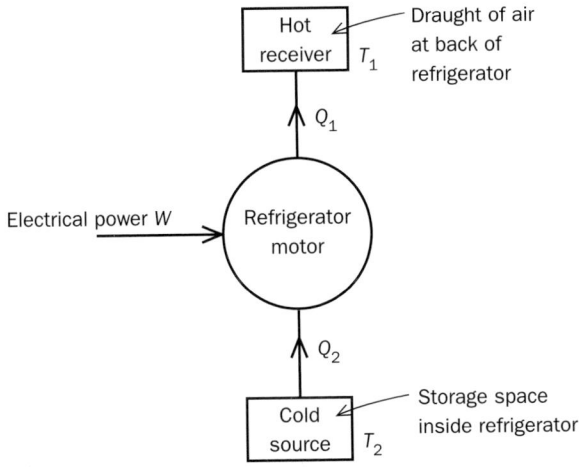


It follows from the theory of the heat engine that:

$$\frac{W}{Q_1} = \frac{Q_1 - Q_2}{Q_1} = \left(\frac{T_1 - T_2}{T_1}\right)$$

If the heat engine being worked backwards is not a perfect engine, the part of the expression involving absolute temperatures (in large brackets) fails.

The purpose of a refrigerator is to reduce the internal energy of the container. The coefficient of performance for a refrigerator is defined with this purpose in view:

$$\frac{Q_2}{W} = \frac{Q_2}{Q_1 - Q_2} = \left(\frac{T_1}{T_1 - T_2}\right)$$

As before, if the engine of the refrigerator is less than perfect, the part of the expression in large brackets fails. (See *heat engine concept, heat pump.*)

**reinforced concrete** is concrete which is poured over a number of steel rods so that it sets to give a beam that can withstand greater bending forces than concrete would be able to on its own. It should not be confused with pre-stressed concrete. (See *composite materials.*)

**relative atomic mass** is the number of times the atom of a *nuclide* is heavier than one-twelfth of the mass of a carbon-12 atom. (A nuclide is a substance whose atomic and mass numbers are specified.) The word equation definition is:

$$\text{relative atomic mass of a nuclide} = \frac{\text{mass of an atom of the nuclide}}{\text{mass of an atom of } {}^{12}_{6}\text{C}} \times 12$$

Alternatively, the relative atomic mass of a nuclide is numerically equal to how many times the mass of an atom of the nuclide is greater than the *unified atomic mass unit.*

**relative molar mass** of a substance is defined by the word equation

$$\text{relative molar mass of a substance} = \frac{\text{mass of one mole of the substance}}{\text{mass of one mole of } {}^{12}_{6}\text{C}} \times 12$$

(See *mole.*)

**relative permeability** $\mu_r$ is the ratio of the *magnetic field strength B* within a material to the magnetic field strength $B_0$ of the magnetising field:

$$\mu_r = \frac{B}{B_0}$$

Its value is slightly less than unity for diamagnetic substances, slightly greater than unity for paramagnetic substances, and large and positive for ferromagnetic substances. (See also *solenoid.*)

**relative permittivity** of an insulating substance is the factor by which the *capacitance* of a vacuum-filled capacitor would increase if the space between the plates were to be filled by the insulating substance. It is defined for a particular material by the following word equation:

$$\text{relative permittivity } \varepsilon_r = \frac{\text{capacitance of a capacitor filled with the material}}{\text{capacitance of the same capacitor filled with vacuum}}$$

$\varepsilon_r$ is defined as a ratio and, as a consequence, has no unit.

Most dielectric materials have relative permittivities less than 10. The success of a dielectric material in increasing the range of capacitor values while keeping the overall dimensions of the capacitor small is mainly due to the ability to manufacture the dielectric material in the form of a very thin sheet. The conducting plates can then be held a very small distance apart without touching.

**relativity:** see *special relativity, general relativity.*

**renewable energy sources** are *energy sources* such as solar energy, *biofuels*, wind power, tidal power and hydroelectric power that draw their power from the recent activity of the Sun, or geothermal power, which are not finite resources in the same sense as something like coal. (See *finite energy sources.*)

**resistance** is the ratio of the *potential difference* (voltage) across a conductor to the current that it carries. The symbol used is $R$ and the SI unit is the ohm ($\Omega$). Resistance and its unit are defined by the word equations

$$\text{resistance} = \frac{\text{potential difference}}{\text{current}}$$

$$\text{ohm} = \frac{\text{volt}}{\text{ampere}}$$

Provided that it carries a stable current for a particular voltage across it, any circuit component or circuit, however complex, has resistance calculated from the definition in the word equation above. *Ohm's law* applies only to some conductors — those that obey it (i.e. those for which $R$ is constant as the voltage varies). (See also *resistivity, internal resistance.*)

**resistance thermometer:** a thermometer which relies on the variation of electrical resistance with temperature. Platinum resistance thermometers are extremely accurate, but are also expensive and bulky and need a lot of care. They are generally used as so-called secondary standards (or, even worse, as sub-standards) for calibrating other thermometers.

**resistivity,** for a material which is available in the form of a wire, is defined by the word equation

$$\text{resistivity} = \text{resistance} \times \frac{\text{area of cross section}}{\text{length}}$$

$$\rho = R \times \frac{A}{l}$$

$$\Omega\text{m} = \Omega \times \frac{\text{m}^2}{\text{m}}$$

Resistance is a property of a circuit component, typically a wire. Resistivity, on the other hand, is a property of the material the component is made from, typically a metal. The graph on page 204 shows the resistivity of tungsten wire at different absolute temperatures.

(Note that, in an examination, you would lose all the marks if in a sentence definition of resistivity you wrote 'per unit area of cross-section per unit length', because 'area' is in the numerator of the fraction and is not a 'per'. The word equation above is unambiguous, easier and quicker to state.) (See *conductivity.*)

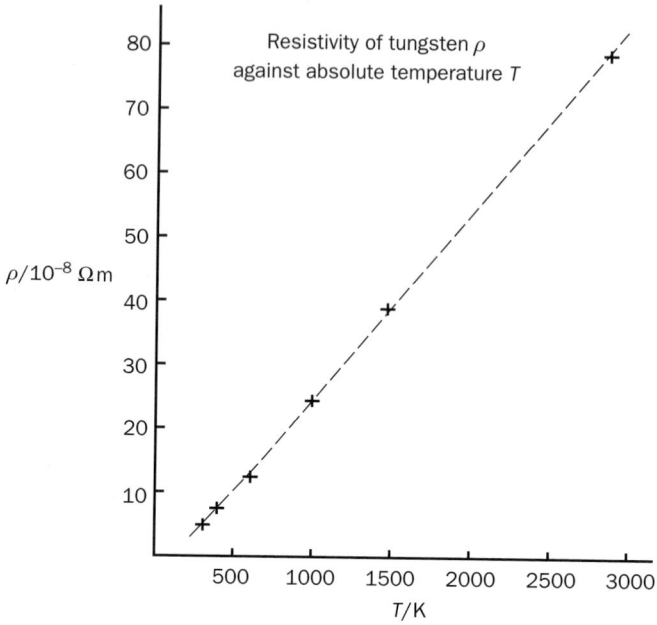


**resistors in parallel** are resistors which are all connected across the same two points as shown in the diagram below. It is useful to know how to replace these three resistors by a single resistor, of resistance $R$, without changing either the total current $I$ drawn from the rest of the circuit or the potential difference $V$ across the arrangement.

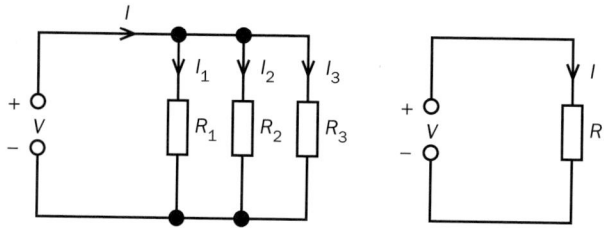


The current $I$ in the single resistor must equal the sum of the three currents in the three resistors:

$$I = I_1 + I_2 + I_3$$

Applying Ohm's law to this condition gives

$$\frac{V}{R} = \frac{V}{R_1} + \frac{V}{R_2} + \frac{V}{R_3}$$

The voltage $V$ cancels throughout and we are left with

$$\frac{1}{R} = \frac{1}{R_1} + \frac{1}{R_2} + \frac{1}{R_3}$$

**Worked example**

**Find the value of the unknown resistance *R* in the circuit shown.**

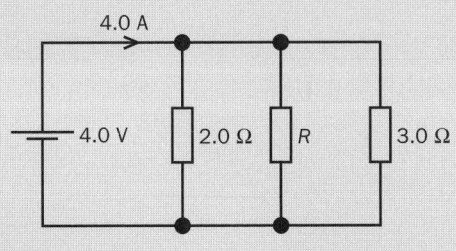


The equivalent resistance of all three resistors equals (4 V)/(4.0 A) = 1 Ω, that is,

$$\frac{1}{1} = \frac{1}{2} + \frac{1}{R} + \frac{1}{3} = \frac{5}{6} + \frac{1}{R}$$

$$\frac{1}{6} = \frac{1}{R} \quad \text{so} \quad R = 6\Omega$$

**resistors in series** are resistors which are connected end to end as shown in the diagram below. It is useful to know how to replace the three resistors by a single resistor, of resistance *R*, without changing either the current *I* drawn from the rest of the circuit or the potential difference *V* across the arrangement.

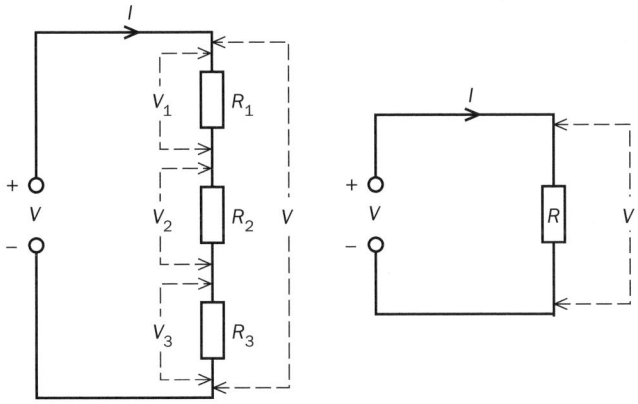


The voltage *V* across the single resistor must equal the sum of the other three voltages:

$$V = V_1 + V_2 + V_3$$

Applying Ohm's law to this condition, we have:

$$IR = I_1R_1 + I_2R_2 + I_3R_3$$

Kirchhoff's first law states that

$$I_1 = I_2 = I_3$$

and all three currents equal *I* if the resistance *R* is to be equivalent to the other three. The currents cancel through and we are left with

$$R = R_1 + R_2 + R_3$$

**Worked example**

**Find the value of the unknown resistance *R* in the circuit shown below.**

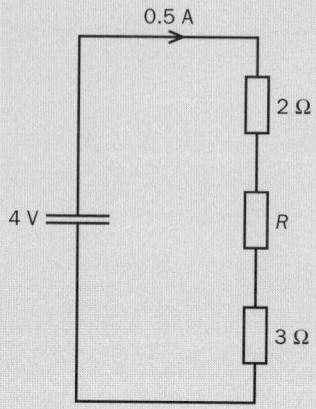


The equivalent resistance of all three resistors equals (4 V)/(0.5 A) = 8, that is,

$2\Omega + R + 3\Omega = 3\Omega$, so $R = 3\Omega$

**resolution of vectors** usually means finding the horizontal and vertical *components* of a single oblique vector. The diagram below shows a velocity vector $v$ inclined at 55° to the ground. The vertical and horizontal directions are given. Constructing two perpendiculars from the far end of the vector results in a rectangular 'parallelogram'. The horizontal component, $v\cos 55°$, and the vertical component, $v\sin 55°$, can both be read from the diagram.

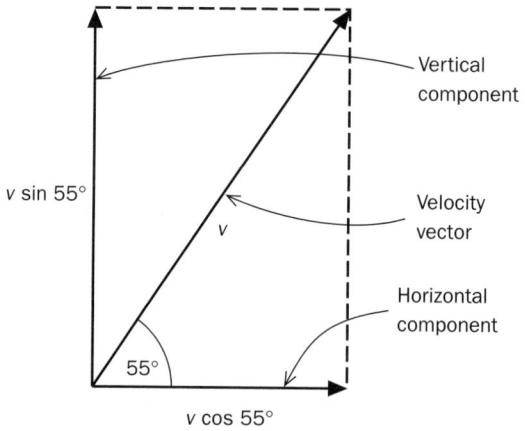


Resolving displacement and velocity vectors in this way simplifies a problem where the vertical motion is subject to gravitational force and acceleration while the horizontal motion continues at constant velocity (see *projectiles*).

A set of ***coplanar forces*** will be in equilibrium provided that the components of all the forces in each of two directions at right angles add up to zero and provided that the sum of the moments of the forces about any point in the plane is zero. (See *forces in equilibrium*.)

**resolving power** is a measure of the fineness of detail distinguishable in the focused image formed by an optical instrument or by something similar, such as a radio telescope.

The definition has a simple mathematical form which is illustrated in the diagram. The resolving power of an image-forming instrument is the minimum angular distance in radians, measured at the instrument, of two small objects in the field of view which can just be distinguished as two separate objects in the image.

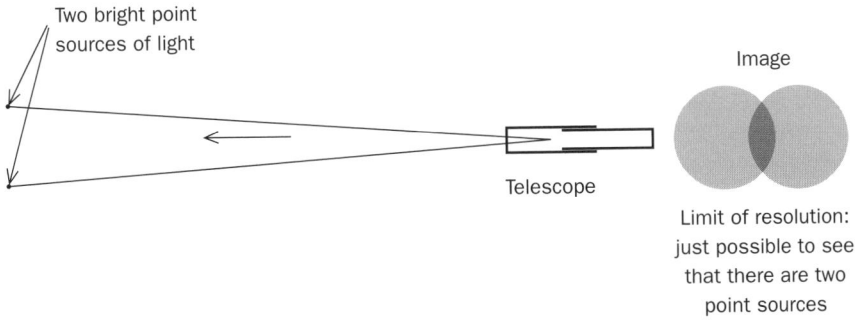


Resolving power is limited by diffraction effects in the instrument. For an optical or radio telescope, the Rayleigh criterion gives the resolving power of a telescope or other optical system in terms of the wavelength and aperture:

$$\text{resolving power } \theta \text{ in radians} = \left\{\frac{1.22\lambda}{d}\right\}$$

$$\text{or, approximately, } \theta \approx \frac{\lambda}{d}$$

where $\lambda$ is the wavelength of the light or of the radio waves focused by the instrument and $d$ is the diameter of the circular hole that limits the width of the beam of radiation entering the instrument. This diameter $d$ is called the aperture. The equation for resolving power explains why the diameters of the dishes of radio telescopes have to be so large, that is, why they need so large an aperture — radio waves have long wavelengths and $\theta$ needs to be small.

**resonance** is the setting up of large amplitude oscillations in a damped oscillator when the driver frequency matches the *natural frequency* of the oscillator. This frequency is then called the resonant frequency. The diagram below shows the change of equilibrium amplitude with driver frequency for the case where driver frequency changes but driver amplitude is constant. Also shown is the effect of heavy damping contrasted with that of light damping. The finite amplitude at zero frequency corresponds to the displacement of the system under the action of a constant displacing force.

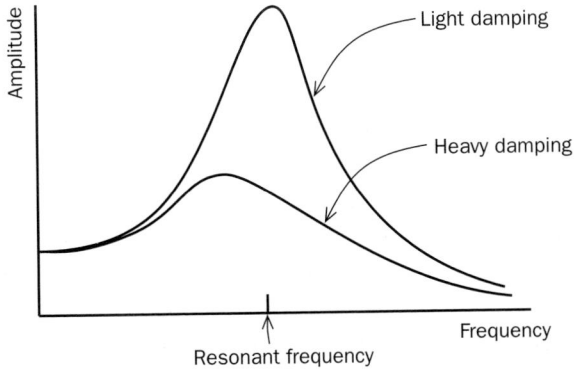

To understand the phenomenon, imagine you are pushing a child on a swing and you want to build up the amplitude with minimum effort. You will find yourself applying a force in step with the displacement and in the direction of motion. The effect of this is to ensure that your driving force matches the period of the swing and the periodic damping forces. Also, by keeping in step with the direction of motion, you ensure that the applied force is always enhancing the motion. Change slightly the frequency of the pushes you apply to the swing and you will find that, after a little while, you are so out of step that your pushes are opposing the motion of the swing and slowing it down. The more you change the frequency the worse this situation gets. The only way to succeed is to match the push frequency to the system it is pushing, and this is resonance. (See *forced oscillations.*)

**resonance in AC circuits** is of two kinds. The impedance of a series circuit has a minimum value at the resonant frequency; the impedance of a parallel circuit has a maximum value at the resonant frequency. (Impedance is the equivalent of resistance for a circuit which combines both resistance and reactance, either capacitive or inductive or both.)

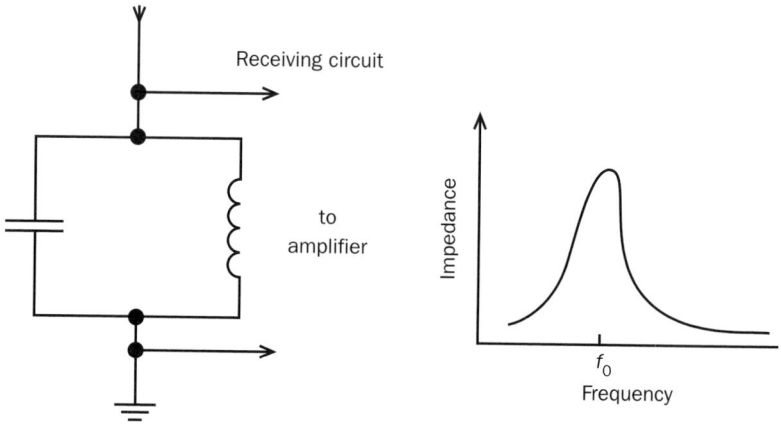


The parallel circuit shown in the diagram above is set up as a tuning circuit. The aerial picks up radio signals of many frequencies. The inductor has impedance $\omega L$; it offers a low-impedance pathway to Earth to the lower-frequency signals. The capacitor has impedance $1/(\omega C)$; it offers a low-impedance pathway to earth to the higher-frequency signals. The impedance of the parallel pair is a maximum at the angular frequency for which the two impedances are equal:

$$\omega L = \frac{1}{\omega C} \quad \text{and} \quad \omega = \frac{1}{\sqrt{(LC)}}$$

This will be the carrier frequency for the radio signal that sets up the maximum-amplitude voltage oscillation across the parallel pair and which is passed to the next stage for amplification.

The series resonant circuit is shown on the following diagram.

Should the value of the angular frequency be such that the voltage across the inductor is equal and in the opposite direction to the voltage across the capacitor, then the supply voltage will be wholly taken up with driving the current in the resistor and the current amplitude will have its maximum value. Once again, this happens at the frequency for which

$$\omega L = \frac{1}{\omega C} \quad \text{and} \quad \omega = \frac{1}{\sqrt{(LC)}}$$

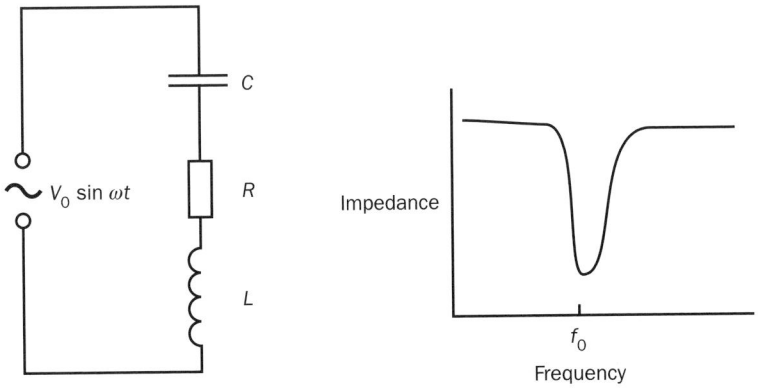


The condition of resonance needs many complete cycles to be properly set up, but since the frequencies are usually measured in kHz, this takes only a short time. Once the resonant condition is achieved, energy oscillates between the electric field in the capacitor and the magnetic field in the inductor, carried by the current. The power supply provides the electrical energy dissipation in the resistor. (See *reactance, capacitive reactance.*)

**resonance with sound waves:** see *waves on strings, waves in pipes.*

**resultant** is the name given to the single vector which equals the sum of two or more other vectors. The diagram below shows the resultant velocity (magnitude $5\,\mathrm{ms^{-1}}$) of two velocities at right angles with magnitudes $3\,\mathrm{ms^{-1}}$ and $4\,\mathrm{ms^{-1}}$. (See *vector addition, parallelogram law.*)

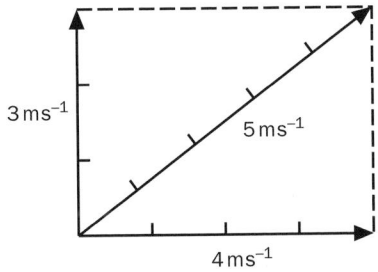


**right hand grip rule:** a rule for finding the direction of the magnetic field near a long straight wire or within a *solenoid.* For a straight wire, grasp the wire with the right hand, with the thumb pointing in the direction of the current; the fingers now curve round to point in the direction of the magnetic field. For a solenoid, grasp the outside of the solenoid with the right hand, with the fingers following the current direction in the wire; the thumb will then be pointing in the direction of the magnetic field *within* the solenoid. Either of these methods can be used for the current ring. (See *ring, solenoid, straight current-carrying wire, Maxwell's corkscrew rule.*)

**rigid bodies** are imaginary bodies which do not change shape or distort in any way when acted upon by a number of forces. The idea allows a mathematician or physicist to concentrate on the external effects of applying a set of forces to a body. Although all bodies distort to some extent when acted on by a force, for practical purposes many solid bodies can be treated as rigid. (See *rigidity.*)

**rigidity** is the ability of a solid body to retain its shape when placed under *stress.*

**ring:** one or several circular turns of a single wire bound together in a single circular loop of radius $r$. If there are $N$ turns and if current $I$ flows in the wire, then the *magnetic field strength* $B$ at the centre of the ring is given by

$$B = \frac{\mu_0 NI}{2r}$$

The shape of the magnetic field is shown in the diagram. The direction of the field can be found from the *right hand grip rule* (imagine that the ring is a short solenoid).

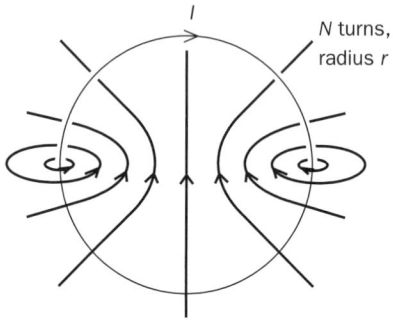


**r.m.s.** (root mean square) values of alternating currents and voltages are the direct currents and voltages which would have the same power dissipation in a resistive load. If $I_0$ and $V_0$ represent the peak values of the *alternating current and voltage*, and $I_{\text{r.m.s}}$ and $V_{\text{r.m.s}}$ represent the root mean square values, then

$$I_{\text{r.m.s}} = \frac{I_0}{\sqrt{2}} \quad \text{and} \quad V_{\text{r.m.s}} = \frac{V_0}{\sqrt{2}}$$

(See *mean power in a resistive load.*)

**rolling** is the motion of a body which moves across a surface without sliding. It involves a combination of translation and spin, such that the part of the body which, at any one time, is in contact with the surface is stationary. Rolling happens only on rough surfaces. On smooth surfaces, bodies slide.

**root mean square speed** (r.m.s. speed) is the square root of the *mean square speed.* It is a measure of the average speed of molecules in a gas; their true average seed is zero. The r.m.s. speed of molecules in a gas increases with temperature. (See also *kinetic theory of gases.*)

**rotational energy** is the kinetic energy associated with a rotating mass. It is calculated from the word equation

$$\text{rotational kinetic energy} = \tfrac{1}{2} \times \text{moment of inertia} \times (\text{angular speed})^2$$

$$W = \tfrac{1}{2} I w^2$$

**rotational motion** is the spinning motion of a body about a fixed axis. The motion is brought about by an unbalanced *torque*, and the rate at which the angular speed increases is controlled by the *moment of inertia* of the spinning mass.

If you are familiar with the equations of linear motion, it is relatively straightforward to solve problems involving rotational motion using the equations of rotational motion in which each linear quantity is replaced by the corresponding rotational quantity; for example, mass is replaced by moment of inertia. (See *rotational motion (equations of)*.)

**rotational motion (equations of):** these follow the same pattern as the equations for straight line motion but with angle, angular velocity and angular acceleration replacing displacement, velocity and acceleration.

There are five variables:

- $\theta$ angular displacement in radians ($\theta$ must be zero at time $t = 0$)
- $t$ time in seconds
- $\omega_1$ initial angular velocity (i.e. at time $t = 0$) in $\text{rad s}^{-1}$
- $\omega_2$ final angular velocity (at time $t$) in $\text{rad s}^{-1}$
- $\alpha$ angular acceleration (which will be constant or zero) in $\text{rad s}^{-2}$

The angular displacement, $\theta$, has positive and negative directions. The positive direction for angular displacement, which must be chosen and then kept to, sets the positive direction of rotation for angular velocity and for angular acceleration. The initial and final angular velocities and the angular acceleration may, like angular displacement, have positive or negative values. This underlines their vector nature. They are 'pseudo-vectors' in the sense that their directions are a matter of convention. Only $t$ is a scalar. Negative values of $t$ would imply times earlier than $t = 0$.

The equations of rotational motion are:

$$\theta = \frac{\omega_1 + \omega_2}{2} \times t \quad (\omega \text{ missing})$$

$$\omega_2 = \omega_1 + \alpha t \quad (\theta \text{ missing})$$

$$\theta = \omega_1 t + \frac{1}{2}\alpha t^2 \quad (\omega_2 \text{ missing})$$

$$\omega_2^2 = \omega_1^2 + 2\omega\theta \quad (t \text{ missing})$$

Notice that each of the equations has one of the five variables missing. The first equation follows from the definition of average angular velocity. The second equation is the definition of uniform angular acceleration. The third is derived by eliminating $\omega_2$ from the first two equations. The fourth equation is derived by eliminating $t$ from the first two equations.

Any problem in rotational motion can be tackled by following a similar procedure to that for straight line motion by using:

| | | |
|---|---|---|
| moment of inertia $I$ | instead of | mass $m$ |
| resultant torque $T$ | instead of | resultant force $F$ |
| $T = I\alpha$ | instead of | $F = ma$ |
| $\frac{1}{2} I\omega^2$ | instead of | $\frac{1}{2} mv^2$ |
| $T \times \theta = \frac{1}{2} I\omega^2$ | instead of | $F \times s = \frac{1}{2} mv^2$ |
| power $= T \times \omega$ | instead of | power $= F \times v$ |
| $I\omega$ | instead of | $mv$ |
| conservation of $I\omega$ | instead of | conservation of $mv$ |
| angular impulse $= T \times t$ | instead of | impulse $= F \times t$ |

Never lose sight of the relevant direction of rotation.

(See *moment of inertia, angular displacement, angular speed, angular velocity, angular acceleration, angular momentum, torque, couple, moment of a force.*)

**rubber** is a naturally occurring polymer with molecules which are tangled and crooked. The molecules straighten when stretched and, once straightened, stop the rubber from stretching any further. If the tension is removed, the molecules curl up again and the rubber recovers its former shape. Natural *cross-linking* between the molecules within the rubber is effective but thinly scattered. The cross-linking is strong enough to enable the rubber to keep its shape in the unstressed condition and to stop it stretching still further once the molecules are straight. But the cross-links are so few that they offer no resistance to the straightening out of the molecules under even modest loads.

Rubber molecules

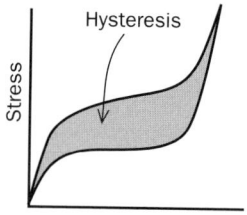

Vulcanisation

The loading curve on the load–extension graph above differs from the unloading curve. The unloading curve shows a faster release of load with falling extension than would be expected. Since energy stored is the area between the curve and the extension axis, less energy is released than is stored. The energy represented by the area enclosed by the loop remains in the specimen in the form of heat. This double curve is called a *hysteresis* loop. If you rapidly stretch and release a short section of rubber band and then test its temperature with your lips, it will be noticeably warmer than the rest of the band which was not stressed in this way. The capacity of a rubber specimen to withstand repeated elastic deformations without deteriorating is a measure of its resilience. (See *vulcanised rubber.*)

**Rutherford scattering:** see *alpha particle scattering experiment.*

**sampling** is the process of reading the instantaneous amplitude of a voltage signal successively at equal and very short intervals of time, usually by storing the instantaneous amplitude of the voltage on a small capacitor. Repetitive switching on and off of the contact between the voltage source and the capacitor creates a time sequence of discrete pulses which carry the information stored on the initial analogue signal from the voltage source. This is called pulse amplitude modulation (PAM). The sampled signal is discrete in time but analogue in amplitude. Sampling is also the first stage in any *analogue-to-digital conversion* process. (See *Nyquist's theorem.*)

**Sankey diagram:** a diagram in the form of a broad arrow which is used to represent energy changes. The arrow divides to show the different forms of energy involved, with the width of each part of the arrow being proportional to the amount of energy represented.

Because the total width of the arrow is constant, the principle of *conservation of energy* is implicit in a Sankey diagram.

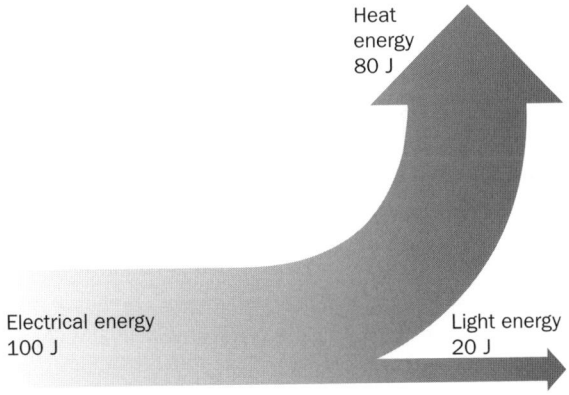


*Sankey diagram for a light-emitting diode*

**satellite** is a term which previously meant a planetary moon but now almost always means an artificial satellite (a spacecraft) in orbit around the Earth. Many of these are reconnaissance satellites in polar orbit between 700 km and 1000 km high with an orbital period of around 90 minutes and a useful life of up to ten years. Others are in *geostationary orbits*, in fixed positions above the equator.

**scalar quantity:** a physical or mathematical quantity which has magnitude but no direction. Scalar quantities can be added algebraically. Examples include distance travelled, speed, density, pressure, energy, power, temperature, electric charge and electric potential. (See *algebraic sum, vector quantity.*)

**Schwarzschild radius:** if an object has its mass compressed into a sphere of radius less than the Schwarzschild radius, it is a *black hole.* The Schwarzschild radius defines the event horizon for a black hole — neither light nor particles can escape from within this horizon because of the strength of the gravitational field. (See *end states of stars.*)

**second,** with symbol s, is a *base unit* in *SI.* It is the SI unit of time, and equals 9 192 631 770 periods of the radiation corresponding to the transition between the two hyperfine ground state levels of the caesium-133 atom.

**second law of thermodynamics:** a principle which underpins the theory of heat engines. One statement of the law is that an engine cannot produce mechanical work solely by extracting heat from the coolest body in the surroundings. Two important consequences of the law are the definition of the *absolute temperature scale* and the well-known expression $[T_1 - T_2]/T_1$ for the efficiency of a perfect heat engine. The law is not tested at A-level. (See *heat engine concept.*)

**secondary energy sources:** see *energy sources.*

**Segrè plot:** see *N–Z curve for stable nuclei.*

**self-inductance** is a measure of the *e.m.f.* induced in a circuit by a change of *flux linkage* brought about by a change of current in the same circuit. The symbol for self-inductance is $L$ and the SI unit is the *henry* (H).

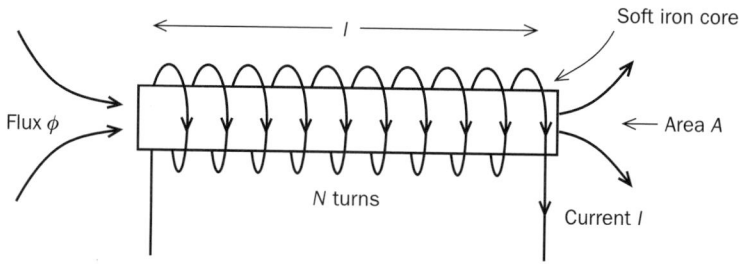


The diagram above shows a coil with $N$ turns of length $l$ and cross-sectional area $A$, wound on a soft iron core. The current $I$ in the coil sets up a magnetic flux $\phi$ in the core and a flux linkage of $N\phi$. If the current $I$ changes, the flux linkage $N\phi$ will also change. Within the coil a back e.m.f. $E$ will therefore be set up, the magnitude of which is given by the laws of *electromagnetic induction*:

$$E = -N\frac{d\phi}{dt}$$

But

$$\phi = BA = \frac{\mu_0 NI}{l} \cdot A$$

where $\mu_0$ is the permeability of free space, so

$$E = \frac{\mu_0 N^2 A}{l} \cdot \frac{dI}{dt}$$

Next, we define the coefficient of self-inductance $L$ of the coil by the equation

$$E = -L \cdot \frac{dI}{dt}$$

We see that

$$N\phi = NI$$

and that

$$L = \frac{\mu_0 N^2 A}{l}$$

The coefficient of self-inductance $L$ of a coil can be defined either as the induced e.m.f. per unit rate of change of current or as the flux linkages in the coil per unit current. These alternatives can be written out in the form of word equations:

$$\text{coefficient of selfi nductance } L = \frac{\text{e.m.f. induced in the coil}}{\text{rate of change of current}}$$

$$= \frac{\text{flux linkage for coil}}{\text{current in coil}}$$

The first of these word equations can be used to define the *henry* (H), the unit of self-inductance:

$$\text{henry} = \frac{\text{volt}}{\text{ampere per second}} = \text{ohm second}$$

That is, the henry (H) is the same as the ohm second.

It is worth going back to the equation $L = \mu_0 N^2 A/l$ and looking at the units. $N$ is a number and has no unit. So the unit for $\mu_0$ is the same as the unit for $Ll/A$, namely $\mathrm{H\,m^{-1}}$.

(See *mutual inductance, inductive reactance, resonance in AC circuits.*)

**semiconductor:** a material which is an insulator at absolute zero but which has valence electrons (the outer electrons) loosely enough bound for a small proportion to be released by thermal motions at room temperature. Such materials are called intrinsic semiconductors. Each electron freed in this way leaves a positive mobile 'hole' in the lattice. Electrons and holes both carry current (although electrons have the higher mobility and so carry more current) and are present in equal numbers.

The semiconducting properties of an intrinsic semiconductor can be drastically changed by the introduction of small quantities of impurity, a process known as doping. These impurities bring about a sharp increase in the number of conduction electrons ($n$-type) or a sharp increase in the number of holes ($p$-type). The resulting material is called an extrinsic conductor.

A major use of semiconducting materials is linked to the electrical behaviour at the junction between two semiconducting materials, one $n$-type and the other $p$-type, sealed together. The properties of the so-called $p$–$n$ junction lie at the root of the semiconductor revolution.

A diode consists of a single *p–n* junction, a transistor consists of two, and an integrated circuit may consist of millions. (See *semiconductor diodes.*)

**semiconductor diodes** are formed by fusing *n*-type and *p*-type semiconducting materials to form a series pair of conductors. Electrons flow across the junction in one direction but not in the other, so the diode conducts current in one direction only.

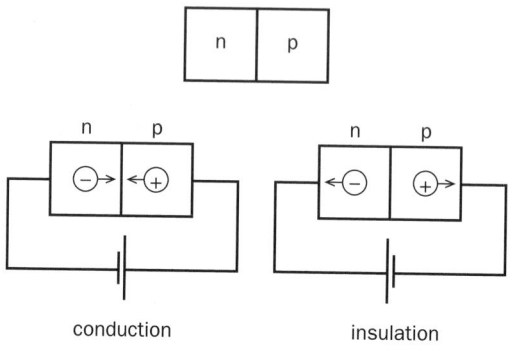


If the *n*-type material is negative with respect to the *p*-type, then electrons flow across the junction from *n* to *p*, holes flow the other way and the diode conducts. For silicon-based materials, the negative bias of the *n*-type material must exceed about 0.6 V before the current climbs to an appreciable level. It then increases strongly with increasing bias. This is illustrated by the following typical current–voltage characteristic. (Note that the positive and negative scales on each axis are different.)

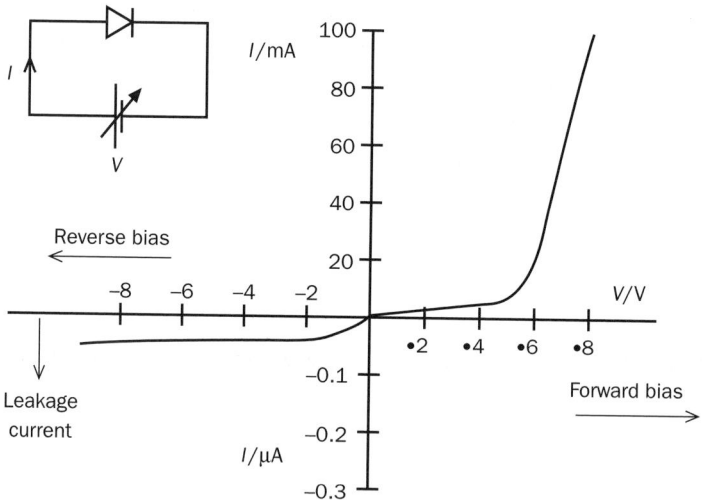


If the *n*-type material is positive with respect to the *p*-type, then electrons in the *n*-type and holes in the *p*-type move away from the junction. Nothing flows across the junction (apart from a residual current of a few microamperes, called leakage current) and a potential difference is set up across the junction which opposes the applied potential difference. If too large a reverse voltage is applied to the diode, it breaks down. Some diodes, called Zener diodes, exploit this effect. (See *semiconductors.*)

**sensitivity** is a measure of the smallest change in a physical quantity that a measuring instrument can detect. This is a separate matter from reliability. A mercury thermometer, for instance, will indicate a change in temperature as small as a tenth of a kelvin, while its reading may differ from the true value by more than a full degree. To assess the sensitivity of an instrument, look for the smallest observable change. This might be a scale division, half a scale division, or even less. *Precision* is an expression of the inherent uncertainty in an instrument and takes into account both the sensitivity and the overall reliability. A good instrument is accompanied by a written definition of the precision guaranteed by the manufacturer.

The word sensitivity is used also as a closely defined technical expression of the scale size for some instruments, particularly *ammeters* and *voltmeters.* Sensitivity is defined as the deflection (in radians) per ampere or per volt or, alternatively, in scale divisions per ampere or per volt. The ratio is called current sensitivity or voltage sensitivity. The numerical value varies enormously with the range of the instrument (is it calibrated in, for example, amperes or microamperes?) and needs careful interpretation.

Some cathode ray oscilloscopes have a control identified as the sensitivity, with a scale in units such as volts per division ($\mathrm{V\,div^{-1}}$). This is the reciprocal of the meaning of sensitivity given above; a better term for this would be the 'gain' of the oscilloscope.

**SI** is the agreed abbreviation for Système International d'Unités. This system provides the international legal framework for the measurement of physical quantities and for the units used to define amounts of physical quantities. In principle, one shouldn't write or say 'SI system', since this repeats the word 'system'; nonetheless, many people do so. (See *base quantity, base unit, derived quantity, derived unit.*)

**simple harmonic motion** is the motion of a body which is acted upon by a resultant force whose magnitude is proportional to the distance of the body from a fixed point and whose direction is always towards that point.

This statement can be put in algebraic form:

$$F = -kx$$

where $F$ is the restoring force on the body, $x$ is the displacement of the body from its rest position and $k$ is the restoring force per unit displacement. The unit for $k$ is $\mathrm{N\,m^{-1}}$.

The algebra becomes simpler if the equation is written in the form

$$F = -m\omega^2 x = -m(2\pi f)^2 x$$

where $m$ is the mass of the body on which the force $F$ acts, $f$ is the frequency of the motion and $\omega$ is the angular frequency of the motion. If $a$ is the acceleration when displacement is $x$, then:

$$a = -\omega^2 x = -(2\pi f)^2 x$$

If this equation is solved with time measured from an instant when the mass is at maximum displacement (i.e. $x = x_0$ when $t = 0$) in the positive $x$ direction, then we get the following important results:

$$x = -x_0 \cos \omega t = x_0 \cos 2\pi ft$$

$$v = -\omega x_0 \sin \omega t = -2\pi f x_0 \sin 2\pi ft = -2\pi f \sqrt{\left(x_0^2 - x^2\right)}$$

$$a = -\omega^2 x = -\left(2\pi f\right)^2 x_0 \cos 2\pi ft$$

$$T = \frac{1}{f} = \frac{2\pi}{\omega}$$

$$E_k = \tfrac{1}{2} mv^2 = \tfrac{1}{2} m(2\pi f)^2 \left(x_0^2 - x^2\right)$$

where $x_0$ is the maximum value of the displacement (i.e. the *amplitude* of the motion) and $T$ is the period. Notice that the peak value of the kinetic energy is proportional to the square of the amplitude.

The diagram on page 219 shows the different graphs which come from these equations and which you should know about.

The secret of solving problems on simple harmonic motion is to concentrate on $\omega$. If you are given the period $T$, then find $\omega$ and use it as part of the data in the other equations to calculate whatever the question asks. If you are required to find $T$, use the data and the earlier equations to find $\omega$ and then $T$.

**Worked examples**

1 **An object which is oscillating with simple harmonic motion has period 2.2 seconds and amplitude 5.1 cm. Assuming that the displacement is maximum at time t = 0, find the displacement and the speed at time t = 0.80 s.**

Using $T = 2.2\,\text{s}$, we have $\omega = 2\pi/T = 2.86\ \text{rad s}^{-1}$.

At $t = 0.80\,\text{s}$, $\omega t = 2.29$ radians or 131°, $\cos \omega t = -0.657$, so

displacement $x = -3.35\,\text{cm}$

Using this value for $x$ in the velocity formula, we have

velocity $v = -11.0\,\text{cms}^{-1}$

We can now state the result in SI units and to the correct number of significant figures:
displacementattime $t = 0.80\,\text{s}$ is $0.034\,\text{m}$

velocity is $-\ 0.110\ \text{ms}^{-1}$

2 **An object which is oscillating with simple harmonic motion of amplitude 0.122 m has speed 0.38 m s⁻¹ when the displacement is 0.076 m. Calculate the period of the motion.**

Using the velocity formula, we have:

$$v = \omega\sqrt{\left(x_0^2 - x^3\right)}$$

$$\omega = \frac{0.38\,\text{ms}^{-1}}{\sqrt{(0.122\,\text{m})^2 - (0.076\,\text{m})^2}} = 3.98\,\text{rads}^{-1}$$

The period can now be found:

$$T = \frac{2\pi \text{ rad}}{3.98 \text{ rad s}^{-1}} = 1.58 \text{ s} = 1.6 \text{ s}^{-1} \text{ (to 2 s.f.)}$$

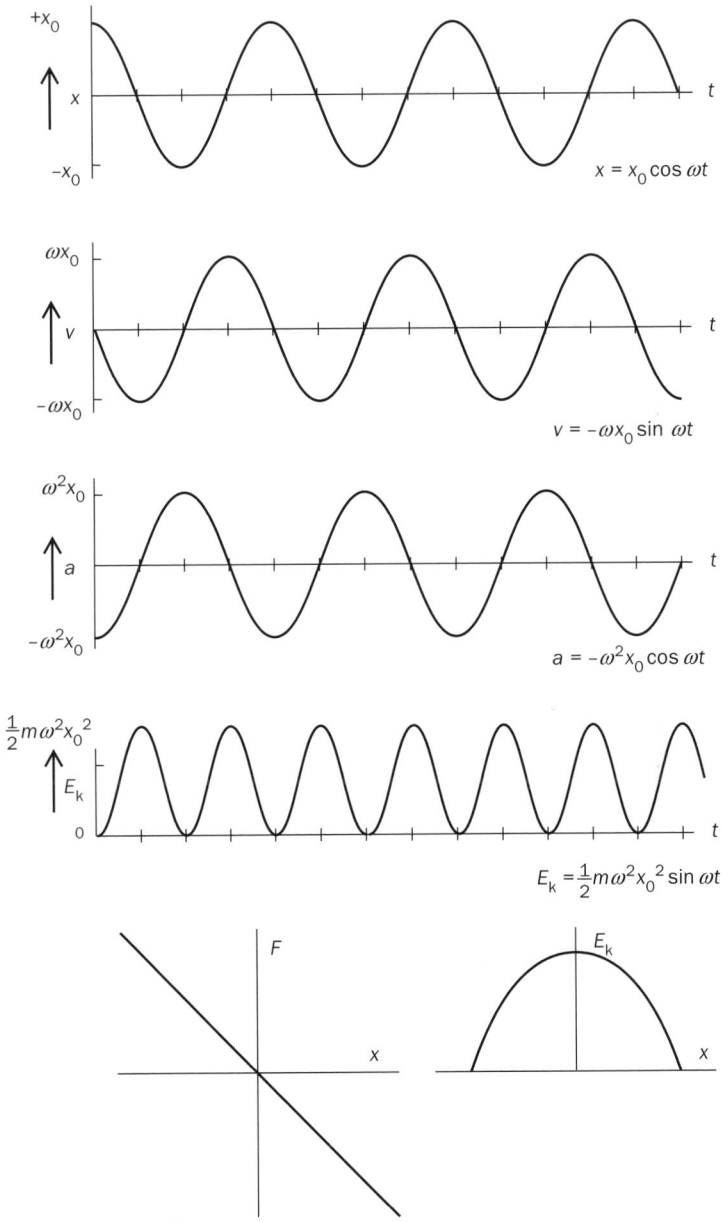


(See *angular frequency, frequency, simple pendulum, mass–spring system, damped harmonic motion, resonance.*)

**simple pendulum:** a small dense object, usually a metal sphere, suspended from a fixed point by a thread and free to move from side to side. If $T$ is the period of the motion, $l$ is the distance from the point of support to the centre of mass of the object and $g$ is the acceleration of free fall, then:

$$T = 2\pi\sqrt{\frac{l}{g}}$$

Note that $T$ is independent of the amplitude. This is an approximate result only, but it is accurate enough for angles of swing smaller than about 5°. Notice too that the definition of the length $l$ is not just the length of the supporting thread; it is a particular distance and should be labelled precisely on any diagram.

**Experiment to measure the acceleration of free fall using a simple pendulum**

**Apparatus**

The diagram should show the simple pendulum suspended from a rigid support. The length $l$, i.e. the distance from the rigid support to the centre of mass of the pendulum bob, must be clearly defined in the diagram and labelled. There should be some kind of visible indicator at the rest position to allow timings to start and stop as the pendulum bob goes through the centre of its swing.

**Measurements**

For each of a series of lengths, measure the distance $l$ with a metre rule and the period $T$. The distance $l$ should be measured carefully three times and an average taken. The period $T$ should be found by measuring the time needed for 25 complete swings three times for each length and then dividing the average of these three measurements by 25.

**Conclusion**

Plot a graph of $T^2$ in seconds squared against $l$ in metres. It will be a straight line of gradient $4\pi^2/g$ which passes through the origin. The acceleration of free fall $g$ is $4\pi^2$ divided by the gradient.

**Comment**

The chief source of error is the random error in the starting and stopping of the clock. This is reduced by taking the average of three measurements and by counting the periods as the pendulum bob passes through the rest position.

A careful student should be able to reach the point at which the uncertainties linked to the measurements are outweighed by the fresh uncertainties introduced, by using an ordinary-sized sheet of graph paper.

(See *simple harmonic motion.*)

**sizes of atoms** are all in the region of $n \times 10^{-10}$ m where $n$ is a small number. (See *oil film experiment.*)

**slip:** a process leading to deformation of the crystal structure of a metal. It happens during the plastic flow stage for a metal stressed beyond its *elastic limit.* It takes the form of adjacent crystal planes sliding over one another in the presence of excessive stress. Slip lines can be seen with a microscope on the surfaces of many metal wires that have been stretched beyond their elastic limits. The extreme case is for a wire of a metal such as cadmium, which can be prepared as a single crystal. The forces within the crystal planes are stronger than the forces holding the planes together. Planes where sliding occurs are called slip planes. (See *plastic deformation*.)

**smoothing capacitor:** see *rectification, half-wave and full-wave.*

**Snell's law:** see *refraction of light.*

**solar constant** is the incident power delivered by radiation from the Sun per square metre at right angles to the direction of flow at the top of the atmosphere near the equator. The accurate value is under review; a working figure is $1.37\,\mathrm{kW\,m^{-2}}$.

It is a difficult measurement to make. The 'top of the atmosphere' needs a closer definition; the distance of the Earth from the Sun varies during the year; the Sun is given to occasional and erratic changes.

Spacecraft in orbit around the Earth use solar panels to generate electricity. These panels can be turned to face the Sun directly, maximising the energy gathered. Because of the low efficiency of solar panels (less than 10%), electricity production at a rate of $100\,\mathrm{W\,m^{-2}}$ is a typical value.

Solar radiation is absorbed by the atmosphere. Hence, when the Sun is directly overhead at the equator, the incident power is reduced to about $1\,\mathrm{kW\,m^{-2}}$ at sea level. When the Sun is not overhead and at other latitudes, the incident power is further reduced.

**solar panels:** a poorly defined term which may refer to:

- devices for absorbing solar radiation across an appreciable area and storing it thermally in water that circulates through the panels
- arrays of photoelectric cells ('solar cells') which absorb sunlight and produce electricity

**solar power** is power drawn directly from the Sun as in *solar panels* used for home heating or solar cells used to produce electricity directly from solar radiation. (See *energy sources*.)

**solenoid:** a tight helix of conducting wire. There may be one or more layers of turns. Provided that the length of the solenoid is more than ten times its diameter, a uniform magnetic field of strength $B$ runs along the inside of the solenoid, where

$$B = \mu_0 nI = \frac{\mu_0 NI}{l}$$

$\mu_0$ is the permeability of vacuum, $I$ is the current, $n$ is the number of turns per metre length of solenoid, $N$ is the total number of turns and $l$ is the length of the solenoid.

The form of the magnetic field set up in a solenoid is shown in the diagram on the next page. The direction of the *lines of force* within the solenoid is given by the *right hand grip rule*: grip the solenoid with your right hand, with your fingers pointing along the direction of the current; your thumb then runs along the solenoid in the same direction as the magnetic field lines inside the solenoid.

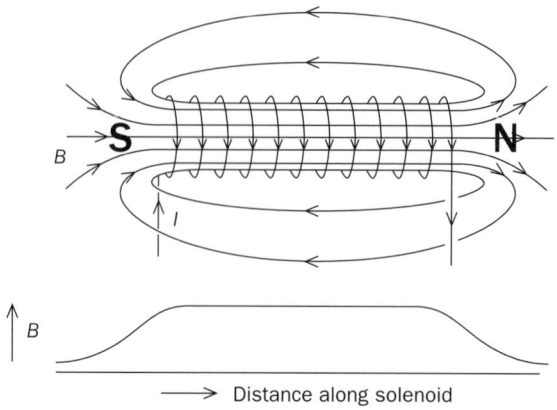


Remember, when copying this diagram, to include at least five equally spaced field lines and to leave breaks in the coils to show the direction of the windings. (Omitting either of these points could cost you all the diagram marks.) The graph in the diagram reminds us that the magnitude of the magnetic field strength begins to tail off just before the end of the solenoid is reached.

The magnetic field strength within a solenoid can be increased by filling the space within the solenoid with a ferromagnetic material. The magnetic field strength within the solenoid becomes:

$$B = \mu_r \mu_0 nI = \frac{\mu_r \mu_0 NI}{l}$$

where $\mu_r$ is called the *relative permeability* of the ferromagnetic material.

This may not seem of much use if the new, stronger magnetic field cannot be accessed because of the ferromagnetic core. It is, however, useful in two ways. Both the magnetic field outside the solenoid and the *self-inductance* of the solenoid are increased in the same proportion. Electromagnets and tuning coils are solenoids with ferromagnetic cores. (See *permeability of free space, relative permeability.*)

**solids:** materials in which the molecules are unable to move around because of the intermolecular forces between them. The molecules are able to vibrate about fixed mean positions.

A solid has a definite shape. When a force is applied to a solid, it responds by resisting the force.

**sound waves** are sets of pressure waves which pass through the air, one after the other, at a speed governed by the density of the air and its elasticity. The following diagram illustrates the essential events leading up to the formation of a single pressure pulse. A loudspeaker cone moves sharply to the right. This affects the air on the right of the loudspeaker. A compression is formed (a localised rise in density and pressure), and the air in the compression has momentum towards the right and potential energy associated with the higher pressure. The momentum equals the impulse imposed on the air by the loudspeaker cone, and the compression will be carried away from the cone as the momentum is passed from one layer of air to the next. There is a flow of sound energy and of momentum. There is no net displacement of air.

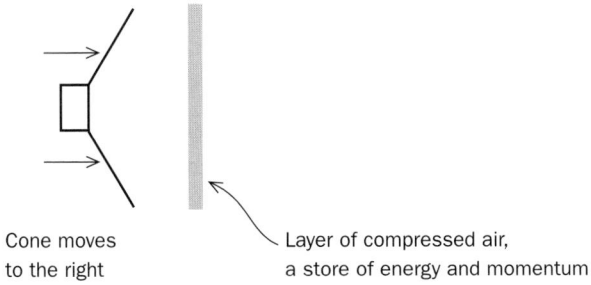


The next step is to consider what happens if the loudspeaker moves repetitively backwards and forwards. Assume that the loudspeaker moves with simple harmonic motion along the axis of its cone. Each time the cone moves to the right it sets up a new compression pulse which follows its predecessors into the air space and away from the cone. The speed of these compressions is fixed by the elasticity and density of the air; it does not depend on the speed of movement of the loudspeaker. The speed of sound in air is a property of air, and of nothing else. A more vigorous motion from the loudspeaker gives a tighter compression with a higher pressure at its centre; the compression will not move through the air any faster but it will carry more energy.

The air particles in the path of the sound wave oscillate backwards and forwards along the line of energy flow. Such waves are called *longitudinal waves*. There is no net motion of the air arising from the passage of the sound wave. The oscillations of the air particles are an ordered motion superimposed upon the disordered motion dealt with in *kinetic theory of gases*. The two motions are independent of one another.

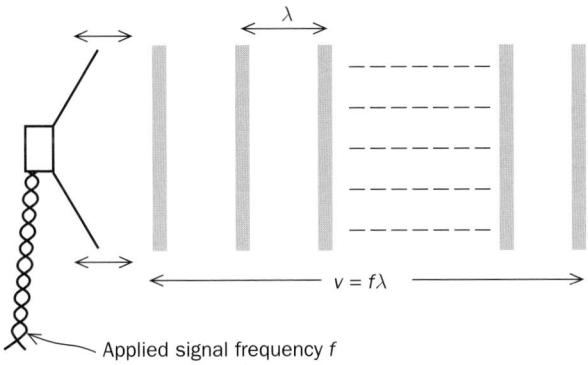


The number of compressions issuing from the loudspeaker per second equals the *frequency* of the motion of the loudspeaker (and this, in turn, equals the frequency of the electrical signal applied to its coil). The distance moved by one compression in a second (the speed) divided by the number of compressions created per second equals the average distance between the centres of successive compressions. This is called the *wavelength* of the sound. It follows that

$$\text{speed of sound} = \text{frequency} \times \text{wavelength}$$

$$c = f \times \lambda$$

This relation is true for any kind of wave. Speed depends on the medium, frequency depends on the source, and wavelength is decided by speed and frequency together. The four graphs in the following figures split into two pairs.

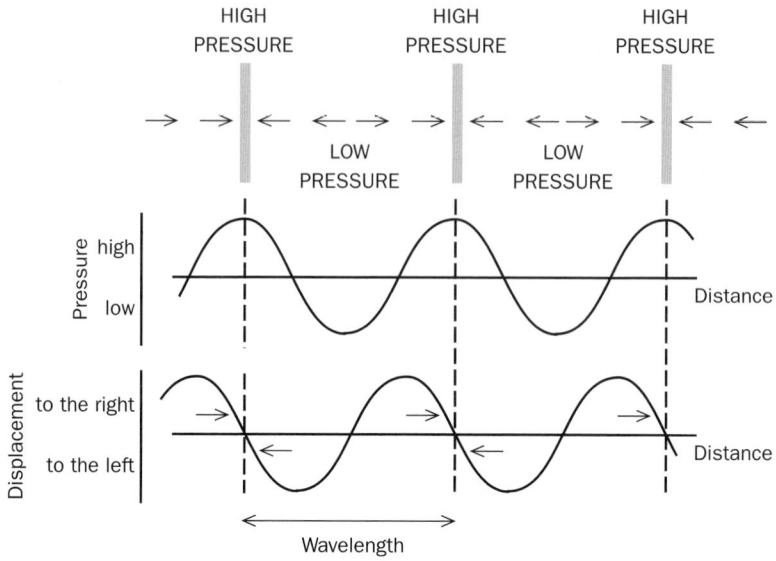


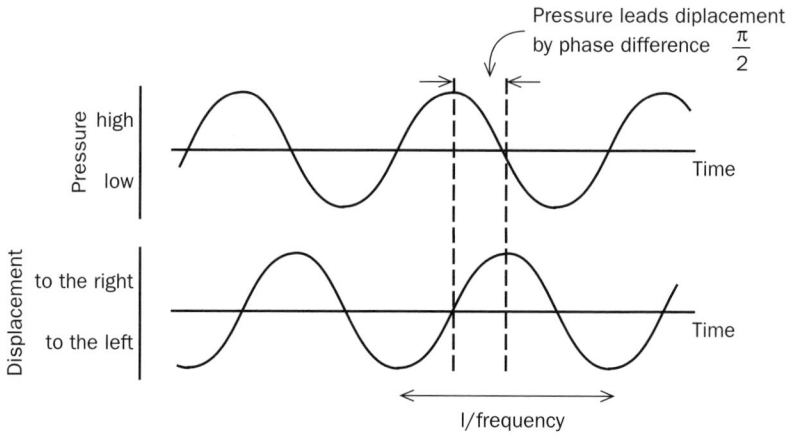


The first pair shows how the pressure and the displacement vary with distance along the path of the sound wave at a particular instant. The second pair shows how the values of the same two variables, pressure and displacement, vary with time at a particular spot in the path of the wave. The first pair of graphs illustrates the meaning of wavelength; the second pair illustrates period and phase. None of the graphs has start or finish points; the sound wave is a continuum.

The pressure amplitude in a sound wave varies between about 50 Pa for a loud sound (*atmospheric pressure* is about 100 000 Pa or two thousand times higher) and $10^{-5}$ Pa for a very weak but still audible sound. Loudness is not expressed as a pressure change, but rather in terms of the power transmitted by the sound wave per unit area. The power transmitted ranges from about 1 W m$^{-2}$ for a loud sound down to $10^{-12}$ W m$^{-2}$ for a barely audible sound. (See *loudness*.)

**special relativity** brings together the physics of motion, optics and electromagnetism into a single scheme of things. The results cannot be applied to systems which are accelerating relative to one another. This is why a theory of *general relativity* is needed.

Imagine an observer called Jack in a laboratory equipped with good-quality measuring instruments. The laboratory appears stationary to Jack – it is his frame of reference for data collection and study.

A second observer, Jill, is in an identical laboratory. This laboratory, Jill's reference frame, is travelling with constant velocity $v$ relative to Jack's reference frame, his laboratory.

Both observers are equipped with identical helical springs having period of oscillation $\Delta t$ and with identical measuring rods of length $\Delta l$. The measuring rods are mounted parallel to the velocity vector $v$ of Jill's frame of reference as seen by Jack.

Jack checks the period of his own spring and the length of his own measuring rod, and finds them unchanged. Jill finds the same.

However, when Jack uses his instruments to check Jill's helical spring, he finds that its period has lengthened to $\Delta t'$. So, clocks in Jill's reference frame seem to be running slow when viewed by Jack from his reference frame. Similarly, Jill's measuring rod appears to have shortened compared with Jack's own measuring rod to a new length $\Delta l'$. Jill's view of Jack's helical spring and of his measuring rod yield exactly the same changes.

This situation is analysed on the basis of two new postulates.

For any two observers whose reference frames are in a state of uniform motion relative to one another (i.e. for any two inertial frames of reference):

- the laws controlling mechanical, optical and electromagnetic events must be the same
- the speed of light in vacuum and in all directions is the same

Two important relationships can be derived on the basis of these two postulates:

$$\Delta t' = \frac{\Delta t}{\sqrt{\left(1 - \frac{v^2}{c^2}\right)}} \qquad \Delta l' = \Delta l \times \sqrt{\left(1 - \frac{v^2}{c^2}\right)}$$

Jack and Jill both record values $\Delta t$ and $\Delta l$ when using their own instruments to measure a given time interval and a given length in their own reference frames. They both record values $\Delta t'$ and $\Delta l'$ when measuring the same time interval and the same distance in the other's reference frame. The velocity of one reference frame relative to the other is $v$, $\Delta l$ is parallel to $v$ in both reference frames and $c$ is the speed of light.

Another important result of special relativity is *mass–energy equivalence* as summarised by the equation

$$\Delta E = \Delta m.c^2$$

This equation tells us that if we warm up a football (i.e. supply energy of $\Delta E$ joules), then the football will be harder to kick a given distance because its inertial mass has increased by an amount of $\Delta m$ kg as calculated from the mass–energy equivalence equation.
A non-trivial example is the fission of a uranium-235 atom following a collision with a slow neutron:

$$^{235}_{92}\mathrm{U} + ^{1}_{0}\mathrm{n} \rightarrow ^{236}_{92}\mathrm{U} \rightarrow ^{140}_{54}\mathrm{Xe} + ^{94}_{38}\mathrm{Sr} + 2\,^{1}_{0}\mathrm{n} + \gamma + 200\,\mathrm{MeV}$$

Mass–energy is conserved throughout this change. But the rest mass of the products is less than the rest mass of the reactants — there has been a transformation. The energy released equals $\Delta m.c^2$, and until that energy is lost from the system, the total mass of the energetic particles is the same as the mass of the reactants. By total mass we mean the mass of the system as decided by the force needed to induce a given acceleration. Equally, the recipient of that lost energy, once it escapes from the system, experiences a corresponding mass increase.

**specific heat capacity** is the heat needed to raise the temperature of one kilogram of a material by one degree kelvin. It is a physical property of a material. The SI unit is $\mathrm{J\,kg^{-1}\,K^{-1}}$. The symbol used is $c$ (note the lower case form). The word equation definition is:

$$\text{specfic heat capacity} = \frac{\text{heat supplied}}{\text{mass} \times \text{temperature rise}}$$

$$\text{unit for specific heat capacity} = \frac{\text{joule}}{\text{kilogram} \times \text{kelvin}} = \mathrm{J\,kg^{-1}K^{-1}}$$

$$c = \frac{\Delta Q}{m \times \Delta\theta}$$

**Worked examples**

1 **Calculate the heat needed to raise the temperature of a 0.250 kg piece of copper (specific heat capacity of copper is 380 J kg$^{-1}$ K$^{-1}$) from 12°C to 47°C.**

$$\Delta Q = mc\Delta\theta = (0.250\,\mathrm{kg})(380\,\mathrm{J\,kg^{-1}K^{-1}})(35\,\mathrm{K}) = 3.3\,\mathrm{kJ}$$

(Note that, by putting the answer in kJ, the problem of too many significant figures is neatly avoided.)

2 **An aluminium vessel of mass 0.035 kg contains 0.052 kg of water at 16°C. A 0.050 kg block of aluminium at 100°C is dropped into the water. The specific heat capacities of aluminium and water are 900 J kg$^{-1}$ K$^{-1}$ and 4200 J kg$^{-1}$ K$^{-1}$, respectively. Calculate the final temperature of the water.**

Let $\theta$ represent the final temperature of the water and the aluminium. Then:

heat lost by aluminium block

$$= \text{mass} \times \{\text{specific heat capacity}\} \times \{\text{temperature drop}\}$$

$$= (0.050\,\mathrm{kg})(900\,\mathrm{J\,kg^{-1}K^{-1}}) \times [(100 - \theta)\mathrm{K}]$$

$$= (4500 - 45\theta)\,\mathrm{J}$$

heat gained by aluminium vessel and water

$$= (0.035\,\mathrm{kg})(900\,\mathrm{J\,kg^{-1}\,K^{-1}}) + (0.052\,\mathrm{kg})(4200\,\mathrm{J\,kg^{-1}\,K^{-1}}) \times (\theta - 16)\,\mathrm{K}$$

$$= (250\,\theta - 4000)\,\mathrm{J}$$

$$(4500 - 45\theta) = (250\,\theta - 4000)$$

$$295\theta = 8500$$

$$\theta = 29^\circ\mathrm{C}$$

The principle used in the second example is to assume that once the aluminium block is dropped in the water, the internal energy of the whole system is constant. The internal energy lost by the block equals that gained by the vessel and the water. This will be true only if the lagging of the apparatus is perfect. (See also *specific heat capacity (measurement of), heat capacity.*)

**specific heat capacity (measurement of):** the two principal kinds of experiment are a 'method of mixtures' and a method based on electrical heating.

The method of mixtures builds on the assumption that the specific heat capacity of water and possibly the heat capacity of a metal vessel (called a calorimeter) are known already. A known mass of water is poured into the calorimeter; its temperature is measured with a thermometer. The mass of the solid or liquid body whose specific heat capacity is needed is found by weighing. The body under examination is then heated to 100°C by immersion in steam or boiling water. It is quickly transferred to the calorimeter and the maximum temperature of the mixture recorded. The gain in internal energy of the water and calorimeter is calculated. This result is divided by both the mass of the body and its drop in temperature to find the specific heat capacity. The principal difficulty is to ensure that there is no serious heat loss to the surroundings while the temperature settles down to its maximum value. This is achieved by having excellent lagging, a lid to discourage evaporation and a sensible choice of liquid and solid masses.

In the electrical method, the temperature of a known mass of material is raised by heating it electrically for a known period of time. The rise in temperature is measured with a mercury thermometer. The thermal energy transferred to the mass is $IVt$, the product of the current $I$ in the heater, the voltage $V$ across the heater and the time $t$ of current flow. Divide the thermal energy transferred, $IVt$, by both the mass $m$ of the body and the temperature rise $\theta$ and you are left with the specific heat capacity $c$ of the body. For a liquid, the experiment is repeated twice using the same vessel but different amounts of liquid. Extra electrical energy is needed to heat the increased mass of liquid by the same amount as before, but the container accounts only for the same amount as before. This extra electrical energy divided by the extra mass and the temperature rise gives the specific heat capacity.

**specific latent heat** is the heat transferred per unit mass when a pure material changes state without changing temperature. The SI unit of specific latent heat is joules per kilogram ($\mathrm{J\,kg^{-1}}$). The symbol used is $L$. The specific latent heat of fusion of ice (or of freezing of water) is $334\,\mathrm{kJ\,kg^{-1}}$, and the specific latent heat of vaporisation of water (or of condensation of steam) is $2.26\,\mathrm{MJ\,kg^{-1}}$. The word equation definition is:

$$\text{specific latent heat} = \frac{\text{heat transferred}}{\text{mass}}$$

$$\text{unit of specific latent heat} = \frac{\text{joule}}{\text{kilogram}} = \mathrm{J\,kg^{-1}}$$

**Worked example**

**Calculate the thermal energy transferred when 350 g of ice at 0°C is transformed into steam at 100°C.**

$$\begin{aligned}\text{heat transferred} &= mL_{\text{ice}} + mc\theta + mL_{\text{steam}}\\ &= (0.350\,\mathrm{kg})(334\,000\,\mathrm{J\,kg^{-1}} + 420\,000\,\mathrm{J\,kg^{-1}} + 2\,260\,000\,\mathrm{J\,kg^{-1}})\\ &= 1.05\,\mathrm{MJ}\end{aligned}$$

1.05 MJ is enough heat to raise the temperature of 2.5 kg of water from the freezing point to the boiling point without change of state. In the above calculation, only a seventh of the heat supplied was used to change the temperature; six sevenths were used to change the state. The large amount of heat stored as latent heat in the water vapour in the atmosphere keeps the Earth's climate manageable by transferring energy from the equator to the poles. If the specific latent heat of vaporisation were appreciably smaller, temperature differences from pole to equator would be greater and storm violence would increase dramatically.

**speed** is a *scalar quantity*. It is defined by the word equation:

$$\text{speed} = \frac{\text{distance travelled}}{\text{time taken}}$$

***Distance travelled*** must be measured along the travel path and cannot decrease. A step backwards is another step — it adds to the total distance travelled. Since distance travelled is always a positive quantity, so is speed. The word equation that defines speed also defines its unit:

$$\text{St unit for speed} = \frac{\text{unit for distance travelled}}{\text{unit for time}} = \frac{\text{metre}}{\text{second}} = \text{ms}^{-1}$$

Uniform speed means equal distances travelled in equal times.

Average speed is defined by the word equation:

$$\text{average speed} = \frac{\text{total distance travelled}}{\text{total time taken}}$$

Instantaneous speed is the average speed over a very small time interval at a given instant. It equals the gradient of the tangent to the *distance–time graph* at that instant.

A graph of instantaneous speed against time is called a speed–time graph. The area between a speed–time curve and the time axis equals the distance travelled between the corresponding times. The gradient of the tangent to a *speed–time graph* equals the rate of change of speed at that instant.

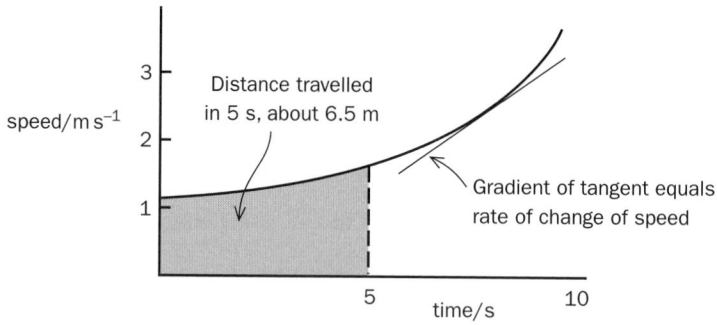


Rate of change of speed is a scalar quantity with units $\text{m s}^{-2}$. Rate of change of speed is not the same as acceleration. Acceleration is a *vector quantity*; it is rate of change of velocity. A body moving along a circular path at constant speed has acceleration even though the rate of change of speed is zero.

**Worked example**

A car, starting from rest at point A, increases its speed from zero to $12.5\,m\,s^{-1}$ at a uniform rate in 12 seconds. It travels at this speed of $12.5\,m\,s^{-1}$ for a further 20 seconds. Finally, it slows down uniformly to rest at B in 20 seconds.

Look at the first speed–time graph below. The line for the first 12 seconds is straight and slopes upwards. The gradient is constant and positive — the speed is increasing at a constant rate. For the next 20 seconds the speed is constant; the gradient of the speed–time curve is zero. For the final 20-second segment, the gradient is constant but negative; the car is slowing down. Speed cannot be negative but its rate of change can.

The area to the left of the upward line at 15 seconds equals the distance travelled by the car in the first 15 seconds. Imagine this line travelling slowly along the time axis from 0 seconds to 52 seconds. The growing area to its left represents the distance travelled and is plotted on the lower graph. This area can only increase; distance once travelled cannot be untravelled.

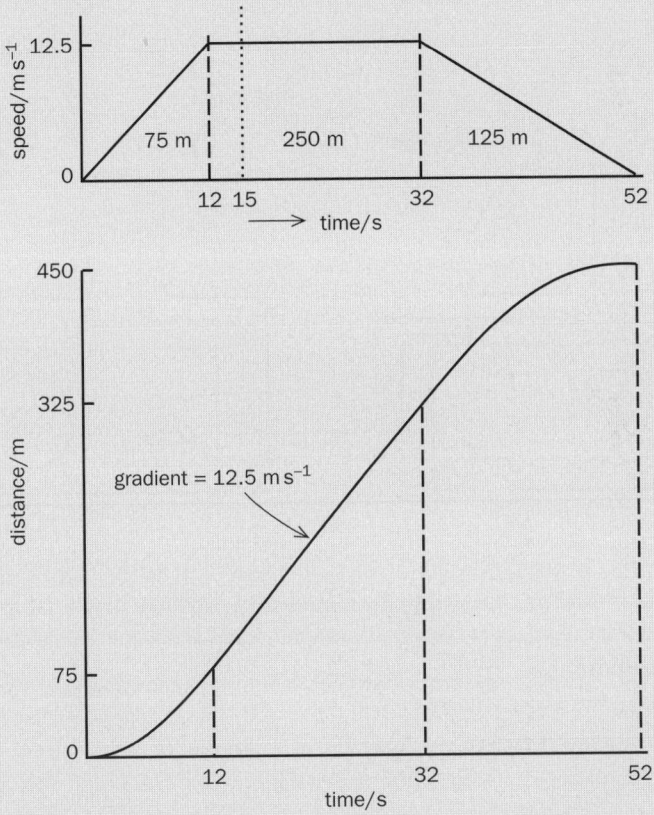


The distance travelled, found in this way, can be plotted against time. The distance–time graph so found cannot have a negative gradient because speed cannot have a negative value. The curved ends of the line represent increasing speed at the beginning and decreasing speed at the end.

From 12 seconds to 32 seconds, the line is straight. The constant gradient corresponds to a constant speed of $12.5\,m\,s^{-1}$.

**speed of a wave:** see *wave speed.*

**speed of light** is, by definition, 299 792 458 m s$^{-1}$ exactly. In SI, the *second* is defined first, then the value of the speed of light is defined (as above), and the length of the *metre* follows from these definitions. In the past, the metre and second were defined first and the speed of light then had to be measured. (See *permittivity of free space, permeability of free space, ampere.*)

**speed of sound:** the distance sound waves travel per unit time. The phrase 'speed of sound in free air' implies the speed at which sound travels across an open laboratory or an open space. Examination questions asking for a description of a method of measuring the speed of sound in free air rarely allow any marks for answers based on a resonance tube method or answers of the 'handkerchief and starting pistol' variety.

**Experiment to measure the speed of sound**

**Apparatus**

A suitable arrangement is shown in the diagram.

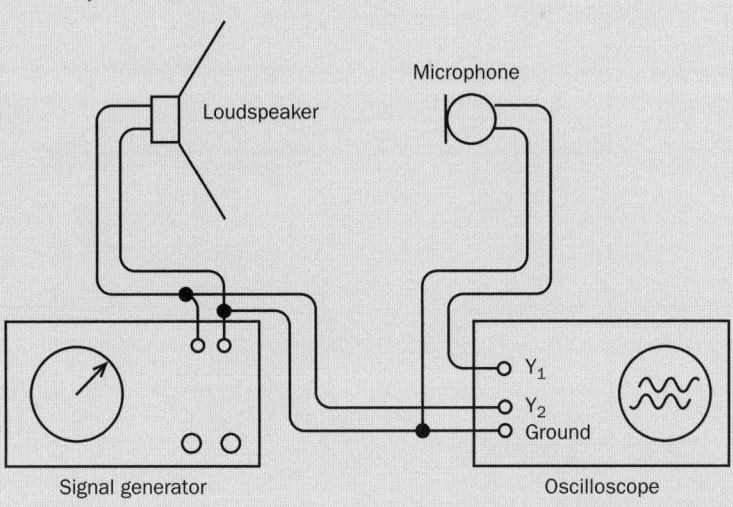


The output from the signal generator is set at about 1 kHz. It is connected to the $Y_2$ input of a double beam oscilloscope and to the loudspeaker. The time base is adjusted to show about three full cycles of the signal from the signal generator. The microphone is connected to the $Y_1$ input.

**Measurements**

Place the microphone, facing the loudspeaker, at a distance for which the two wave traces on the oscilloscope screen are in phase. Mark the position of the microphone.

Move the microphone away from the loudspeaker slowly and note how the signals get increasingly out of phase until they are back in phase again. Continue moving the microphone until this has happened four times. Measure the total distance moved by the microphone with a metre rule. This equals four wavelengths. Repeat this measurement three or four times and find an average value for the wavelength. Read the frequency from the scale of the signal generator (you may need to check this using a frequency meter).

**Conclusion**
The product of the wavelength and the frequency equals the speed of sound.

**Comment**
It would be a simple matter to repeat the experiment with different frequency settings. The measurements could be used to check that the speed of sound is the same for all frequencies.

**speed–time graph:** a graphical display of the time variation of *speed*. The area between the speed–time curve and the time axis gives *distance travelled*. The gradient of the tangent to the curve gives the rate of change of speed with time. This is not the same thing as *acceleration*; acceleration is a *vector quantity*.

It sometimes helps to remember that speed is what a speedometer in a car records. It tells you how fast a car is going but not its direction of travel. The magnitude of speed can rise or fall but it cannot have a negative value, and so a speed–time graph cannot cut the time axis.

(See *distance, displacement, velocity–time graph*.)

**spherical aberration** is a distortion of an image formed by a lens or mirror. It happens when mirrors or lenses are made with surfaces which are parts of spheres. Spherical surfaces are not of the correct shape if rays parallel to the principal axis are to be focused at a point; the *focal length* at the edge of the lens or mirror is shorter compared with the focal length of the part near the principal axis. The fault can be corrected by a small change in the shape of the lens, but this is costly. The reduction of spherical aberration is just one more reason why higher-quality telescopes or binoculars are expensive.

**spontaneous** is a word that is often used in connection with *radioactive decay*. The word implies that the decay of a particular nucleus is instantaneous, that there is no warning and that there seems to be no external trigger. It is linked to the idea of randomness. Radioactive decay is controlled by strong or weak interactions and these have short ranges with influences that do not extend outside the nucleus or beyond isolated nuclear particles.

**spring constant,** $k$, is defined by the equation $F = kx$ where $F$ is the *tensile force* applied to a spring and $x$ is the extension of the spring. The unit of $k$ is $\mathrm{N\,m^{-1}}$. (If you are studying mechanics in A-level mathematics, take care not to confuse the spring constant $k$ with the spring modulus $\lambda$ defined by the equation $F = \lambda x/L$, where $L$ is the relaxed length of the spring.) See *mass–spring system*.

**standard pressure** is the bar which is defined as exactly $10^5$ Pa. The quantity $1.01325 \times 10^5$ Pa is called the standard atmosphere. (See also *bar, standard temperature and pressure (s.t.p.)*.)

**standard temperature and pressure (s.t.p.)** means a temperature of 273.15 K (or 0°C) and a pressure of $1.01325 \times 10^5$ Pa exactly.

Chemists often choose 298.15 K (or 25°C) instead of 273.15 K (or 0°C) as their standard, because when exact measurements are to be made of physical constants, it is much easier to control accurately a temperature which is slightly warmer than the surroundings than to cool a mass of gas, say, to 0°C before making the measurements.

**standing wave:** see *stationary wave*.

**star:** a large incandescent mass whose core pressures, densities and temperatures are high enough to sustain nuclear fusion reactions which provide a continuous and enormous output of radiant power. When the fuel begins to run out, other reactions cause the core to overheat and the star embarks upon the *red giant* phase.

The observable properties of stars include surface temperature $T$, distance $D$, mass $m$, luminosity $L$, intensity $I$, radius $r$ (indirectly), velocity, spectrum and spectral type.

- Temperature is measured from the *total radiation curve* for the star using *Wien's law* (1893).
- Distance $D$ can be measured directly only for those stars which are close enough to the Earth for their parallaxes to exceed 0.02 seconds of arc. Parallax is the maximum angle subtended at the star by the radius of the Earth's orbit. It is found by measuring the position of the star against a background of faint and generally distant stars over a six-month period. The distances of a few thousand nearby stars have been measured in this way (i.e. about one star in a hundred million for our galaxy). The distance of a star for which the parallax would be exactly one second of arc is called a *parsec* ($3.09 \times 10^{16}$ m or 3.26 light years). The nearer stars are a few parsecs away.
- Mass can be determined for any star which is one member of a double star and close enough for the separation of the two stars to be measured. This is the case for about 200 stars.
- Luminosity $L$ of a star is the total radiant power output in watts. If luminosity and surface temperature are both known, then by using *Stefan's law* the radius of the star can be found: $L = A\sigma T^4 = 4\pi r^2 \cdot \sigma T^4$.
- The intensity $I$ of a star is the radiant power per square metre of star surface, reaching the Earth's surface. If $D$ is the distance of the star from the Earth, then $I = L/(4\pi D^2)$.

(Avoid the ambiguous word 'brightness'. Luminosity is actual brightness; intensity is apparent brightness.)

Intensity is sometimes expressed in terms of two ancient parameters, the apparent magnitude $m$ and the absolute magnitude $M$. Apparent magnitude is related to intensity $I$ as follows:

$$m = -2.5\log_{10} I + \text{constant} \quad \text{or} \quad m_1 - m_2 = 2.5\log_{10}(I_2/I_1)$$

The absolute magnitude of a star equals the apparent magnitude of the star were it a distance of ten parsecs from the Earth. Since intensity is inversely proportional to distance squared, we can substitute $M$ for $m_2$ on the left-hand side of the last equation and, on the right-hand side, replace $(I_2/I_1)$ by $(r/10)^2$. The equation now links $m$ to $M$ for a particular star:

$$m - M = 5\log_{10}(r/10)$$

where $r$ is the distance of the star from the Earth in parsecs. These same two quantities, $m$ and $M$, are used with galaxies as well as stars.

Spectral types (O, B, A, F, G, K, M) are a way a classifying the spectra of stars by broad visual character. The method was essential before Wien's law was known; it is retained because it is useful.

| Class | Temperature | Surface character |
|---|---|---|
| O | > 25000 K | Ionised helium lines dominant |
| B | 25000 K to 11000 K | Neutral helium, excited hydrogen visible |
| A | 11000 K to 7500 K | Hydrogen lines dominant |
| F | 7500 K to 6000 K | Hydrogen lines weaker, calcium gaining strength |
| G | 6000 K to 5000 K | Calcium dominant, ions much weaker |
| K | 5000 K to 3500 K | Neutral metals predominate |
| M | < 3500 K | Molecular bands apparent |

(See *end states of stars, Hertzsprung–Russell diagram, Hubble's law, parallax (stellar).*)

**states of matter** are the set of states that the atoms or molecules in a lump of matter can exist in. At one time there were thought to be three states of matter: solid, liquid and gas. More recently the gaseous state has been joined by the plasma state in which a gas has become ionised so that it consists of atoms, ions and free electrons. The distinction between the solid and liquid states has also broken down following the recognition that *glasses* form an intermediate group. It is not simply that there are kinds of solid; there is an increasing number of structures which do not fit the definition of the solid state as an ordered arrangement with the atoms or molecules attached to their neighbours. (See *solids, liquids, gases, metals, crystalline solids, polycrystalline solids, amorphous solids, polymeric solids.*)

**stationary wave:** an extended oscillation in which vibrational energy is stored. Stationary waves are sometimes called standing waves. A stationary wave can be resolved into two *progressive waves* of the same frequency, travelling along the same line but in opposite directions. The sequence of events leading to the formation of a stationary wave is illustrated in the diagram.

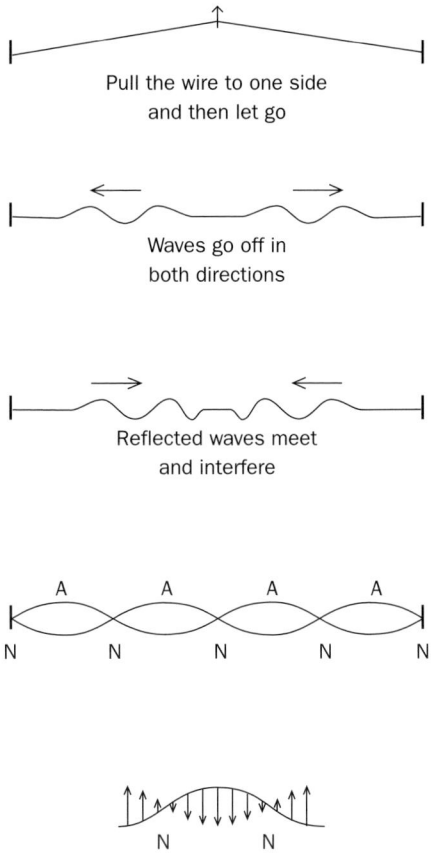


An initial disturbance sends out waves in both directions along a taut wire. They are reflected from both ends of the wire and overlap on their return paths. At certain points marked as

N *(nodes)* the waves always meet out of phase and interfere destructively. At other points marked as A *(antinodes)* the waves always meet in phase and interfere constructively. The wire is stationary at the nodes and oscillates with maximum amplitude at the antinodes.

The waves are stationary in two senses: there is no flow of energy, and the node–antinode system is fixed in position. The final panel of the diagram above illustrates what is meant by all points between adjacent nodes moving in phase and by a phase change of $\pi$ on moving through a node.

Most musical instruments work by setting up a stationary wave on a thread, in a pipe or on a diaphragm. The energy arrives in an erratic way but is stored smoothly and is transmitted to the air in a smooth fashion. The dying away of the note from a single piano string is an example of *damped harmonic motion*.

A stationary wave is an *interference* pattern set up by two waves of the same frequency moving in opposite directions. It is also an example of *resonance*. Imagine a power source of variable frequency applied to a taut wire. Let the frequency slowly increase from zero. At most frequencies, the two waves moving in opposite directions along the wire will self-destruct. At some frequencies (the resonant frequencies) they enhance one another. This happens when a stationary wave can form on the wire with a node at either end. These waves are the result of *constructive interference* and are an example of resonance. Resonance can happen only on a wire whose length is a whole number of half-wavelengths. The situation with pipes is more complicated. (See *waves in pipes*, *waves on strings*.)

The table below lists the important properties of stationary waves and contrasts them with progressive waves.

| **Stationary wave** | **Progressive wave** |
|---|---|
| Stores vibrational energy | Transmits vibrational energy |
| The amplitude increases smoothly from a minimum value at the nodes to a maximum value at the antinodes | The amplitude is constant along the length of the wave |
| All points along the wave between any two adjacent nodes move in phase | Phase varies linearly with distance along the path of the wave |
| There is an abrupt phase change of $\pi$ on moving through a node | There are no sudden changes of phase |
| Nodes are set half a wavelength apart, antinodes are set half a wavelength apart, an antinode is set midway between two nodes | There are no nodes or antinodes |

**steady state** is the condition of a body when the various temperatures throughout the body are constant, and during which there is no net loss or gain of heat to or from the surroundings (note, however, that the temperatures are not necessarily everywhere the same).

Imagine a long-handled metal spoon dipping into water kept at boiling point. Heat energy flows into the bowl of the spoon and out along the handle. The spoon loses heat energy to the surroundings along its length and the top end of the handle will be cool enough to hold. The spoon loses as much heat as it gains; all the temperatures throughout the spoon are steady but the temperatures are not everywhere the same. Furthermore, heat energy is flowing through the spoon without there being any net gain or loss to the spoon. This is a steady state, not a *thermal equilibrium* state.

**steam point:** the temperature at standard atmospheric pressure of steam in *thermal equilibrium* with water. It is 373.15 K.

**Stefan's law** (also known as the Stefan–Boltzmann law) states that the power $P$ radiated (i.e. energy radiated per second) from a body is proportional to the area, $A$, and to the fourth power of the absolute temperature $T$ of the surface. For a perfect radiator (a total radiator or a black body), Stefan's law is written:

$$P = \sigma A T^4$$

This equation gives only the heat radiated. The heat absorbed from the surroundings must obey the same law, otherwise a body at the same temperature as its surroundings would not be in *thermal equilibrium*.

For example, take a black pot in surroundings at 300 K and raise the temperature of the pot to 600 K. The net power loss is the difference between the power radiated and the power absorbed:

$$P = \sigma A\left(600^4 - 300^4\right) = \sigma A \times 300^4\left(2^4 - 1\right)$$

Since $2^4$ is 16, we see that a body which is twice the temperature of its surroundings emits 16 times as much radiation per second as it absorbs.

Stefan's law is extended to cover real surfaces by writing it in the form

$$P = \varepsilon \sigma A T^4$$

where $\varepsilon$ is a constant between 0 and 1. $\varepsilon$ is called the total emissivity and it takes different values for different surfaces.

**stiffness** is the quality of a material which enables it to respond to a high tensile stress with a small tensile strain: its *Young modulus* is large. If various materials are made into beams, all of the same size, the stiffer materials will bend least. A stiff material has low *flexibility*. (See *stress–strain curves*.)

**Stokes' law** states that the viscous force opposing the motion of a sphere of radius $r$ moving at terminal speed $v$ through a fluid medium of viscosity $\eta$ in conditions of streamline flow is $6\pi r\eta v$. Imagine a small steel sphere, of mass $m$ and radius $r$, falling through a light oil in a tall measuring cylinder. Its speed increases slowly up to a maximum and constant value called the *terminal speed*. At this point the apparent weight of the steel sphere (which is equal to weight minus upthrust), pulling downwards, and the resistive *drag*, acting upwards, are equal and opposite. The resistive drag at the terminal speed $v$ equals $6\pi r\eta v$. (See *streamline flow*, *viscosity*.)

**straight current-carrying wire:** for a long straight wire isolated from its surroundings and carrying current $I$, the magnitude of the *magnetic field strength* $B$ at a point a perpendicular distance $r$ from the wire is given by:

$$B = \frac{\mu_0 I}{2\pi r}$$

The magnetic lines of force are all circular, and the spacing increases away from the wire as the field strength weakens. The direction of the magnetic lines of force is shown in the following diagram. This direction is given by the *right hand grip rule*.

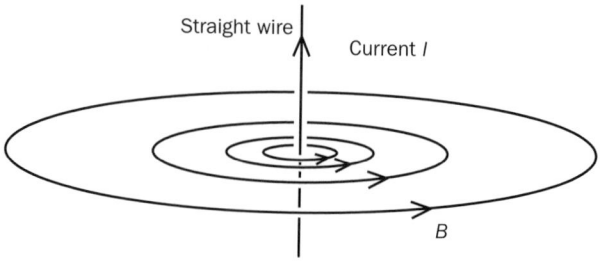


Remember when copying this diagram that the magnetic lines of force must be broken to show where they pass behind the wire and that you should draw a minimum of four magnetic lines of force to show the increased spacing with distance. (See *magnetic effect of current.*)

**straight line motion** is the fundamental motion on which Newtonian mechanics and classical physics are built. Some books and specifications call it rectilinear motion. Kinematics, the study of motion without reference to force or energy, takes the topic beyond straight line motion to curved paths of almost any shape. Straight line motion in A-level physics is covered by the entry *equations of motion*. One danger with straight line motion is that, because direction is often irrelevant, the distinctions between distance and displacement and between speed and velocity become obscured. Once force or energy are involved, the topic becomes part of dynamics.

**strain,** or more accurately tensile strain, is the increase in length of a specimen per unit length in response to a tensile *stress*. Strain is a ratio of two lengths; it is a number with no unit. It is a property of a material and its value depends only on the magnitude of the applied stress and not at all on the dimensions of the specimen. (See *stress, stress–strain curves, Young modulus.*)

**strain energy:** see *elastic strain energy.*

**strain gauge:** a sensor, often consisting of a metal wire, which is attached to a structure. As the structure is put under strain, the sensor is also strained and its electrical *resistance* changes. Measurement of the resistance allows the strain to be determined.

**streamline flow** (or laminar flow) is the smooth flow of a fluid along a channel without the disturbing action of small eddies. Streamlines are the imaginary lines which mark the path of the fluid. In streamline flow these lines are smooth curves or straight lines. *Stokes' law* is valid for streamline flow only. (See *turbulent flow.*)

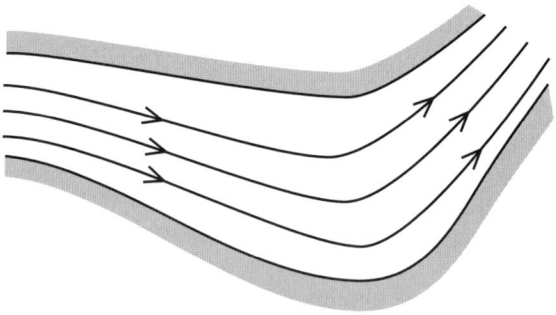

**strength** of a specimen is the tensile force or the tensile *stress* needed to break it. (See *ultimate tensile stress, breaking stress.*)

**stress** may compress a volume, distort a shape or stretch a thread. Only the stretching action matters at A level. The specimen must be pulled by equal tensions in opposite directions. Tensile stress, as it is called, equals the tensile force per unit area applied to a specimen. The SI unit for tensile stress is the pascal (Pa). (See *strain, stress–strain curves, compressibility, Young modulus.*)

**stress–strain curves** are graphs that show how the tensile *strain* of a specimen varies with the tensile *stress* applied to it. The graph below applies to no material in particular; this is why there are no numerical values on the axes. Its purpose is to display typical features of these curves and to define some of the parameters which are used when discussing the elastic properties of materials.

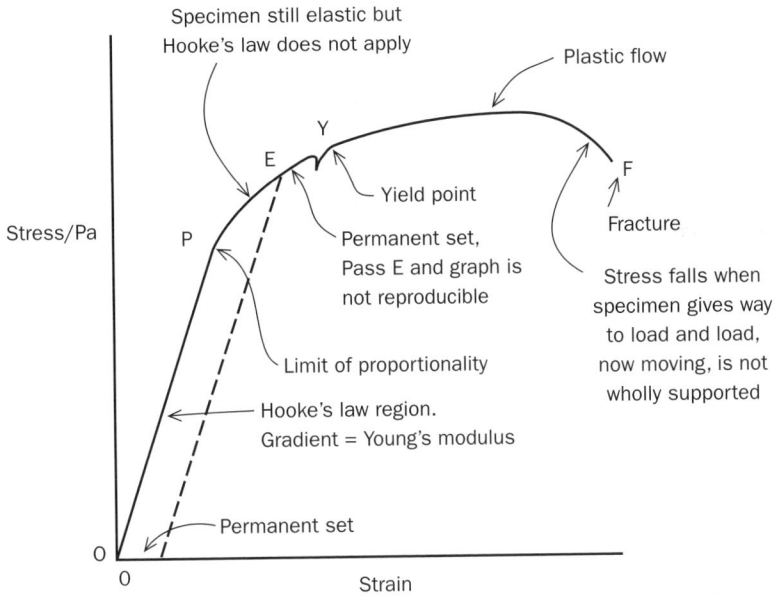


Starting at O, the point of zero stress and zero strain, the curve rises along a straight line to the point P. Along OP, stress is proportional to strain, and *Hooke's law* applies to the specimen. OP is called the Hooke's law region and P is called the *limit of proportionality.* The gradient of the straight portion OP is the *Young modulus* for the specimen. Along the section PE, the specimen is still elastic in the sense that if the strain is removed the specimen will return to O and recover its original length. The point E is the *elastic limit.* If the specimen is stretched beyond E, it will not return to O when the stress is relaxed; it will never quite recover its original length. There is now a permanent set. Increase the stress a little more and the specimen is subject to sudden internal slippage. This point Y is called the *yield point.* The curve drops and rises because, with the sudden increase in length (increase in strain), the wire moves and does not altogether support the load for a moment. This part of the curve cannot be repeated or traced backwards. Once the yield point is passed, any further increase in the level of stress invites a continuum of small yields which is known as plastic flow. Atoms are slipping over one another, the specimen is about to break and, since the load is no longer being supported (it is falling and gathering speed), the stress decreases. The area between the curve and the strain axis is the energy transferred per unit volume to the specimen during the whole process.

The set of curves below is chosen to highlight different elastic properties. Each curve starts at zero stress. An asterisk at the end of the graph indicates where the specimen breaks.

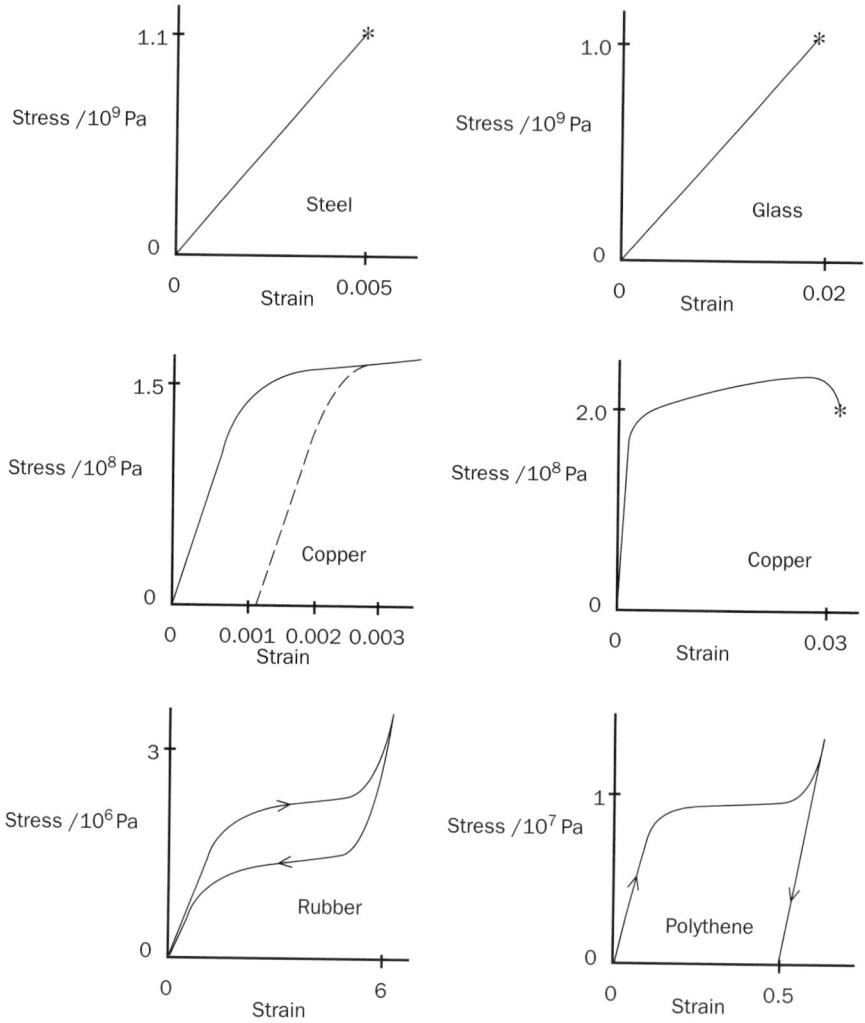


Mild steel and glass have high breaking stresses and are said to be strong. *Stiffness* is linked to the gradient of the graph and is higher for steel than for glass. Glass gives no warning that it is about to break; it is said to be brittle. Copper, with its large extension and large area 'under the curve', absorbs a lot of energy before it breaks and is said to be tough.

Copper exhibits a large plastic flow while rubber has a strong *hysteresis* effect. The numerical values on the axes of these curves are orders of magnitude; they should be known. (See *brittleness, strength, toughness, plastic deformation.*)

**stroboscope:** a device used to observe repetitive motions. An electronic stroboscope (or 'strobe') is a flashing lamp whose frequency can be controlled precisely. It is directed at a vibrating object and its frequency is adjusted. If the frequency of the stroboscope exactly matches that of the vibrating object, the object will appear stationary because the observer will see a succession of views of the object, each showing it at the same point in its vibration cycle. If the frequency of the stroboscope is slightly different from that of the object, then to the observer, the object will apparently be moving slowly through its vibration.

The same effect can be obtained using a mechanical stroboscope consisting of a rotating wheel with equally spaced slots in its rim. The wheel is turned by hand or motor and the vibrating object is viewed through the slots. When the frequency of the slots passing the eye matches the frequency of the vibrating object, the object will appear stationary.

**structure** is a term used to describe manufactured objects such as *beams*, girders, *cantilevers*, pipes, walls or embankments where the design process has made use of the physical properties of the component materials.

**subatomic particle** is a term which covers any particle smaller than an atom in size. Atoms are roughly $10^{-10}$ m across. Atomic nuclei are typically $10^{-14}$ m across unless the mass number is low, in which case, like the neutron and proton, they are closer to $10^{-15}$ m across. ***Elementary particles*** such as *leptons* (e.g. electrons) or *quarks* are known to be less than $10^{-18}$ m across — that is about as small as can be measured. A distance of $10^{-15}$ m is just within the range of operation of the strong nuclear force.

**superconductors** are substances with a resistance to current that falls to zero at a transition temperature. The first superconductors were *metals* which were found to have transition temperatures a few degrees above absolute zero. More recently, ceramic superconductors have been discovered that become superconducting at temperatures on the order of 100 K. Magnets powered by coils of superconducting materials are in widespread use, for example, in *particle accelerators* and *MRI* scanners. Transmission of electric power by superconducting cable will await the development of materials that are modestly priced, available in bulk and which retain their superconducting properties at temperatures higher than the boiling point of liquid nitrogen.

**superposition** is the process by which two waves combine into a single wave form when they overlap. (See *principle of superposition.*)

**symbol:** an agreed abbreviation for a physical or mathematical quantity. It may represent either a constant or a variable. See the appendices on pages 289 and 296 for lists of symbols used in physics for variables and constants.

**synchrotron:** see *particle accelerators.*

**systematic error:** an inherent error in an instrument or technique which cannot be reduced or eliminated by averaging the results of several measurements. Systematic error is guarded against by analysis and care. Examples include *zero error*, measuring the wrong distance for a pendulum length or a falling body, poor instrument *calibration*, and failing to correct for background radiation. (See *error, uncertainty, random error, zero error.*)

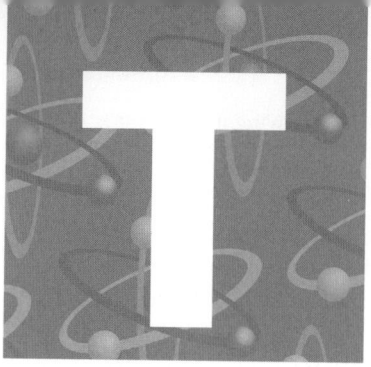

**telescopes** are devices used to collect radiation coming from beyond the Earth. Optical telescopes gather light, radio telescopes gather radio waves, and so on.

Optical telescopes magnify by collecting light confined to a small visual angle and spreading it out over a much larger angle. In terrestrial terms, the same effect is achieved by walking closer to the object of interest. If you get too close to the object for the eyes to focus, then you throw the image back and away from the eye with a magnifying glass or, still better, a microscope. The ray diagram for an astronomical telescope in normal adjustment (i.e. with the image at infinity) is shown in the diagram.

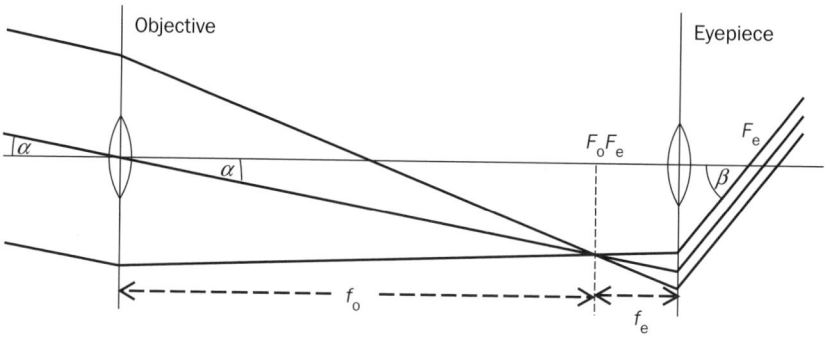


The magnification is calculated as follows:

$$M = \frac{\text{angle subtended by image at eye}}{\text{angle subtended by object at eye}} = \frac{\beta}{\alpha} = \frac{f_0}{f_e}$$

The image is never perfect. Two principal sources of imperfection are *chromatic aberration* (change of *focal length* with wavelength of light used) and *spherical aberration* (change of focal length with distance from the principal axis). The elimination of chromatic aberration is a pleasing feature of reflecting telescopes, but the main attraction of reflectors has to do with resolving power.

The angle $\theta$ between two point sources of light which can just be separated by a telescope can be shown to equal $1.22\lambda/D$, where $D$ is the diameter of aperture limiting the width of the light beam collected and $\lambda$ is the wavelength of the radiation used. In practice, $D$ is the diameter of the objective lens or of the mirror. The angle $\theta$ is called the resolving power; it governs how much detail can be seen. Mirrors can be made much larger than lenses without distorting under their own weight. For high resolution, reflectors win every time. The long wavelength of radio waves explains the huge size of radio telescopes. (See *diffraction at a small circular hole, resolving power.*)

The next diagram shows the optical system for a reflecting telescope. This system is known as the *Cassegrain arrangement.* Without the small central mirror or something similar, the light cannot leave the telescope and the image will not be seen. The light loss associated with the mirror is hugely compensated for by the larger diameters possible with reflectors. The focusing of either refracting or reflecting telescopes can be adjusted to give real images which can then be observed electronically on PC monitors using *charge-coupled devices* (CCDs) as image sensors. With radio telescopes, the small mirror is replaced by an aerial tuned to the radio frequency that the astronomer is interested in, usually around 1.5 GHz. For resolving powers well below one degree, the radio reflector needs a diameter of 100 m or more. Resolution can be improved by using arrays of smaller radio telescopes. The downside to this is a loss of collecting beam cross-section.

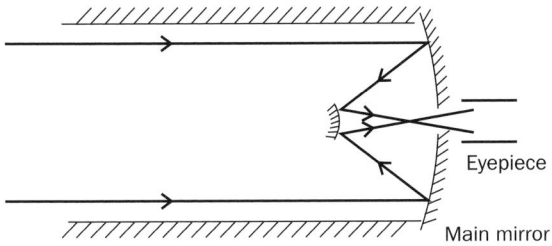


The reason for the concentration of work within the visible and radio wavebands is that these are the wavelengths for which the atmosphere is transparent. Mounting telescopes on satellites extends the work to other wavebands such as X-ray, UV, IR and microwave. There is the further advantage in using satellites, which applies equally to the visible region, that there is little atmospheric absorption or refraction. However, modern Earthbound telescopes use 'adaptive optics' to reduce or eliminate many of these distortion effects so that the resolution obtained is comparable with that of space telescopes.

**temperature** is the hotness of a body expressed on a numerical scale. Temperature scales were, at one time, set up in an arbitrary way and different people used different scales. It is now recognised that temperature is not an arbitrary quantity. The *absolute temperature scale* is defined within thermodynamics in a way which is independent of the properties of any substance but applicable to all substances. It turns out that this scale is identical to the temperature scale that is written into the gas laws. Using these ideas as a basis, another temperature scale, the *International Practical Temperature scale,* has been defined, which specifies how temperatures are to be measured before they can be part of a legally enforceable specification.

One advantage of basing everything on thermodynamics is that there is no need to make assumptions about mercury in a mercury thermometer, platinum in a *resistance thermometer* or any other substance. Each of these, if assumed to vary linearly with temperature, would define its own temperature scale. This is an altogether different thing from the Celsius and Fahrenheit scales, which merely involve shifting the zero of the absolute scale, changing the temperature interval belonging to one degree, or both.

**temperature coefficient of resistance** is the increase in the resistance of a conductor, as a fraction of its resistance at 0°C, per degree absolute rise in temperature. The word equation definition is:

$$\text{temperature coefficient of resistance} = \frac{\text{increase in resistance}}{\text{resistance at } 0°\text{C} \times \text{ temperature rise}}$$

$$\alpha = \frac{R_2 - R_1}{R_0\left(T_2 - T_1\right)}\,\text{K}^{-1}$$

**temperature gradient** is defined by the word equation

$$\text{temperature gradient} = \frac{\text{temperature difference between two points}}{\text{distance between the points}}$$

The unit for temperature gradient is $\text{K m}^{-1}$. A temperature gradient gives rise to heat transfer when two bodies are in thermal contact (i.e. when there is a path between them along which heat can be transferred).

**tensile force** is a stretching force usually applied to a material that is in the form of a strand, such as a wire, an elastic string or a spring. For the material to stretch, there must be two tensile forces of equal magnitude, acting in opposite directions. The ratio of force to extension depends both on the material and on its dimensions. To remove the dimensional factor, it is usual to work with (tensile) *stress* and (tensile) *strain*.

**tensile strain:** see *strain*.

**tensile stress** is a force per unit area acting on the ends of a material in bar form to stretch it. It is the opposite of *compressive stress* and is caused by a pair of equal and opposite *tensile forces* acting on the bar. The ratio of tensile stress to tensile strain (fractional increase in length) for an elastic material is its *Young modulus*.

**terminal speed** (sometimes referred to, incorrectly, as terminal velocity) is the speed of fall of a body in air for which the air resistance, acting upwards, is equal in magnitude but opposite in direction to the downward-acting weight. The resultant force is zero and the body continues its path towards the ground at constant speed. For a large but light body, such as a parachutist, the Archimedean upthrust has to be taken into account. It acts upwards and 'helps' the air resistance. There are then three forces drawn and labelled on the *free-body force diagram*.

Terminal speeds in liquids are much slower than terminal speeds in air. The Archimedean upthrust is generally a much larger fraction of the weight, and the *drag* forces supplied by the liquid are much larger than those provided by air.

An important special case is illustrated by a solid sphere falling through liquid at rest. Provided that the liquid is not held in a narrow tube, the drag force is given by *Stokes' law*. It equals $6\pi r\eta v$ where $r$ is the radius of the sphere, $\eta$ is the coefficient of viscosity and $v$ is the terminal speed. Stokes' law provides a method for measuring the coefficient of viscosity and, if the value of the coefficient is known already, a method for estimating average particle size.

**tesla** is the SI unit for *magnetic field strength*. The symbol for the unit is T. Following on from the equation used to define magnetic field strength, $F = BIl$, the tesla is defined by the word equation

$$\text{tesla} = \frac{\text{newton}}{\text{ampere} \times \text{metre}}$$

**thermal conduction** is the process by which heat flows through matter along a temperature gradient. The mathematics for three-dimensional flow quickly gets out of hand, so we restrict ourselves to the case of one-dimensional flow of heat along a uniform bar of cross-sectional area $A$. We further restrict ourselves to the *steady state* condition, wherein temperatures along the bar, although they may be different, are all constant. The situation is illustrated in the diagram below.

One end of the bar is kept at 100°C with a current of steam, the other at 0°C with a current of ice-cold water. The bar is in a steady state once all the temperatures along its length have become constant (note that this is not a *thermal equilibrium* state, in which all the temperatures along its length would be the same and there would be no heat flow). If the sides of the bar are efficiently lagged, the rate of heat flow into the hot end of the bar equals the rate of heat flow out of the cold end. The rate of heat flow will be the same at all points along the length of the bar, and the temperature gradient $d\theta/dx$ is constant along the length of the bar. The graph shows the temperatures at various distances from the hot end of the bar to follow a straight line. The heat flow is governed by the equation

$$\frac{dQ}{dt} = kA\frac{d\theta}{dx}$$

where $dQ/dt$ is the heat flowing per second into or out of the bar, $A$ is the area of the cross-section of the bar, $d\theta/dx$ is the temperature gradient and $k$ is the coefficient of thermal conductivity of the material of the bar. The unit for $k$ is $W\,m^{-1}\,K^{-1}$. The above equation defines the coefficient of thermal conductivity $k$.

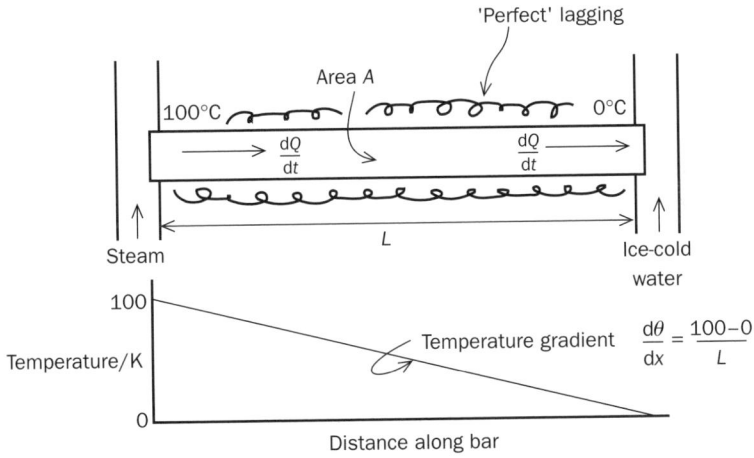


**Worked example**

**Imagine that the bar shown in the diagram is made of brass (thermal conductivity $109\,W\,m^{-1}\,K^{-1}$), with length 25.6 cm and cross-sectional area $9.2\,cm^2$. The temperature difference between the ends is 100 K. Find the rate of flow of heat along the bar.**

$$\text{rate of flow of heat} = \frac{dQ}{dt} = kA\frac{\theta_1 - \theta_2}{x}$$
$$= (109\ W\ m^{-1}K^{-1})(9.2 \times 10^{-1}m^2)(100\ K/0.256\ m)$$
$$= 39\ W\ (\text{to 2 s.f.})$$

(See *thermal conductivity, temperature gradient, U value.*)

**thermal conductivity** is the rate of heat flow per unit area per unit temperature gradient. Its value is a property of the substance involved. The symbol used is $k$ and the SI unit is $\mathrm{W\,m^{-1}\,K^{-1}}$. The word equation definition is derived from the thermal conductivity equation, thus:

$$k = \frac{\mathrm{d}Q}{\mathrm{d}t} \div \left(A\frac{\mathrm{d}\theta}{\mathrm{d}x}\right)$$

$$= \frac{\text{rate of flow of heat}}{\text{area} \times \text{temperature gradiant}}$$

$$\mathrm{Wm^{-1}K^{-1}} = \frac{\mathrm{Js^{-1}}}{\mathrm{m^2} \times (\mathrm{Km^{-1}})}$$

There are two groups of substances: good thermal conductors and poor thermal conductors. The values of the coefficient $k$ for good thermal conductors are typically a thousand times the values of $k$ for poor thermal conductors. Most good thermal conductors are electrical conductors (i.e. metals). The reason is that the conduction electrons carry heat through the material far faster than do atomic vibrations within the solid mass. Compare this with the electrical case: crystal structures do not transmit electrical charge. The distinction is between *conductors and insulators* and the ratio of their electrical conductivities is typically around $10^{21}$.

**thermal energy** is an uncertain term which is best avoided. The word 'thermal' is an adjective relating to heat. The term 'thermal energy' may be used to refer to:

- *internal energy*: that part of the energy content of a body which is associated with the disordered motion of the atoms (kinetic in part and potential in part)
- *heat*: energy flowing down a temperature gradient

Because these are distinct concepts which should not be confused, it is best to avoid using the term 'thermal energy'.

**thermal equilibrium** is a state in which every part of a body has the same temperature and in which there is no net loss or gain of thermal energy by the body to or from the surroundings. A body is known to be in a state of thermal equilibrium if the independent physical properties of the system (pressure and volume) are constant. Once other observable physical properties are known to be constant, the temperature of the body must be constant.

Two bodies will be in thermal equilibrium with one another (with their temperatures equal) provided: (i) they are in thermal contact, and (ii) they are both in thermal equilibrium states. Do not confuse a thermal equilibrium state with a *steady state*.

(See *zeroth law of thermodynamics*.)

**thermal fission reactor** (nuclear reactor) is an electricity-generating plant which exploits the energy released when nuclei of heavy elements such as uranium are broken down into lighter elements. The mass–energy conversion process which underpins the process is discussed under *binding energy*. The principle of a thermal fission reactor involves three ongoing activities: a stable *chain reaction*, an energy removal process and maintenance.

For the chain reaction, start with a stray neutron which collides with a uranium nucleus. The nucleus absorbs the neutron, becomes unstable and breaks up into two nuclei,

X and Y, some neutrons (two or three but averaging 2.6) and a lot of energy (mostly in the form of kinetic energy for X and Y). We can write a generalised nuclear equation for one fission process:

$$n + {}^{235}U = X + Y + 2.6n + \text{about } 200 \text{ MeV}$$

This is not as dangerous as it looks. The incident neutron must be 'slow', that is, its kinetic energy must correspond to the prevailing temperature. But the 2.6 neutrons are 'fast'; their kinetic energies are five or six orders of magnitude too high for them to trigger further fission reactions.

To achieve a stable chain reaction, the 2.6 fast neutrons must be slowed down, with one neutron returning to cause a successful fission reaction and the rest being absorbed or escaping from the structure. This slowing-down process occurs in the *moderator*. The uranium fuel is held in long narrow *fuel rods* which slot into columns of graphite moderator at regular intervals. When fast neutrons escape from the fuel rods into the moderator, they crash into carbon nuclei and give up most of their energy after several such collisions. The moderator gets hot; a proportion of the neutrons diffuses out of the system, but some re-enter the fuel rods. The number returning is just large enough to sustain a constant rate of nuclear fission processes (see diagram).

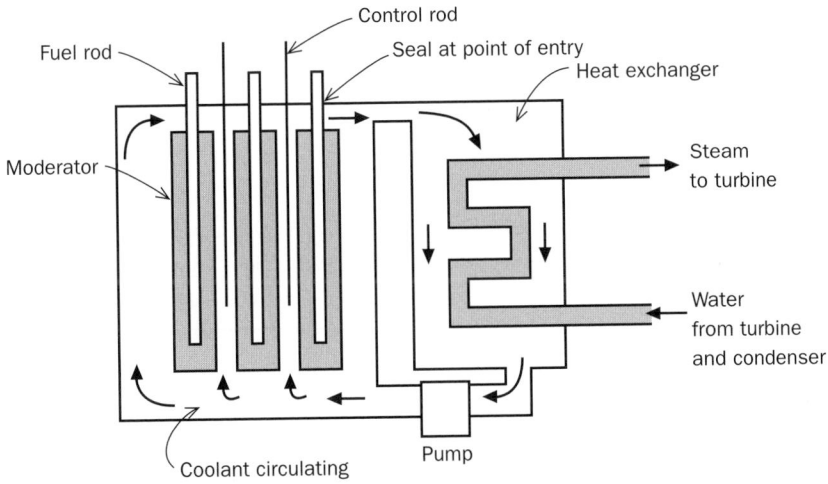


The stability of the chain reaction is a consequence of the design, the amount of uranium in the fuel rods and the spacing of the fuel rods in the moderator. There is one more vital component: a set of *control rods*. These control rods contain material such as boron which is highly efficient at absorbing neutrons. The rods are lowered into the moderator at regular intervals and just deep enough for the reactor to 'go critical'. If they are lowered further the reaction slows down; if they are raised slightly the reaction speeds up.

The energy removal process uses a fluid, possibly carbon dioxide gas under high pressure, pumped through the reactor. The coolant picks up by conduction the heat generated in the fuel rods and transmits it to the heat exchanger where it powers the conversion of water into high-pressure steam that is used to drive turbines and generate *electrical power*. Since most of the energy released in the fission processes appears as kinetic energy of the heavy fission products, the coolant pipes must be as close as possible to the fuel rods, otherwise the moderator material will overheat. Notice that the fission products, excepting the neutrons, stay in the fuel rods. The neutrons cannot pick up the kinetic energy from these fission products: they are too light and they are already far too fast so that collisions would tend to slow them down. Only a conduction process can remove the energy from the fuel rods, and for this to occur the coolant must not be far away.

The maintenance work includes replacing the fuel rods at regular intervals and monitoring the coolant, coolant support system, moderator and control rods.

**thermal power** is *power* drawn from any device for which the starting point is the burning of some kind of fuel or the process of nuclear *fission*. (See *fuels, thermal power station*.)

**thermal power station:** an installation where fuel is burned and part of the heat released, used to generate *electrical power*. The overall efficiency of a thermal power station is the ratio of the electrical energy reaching the consumer to the internal energy released when the primary fuel burns.

**thermionic emission** is the flow of electrons through and away from the surface of a hot metal. The metal has to be heated to a dull red heat and a battery is needed to sustain the flow; otherwise the build up of positive potential on the metal inhibits and eventually suppresses the electron flow. A heated cathode provides the electrons in the *electron guns* used in X-ray tubes, oscilloscopes and television sets.

**thermistors** are resistors with strongly temperature-dependent resistance values. The current $I$ in a conductor of cross-sectional area $A$ is given by the relationship

$$I = nAqv$$

where there are $n$ charge carriers per unit volume moving with an average drift velocity $v$, each carrying charge $q$. For some semiconducting materials, the number of charge carriers per unit volume, $n$, increases sharply with rising temperature. For a given potential difference across the specimen, the current increases sharply with increasing temperature. The resistance will have dropped. These thermistors have a negative *temperature coefficient of resistance*; they are the most common sort.

Other thermistors can be manufactured in which the increase of $n$ with rising temperature is slight but in which lattice vibrations impose a much stronger brake on charge carrier motion if the temperature rises. There is a sharp decrease in $v$ and the resultant fall in current swamps any tendency for the current to rise because of an increase in $n$. The resistance of these thermistors increases if their temperature rises: they have positive temperature coefficients of resistance.

**thermocouple:** a thermometer which uses the thermoelectric effect to sense and measure a difference in temperature. The diagram below shows an idealised thermocouple. A series circuit is set up consisting of a digital voltmeter, two wires of metal X and a single wire of metal Y. The junctions at either end of metal Y, labelled A and B, are set in two objects of temperatures $\theta_A$ and $\theta_B$, respectively. Experiment shows that the reading of the digital voltmeter depends on $(\theta_A - \theta_B)$. If $\theta_B$ is fixed at thermal equilibrium state 0°C by immersing the end B in iced water, the digital voltmeter can be calibrated to give a direct reading of the temperature $\theta_A$.

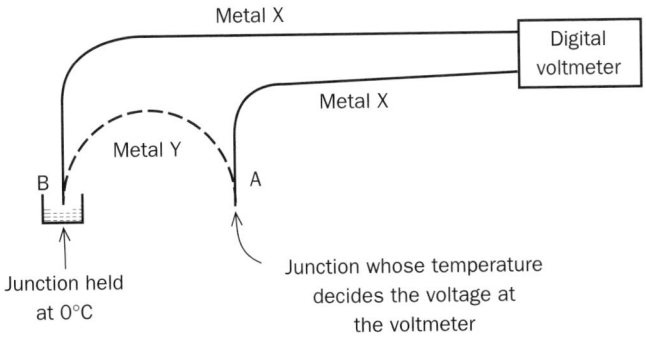


Thermocouple thermometers are not easy to build because their *calibration* depends on too many factors, such as the purity of the metals used for the wires and the quality of the junctions. The metals used often need special solder. In commercial thermocouples, the metals are chosen to suit the temperature range for which they will be used.

Thermocouples are widely used because of their many valuable qualities:

- they are rugged, accurate and sensitive
- they are usually small enough not to interfere with the object whose temperature is being measured
- output can be fed directly to a data recording device
- the instrumentation can be remote from any hot object under investigation

**thermodynamic temperature scale:** another name for the *absolute temperature scale.*

**thermodynamics:** the mathematical study of the relationship between heat and other forms of energy, particularly in relation to *heat engines.* (See *first law of thermodynamics, second law of thermodynamics, zeroth law of thermodynamics.*)

**thermoplastic polymers** are *polymeric solids* with molecular chains that are weakly bound together by Van der Waals' forces. Such polymers soften on heating and harden again on cooling. They are easily moulded into shape. (See *Van der Waals' bond.*)

**thermosetting polymers** are *polymeric solids* in which strong covalent cross-links are formed between the molecular chains when the material first cools but which do not break up when the material is reheated. They are good for making saucepan handles and suchlike, but can be brittle. (See *covalent bond.*)

**threshold frequency:** the minimum frequency of electromagnetic radiation capable of triggering the *photoelectric effect* for a given material.

**thrust** is a force spread over an area instead of acting through a point of application. The thrust exerted by a fluid on a surface equals the product of the *pressure* and the area of the surface. It is a contact force which acts normal to the surface and into the surface.

**time** is a base *physical quantity* in SI. Its symbol is $t$ and the SI unit is the *second.* The time scale that clocks measure and which we use without too much fuss in mechanics and in the rest of A-level physics is defined implicitly within Newton's laws of motion. (See *base quantity.*)

**time constant** $\tau$ is the time interval during which the charging or discharging current for a capacitor in series with a resistor falls to a fraction 1/e of an earlier value. The phrase 'an earlier value' is used because the current–time graph is exponential and the time needed for any given fractional change is constant along its length.

The charging current for capacitance $C$ in series with resistance $R$ changes with time according to the following formula:

$$I = I_{max}e^{-t/RC}$$

The definition of time constant tells us that when $t = \tau$,

$$I = I_{max}e^{-1}$$

Therefore, putting $t = \tau$ in the first formula above and equating it with the second, we have

$$\tau/RC = 1 \quad \text{or} \quad \tau = RC$$

This last equation is an important result, but it is not the definition of time constant. The definition of time constant is the first sentence of this entry; learn it.

**time dilation** is the increase in the time interval between two events when they occur in a reference frame which is moving relative to the observer. A classic example is the decay of muons. Muons are leptons which decay with a half-life of about 2 μs as measured in the laboratory. But if the half-life of fast-moving muons arriving from space is measured, it is found to be considerably longer. So, as observed by a stationary observer, fast-moving clocks appear to run slow. However, if you travel at speed with a clock, it will appear to advance at its normal rate because you are at rest relative to the clock. (See *special relativity.*)

**time division multiplexing** is a technique for enabling one telephone cable or transmission channel to carry many separate messages in digital form simultaneously. Imagine the time scale for such a cable to be split into intervals, each one microsecond long. Next, imagine each of these 1 μs divisions to be divided into 20 slots, each of length 50 ns. One digital message can be transmitted in the third slot of each microsecond, another can be transmitted in the fourteenth slot. If one slot is retained for managing the use of the cable, 19 messages can be transmitted simultaneously. (See also *frequency division multiplexing, pulse code modulation.*)

**time interval** is a measure of duration. It is measured in seconds.

**torque** is the moment of a couple. The SI unit for torque is the newton metre (N m). The symbol used is $T$. It is a pseudo-vector quantity but its vector qualities are usually ignored at A-level (these vector properties matter only if a body is acted upon by two non-parallel torques). Torque plays the same part in rotational motion that force plays in translational motion. The vital relationships are:

$$\text{torque} = \text{moment of inertia} \times \text{angular acceleration}$$

$$T = I \times \alpha$$

torque × angle turned in radians = increase in rotational kinetic energy

$T \times \theta = \frac{1}{2} I\omega_2^2 - \frac{1}{2} I\omega_1^2$

torque × angular speed = power

$T \times \omega = p$

The word torque is often used in an informal sense to mean a 'turning force' as opposed to a push or a pull.

**Worked example**

**A torque of 0.20 Nm is applied to a stationary flywheel of moment of inertia 1.42 kg m². Calculate the speed of the flywheel at the end of the fifth revolution.**

$\theta$ after 5 revolutions is $10\pi$ radians; $\omega_1$ is zero. Hence:

$$\omega_2 = \sqrt{\frac{2T\theta}{I}} = \sqrt{\frac{2 \times (0.20\,\text{Nm}) \times (10\pi\,\text{rad})}{(1.42\,\text{kg m}^2)}} = 3.0\,\text{rads}^{-1} \text{ (to 2 s.f.)}$$

(See *moment of inertia, angular acceleration.*)

**total internal reflection** occurs when light approaches a refracting surface at such an angle that there is no angle of refraction that would satisfy Snell's law (see *refraction of light*). This is best illustrated with a worked example.

**Worked example**

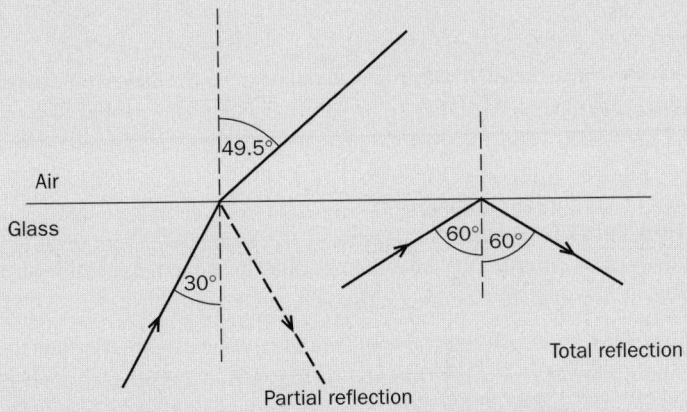


**The diagram shows two rays of light in glass travelling towards a flat surface, one with an angle of incidence of 30° and the other with an angle of incidence of 60°. Find the angle of refraction in air corresponding to the angle of incidence in glass of 30°.**

$$\frac{1}{1.52} = \frac{\sin 30°}{\sin r} = \frac{0.5}{\sin r}$$

$$r = \sin^{-1}(1.52 \times 0.5) = \sin^{-1}(0.76) = 49° \quad \text{(to 2 s.f.)}$$

Sin 60°, on the other hand, is 0.8660 and so $r$ would come out as $\sin^{-1}(1.52 \times 0.8660)$ or $\sin^{-1}(1.32)$; but there is no angle whose sine has value 1.32. Therefore, light in glass approaching the flat surface at an angle of incidence of 60° cannot be refracted.

Since it cannot be refracted, all the light is reflected. This is total internal reflection. The light which approaches the surface at 30° is partially reflected and partially refracted. Between these two angles there is a so-called critical angle which marks the onset of total internal reflection. The critical angle is shown in the diagram below.

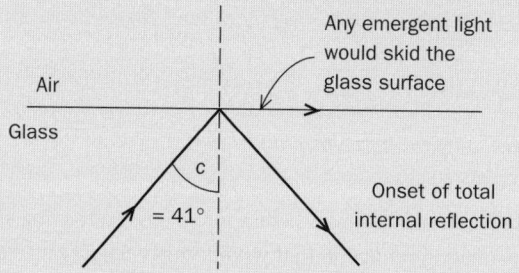


The critical angle $c$ must be the angle for which $r$ is $\sin^{-1}(1)$. For this example, $r$ is $\sin^{-1}(1.52 \times \sin c)$. We then have

$$1.52 \times \sin c = 1 \quad \text{or} \quad c = \sin^{-1}\left(\frac{1}{1.52}\right) = 41° \quad \text{(to 2 s.f.)}$$

More generally, the critical angle $c$ within a material of refractive index $n$ relative to vacuum is calculated from the relationship

$$c = \sin^{-1}\left(\frac{1}{n}\right)$$

**total radiation curve** (also known as the 'black body radiation curve') is a graph showing how $W_\lambda$, the power radiated per unit area per unit wavelength interval from a hot surface, varies with wavelength (see the graph on page 251).

The phrase 'per unit wavelength interval' can be a little troublesome. It means the following: measure the power carried away from the surface within the wavelength band $\lambda$ to $\lambda + d\lambda$ and divide this amount of power by $d\lambda$; then make $d\lambda$ as small as possible. It is just another example of a limiting value.

There are a few points to make about the graph on page 251.

The word 'total' emphasises that all wavelengths are represented. The term 'black body' emphasises that perfect radiators (surfaces which give the smooth curve shown with nothing missing) are black when cold; that is, they are not only complete radiators, they are also perfect absorbers.

Two curves are shown, one corresponding to a higher temperature than the other. The surface at the higher temperature emits radiation more powerfully than the surface at the lower temperature; this is true for all wavelengths but is exaggerated in the short-wavelength region.

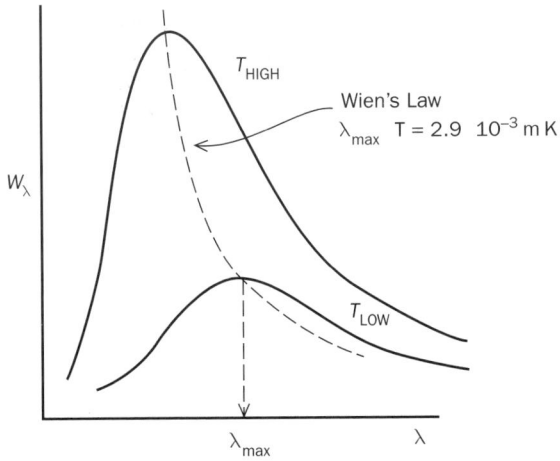


The area between the curve and the wavelength axis equals the power radiated from unit area of the surface over the whole wavelength range. This area increases in proportion to $T^4$. This is *Stefan's law.*

The wavelength $\lambda_{max}$ at which the curve peaks is proportional to $1/T$, i.e. it gets shorter as the temperature of the radiating surface increases. This is called *Wien's law.*

The graph provides a way of illustrating the *electromagnetic spectrum.* To complete this task, the high temperature would have to be identified, say 6000 K, and the wavelength axis divided into sections and labelled UV, visible, IR and so on.

**toughness** is a measure of the amount of *work* which is needed to break a material. Materials such as leather are tough. Toughness contrasts with *stiffness* and *brittleness.*

**tracer elements:** radioactive isotopes used to monitor the progress of an element or its compounds through a living organism or process pathway (such as in the soil or through a gas pipe) by providing non-radioactive isotopes of the same element with a radioactive 'tag'. The movement of the tracer is monitored by detecting the radiation it emits. To avoid long-term contamination of a patient or the environment, it is usual to select a radioisotope whose half-life is similar to the timescale of the investigation.

**transformer:** two coils wound on a single core thereby enabling electrical power to be transmitted between two circuits which are electrically isolated from one another.

The diagram on page 252 shows an idealised transformer. The primary coil has $N_p$ turns, the secondary coil $N_s$ turns. The primary coil is used to supply energy to the transformer, the secondary coil to carry the energy away. The theory is simplified by assuming that coils are perfect conductors and that there is no leakage of *magnetic flux* from the transformer core.

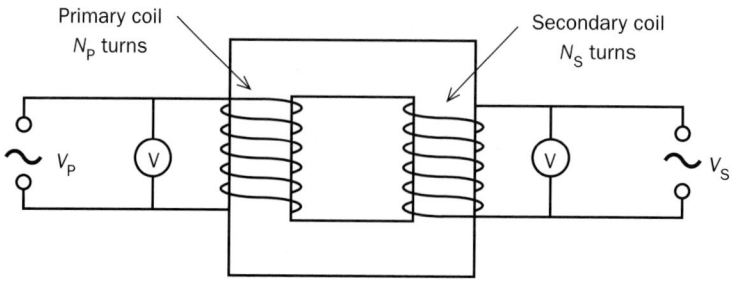


Assume, as a starting point, that an alternating current in the primary coil creates a changing magnetic flux $d\phi/dt$ within the core. There will be an *induced e.m.f. E* in every turn of wire in either coil, where

$$E = -\frac{d\phi}{dt}$$

The primary coil consists of $N_p$ turns of wire in series and the induced e.m.f. will be $N_pE$. This induced e.m.f. is equal and in the opposite direction to the alternating voltage $V_P$ applied to the primary coil by an external power source.

The secondary coil consists of $N_S$ turns of wire in series. The induced e.m.f. (the only e.m.f.) will be $N_SE$. This will be the voltage across the secondary coil, $V_S$. We have, then:

$$V_P = -N_PE = N_P\frac{d\phi}{dt}$$

$$V_S = N_SE = -N_S\frac{d\phi}{dt}$$

$$\frac{V_P}{V_S} = -\frac{N_P}{N_S}$$

The negative sign indicates that the primary and secondary voltages are in antiphase.

There is the additional requirement that any power drawn from the secondary coil must be provided by the power source for the primary coil. If $I_p$ and $I_S$ represent the primary and secondary currents, respectively, then:

$$I_PV_P = I_SV_S$$

provided that the transfer of energy from primary to secondary is 100% efficient; otherwise, $I_PV_P < I_SV_S$. (See *mutual inductance.*)

**translational motion:** the motion of a body which moves from one point to another rather than undergoing a repetitive motion such as *simple harmonic motion* or *circular motion.*

**transmission line:** a cable or collection of cables used to transfer electrical energy over significant distances between a power station and a local distribution centre. Transmission lines may be below ground or supported above ground by pylons. High voltages are used because this results in smaller currents, giving reduced power losses in the resistance of the cables.

**transverse waves** are *progressive waves* whose displacements are at right angles to the direction of energy flow. (See *longitudinal waves, stationary wave.*)

**triple point:** the one temperature at which ice, water and water vapour, all in their pure form, may be in *thermal equilibrium* with one another. It is 273.16 K. Other substances also have a triple point at which solid, liquid and vapour are in thermal equilibrium. (See *ice point.*)

**turbulent flow** is the churning motion in a fluid which occurs when *streamline flow* has broken down. It happens when a fluid is travelling too fast or when it passes an obstacle in its path.

**two-dimensional motion** describes the many situations in which a body moves along a curved path in a plane. *Projectiles* provide a common example. Problems are usually tackled by treating the two velocity *components* separately – for projectiles, the vertical and horizontal motions are treated separately because only the vertical motion is accelerated by gravity. An exception is *circular motion*: this is a two-dimensional motion but problems are usually tackled from a different standpoint. The two components of circular motion would, as it happens, be two simple harmonic motions 90° out of phase, along paths at right angles to one another and bisecting one another.

**two slits experiment:** a demonstration of the *wave nature of light* by showing the *interference* pattern where two coherent beams of light meet on a screen. The diagram below illustrates the minimal set up. The two slits are parallel, a distance *s* apart, in an opaque sheet. These slits are illuminated normally by light from a laser. The light which gets through the slits illuminates a screen a perpendicular distance *D* beyond the slits.

The pattern on the screen consists of a dozen or so equally spaced bright lines. The lines are parallel to the slits in the opaque sheet and their centres are a distance *x* apart. The graph on the diagram shows how the intensity of light varies across the screen. The central bright line, A, is equidistant from both slits in the opaque screen. The beams of light from the two slits reach A in phase; there is constructive interference and the screen is bright. Each point B on either side of A is one wavelength further from one slit than the other. The beams of light from the two slits arrive at the screen in phase; there is constructive interference and the screen is bright at the points B.

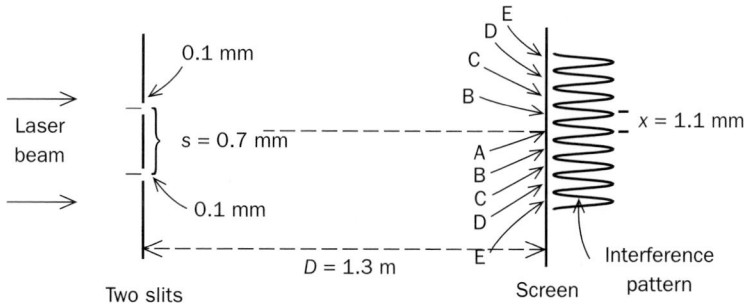


Midway between A and either of the points B, one beam travels half a wavelength further than the other; the beams are out of phase when they meet and the interference is destructive.

The points C are two wavelengths further from one slit than the other, the points D are three wavelengths apart and so on.

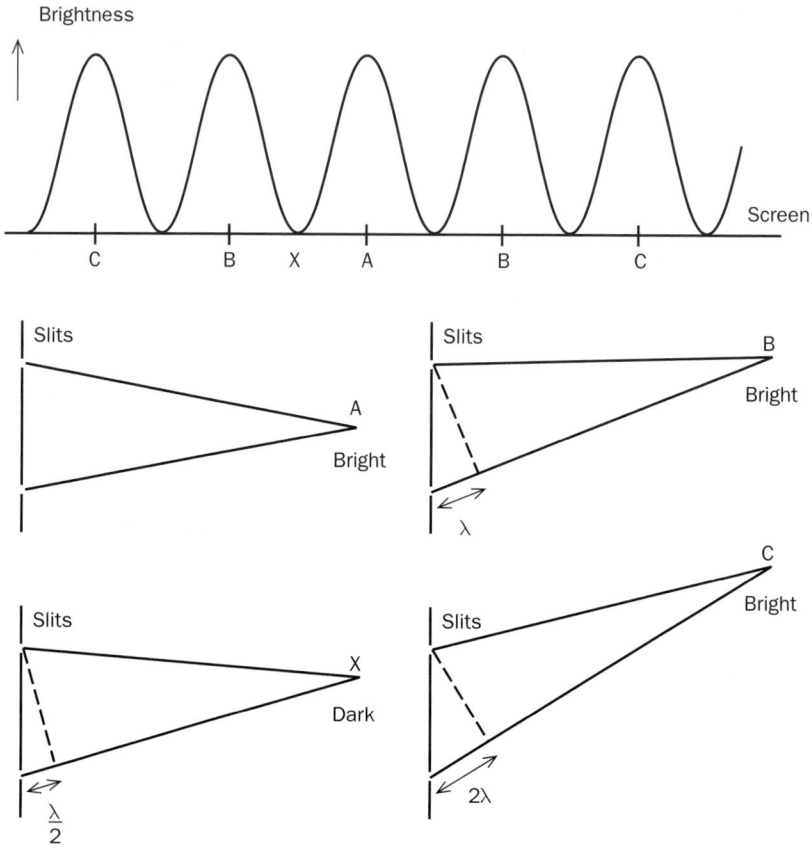


It can be shown that if $\lambda$ is the wavelength of the laser light, then

$$\lambda = \frac{xs}{D}$$

In a typical experiment, the slits are about a tenth of a millimetre wide and about 0.7 mm apart. Distance $D$ would be about 1.3 m and $x$ about 1.1 mm. The wavelength $\lambda$ of the laser light would be around 600 nm. Values of $s$ and $x$ would be measured with a micrometer eyepiece; $D$ would be measured with a ruler. Four lengths are involved in this experiment. If we rewrite the equation as $xs = \lambda D$, you will see that the right-hand side consists of the product of the longest and shortest lengths, while the left-hand side is the product of the two intermediate lengths.

The slit width ($\approx$ 0.1 mm) is of some significance. If it is too large, the interference pattern loses definition; if it is too small, the pattern is sharp but too faint to see. This is why the best images are recorded photographically; a long exposure time brightens a sharp but too-faint image.

Consider the part played by diffraction in the formation of the interference pattern. There are two diffraction patterns on the screen, one for each slit. These patterns are each a couple of centimetres wide but only $s$ apart at their centres (in this case, 0.7 mm). The envelope formed by merging these two diffraction patterns decides the brightnesses of the different bright fringes in the interference pattern. Briefly, the two diffraction patterns overlap and interfere with each other, constructively along the bright fringes and destructively in between. Consequently, the central fringe is the brightest, and the brightnesses of the other fringes fall away on each side. This falling away of brightness has not been shown on either diagram. (See *diffraction at a single slit.*)

Another way of looking at this experiment is to regard the slits as point sources of light in the plane of the diagram. (In fact, Thomas Young used pin holes rather than slits as point sources.) There will be constructive interference at any point on the screen which is one or more whole wavelengths further from one slit than the other. A little calculation shows that these points are a distance $\lambda D/s$ apart and this gives us the equation for the distance $x$ between the centres of adjacent fringes. Destructive interference occurs at any point which is an odd number of half-wavelengths further from one slit than the other. These points of darkness are midway between the points of maximum brightness. This treatment explains how the bright and dark bands are formed and leads to the expression for fringe width, but it does not explain why the bands extend only a centimetre or so on either side of the principal axis. This point is discussed in detail under *diffraction at a single slit.*

Historically, the important feature of this experiment is the dark lines — the *destructive interference.* They mark out parts of the screen which would be illuminated by either slit on its own but are in darkness when illuminated by both slits at the same time. The observation that one beam of light can cancel another was altogether original.

**Are you studying other subjects?**

The *A–Z Handbooks (digital editions)* are available in 14 different subjects. Browse the range and order other handbooks at **www.philipallan.co.uk/a-zonline.**

**U value** is the rate of heat flow through a thermal barrier per unit area, per unit temperature difference across the barrier. The symbol is $U$ and the SI unit is $\mathrm{W\,m^{-2}K^{-1}}$. The word equation definition for U value is:

$$\text{U value} = \frac{\text{rate of heat flow through a thermal barrier}}{\text{area} \times \text{temperature difference}}$$

Compare the U value equation with the *thermal conductivity* equation:

$$\frac{\mathrm{d}Q}{\mathrm{d}t} = kA\frac{\mathrm{d}\theta}{\mathrm{d}x} = UA\mathrm{d}\theta$$

In purely mathematical terms, we should be able to define $U$ as the quotient $k/\mathrm{d}x$. But this would obscure the fact that $k$ is a property of a homogeneous material while $U$ is a property of a structure such as a window or a wall treated as a thermal barrier. U values are used in the building trade.

**Worked example**

**A small detached house has $220\,\mathrm{m^2}$ of double cavity walling (U value $0.51\,\mathrm{W\,m^{-2}K^{-1}}$) and $21\,\mathrm{m^2}$ of double glazing (U value $4.8\,\mathrm{W\,m^{-2}K^{-1}}$). On a cold day, there is a temperature difference of 20°C between the inside and the outside of the house. Calculate the rate of heat loss through the windows and find the ratio of this to the heat loss through the walls.**

$$\text{rate of heat loss through windows} = 4.8 \times 21 \times 20 = 2016\,\mathrm{W}$$

$$\text{rate of heat losses} = \frac{[U \times A]_{\text{windows}}}{[U \times A]_{\text{walls}}} = \frac{(4.8\,\mathrm{W\,m^{-2}\,K^{-1}})(21\,\mathrm{m^2})}{(0.51\,\mathrm{W\,m^{-2}\,K^{-1}})(220\,\mathrm{m^2})} = 0.90$$

(See *thermal conduction*.)

**ultimate tensile stress** is a measure of the *strength* of a material. It is the greatest tensile stress applied to a sample of the material as it undergoes tensile testing. It corresponds to the stress at the highest point on a stress–strain curve. See *stress–strain curves*.

**ultrasound** is high-frequency (a few MHz), short-wavelength (≈ 1 mm) sound used for non-destructive exploration of the inside of the human body. The two basic ideas are:

1 The distance of a reflecting surface from a transmitter/receiver is the journey time of a pulse multiplied by the speed of the ultrasound.
2 The reflection coefficient of a surface is defined and calculated as follows:

$$\alpha = \frac{\text{reflected intensity}}{\text{incident intensity}} = \left(\frac{z_2 - z_1}{z_2 + z_1}\right)^2$$

where $Z$, the specific *acoustic impedance* of a medium, is the product of the density $\rho$ of the medium and the speed $c$ of ultrasound within the medium: $Z = \rho c$. The value of $Z$ is typically $1.6 \times 10^6 \text{kg m}^{-2}\text{s}^{-1}$ for soft tissues but changes by as much as 20% in passing from, say, fat to muscle and increases by a factor of four at a tissue/bone boundary.

The strong dependence of reflection coefficient on density change explains the necessity for the coupling gel between the probe and the skin surface.

The ultrasound transmitter, usually a *piezoelectric transducer*, also acts as the receiver. The circuitry has four functions:

- to generate the signal which becomes the pulse
- to detect and amplify the reflected pulse
- to record the time lapse between transmission and reception
- to display the result on a screen

The display may be an oscilloscope trace showing the receiver signal intensity against time. This is called an A-scan. Alternatively, the oscilloscope trace may be a straight line whose length indicates time and whose brightness indicates signal strength; this is called a B-scan. The advantage of the B-scan is that it can be built up into a two-dimensional picture of, say, a fetus within the mother's womb.

*Doppler ultrasound* scanning can give information about the speed of movement of organs or tissues in the body.

**ultraviolet light:** see *UV*.

**uncertainty** is the range of values on either side of a measurement within which the true value is expected to be located. There is, however, no more than a probability that the true value lies within this range. This is why some people prefer the term 'probable error'.

Imagine that you want to know the diameter of a coin and that all you have is a plastic ruler and a magnifying glass. The diameter looks just less than 25.5 mm but you are not too sure by how much. You can write 'diameter = (25.4 ± 0.1) mm' or you might prefer the form 'diameter = 25.4 mm ± 0.4%'. The ± sign is characteristic of uncertainties, whereas an *error* is either positive or negative. An uncertainty is a range of values; an error is one particular amount.

Imagine 100 careful people making 100 such measurements with your ruler. The 100 values will lead to a more precise statement. Some measurements may be as high as 25.6 mm and some may be as low as 25.2 mm, but the average value about which all these measurements centre can be decided with much greater certainty (i.e. a smaller uncertainty) as something like (25.39 ± 0.02) mm.

Individual measurements above and below the mean value occur randomly and this contribution to the uncertainty is described as *random error*. A feature of a random error is that it can be reduced by averaging several independent measurements.

Imagine, next, that a friend repeats the experiment using an old ruler that has shrunk over the years. The hundred measurements may yield a result like (25.43 ± 0.02) mm. The random error is unchanged but all the measurements are 0.04 mm too large. This is called a *systematic error*. Its cause is a fault in the instrument and no amount of repetition will indicate its size or reduce it. (See also *precision*.)

**uncertainty principle:** a statement that the product of the uncertainty $\Delta E$ in the energy of a body and the time interval $\Delta t$ for which the body has this energy is less than or equal to $h/(2\pi)$, where $h$ is the Planck constant. This principle touches A-level physics in the *particle physics* area. An *exchange particle* can come into being for a time so short that the uncertainty principle is not violated. This works out at about $10^{-24}$ s for the weak interaction. Light can travel no further than about $10^{-16}$ m in such a time interval. This explains why the weak interaction is a short-range force which acts within, but not between, neutrons and protons.

**unified atomic mass unit** is the modern unit for what used to be called the atomic mass unit. It is defined as one-twelfth of the mass of a carbon-12 atom, and the symbol used is 'u' where $1\,\text{u} = 1.660\,540 \times 10^{-27}$ kg. The energy equivalent ($\Delta m{\cdot}c^2$) is 1.492 419 J or 931.494 MeV. The unwieldy name of this unit distinguishes it from an older unit, the *atomic mass unit*, which was defined as one-sixteenth of the mass of an oxygen-16 atom.

An alternative name for the unified atomic mass unit is the Dalton, symbol Da. This name is frequently used in biochemistry, so a large protein molecule may be described as having a mass of 200 kDa.

**uniform acceleration:** constant acceleration. The word 'uniform' generally means 'constant', as in 'uniform velocity'. The phrase 'uniform motion' is not well-defined but can usually be taken to mean that a body is moving with constant velocity, i.e. with constant speed in a straight line. (See *velocity*.)

**uniform electric field:** an electric field with magnitude and direction that are everywhere the same. The diagram below shows the uniform electric field between the plates of a parallel plate capacitor. Notice the 'edge effects' at each side. The field lines are equally spaced. So too are the lines of equal potential, i.e. the *equipotential lines*, which are shown as broken lines.

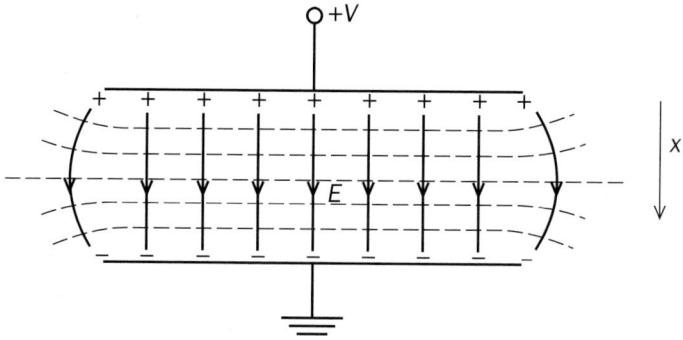


If you have to draw this diagram in an examination, never show fewer than three equipotential lines or five electric field strength lines. Be sure to have the spacing approximately correct.

The relationship between electric field strength, $E$, and the rate of change of potential with distance, $-\,\mathrm{d}V/\mathrm{d}x$, is simpler for a uniform field. In general:

$$E = -\frac{\mathrm{d}V}{\mathrm{d}x}$$

But for a uniform field:

$$E = -\frac{dV}{dx} = -\frac{V}{d}$$

where $d$ is the distance measured parallel to and in the same direction as $E$, along which the drop in potential is $V$. It is because $V$ diminishes along the direction of $E$ that the negative sign appears. Often, the direction in which $d$ is measured is unimportant. Only the magnitudes are of interest. We then write:

$$E = \frac{V}{d}$$

**unit:** an agreed amount of physical quantity used to express the result of a measurement. It has to be assumed that instruments are available which can compare the magnitudes of two different amounts of the physical quantity. A ruler, for instance, will tell you that one length is 5.65 times as long as another length. If the shorter length is one metre, then the greater length is 5.65 m.

The magnitude of any physical quantity is expressed as the product of a number and a unit.

The *SI* system defines seven base (physical) quantities and their corresponding seven *base units*. All other units are defined in terms of these seven base units and are called *derived units*.

The SI unit for acceleration is $m\,s^{-2}$. The $m\,s^{-2}$ is a derived unit. Note that acceleration does not have units; it has a unit. The unit of force is $kg\,m\,s^{-2}$, and this unit has a name of its own, the newton (N). Some derived units have their own names, but most do not. (see also *kilowatt-hour*)

**upthrust** is a term that can refer to any upward thrust, but it is usually taken to mean the upward force acting on an object immersed in a fluid. (See *Archimedes' principle*.)

**UV** or ultraviolet light is that segment of the *electromagnetic spectrum* which is emitted when the outer electrons of atoms in excited states return to their ground states, provided that their wavelengths are too short to be visible. Typical UV photons have energies in the region of several electron volts and this is more than sufficient to break up many atomic bonds. It follows that UV radiation is chemically active in a destructive sense and can be very damaging.

UV radiation consists of *photons* whose energies are just low enough for them to be present in the Sun's spectrum. Most of the energy in the UV waveband carried in the solar spectrum is absorbed by ozone in the stratosphere, so that life on Earth is protected from its damaging effects. This also explains why the temperature of the stratosphere increases with height. This increase of temperature with height eliminates *convection* currents and largely contains weather within the troposphere (the lowest 20 kilometres or so of the atmosphere).

The UV segment of the electromagnetic spectrum ranges from about 1 nm to about 400 nm where it meets the visible spectrum. The corresponding frequencies range from about 0.3 EHz ($0.3 \times 10^{18}$ Hz) down to about 0.75 PHz ($0.75 \times 10^{15}$ Hz), and the corresponding photon energies range from about 1.24 keV to about 3 eV. Three sub-bands can be identified according to their wavelength ranges:

- UV-A (320–400 nm), which causes skin wrinkling
- UV-B (280–320 nm), which can damage DNA in skin cells, leading to cancer
- UV-C (< 280 nm), which is mostly absorbed by the atmosphere's ozone layer

The high-frequency end of the Sun's spectrum is close to 10 PHz ($10 \times 10^{15}$ Hz, with a photon energy of around 40 eV); photons of this energy, although few in number, would be very damaging if they were to reach the Earth's surface.

UV radiation is detected mostly photographically or with photocells. Many substances fluoresce when irradiated with UV. (See *electromagnetic spectrum*, *photoelectric effect*.)

**Aiming for a grade A*?**

Don't forget to log on to **www.philipallan.co.uk/a-zonline** for advice.

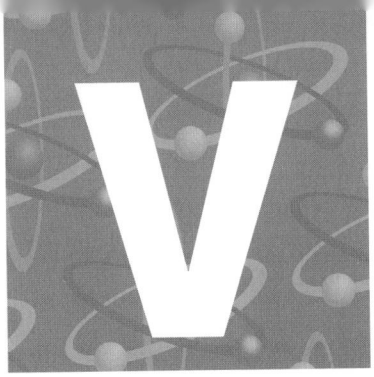

**Van der Waals' bond** is a weak intermolecular bond. An atom consists of a positive nucleus surrounded by electron shells. When isolated, the atom is electrically neutral and creates no electric field. But in the liquid or solid state, an atom can be so distorted by the close presence of its neighbours that the 'centre of charge' of the electrons is displaced away from the nucleus. The atom thus becomes a dipole, that is, a positive charge and an equal negative charge separated by a short distance.

The negative pole of the distorted atom would be attracted to a positively charged component of a neighbouring molecule; the positive pole would be attracted to negatively charged components of neighbouring molecules. Neighbouring atoms or molecules are similarly distorted and so tend to stick to the atoms in a neighbouring molecule. The net result is an inter-atomic bond which is much weaker than an *ionic bond* or *covalent bond* but which is strong enough to be significant. This is particularly so with *polymeric solids* in which a single polymer molecule can be held down by hundreds of Van der Waals' bonds along its length. Surface tension and viscosity begin with Van der Waals' bonds.

Molecular substances such as nitrogen and hydrogen become gaseous at low temperatures because the Van der Waals' bonds between their molecules are weak and little thermal energy is required to overcome them.

**vector addition:** see *parallelogram law.*

**vector quantity:** a physical or mathematical quantity which has both direction and magnitude. Examples include displacement, velocity, acceleration, force, magnetic field strength and electric field strength. Force is different from other vectors: it acts through a point. (For a discussion of force as a vector, see *force: a localised vector.*) The phrase 'composition of vectors' means no more than how vectors add together. Two vectors must represent the same physical quantity before they can be added together (i.e. both must be forces, or both must be velocities, etc.).

Vector quantities are often represented by arrows. The length of an arrow represents vector magnitude and the direction of the arrow represents vector direction. Forces are a little more difficult; the arrows have to point along the correct lines of action. (See also *parallelogram law, resultant, resolution of vectors.*)

**velocity** is defined by the word equation

$$\text{velocity} = \frac{\text{change of displacement}}{\text{time interval}}$$

The unit for velocity is $\mathrm{m\,s^{-1}}$.

The graph on the left, below, illustrates the ideas of uniform velocity and uniform acceleration. The graph on the right illustrates average velocity and instantaneous velocity.

The term 'uniform velocity' implies equal changes of displacement in equal times. Since velocity is a *vector quantity*, velocity can be uniform only for *straight line motion*. The term 'uniform acceleration' means that the velocity increases by equal amounts in equal times without changing direction.

The magnitude of a velocity equals the *gradient* of a *displacement–time graph*. Look at the second graph: average velocity during the period $t_A$ to $t_B$ is the gradient of the straight line AB, and instantaneous velocity at time $t_C$ is the gradient of the tangent at C.

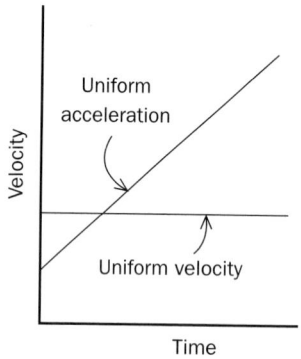


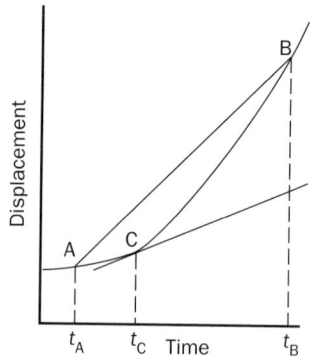


Average velocity during a specified time interval is defined by the word equation

$$\text{average velocity} = \frac{\text{change of displacement}}{\text{time interval}}$$

Instantaneous velocity is defined as the limiting value of the ratio on the right-hand side of this equation evaluated for a very short time interval.

The *equations of motion* apply to motion along a straight line with uniform acceleration. Velocity changes in magnitude but not in direction.

(See *displacement*, *acceleration*, *straight line motion*, *velocity–time graph*.)

**velocity–time graph:** a graphical display of the time variation of *velocity*. Velocity is a *vector quantity* and its value can be positive or negative, so the graph can cut the time axis. The graph cannot indicate the changing direction of a moving body; if the body is following a curved path of some sort, then each *component* of the velocity must have its own velocity–time graph.

The area between the velocity–time curve and the time axis equals change of displacement during the relevant time interval and this can be positive or negative. Each graph is linked to a particular direction and the gradient of a tangent to the graph gives *acceleration* in that direction at that instant; it may be positive or negative.

The velocity–time graph on page 263 is for a car which is driven away from the observer (reference point) along a straight line with increasing acceleration. The gradient of the graph is the instantaneous acceleration, and the area between the graph and the time axis is the change of *displacement* during the relevant time interval.

Notice that the area between the curve and the time axis is change of displacement and not simply displacement. It will equal displacement if the area starts at an instant when the displacement is zero.

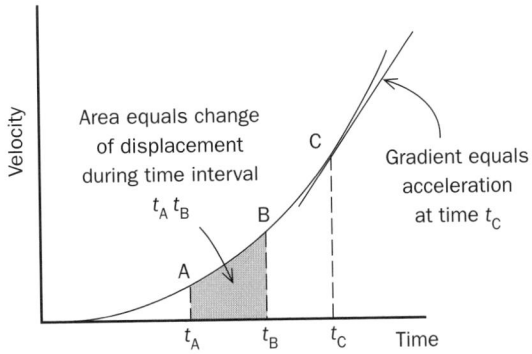


**Worked example**

**A glider on a horizontal air track travels towards one end at a speed of 0.60 m s$^{-1}$. It is reflected elastically and returns along the same path at the same speed. The clock is started when the glider is 1.2 m from the reflector and is stopped when the glider returns through the same point. Draw and label a velocity–time graph for the motion.**

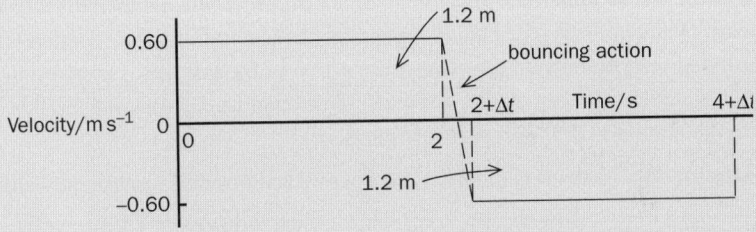


Notice that the average velocity calculated over the $4 + \Delta t$ seconds time interval is zero and the net displacement is zero.

**Vernier callipers:** an instrument used to measure lengths such as the external or internal diameter of a tube or the thickness of a metal block. Measurements can often be made to within ±0.1 mm. The callipers have two scales: a long fixed scale, marked in millimetres, and a moveable Vernier scale. The Vernier scale has ten divisions in the space occupied by nine divisions on the main scale.

The object to be measured is placed between the jaws of the callipers and the jaws closed so that they just touch the sides of the object. Excessive pressure must be avoided.

To read the callipers, look at the zero mark on the Vernier scale and identify the scale mark on the main scale which is just below this. This gives a reading to the nearest millimetre below the true reading.

Luton Sixth Form College
Learning Resources Centre

Now look at the Verrnier scale and identify the mark on the scale which aligns exactly with a division on the fixed scale. This marking gives the additional fraction of a millimetre which must be added to the whole number of millimetres previously recorded to give the final measurement. (See *micrometer screw gauge.*)

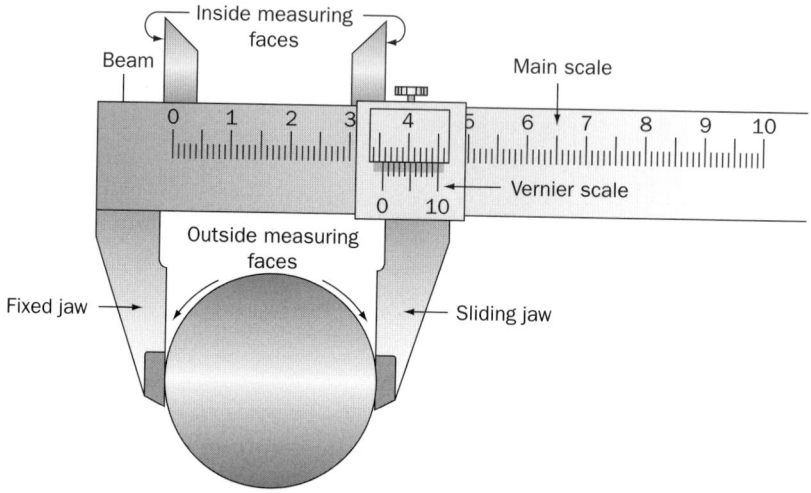


Diameter of object = 3.59 mm

**viscoelasticity** is the liquid-like flow within a polymer or glass under the action of a long-term continued stress. The effect is more noticeable at high temperatures than at low ones. The separate effects of the time-dependent element and the stress-dependent element are illustrated with bouncing putty. Under the action of the fast forces involved in bouncing, the putty is almost perfectly elastic; but under slow continued pressure it moulds quite easily in the hand and is almost perfectly plastic.

**viscosity** (or viscous drag) is the frictional force which opposes movement within a fluid. It is what stops tea swirling around a cup forever once it has been stirred. It acts between two adjacent layers of fluid which are moving parallel to one another but at different speeds. There are materials such as toffee or glass which have no clear-cut melting point: they get softer as the temperature rises; the viscosity has so high a value at the lower temperatures that the liquid material behaves in many ways like a solid. The Earth's mantle is a fluid with a high viscosity and this is why the drift of continents is so slow. Honey and treacle have much higher viscosities when cold than when hot. Gases, too, have viscosity.

The flow of a viscous fluid is analysed with reference to a coefficient of viscosity. To understand how the coefficient of viscosity, $\eta$, is defined, look at the situation in the diagram below.

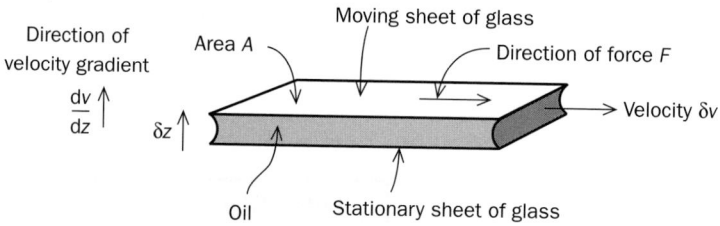

A thin flat sheet of oil of area $A$ and thickness $\delta z$ lies between two sheets of glass. The tangential force $F$ needed to keep the upper sheet moving across the lower sheet with a steady speed $\delta v$ is given by the word equation

tangential force = coefficient of viscosity × area × normal velocity gradient

$$F = \eta A\left(\frac{dv}{dz}\right)$$

Notice that the force $F$ is parallel to the area $A$ and that the velocity gradient is measured at right angles to $A$. This equation, which defines coefficient of viscosity, is valid for *streamline flow* only. Any small eddies (known as 'turbulence') within the fluid between the two sheets of glass will have a dramatic effect on the magnitude of the force $F$.

From this definition it is possible to derive *Stokes' law*, which applies to a sphere falling through a fluid at its terminal speed.

**visible spectrum:** the segment of the *electromagnetic spectrum* which can be detected by the normal human eye. The wavelength range is from close to 400 nm to close to 700 nm. The corresponding frequencies are 750 THz ($7.5 \times 10^{14}$ Hz) to 430 THz ($4.3 \times 10^{14}$ Hz). The *photon* energies range from 3.1 eV to 1.8 eV and are just high enough to ensure that visible light has some destructive power at the molecular level; this is why some dyes fade so quickly in bright sunlight.

Visible radiation is emitted when excited or ionised atoms return to their ground states in stages. For the direct transition the radiation would be in the UV range. The precise wavelength values associated with these transitions form the main source of detailed information about atomic structure. This is the origin of the study known as spectrum analysis.

**volt** (V) is the SI unit of *potential difference*. It is another name for the joule per coulomb.

**voltage:** a term that can refer to either a *potential difference* (p.d.) or an electromotive force (*e.m.f.*). In general, it is preferable to use either one of these separate terms, although most physicists are happy to talk about 'voltage' when they are confident that the listener will understand which type of voltage is being referred to.

**voltage–current characteristics:** see *current–voltage characteristics*.

**voltmeters** measure *potential difference*. Digital voltmeters are accurate and cheap. There is no point wondering how they work unless you have a special interest. They must be connected across the required two points and in parallel with the rest of the circuit. The diagram on the next page shows how a voltmeter and ammeter should be connected when measuring the current in, and the potential difference across, a resistor R.

The presence of meters in a circuit can have an effect on the quantities being measured. A voltmeter, connected in parallel with a component, provides an additional path for current to flow. To minimise this effect, the voltmeter must have as high a resistance as possible.

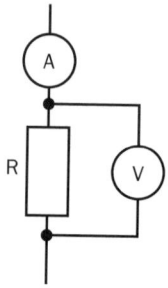


**vulcanised rubber** is rubber which is hardened by mixing the raw rubber with sulfur and then exposing it to a slow heating process. The sulfur binds the polymer molecules together by providing cross-links. The hardening which results is in rough proportion to the concentration of sulfur. (See *rubber.*)

**water waves** are waves which run across the surface of a mass of water. Water waves are sometimes incorrectly described as transverse. A molecule on the surface of water across which a wave is travelling follows a circular path in a vertical plane. This means that its motion can be resolved into two *simple harmonic motions*, one vertical (transverse) and the other horizontal (longitudinal).

**watt:** a rate of *energy transfer* of one joule per second ($1\,W = 1\,J\,s^{-1}$). It is the SI *derived unit* for *power* and its symbol is W. The *base unit* equivalent of the watt is $kg\,m^2\,s^{-3}$.

**wave behaviour** is the set of properties (reflection, refraction, diffraction, interference, dispersion) which are shared by all wave motions (and the *polarisation phenomena* shared by some). The diagrams below summarise how most of these phenomena can be demonstrated with a ripple tank.

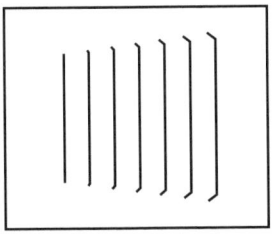

Rectilinear propagation

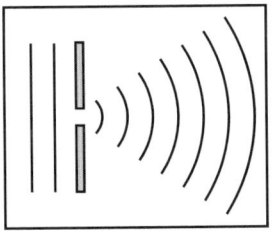

Diffraction

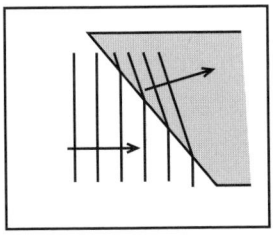

Refraction

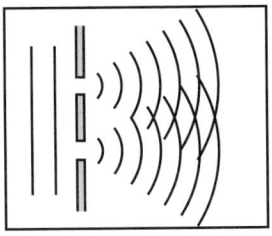

Interference

(See *reflection of light, refraction of light, diffraction, interference, dispersion of light, dispersion of sound.*)

**wave nature of light:** the capacity of a light beam to behave like a succession of waves progressing through a medium. Light shares its wave-like properties with the whole of the *electromagnetic spectrum*, but the phrase 'wave nature of light' pre-dates the discovery of the rest of the electromagnetic spectrum, apart from the near-infrared and the near-ultraviolet. The key properties which betray the wave nature of light are *interference*, *diffraction* and the relationship of refractive index to wave speed. Polarisation establishes the transverse nature of these waves. The straight line motion of light and its reflection by polished surfaces can be reconciled with the wave idea but sits more easily with a particle interpretation (see *wave–particle duality*).

Wave theory cannot accommodate those properties of light which link up with its interaction with matter and with the *photon* concept. These properties are principally the *photoelectric effect*, the formation of absorption and emission spectra and the character of the total radiation (black body) spectrum. (See *absorption spectrum, emission spectrum, total radiation curve.*)

**wavefront:** a surface which travels with a wave, drawn everywhere at right angles to the direction of the wave and across which the phase of the wave is everywhere the same. In two-dimensional diagrams, a wavefront appears as a one-dimensional line or curve.

**wavelength:** the shortest distance along the path of a wave between two points where the wave displacements are changing in phase. (See *sound waves, electromagnetic waves.*)

**wave speed:** the speed at which energy is transmitted by the wave. The speed $v$ of a wave is related to its frequency $f$ and wavelength $\lambda$ by the relationship:

$$\text{speed} = \text{frequency} \times \text{wavelength}$$
$$v = f\lambda$$

(See *speed of sound, speed of light.*)

**wave–particle duality** expresses the need to treat both photons and atomic or subatomic particles as either particles or wave trains, according to circumstances. Electrons act mostly like particles, but they can be diffracted. Electromagnetic radiation is known best for its wave properties, but the photoelectric effect underlines the particle nature of this radiation.

**waves in pipes** are *stationary waves*. They form at particular frequencies only. This is because their formation is an example of *resonance*. There is a resonant frequency when the air in a pipe is set into vibration with a *node* at any closed end of the pipe and an *antinode* at an open end of the pipe. If $n$ is the number of antinodes within the pipe, $l$ is the length of the pipe and $\lambda$ is the wavelength of the wave motion, then, for a pipe open at one end and closed at the other (as in the diagram),

$$l = (2n+1)\left(\frac{\lambda}{4}\right)$$

Notice that $(2n + 1)$ equals 1 or 3 or 5 etc. — it is always an odd number. For resonance, the length of the pipe must be an odd number of quarter-wavelengths.

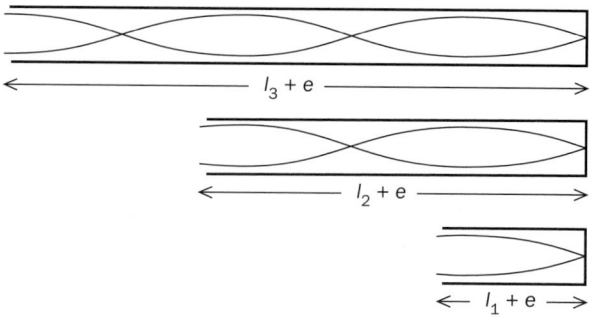

In practice, the position of the exterior antinode is a short distance $e$ beyond the open end of the pipe. The equation relating the length of pipe to the wavelength of the sound therefore needs modifying slightly:

$$l + e = (2n + 1)\left(\frac{\lambda}{4}\right)$$

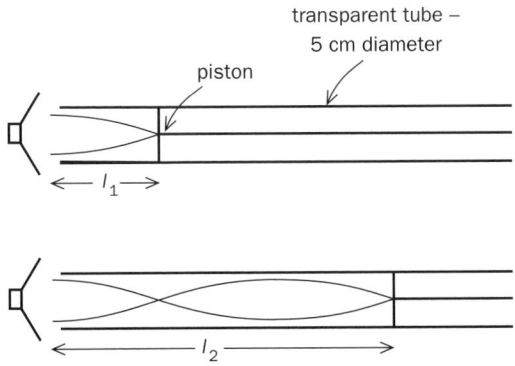


In the arrangement shown above, the position of the piston is adjusted for resonance. The frequency $f$ applied to the loudspeaker is held constant and the two shortest resonance lengths, $l_1$ and $l_2$, are measured. Since

$$l_2 - l_1 = \left(\frac{\lambda}{2}\right)$$

once these two pipe lengths are measured, the wavelength of the sound from the loudspeaker can be calculated without needing to know the end correction $e$. If the frequency of the sound is known, the speed of sound in the pipe can be found. (But remember that this experiment is not accepted as a method of measuring the *speed of sound* in free air.)

**waves on strings** are *stationary waves*. They form when a string is set into vibration with a node at each end of the string. If $n$ is the number of antinodes, $l$ is the length of the string and $\lambda$ is the wavelength of the wave motion on the string, then, since nodes are half a wavelength apart, we have

$$2l = n\lambda$$

But wavelength equals speed/frequency ($\lambda = c/f$) and the speed of waves along a string is $\sqrt{(T/\mu)}$ where $T$ is the tension in the string and $\mu$ is the mass per unit length of the string. It follows that a stationary wave will form on a string at those frequencies for which

$$f = \frac{n}{2l}\sqrt{\frac{T}{\mu}}$$

Taut strings will support stationary waves at these frequencies and at no others. This is what is meant by *resonance*.

**weight** is the *force* acting on a mass due to the gravitational field in which it is placed. The SI unit of weight is the newton (N).

$$\text{weight} = \text{mass} \times \text{gravitational field strength}$$
$$W = mg$$

Because it is a force, weight is a *vector quantity*. Its direction is given by the direction of the gravitational field producing it.

It is useful to recall that, close to the Earth's surface, a mass of 0.1 kg has a weight of about 1.0 N.

**weightlessness** is the condition of a body when the only force acting on it is its *weight*. This is the case for a satellite high up above the Earth's atmosphere. If you jump into the air, you will be near enough weightless until you touch the ground again.

**white dwarf:** the end state of a main sequence star whose mass is less than eight solar masses. (See *end states of stars.*)

**Wien's law** states that the wavelength $\lambda_{max}$ at which the power radiated from a total radiator peaks is related to the surface temperature $T$ of the radiator as follows:

$$\lambda_{max}T = 2.9 \times 10^{-3}\,\text{mK}$$

The law enables the temperature of a bright but distant object to be determined spectroscopically. (See *total radiation curve.*)

**word equation:** an equation in which the mathematical symbols are replaced by the names of the variables they represent. Word equations are frequently used for definitions of physical quantities.

**work** is the amount of energy transferred to an object when it is moved by a force applied to it by a different object. It is a *scalar quantity*. The SI unit of work is the joule (J). The symbol for work is $W$, the same as for energy. Amount of work and the joule are defined by the word equations

work = force × component of displacement in direction of force

joule = newton × metre

This definition shows that the joule is a convenient name for the newton metre.

The definition of work also gets to the root of what we mean by energy. Energy is that which is transferred when a force moves through a distance along its line of action. The equation for work tells us how to calculate the amount of energy transferred.

*Newton's third law of motion* states that forces occur in equal and opposite pairs acting on different bodies. The force a bow exerts on an arrow equals the force the arrow exerts on the bow. However, there is an essential lack of symmetry: the arrow moves in the direction of the force applied to it and receives (kinetic) energy; the bow releases (potential) energy and does not have to move. Because energy is transferred from the bow to the arrow, it is the bow which works on the arrow and not the other way round. *Conservation of linear momentum* demands that the archer receives a slight backwards push.

So far we have dealt with work and mechanical energy; let us enlarge the discussion to include other forms of energy. We started with the idea that work is an energy transfer process, and so it is. Heating is an energy transfer process but heating is not working, so what exactly is the difference?

The fundamental energy transfer principle is the *first law of thermodynamics* which is usually stated in the following abbreviated form:

$$\Delta U = \Delta Q + \Delta W$$

$\Delta U$ is the energy transferred to a system and it can arrive in two forms, $\Delta Q$ and $\Delta W$.

Energy included in $\Delta Q$ is disordered energy such as the kinetic energy stored in a gas.

Energy included in $\Delta W$ is ordered energy such as the mechanical energy stored in a spring or the electrical energy stored in a capacitor. Transferring disordered energy is called 'heating'. Transferring ordered energy is called 'working'. The distinction is vital in thermodynamics because disordered energy can only be partially recovered in a useful way whereas ordered energy can be fully recovered. (See also *heating and working.*)

Sometimes, as in frictional heating, the energy changes form on transfer. The object which provides the energy exerts a force, and therefore does work. Frictional heating contributes to $\Delta W$ and not to $\Delta Q$. Similarly, electrical heating $IVt$ contributes to $\Delta W$ and not to $\Delta Q$.

Next, how is an amount of work calculated? The cases that follow relate to a force applied to a system (such as a spring being stretched), a gas expanding against some resistance from the system (like compressed air in an air gun driving out a slug) and a battery driving electric current through a resistor (as in an electric fire).

- Mechanical work: force × component of the displacement parallel to the force
- Gas expansion work: pressure × increase in volume
- Electrical work: voltage × current × time (or voltage × charge)

**Worked examples**

**1 A 3.2 kg mass falls through 1.6 m. How much work is done on it?**

$$\text{Work done } W = \text{force} \times \text{displacement} = (3.2\,\text{kg})(9.8\,\text{ms}^{-2}) \times (1.6\,\text{m})$$
$$= 50\,\text{J (to 2 s.f.)}$$

The work is done by the gravitational field (for that is where the energy comes from). The immediate destination for this energy is probably the kinetic energy of the falling mass.

**2 A force of 56 N pushes a heavy box 1.9 m across a floor. Calculate the work done.**

$$W = (56\,\text{N}) \times (1.9\,\text{m}) = 106\,\text{J}$$

Notice that in the first example, the 50 J is probably stored as recoverable kinetic energy and $\Delta U = \Delta W$ for the falling mass. In this second example, however, the energy transferred by the working process is probably transformed into heat by friction. It is still part of $\Delta W$ in a first law of thermodynamics application because the energy provider is using ordered energy; but the energy gets stored in the receiving system as disordered (internal) energy and so contributes to a rise in temperature.

**3 Estimate the work done when 60 cm³ of air at atmospheric pressure is compressed to 58 cm³.**

$$W = -p\Delta V = (1 \times 10^5\,\text{Pa}) \times (2 \times 10^{-4}\,\text{m}^3) = 20\,\text{J}$$

For this process, $\Delta U = \Delta W$, i.e. the energy arrives in the ordered form. Whether or not it is transformed to disordered energy in the gas, in whole or in part, is another matter. Notice that the work done on the gas is positive and the volume change is negative. (We have to assume that the pressure remains constant.)

**4 A 9 V battery drives a current of 0.4 A through a resistor for three minutes. Calculate the work done by the battery.**

$$W = IVt = (0.4\ \text{A}) \times (9\ \text{V}) \times (180\ \text{s}) = 648\ \text{J}$$

Notice, again, that the energy provided by the battery is ordered energy (it can drive a motor or heat a resistor), so it will be part of $\Delta W$ and not $\Delta Q$.

**word function:** $\phi$ joules, is the energy needed by a conduction electron to escape through the surface of a conductor. (See *photoelectric effect.*)

**work hardening** is the hardening or strengthening of a wire by subjecting it to repeated loading or *stress*, causing cold plastic deformation. It is a consequence of the increased number of tiny dislocations introduced into the metal. (See *hardness.*)

**A–Z Online**

Log on to A–Z Online to search the database of terms, print revision lists and much more. Go to **www.philipallan.co.uk/a-zonline** to get started.

**X-rays** are electromagnetic radiation of very short wavelength. They are produced naturally in space by a number of processes which result in the deceleration of electrons or other charged particles. However, here we will focus on man-made X-rays, which we will consider in terms of production, properties, detection and medical applications.

***1 Production.*** The essential components of an X-ray tube are an *electron gun* and a tungsten anode at opposite ends of an evacuated tube with a high voltage (e.g. 50 kV) source connected across them. A narrow beams of electrons streams across the tube onto the tungsten anode and X-rays are produced by the collisions. Most of the energy in the electron beam heats up the tungsten target; a small motor rotates the target to keep one spot from overheating. The ratio of X-ray energy output to electrical energy input (i.e. the tube efficiency) is very low because most of the electron beam energy is absorbed in the tungsten target, increasing its temperature.

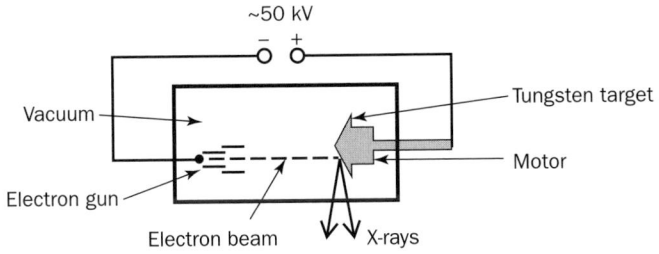


The second diagram shows a graph to illustrate how the X-ray intensity varies with X-ray photon energy for a tube voltage of 50 kV. Increasing the tube voltage widens the graph; increasing the tube current heightens it. The maximum photon frequency, $f_{max}$, is calculated from the relationship

$$eV = hf_{max} = \text{kinetic energy of electron at anode}$$

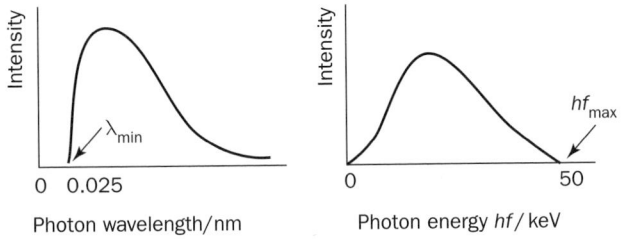

Should the electron beam energy be sufficient to excite electrons in the inner K-shells of the target material, then a line spectrum in the form of spikes is added to the continuous spectrum.

***2 Properties.*** X-ray photon energies range from about 0.12 keV at the low end to about 1.2 MeV at the high end. Wavelengths range from about 10 nm down to about 1 pm.

X-rays share all the properties of electromagnetic radiation. Because X-ray wavelengths are much the same size as atomic diameter, *diffraction* effects can be observed only by using crystals or thin sheets of metal as the diffracting elements; this leads into a major technique for examining crystal structure. Interference and polarisation effects are not of much relevance with X-rays but they have been observed. The short wavelengths of X-rays ensure that the inverse square law is followed closely.

***3 Detection.*** The two principal means of X-ray detection are photography and the *GM tube*. GM tubes are used when little more than an estimate of X-ray intensity is needed, usually for safety monitoring purposes. Photography gives a permanent record. Accurate work is mostly carried out with scintillation counter–photomultiplier assemblies which can both count the number of photons and record their energies (see *radiation detectors*).

***4 Medical applications.*** The medical uses are of two kinds: diagnostic and therapeutic.

- Diagnosis: X-ray photographs of bones or lung tissues are used to identify fractures or other troubles. X-ray tubes for this kind of work are run at a few tens of thousands of volts, and the X-ray photons of this energy are largely absorbed in photoelectric events. Since the probability of these events increases with $Z^3$, where $Z$ is the atomic number of the absorbing material, absorption in bones is strong but absorption in the soft tissues weak.

  The quality of the X-ray photograph lies in its clarity, and this improves with the intensity of the X-ray beam. But high beam intensity is bad for the subject of the photograph. So, to achieve a satisfactory image with a low-intensity beam, the unexposed film is mounted between two fluorescent sheets which act as image intensifiers. Each X-ray photon that is absorbed in the screen triggers the emission of as many as two or three hundred visible photons (of energy a few eV). The advantage is a useful X-ray picture with a reduced X-ray dose. The cost is the blurring of the picture. In practice, a compromise has to be found.
- Therapy: X-ray photons produced at approximately a megavolt or above are mostly absorbed by *Compton scattering*, and this effect is independent of $Z$ — there is no preferential absorption by any one tissue type. A beam of these X-rays, if focused upon some offending tissue, will destroy innocent tissue in its path. However, if at the same time the body is rotated about the offending tissue, then this will be the only tissue which gets a high enough dose to be destroyed. (See *electromagnetic spectrum, photon.*)

**yield point:** the point along a *stress–strain curve* at which random and erratic movement occurs between planes of atoms within the specimen. It marks the onset of plastic flow.

**Young modulus** is defined by the word equation

$$\text{Young modulus} = \frac{\text{tensile stress}}{\text{tensile strain}}$$

$$\text{unit for Young modulus} = \frac{\text{pascal}}{\text{no unit}} = \text{pascal}$$

For a specimen in the form of a wire of length $l$ and area of cross-section $A$ subjected to a tensile force $F$ which causes an extension $e$, the Young modulus $E$ is calculated from the expression

$$E = \frac{Fl}{Ae}$$

A rough order of magnitude can be found by putting typical values into the expression. With $F = 50\,\text{N}$, $l = 3\,\text{m}$, $A = 0.50 \times 10^{-6}\,\text{m}^2$ and $e = 0.003\,\text{m}$, we will have $E = 1 \times 10^{11}\,\text{Pa}$.

**Young's two slits experiment:** see *two slits experiment.*

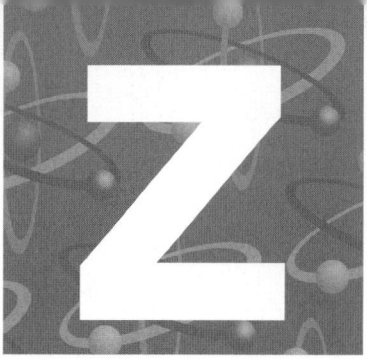

**zero error** arises when the scale reading of a *voltmeter* or *ammeter* is significantly different from zero when zero current is flowing through the instrument. It can also happen that the needle zeroes correctly but needs more than a finite current or voltage to shift it away from the zero. A zero error can occur with any instrument which has a scale — a thermometer, a *micrometer screw gauge*, a pressure gauge, an electrometer. Zero error cannot be reduced by averaging the results of several measurements: it is a *systematic error*. (See *error, uncertainty, random error.*)

**zeroth law of thermodynamics:** this states that if two bodies are each in *thermal equilibrium* with the same third body, then they are in thermal equilibrium with one another. There must be some physical quantity which decides whether or not two bodies can be in thermal equilibrium with one another. This physical quantity is called *temperature*. The zeroth law of thermodynamics is a formal way of defining temperature with reference to the concept of a thermal equilibrium state. The attraction of the thermal equilibrium state concept is that it can be recognised without recourse to thermometers.

This law is sometimes referred to as the 'mother, baby and bathwater' law. A mother knows that her temperature is the same as that of her baby. She tests the bathwater with her elbow. When the water is at the same temperature as her elbow, she knows that it will also be at the same temperature as the baby.

# Physics revision lists

## Using A–Z Online

In addition to the revision lists set out below, you can use the A–Z Online website to access revision lists specific to your exam board and the particular exam you are taking. Log on to **www.philipallan.co.uk/a-zonline** and create an account using the unique code provided on the front inside cover of this book. Once you have logged on, you can print out lists of terms together with their definitions, which will help you to focus your revision.

On the pages that follow, we have listed revision terms for the AS and A-level examinations for the three main awarding bodies:

- AQA (Specification A), see pages 278–281
- OCR (Specification A), see pages 282–285
- Edexcel, see pages 286–288

This is to help you use this handbook as effectively as possible. On the website, we have set out revision lists for other examination bodies which may provide the physics exams at your school or college, including:

- AQA (Specification B)
- OCR (Specification B)
- Cambridge International Examinations (CIE)
- Council for the Curriculum, Examinations and Assessment (CCEA)
- Welsh Joint Education Committee (WJEC)
- Scottish Higher
- International Baccalaureate (IB)

# AQA (Specification A) revision lists

## AS Physics

### Unit 1 Particle, quantum phenomena and electricity

#### PART 1 PARTICLES AND RADIATION

annihilation
antimatter
de Broglie wavelength
electron capture
exchange particles
Feynman diagrams
fundamental interactions
hadrons
leptons
neutrino
nuclear atom
pair production
photon
Planck constant
positron
quarks

#### PART 2 ELECTROMAGNETIC RADIATION AND QUANTUM PHENOMENA

electron volt
emission spectrum
energy level
ionisation
photoelectric effect
wave–particle duality

#### PART 3 CURRENT ELECTRICITY

alternating current and voltage
current–voltage characteristics
e.m.f. (electromotive force)
electric circuit calculations
electric current
internal resistance
Ohm's law
potential difference
potential divider
resistance
resistivity

## Unit 2 Mechanics, materials and waves

### PART 1 MECHANICS

acceleration due to gravity
centre of mass
conservation of energy
displacement–time graph
efficiency (machines)
equations of motion
equilibrium
kinetic energy
moment of force
Newton's laws of motion
parallelogram law
potential (gravitational)
power
projectiles
resolution of vectors
scalar quantity
vector quantity
velocity–time graph
work

### PART 2 MATERIALS

breaking stress
density
elastic strain energy
fracture
Hooke's law
plastic deformation
stress–strain curves
Young modulus

### PART 3 WAVES

diffraction at a single slit
electromagnetic waves
frequency
interference
longitudinal waves
optical fibre systems
path difference
phase
polarisation phenomena
progressive waves
refraction of light
sound waves
stationary wave
superposition
total internal reflection
transverse waves
two slits experiment
wave speed

# A2 Physics

## Unit 4 Fields and further mechanics

### PART 1 FURTHER MECHANICS

centripetal force
circular motion
conservation of linear momentum
damped harmonic motion
elastic collision
impulse
linear momentum
mass–spring system
resonance
simple harmonic motion
simple pendulum

### PART 2 GRAVITATION

geostationary orbit
gravitational field strength
Newton's law of universal gravitation
planetary motion
potential (gravitational)
work

### PART 3 ELECTRIC FIELDS

Coulomb's law
electric field strength
electric potential
potential difference

### PART 4 CAPACITANCE

capacitance
energy stored in a capacitor
exponential decay
time constant

### PART 5 MAGNETIC FIELDS

electromagnetic induction
electromagnetic induction (laws of)
electron beams
Fleming's left hand rule
flux linkage
magnetic flux
magnetic flux density
transformer

## Unit 5 Nuclear physics, thermal physics, options

### PART 1 NUCLEAR AND THERMAL PHYSICS

alpha particle scattering experiment
electron capture
half-life
inverse square law
nuclear atom
nuclear radius
*N–Z* curve for stable nuclei
randomness and radioactive decay

### PART 2 NUCLEAR ENERGY

atomic mass unit
binding energy
binding energy per nucleon
electron volt
mass–energy equivalence
thermal fission reactor

### PART 3 THERMAL PHYSICS

ideal gas equation
kinetic theory of gases
mole
specific heat capacity
specific latent heat

## Unit 5A Astrophysics

charge-coupled device
end states of stars
Hertzsprung–Russell diagram
Hubble's law
lens equation
resolving power
red shift
stars
Stefan's law
Wien's law

## Unit 5B Medical physics

CT scanner
ear
ECG waveform
eye
intensity of radiation
lens equation
MRI
optical fibre systems
resolution
ultrasound
X-rays

## Unit 5C Applied physics

adiabatic change
angular momentum
engine cycle
first law of thermodynamics
heat engine concept
heat pump
isothermal change
moment of inertia
rotational motion (equations of)

## Unit 5D Turning points in physics

thermionic emission
Millikan's oil drop experiment
wave–particle duality
electromagnetic waves
photoelectric effect
de Broglie wavelength
Michelson–Morley experiment
special relativity
time dilation
mass–energy equivalence

# OCR (Specification A) revision lists

## AS Physics

### Unit 1 Mechanics

#### MODULE 1 MOTION

displacement
displacement–time graph
equations of motion
parallelogram law
resolution of vectors
velocity–time graph

#### MODULE 2 FORCES IN ACTION

acceleration of free fall
density
equilibrium
force
moment of force
pressure
special relativity
weight

#### MODULE 3 WORK AND ENERGY

efficiency (machines)
energy
Hooke's law
kinetic energy
plastic deformation
polymeric solids
potential (gravitational)
power
Sankey diagram
stress–strain curve
work
Young modulus

### Unit 2 Electrons, waves and photons

#### MODULE 1 ELECTRIC CURRENT

coulomb
drift speed
electric current
Kirchhoff's first law

### MODULE 2 RESISTANCE

electric circuit calculations
e.m.f. (electromotive force)
Ohm's law
potential difference
resistance

### CURRENT–VOLTAGE CHARACTERISTICS

kilowatt-hour
resistivity
thermistors

### MODULE 3 DC CIRCUITS

internal resistance
Kirchhoff's second law
light-dependent resistor
potential divider
resistors in parallel
resistors in series

### MODULE 4 WAVES

coherence
diffraction grating
electromagnetic spectrum
intensity (stellar)
interference
longitudinal waves
Malus' law
path difference
phase difference
polarisation phenomena
stationary wave
superposition
transverse waves
two slits experiment
UV
wave speed

### MODULE 5 QUANTUM PHYSICS

de Broglie wavelength
electron diffraction
electron volt
emission spectrum
energy level
photoelectric effect
photon
wave–particle duality

# A2 Physics

## Unit 4 The Newtonian world

### MODULE 1 NEWTON'S LAWS AND MOMENTUM

collision
conservation of linear momentum
force
impulse
linear momentum
Newton's laws of motion

### MODULE 2 CIRCULAR MOTION AND OSCILLATIONS

centripetal force
circular motion
damped harmonic motion
forced oscillations
geostationary orbit
gravitational field strength
Kepler's laws
Newton's law of universal gravitation
radian
resonance
simple harmonic motion

### MODULE 3 THERMAL PHYSICS

absolute temperature scale
absolute zero
Boltzmann constant
Boyle's law
Brownian motion
heat transfer
ideal gas equation
internal energy
kinetic theory of gases
mole
specific heat capacity
specific latent heat
thermal equilibrium

## Unit 5 Fields, particles and frontiers of physics

### MODULE 1 ELECTRIC AND MAGNETIC FIELDS

Coulomb's law
electric field
electromagnetic induction
electromagnetic induction (laws of)
electron beams
Fleming's left hand rule
flux linkage
generator
magnetic field strength
magnetic flux
magnetic flux density
mass spectrometer
transformer
uniform electric field

### MODULE 2 CAPACITORS AND EXPONENTIAL DECAY

capacitance
energy stored in a capacitor
exponential decay
time constant

### MODULE 3 NUCLEAR PHYSICS

activity
alpha particle scattering experiment
beta decay
binding energy
binding energy per nucleon
decay constant
fundamental interactions
half-life
isotope
leptons

mass–energy equivalence
neutrino
nuclear atom
nuclear reactions
nuclide
positron
quarks
radioactive decay
randomness and radioactive decay
stars
thermal fission reactor

## MODULE 4 MEDICAL IMAGING

acoustic impedance
attenuation
barium meal
Doppler effect
intensity of radiation
MRI
pair production
PET scanning
piezoelectric transducer
ultrasound
X-rays

## MODULE 5 MODELLING THE UNIVERSE

Big Bang theory
cosmological principle
end states of stars
galaxies
Olber's paradox
parsec
red shift
stars

# Edexcel revision lists

## AS Physics

### Unit 1 Physics on the go

#### PART 1 MECHANICS

centre of gravity
displacement
displacement–time graph
equations of motion
free-body force diagram
gravitational field strength
kinetic energy
light gates
Newton's laws of motion
parallelogram law
potential (gravitational)
projectiles
velocity–time graph
work

#### PART 2 MATERIALS

brittleness
density
elastic strain energy
force–extension curve
Hooke's law
laminar flow
limit of proportionality
plastic deformation
Stokes' law
stress–strain curve
turbulent flow
upthrust
viscosity
Young modulus

### Unit 2 Physics at work

#### PART 1 WAVES

amplitude
coherence
diffraction
Doppler effect
electromagnetic spectrum
electron diffraction
longitudinal waves
path difference
phase difference
polarisation phenomena

refraction of light
stationary wave
superposition
total internal reflection
transverse waves
ultrasound
wave speed
wavefront

### PART 2 DC ELECTRICITY

current–voltage characteristics
drift speed
e.m.f. (electromotive force)
electric circuit calculations
electric current
Ohm's law
potential difference
potential divider
resistance
resistivity
thermistors
voltage

### PART 3 NATURE OF LIGHT

electron volt
energy level
photoelectric effect
photon
photovoltaic cells
wave nature of light
wave–particle duality

# A2 Physics

## Unit 4 Physics on the move

### PART 1 FURTHER MECHANICS

angular displacement
angular velocity
centripetal force
circular motion
conservation of linear momentum
kinetic energy
linear momentum
Newton's second law of motion
radian

### PART 2 ELECTRIC AND MAGNETIC FIELDS

capacitance
Coulomb's law
electric field
electromagnetic induction
electromagnetic induction (laws of)
electron beams
energy stored in a capacitor
exponential decay
field lines (electric)
Fleming's left hand rule
flux linkage
magnetic flux
time constant
uniform electric field

### PART 3 PARTICLE PHYSICS

alpha particle scattering experiment
annihilation
antimatter
de Broglie wavelength
mass–energy equivalence
MeV
nuclear atom
particle accelerators
quarks
thermionic emission
unified atomic mass unit

## Unit 5 Physics from creation to collapse

### PART 1 THERMAL ENERGY

absolute temperature scale
internal energy
kinetic theory of gases
specific heat capacity
thermal energy

### PART 2 NUCLEAR DECAY

alpha radiation
background radiation
beta radiation
decay constant
exponential law of radioactive decay
half-life
gamma radiation
ionising radiation
radioisotopes
randomness and radioactive decay

### PART 3 OSCILLATIONS

damped harmonic motion
forced oscillations
resonance
simple harmonic motion

### PART 4 ASTROPHYSICS AND COSMOLOGY

binding energy
black body radiation
gravitation
gravitational field strength
Hertzsprung–Russell diagram
Hubble's law
luminosity
mass defect
Newton's law of universal gravitation
parallax (sellar)
red shift
stars
Stefan's law
Wien's law

# Physical quantities and their units

This appendix lists most of the physical quantities included in A-level physics specifications, together with their units. For emphasis, base physical quantities of the SI system and their units are shown in bold. Quantities have been listed so that, apart from the occasional exception, the definition of any physical quantity or its unit depends only on those listed above it. In this way, you can see how physics is built up on the basis of quantities, each defined in terms of more fundamental quantities.

As you study physics, you will come across new quantities. This appendix will help you see how these are related to quantities with which you are already familiar.

Many questions begin by asking the candidate to explain a term of some sort and the term is often a physical quantity. You need to familiarise yourself with these physical quantities by referring to them frequently. Read the following lists every so often and remind yourself of the definitions and interconnections.

The scalar or vector nature of a physical quantity is listed alongside each entry. Pseudo-vectors (rotational vectors like torque) are not covered by any specifications; the labels have been included here for completeness. Some scalar quantities, such as current and e.m.f., are regarded as vectors in more advanced work. However, they are treated as scalars at A-level. Whether or not a physical constant such as the Boltzmann constant is a scalar depends on the strict definition of a scalar; but such constants are certainly not vectors.

| **Length** | ***l*** | **m** | **scalar** |
|---|---|---|---|
| angle | $\theta$ | rad, ° | pseudo-vector |
| distance | $d$ | m | scalar |
| distance travelled | $d$ | m | scalar |
| displacement | $s$, $x$ | m | vector |
| amplitude | $x_0$, $y_0$ | m | scalar |
| wavelength | $\lambda$ | m | scalar |
| area | $A$ | $m^2$ | pseudo-vector |
| volume | $V$ | $m^3$ | scalar |

| **Time** | ***t*** | **s** | **scalar** |
|---|---|---|---|
| frequency | $f$ | Hz | scalar |
| angular frequency, angular speed | $\omega$ | $rad\,s^{-1}$ | scalar |

| | | | |
|---|---|---|---|
| speed | $c$ | $\mathrm{m\,s^{-1}}$ | scalar |
| rate of change of speed | $\frac{dv}{dt}$ | $\mathrm{m\,s^{-2}}$ | scalar |
| uniform, average, or instantaneous velocity | $u$, $v$ | $\mathrm{m\,s^{-1}}$ | vector |
| acceleration | $a$ | $\mathrm{m\,s^{-2}}$ | vector |
| acceleration of free fall | $g$ | $\mathrm{m\,s^{-2}}$ | vector |
| gravitational field strength | $g$ | $\mathrm{N\,kg^{-1}}$ | vector |
| **Mass** | $\boldsymbol{m}$ | **kg** | **scalar** |
| density | $\rho$ | $\mathrm{kg\,m^{-3}}$ | scalar |
| momentum | $p$, $mv$ | $\mathrm{kg\,m\,s^{-1}}$ | vector |
| force | $F$ | N | vector |
| impulse | $\Delta p$ | N s | vector |
| moment of force | $M$ | N m | pseudo-vector |
| torque | $T$ | N m | pseudo-vector |
| pressure | $p$ | Pa | scalar |
| stress | $\sigma$ | Pa | scalar |
| strain | $\varepsilon$ | no unit | scalar |
| Young modulus | $E$ | Pa | scalar |
| gravitational constant | $G$ | $\mathrm{N\,kg^{-2}\,m^{2}}$ | scalar |
| work | $W$ | J | scalar |
| energy | $W$, $E$ | J | scalar |
| kinetic energy | $E_k$ | J | scalar |
| potential energy | $E_p$ | J | scalar |
| power | $P$ | W | scalar |
| **Temperature** | $\boldsymbol{T}$ | **K** | **scalar** |
| internal energy | $U$ | J | scalar |
| heating | $q$ | J | scalar |
| heat capacity | $C$ | $\mathrm{J\,K^{-1}}$ | scalar |
| specific heat capacity | $c$ | $\mathrm{J\,kg^{-1}\,K^{-1}}$ | scalar |
| specific latent heat (specific enthalpy) | $L$ | $\mathrm{J\,kg^{-1}}$ | scalar |
| temperature gradient | $\Delta T/\Delta x$ | $\mathrm{K\,m^{-1}}$ | scalar |
| thermal conductivity | $k$ | $\mathrm{W\,m^{-1}\,K^{-1}}$ | scalar |
| U value | $U$ | $\mathrm{W\,m^{-2}\,K^{-1}}$ | scalar |
| **Amount of substance** | $\boldsymbol{n}$ | **mol** | **scalar** |
| molar mass | $M$ | $\mathrm{kg\,mol^{-1}}$ | scalar |
| molar heat capacity | $C_m$ | $\mathrm{J\,mol^{-1}\,K^{-1}}$ | scalar |
| molar gas constant | $R$ | $\mathrm{J\,mol^{-1}\,K^{-1}}$ | scalar |
| Avogadro constant | $N_A$ | $\mathrm{mol^{-1}}$ | scalar |
| Boltzmann constant | $k$ | $\mathrm{J\,K^{-1}}$ | scalar |

| | | | |
|---|---|---|---|
| **Current** | $I$ | **A** | **scalar** |
| charge | $Q$ | C | scalar |
| electric field strength | $E$ | $NC^{-1}$, $Vm^{-1}$ | vector |
| electric potential | $V$ | V | scalar |
| permittivity of free space | $\varepsilon_0$ | $Fm^{-1}$ | scalar |
| relative permittivity | $\varepsilon_r$ | no unit | scalar |
| permeability of free space | $\mu_0$ | $Hm^{-1}$ | scalar |
| potential difference | $V$ | V | scalar |
| electromotive force (e.m.f.) | $E$ | V | scalar |
| capacitance | $C$ | F | scalar |
| resistance | $R$ | $\Omega$ | scalar |
| resistivity | $\rho$ | $\Omega$m | scalar |
| conductance | $G$ | S | scalar |
| conductivity | $\sigma$ | $Sm^{-1}$ | scalar |
| inductance | $L$ | H | scalar |
| reactance | $X$ | $\Omega$ | scalar |
| impedance | $Z$ | $\Omega$ | scalar |
| time constant | $\tau$ | s | scalar |
| magnetic field strength | $B$ | T | vector |
| magnetic flux | $\phi$ | Wb | scalar |
| magnetic flux linkage | $N_\phi$ | Wb turn | scalar |
| **Planck constant** | **h** | **J s** | **scalar** |
| photon energy | $hf$ | J | scalar |
| work function | $\phi$ | J | scalar |
| activity | $A$ | Bq | scalar |
| decay constant | $\lambda$ | $s^{-1}$ | scalar |
| half-life | $T_{1/2}$ | s | scalar |
| mass excess | $\Delta m$ | kg, u | scalar |
| binding energy | $E_b$ | J | scalar |
| binding energy per nucleon | $E_b/A$ | J nucleon$^{-1}$ | scalar |
| mass number | $A$ | no unit | scalar |
| atomic number, proton number | $Z$ | no unit | scalar |
| neutron number | $N$ | no unit | scalar |

# Useful formulae and equations

Most of the formulae that you may need in an A-level examination are provided in 'formula sheets'. You have to be familiar with these formulae and be able to select the appropriate formula for a particular problem.

A formula encapsulates an idea. The fact that you can recite a formula does not indicate understanding. However, if you are also able to use the formula correctly, it shows that you have understood the idea.

The formulae are presented under a number of topic headings. This will help you to see how they are related. It may also help you with revision.

Make sure that you know which formulae are relevant to the specification you are studying, and which examinations they will be needed in.

## Mechanics

$$\text{pressure} = \frac{\text{force}}{\text{area}} \qquad p = F/A$$

$$\text{speed} = \frac{\text{distance travelled}}{\text{time taken}} \qquad v = \Delta s/\Delta t$$

$$\text{acceleration} = \frac{\text{increase in velocity}}{\text{time taken}} \qquad a = \Delta v/\Delta t$$

$$\text{momentum} = \text{mass} \times \text{velocity} \qquad p = mv$$

$$\text{resultant force} = \text{mass} \times \text{acceleration} \qquad F = ma$$

$$\text{work done} = \text{force} \times \text{distance moved in the direction of the force} \qquad W = Fs \cos\theta$$

$$\text{power} = \frac{\text{energy transferred}}{\text{time taken}} = \frac{\text{work done}}{\text{time taken}} \qquad P = \frac{\Delta E}{\Delta t} = \frac{\Delta W}{\Delta t}$$

$$\text{kinetic energy} = \tfrac{1}{2}\text{mass} \times \text{velocity}^2 \qquad E_k = \tfrac{1}{2}mv^2$$

centripetal force = $\dfrac{\text{mass} \times \text{speed}^2}{\text{radius}}$ $\qquad F = mv^2/r$

moment of force $F$ about point O
= $F \times$ perpendicular distance from $F$ to O $\qquad M = F \times d$

sum of clockwise moments about any point in a plane = sum of anticlockwise moments about that point

pressure × volume = number of moles × molar gas constant × absolute temperature $\qquad pV = nRT$

$$\frac{p_1V_1}{T_1} = \frac{p_2V_2}{T_2}$$

$$s = \frac{u + v}{2}t \qquad \omega = \frac{\Delta\theta}{\Delta t} = \frac{v}{r} \qquad T = 2\pi\sqrt{\frac{m}{k}}$$

$$v = u + at \qquad T = \frac{1}{f} = \frac{2\pi}{\omega} \qquad p = \frac{m}{v}$$

$$s = ut + \tfrac{1}{2}at^2 \qquad a = \omega^2 r = \frac{v^2}{r} \qquad F = k\,\Delta x$$

$$v^2 = u^2 + 2as \qquad x = x_0 \cos \omega t \qquad \sigma = \frac{F}{A}$$

$$F = \frac{\Delta p}{\Delta t} \qquad v = -\omega x_0 \sin \omega t \qquad \varepsilon = \frac{\Delta l}{l}$$

$$F\Delta t = \Delta(mv) \qquad a = -\omega^2 x \qquad E = \frac{\sigma}{\varepsilon} = \frac{Fl}{A\Delta l}$$

$$P = F \times v \qquad T = 2\pi\sqrt{\frac{l}{g}} \qquad W = \tfrac{1}{2}F\Delta x = \tfrac{1}{2}k\Delta x^2$$

$$T = I(\omega_2 - \omega_1)/t \qquad W = T\theta = \Delta(\tfrac{1}{2}I\omega^2)$$

## Fields

weight = mass × gravitational field strength $\qquad W = mg$

inverse square laws of force: $F = G\dfrac{m_1m_2}{r^2}$ $\qquad F = \dfrac{Q_1Q_2}{4\pi\varepsilon_0 d^2}$

change in potential energy =
mass × gravitational field strength
× change in height $\qquad E_p = mg\Delta h$

$E = F/Q$

$E = V/d$ (uniform)

$E = Q/4\pi\varepsilon_0 r^2$ (radial)

$V = Q/4\pi\varepsilon_0 r$ (radial)

$e\Delta V = \Delta(\frac{1}{2} m_e v^2)$

$C = \varepsilon_0 \varepsilon_r A/d$

$F = BIl$

$F = BQv$

$B = \mu_0 I/2\pi r$

$B = \mu_0 NI/l = \mu_0 nI$

$B = \mu_0 NI/2r$

$F = \dfrac{\mu_0 I_1 I_2}{2\pi r}$

$\phi = BA$

$E = -N\dfrac{d\phi}{dt}$

$E = Blv$

$E = \omega BAN \sin 2\pi ft$

$g = F/m$

$g = Gm/r^2$ (radial)

$V = -Gm/r$ (radial)

## Waves

wave speed = frequency × wavelength $\quad c = f \times \lambda$

## Thermal physics

$\theta/°C = T/K - 273.15$

$\theta = \dfrac{X_\theta - X_0}{X_{100} - X_0} \times 100°C$

$\Delta W = -p.\Delta V$

$\Delta U = mc\Delta T$

$\Delta U = L.\Delta m$

$\Delta U = \Delta Q + \Delta W$

$C_p - C_V = R$

$\dfrac{\Delta Q}{\Delta t} = kA\dfrac{\Delta T}{\Delta x}$

$\dfrac{\Delta Q}{\Delta t} = UA\Delta T$

$pV = \frac{1}{3} Nm \langle c^2 \rangle$

$T \propto \langle molecular\ k.e. \rangle$

$\langle molecular\ k.e. \rangle = \frac{3}{2} kT$

$R = kN_A$

$\Delta p = \rho g \Delta h$

$\eta = \dfrac{Q_1 - Q_2}{Q_1} = \dfrac{T_1 - T_2}{T_1}$

## Electricity and magnetism

current = charge / time interval $\quad I = \Delta Q/\Delta t$

potential difference = work done / charge $\quad V = W/Q$

electrical energy transfer =
current × potential difference × time interval $\quad \Delta W = IV\Delta t$

electrical power = potential difference × current $\quad P = VI = I^2R$

$$\text{resistance} = \frac{\text{resistivity} \times \text{length}}{\text{cross-sectional area}} \qquad R = \frac{V}{I} = \frac{\rho l}{A}$$

$$\text{capacitance} = \frac{\text{charge stored}}{\text{potential difference}} \qquad C = \frac{Q}{V}$$

$I = nAQv$

$V = E - Ir$

$R = R_1 + R_2 + R_3$

$$\frac{1}{R} = \frac{1}{R_1} + \frac{1}{R_2} + \frac{1}{R_3}$$

$$\frac{1}{C} = \frac{1}{C_1} + \frac{1}{C_2} + \frac{1}{C_3}$$

$C = C_1 + C_2 + C_3$

$W = \frac{1}{2}CV^2$

$Q = Q_0 e^{-t/CR}$

$Q = Q_0\left(1 - e^{-t/CR}\right)$

$\tau = CR$

$X_C = 1/\omega C = 1/2\pi f C$

$X_L = \omega L = 2\pi f L$

$I = I_0 \sin 2\pi f t$

$I_{\text{r.m.s}} = I_0/\sqrt{2}$

$V_{\text{r.m.s}} = V_0/\sqrt{2}$

$$f_{\text{resonance}} = \frac{1}{2\pi\sqrt{(LC)}}$$

$\langle P \rangle = I_{\text{r.m.s}} V_{\text{r.m.s}} = I_0 V_0/2$

## Waves, quantum phenomena and radioactivity

$$I = \frac{P}{4\pi r^2} \qquad f = \frac{1}{2t}\sqrt{\left(\frac{T}{\mu}\right)} \qquad A = \frac{dN}{dt} = -\lambda N$$

$$\lambda = \frac{xs}{D} \qquad \Delta E = c^2.\Delta m \qquad N = N_0 e^{-\lambda t}$$

$$n\lambda = d \sin\theta \qquad E = hf \qquad T_{1/2} = \frac{0.693}{\lambda}$$

$$\frac{\sin\theta_1}{\sin\theta_2} = \frac{\lambda_1}{\lambda_2} = \frac{C_1}{C_2} = \frac{n_2}{n_1} = {}_1n_2 \qquad hf = \phi + \left(\tfrac{1}{2}mv^2\right)_{\max}$$

$$\sin\theta_C = \frac{C_2}{C_1} = \frac{1}{{}_1n_2} \qquad \lambda = \frac{h}{P} = \frac{h}{mv}$$

$$n_1 = \frac{C}{C_1} \qquad hf = E_1 - E_2$$

# Physical constants

| Physical quantity | Symbol | Value | Unit |
|---|---|---|---|
| speed of light in vacuum — exact value as defined | $c$ | $2.997\,924\,58 \times 10^{8}$ | $m\,s^{-1}$ |
| speed of light in vacuum — value to use in calculations | $c$ | $3.00 \times 10^{8}$ | $m\,s^{-1}$ |
| permeability of vacuum — exact value as defined | $\mu_0$ | $4\pi \times 10^{-7}$ | $H\,m^{-1}$ |
| permittivity of vacuum — defined to be $1/(\mu_0 c^2)$ | $\varepsilon_0$ | $8.854\,187\,817 \times 10^{-12}$ | $F\,m^{-1}$ |
| gravitational constant | $G$ | $6.673 \times 10^{-11}$ | $m^3\,kg^{-1}\,s^{-2}$ |
| molar gas constant | $R$ | 8.315 | $J\,K^{-1}\,mol^{-1}$ |
| Avogadro constant | $L$ or $N_A$ | $6.022 \times 10^{23}$ | $mol^{-1}$ |
| Boltzmann constant (= $R/L$) | $k$ | $1.381 \times 10^{-23}$ | $J\,K^{-1}$ |
| elementary charge | $e$ | $1.602 \times 10^{-19}$ | C |
| Faraday constant (= $eL$) | $F$ | $9.649 \times 10^{4}$ | $C\,mol^{-1}$ |
| Stefan–Boltzmann constant | $\sigma$ | $5.671 \times 10^{-8}$ | $W\,m^{-2}\,K^{-4}$ |
| Wien's law constant | $c_w$ | $2.898 \times 10^{-3}$ | m K |
| unified atomic mass unit | $u$ or $m_u$ | $1.661 \times 10^{-27}$ | kg |
| electron rest mass | $m_e$ | $9.109 \times 10^{-31}$ | kg |
| proton rest mass | $m_p$ | $1.673 \times 10^{-27}$ | kg |
| neutron rest mass | $m_n$ | $1.675 \times 10^{-27}$ | kg |
| alpha particle rest mass | $m_\alpha$ | $6.646 \times 10^{-27}$ | kg |
| specific charge of electron | $e/m_e$ | $1.759 \times 10^{11}$ | $C\,kg^{-1}$ |
| specific charge of proton | $e/m_p$ | $9.579 \times 10^{7}$ | $C\,kg^{-1}$ |
| Planck constant | $h$ | $6.626 \times 10^{-34}$ | J s |
| Rydberg constant | $R_\infty$ | $1.097 \times 10^{7}$ | m |

# Useful data

| Physical quantity | Value | Unit |
|---|---|---|
| acceleration of free fall near Earth's surface | 9.81 | $m\,s^{-2}$ |
| gravitational field strength near Earth's surface | 9.81 | $N\,kg^{-1}$ |
| standard pressure | 100 000 | Pa (or 1 bar) |
| standard atmosphere | $1.013\,25 \times 10^5$ | Pa |
| standard temperature | 273.15 | K (or 0°C) |
| ice point | 273.15 | K (or 0°C) |
| triple point of water | 273.16 | K |
| density of dry air at s.t.p. | 1.293 | $kg\,m^{-3}$ |
| density of water at s.t.p. | $1.000 \times 10^3$ | $kg\,m^{-3}$ |
| molar mass of air | 0.028 98 | $kg\,mol^{-1}$ |
| molar volume at s.t.p. (= $RT/p$) | $22.414 \times 10^{-3}$ | $m^3$ |
| molar volume at standard atmospheric pressure and 298 K | $24.467 \times 10^{-3}$ | $m^3$ |
| radius of Sun | $6.96 \times 10^8$ | m |
| mass of Sun | $1.99 \times 10^{30}$ | kg |
| power radiated from Sun | $3.85 \times 10^{26}$ | W |
| temperature of Sun's surface | 5770 | K |
| distance of Sun from Earth | $1.496 \times 10^{11}$ | m |
| radius of Earth at equator | $6.378 \times 10^6$ | m |
| radius of Earth at poles | $6.357 \times 10^6$ | m |
| mass of the Earth | $5.976 \times 10^{24}$ | kg |
| radius of the Moon | $1.739 \times 10^6$ | m |
| mass of the Moon | $7.36 \times 10^{22}$ | kg |
| distance of Moon from Earth | $3.844 \times 10^8$ | m |

# Conversion factors

1 day = $8.64 \times 10^4$ s

1 year ≈ $3.16 \times 10^7$ s

1 light year ≈ $9.5 \times 10^{15}$ m

1 parsec ≈ $3.1 \times 10^{16}$ m

1 u ≈ 931.3 MeV

# Preparing for the examination

This appendix begins with some ideas for planning your revision. It continues with some notes on how to answer examination questions or work through calculations, and ends with some detailed discussion about describing experiments.

## Planning your revision

Students always have their own preferences and their own work patterns. However you manage your own affairs, don't do less than is recommended here.

Your revision period starts about two months before the examination. This is still true even if you are taking just one module; the brain needs time to mull over the important ideas, to become familiar with all the details and to be fluent with its responses. One module will not need so much time per day but it will need the same stretch of time.

Begin your revision by dividing the specification into bite-sized pieces. About 30 of these will cover the complete specification. Your list will look something like this:

- physical quantities and their units
- straight line motion
- force, motion, energy and power
- motion in a circle
- simple harmonic motion

  .

  .

  .
- photoelectric effect
- radioactivity

  .

  .

  .

Get some small white cards, and as you revise each area of the specification, list what you need to know about that topic on its own card.

For example, the simple harmonic motion card should include these reminders of definitions, formulae, graphs and experiments:

- s.h.m. — definition (magnitude and direction)
- definitions — amplitude, frequency, period, restoring force, spring constant
- formula sheet — $x$, $a$, $T$, maximum speed and acceleration
- know formulae for $v$, $E_k$
- graphs — $x$, $v$, $a$, $F$, $E_k$ against time; $a$, $F$ and $E_k$ against displacement
- trace conservation of energy through energy transformations
- energy variation with displacement for simple pendulum and helical spring
- experiments — simple pendulum, helical spring

The photoelectric effect card will have a similar set of reminders, such as:

- photoelectric effect — definition
- definitions — work function, stopping potential, threshold frequency
- photoelectron, photon, photon energy $hf$
- Einstein's photoelectric equation
- experiment — vacuum, incident photons, collector grid, electrometer, voltmeter
- graphs — stopping potential against frequency: gradient = $h/e$, ...; photoelectric current against grid voltage: vary incident intensity...; photoelectric current against incident intensity: grid voltage fixed...

Write out these cards as you work through the specification section by section. Go back to the specification and make sure nothing is left out. Read the cards frequently and keep your grip on each specification section you have worked through. Always learn whole sections, and don't leave things out.

## Answering questions

Questions in modular examinations are broken down into short sections; all the candidate has to do is write out the answers carefully. But this is easier said than done, and it is worthwhile asking why so many candidates end up with lower marks than they think they deserve.

Consider the following imaginary question:

- Explain why a metal block gets hot when it is rubbed on a concrete floor. [2 marks]

Two marks implies that you have to include two distinct points in your answer. The candidate who writes 'Because the energy transferred by working against friction is transformed into heat' gets one mark. The second mark will be awarded for something along the lines of 'This heat flows into the metal block because the metal is a much better thermal conductor than the concrete'. Half or more of the candidates will lose that second mark. Don't omit an essential step because it seems too 'obvious'.

Many questions involve a contrast. Consider:

- Why does A warm up faster than B? [2 marks]

Your answer must include a statement about A, a statement about B and a reason for the difference. 'Because A is inside the furnace' gets one mark. 'Because A is inside the furnace where it is hot but B stays outside the furnace where it is cool' gets two marks.

There are many candidates who could answer these last two questions, but who would earn only two out of the four marks. An average candidate will repeatedly lose marks by giving only half of any answer, often thinking that the rest of the answer is too obvious to bother writing down. Don't fall into this trap. You can drop by as much as two or three grades through not paying attention to the details in your answers. You may not like this way of doing things, but you have no choice if you want to earn a high grade.

If, in answer to a question such as 'define resistivity' or 'state the law of universal gravitation' you write down an equation without stating what the symbols mean, you will score nothing. List the symbols and their meanings immediately below the equations. Use word equation definitions wherever possible — they avoid many of these problems.

Often you will be asked to sketch a graph. There will be one mark for labelling the axes with variables and their units and, possibly, for marking the scale values along the axes. Another mark will be allocated for having the shape of the curve roughly correct (e.g. don't let a decay curve cut the time axis). There will also be one mark for giving the numerical value of an intercept, if the necessary information is available, and one mark for stating the value of the gradient or of an identified area. These are the aspects you should try to include in your sketch.

There is an increasing tendency to provide a graph in a question paper and ask candidates to use it to estimate the value of some quantity. The word 'estimate' indicates that answers may vary somewhat from one candidate to another. These questions mostly require either the evaluation of a gradient or the evaluation of an area. To evaluate a gradient, draw the tangent carefully and at the right point on the curve. Draw as large a right-angled triangle as possible and measure the rise and the run according to the scales on the axes. Don't forget to give the unit of the gradient: it is the ratio of the $y$-axis unit to the $x$-axis unit. Estimating an area is often a little troublesome. If the easiest way of finding the relevant area is to count squares, then count squares; but don't forget to use the axes scales to evaluate the area of one square. The unit for the area will be the product of the units on the two axes.

When you are asked to draw a diagram, the marks will be awarded for correctly labelled parts of the diagram. A part that is not labelled, however obvious its meaning, will not get a mark.

## Calculations

Many calculations are short and you will earn all the marks if you get the right answer and remember to include the unit. There is no problem with that — but you need to guard against losing marks unnecessarily when you don't get the right answer. This is why your method needs to be clear without being overdetailed.

Marking schemes vary occasionally, but usually there is one mark for a correct statement of principle, one mark for manipulating the equation, another for substituting the data correctly and a final mark for the right answer with its unit. Where there are only three marks, it is the middle two marks that are combined.

Candidates who don't know the principle on which a calculation is based cannot start the calculation; it is all too late for these candidates. More worrying is the failure of other candidates to put the data correctly into an equation. Equations are correct provided that the data are all in standard SI units. Current must be in amperes, not milliamps. Mass must be in kilograms, not grams. Be very careful with areas: a radius of 2.2 cm gives the circle's area as $\pi(2.2 \times 10^{-2})^2\,m^2$, and a radius of 8.1 mm gives an area of $\pi(8.1 \times 10^{-3})^2\,m^2$. Calculations like these are often done incorrectly. For instance, candidates frequently replace $1.0\,mm^2$ with $1.0 \times 10^{-3}\,m^2$ instead of $1.0 \times 10^{-6}\,m^2$.

## Describing experiments

It is rare to find an examination paper which does not include one question largely given over to a description of an experiment. A typical question gives you ten minutes or so to earn about eight marks. The way that the marks are distributed will, of course, vary from one occasion to another but the broad pattern is always the same.

Follow these rules:

- **Apparatus.** Put as much information as you can into a fully labelled diagram. Labels need to be brief but informative, e.g. 'timer runs while this light beam is broken', 'fixed mass of gas', 'grid at low negative potential to slow down and repel electrons'. Identify precisely any length, area or volume that is going to be measured.
- **Measurements.** List each measurement and name the instruments used, e.g. 'measure the length of the pendulum with a metre rule', 'add the barometer reading to the pressure gauge reading to find the gas pressure', 'measure the terminal voltage with the digital voltmeter and, at the same time, record the current in the ammeter'. Whenever possible, state that a measurement is repeated so that an average value can be worked out and used.
- **Conclusion.** Frequently, an experiment concludes by requiring the candidate to draw a graph and check whether or not it is straight, check whether or not it goes through the origin, or find a gradient. Always sketch the graph you expect to get, label the axes and identify the feature of interest.

Check your course specification to find out which experiments are mentioned. Look through past examination papers to see how questions relating to these experiments are presented.

# Examiners' terms

We are all familiar with the advice to 'read the question'. However, you need to understand the terminology used by examiners if you are to make the most of reading the question. In particular, there are some introductory words and phrases which, if you understand what the examiner means by them, will help you to understand what the examiner is looking for.

The allocation of marks is also a useful guide. A single mark may require an answer which is a single word or a brief phrase. A three-mark question probably expects an answer with three main points; you may be able to present these as a list. Remember that the examiner's mark scheme is usually presented as a list with one mark's worth of answer on each line.

Here is a list of some frequently used examination terms.

## Define...

Define always means write out a definition. A word equation may be sufficient and is often easier to write out accurately than a sentence. If you use an algebraic definition, remember to define the symbols in your equation.

## Explain the meaning of... or Explain what is meant by...

A definition is sometimes enough. If the mark allocation suggests that a simple definition isn't enough, then give an example. Perhaps draw a diagram. The term 'gradient' for instance, is better explained with a sketch graph than with a few fine words. Terms such as 'equilibrium' are best explained by giving an example.

## Describe...

Have a look at a few questions. You won't be asked to describe a helical spring or an electric field or a set of expensive dinner plates. You will be asked to describe a process such as the energy transformations occurring in a simple pendulum or an experiment to illustrate something. Say how things are at the start, in the middle and at the end. Concentrate on getting the sequence right. The mark allocation is the best clue to how many steps you should include. Draw a labelled diagram whenever possible.

## Explain why...

The question will indicate the phenomenon that needs explanation. The explanation will always involve a principle of some sort. Identify and state the relevant principle, e.g. 'impulse equals change of momentum' or 'total charge stored is constant'. Apply the principle to the initial state of the situation and show how it leads to the outcome.

## Explain what happens when...

State clearly what happens and then 'Explain why' as above.

## Calculate... or Find...

These words ask you to work out a numerical problem. State clearly the principle or the basic equation. Rearrange the equation. Put in the data in SI units, not their multiples or submultiples. Then calculate the result. A tidy calculation can score most of the marks even when the final answer is wrong; but a jumble of figures and a wrong answer scores nothing.

Use as many significant figures as you like but reduce the number to match the initial data when you state the answer. Never omit the unit.

## Estimate...

Estimate usually means that you supply some typical data yourself and calculate a typical value. Sometimes all the data are given in the question but you need to make an approximating assumption, e.g. assume that steam behaves like a perfect gas or that a frictional force is zero.

## State... or List...

These words should be taken literally. A list is best presented with one item below another, rather than as continuous text.

## Sketch...

Whether it is a graph that needs sketching or apparatus for an experiment, the marks will always be associated with the labels.

When sketching a graph, label the axes, get the shape of the curve roughly correct and put in any magnitudes you can, such as the value of an intercept or the meaning of a gradient. If the axes cross at the origin, then mark the origin 0,0. Don't let a decay graph touch the time axis.

When sketching apparatus for an experiment, first draw the two or three important parts in roughly the right places, then join them up and label them. Avoid using rulers — the lines are rarely in the right places, they look wrong, the rulers take up valuable time and the marks are given for correct labels not for accurate drawing.

# Synoptic questions in A-level physics

There is a general requirement that A-level specifications should include a synoptic element in the examinations. As far as physics is concerned, this means that questions in one part of the examination will call on knowledge from more than one area of the specification. This is one of the more demanding aspects of your course, but when the time comes you should find yourself prepared to tackle these questions.

What form will synoptic questions take? We can cover most of the possibilities under three headings: mathematical questions, topic questions and comprehension questions.

## Mathematical questions

The examiner exploits two situations which involve similar mathematical equations — not difficult, just similar. The following examples are well known:

1 **Inverse square laws.** There are two inverse square laws of force that are covered by all A-level physics specifications: gravitational and electrical. Similarities include the vector nature of the force, the scalar nature of the potential (unlikely to be examined) and a uniform field on a local scale. In both cases, the force acts along a radius; there is no component along a tangent. Differences largely centre on electric fields being either attractive or repulsive and gravity being the important force at the astronomical level because matter in sufficient bulk is electrically neutral. Another important difference is that charge can be moved around and stored on conductors, thereby creating the possibility of manipulating the shape of the field.

   There is a second set of inverse square laws, namely the laws connected with particle or radiation flow. Any electromagnetic radiation from a point source weakens inversely with the square of the distance; this is the case, too, with concentrated alpha and beta radiation sources in vacuum.

2 **Exponential decay.** Exponential decay occurs whenever the rate at which some quantity diminishes is in proportion to its present value. This point is stressed in the diagram for *exponential decay*. Three situations likely to be tested are radioactive decay, capacitor discharge through a resistor and damped harmonic motion. Similarities involve the causes — activity proportional to undecayed mass, discharge current proportional to charge stored and work done against friction per cycle proportional to the square of amplitude, respectively. Be ready to compare activity and half-life on the one hand with discharge current and time constant on the other. A graph of ln(activity) against time or ln(discharge current) against time enables half-life or time constant to be evaluated.

A question could pick up on the contrast between the exponential decay with distance brought about by the absorption of, say, $\gamma$-rays in aluminium and the exponential decay with time brought about by radioactive decay. Both ideas are within your syllabus.

3 **Stored energy.** Compare $\frac{1}{2}kx^2$ for a helical spring with $\frac{1}{2}CV^2$ for a capacitor. Both laws derive from a certain linear property of the hardware, $F = kx$ and $Q = CV$, respectively. Both are important because the energy can be recovered without it transforming into the disordered form (what used to be called heat). In terms of the first law of thermodynamics, $\Delta W$ is transferred to the system and $\Delta U$ increases; it is the other way round when the energy is recovered. $\Delta Q$ is zero at all times. This last point can turn up with non-ideal systems: $\Delta Q$ is not zero and not all of the input energy is recoverable.

## Synoptic topics

The examiner chooses a topic which impinges on the specification in more than one area. The only way to prepare for this style of question is to watch for possibilities while you are working through the course. Synoptic topics mostly turn up towards the end. Common examples are found with important instruments. The mass spectrometer involves a velocity selector and, like the cyclotron, a centripetal force which derives from the motion of a charged particle in a magnetic field. All radiation detectors rely on absorption processes. A question on the nuclear fission reactor can drift into thermal efficiency, energy conversion at the nuclear level ($\Delta m.c^2$) and energy conversion processes in the turbines, generators, transformers and the transmission system. The idea of efficiency is relevant to anything involving energy conversion processes, from X-ray tubes to electric motors. It is always the sources of inefficiency that matter.

## Comprehension passages

These questions do no more than test whether or not you have made an honest attempt to cover the specification. A familiar topic is tested in an unfamiliar situation, such as wet hands under a hand drier switching on the drier by changing the capacitance of a capacitor inside the box. Why do you suppose the hands have to be underneath and not to one side? You can't prepare for the particular question you are going to get, but you can be prepared in general. Know exactly what you are going to do when you encounter such a question.

Read each part of the question carefully and identify the part of the passage it relates to — is the answer in the passage or are you going to need to involve part of what you've learned across the specification? When you have finished writing out your answers you will know much more about the passage; perhaps your earlier answers will need to be changed a little, so remember to leave yourself a bit of space to do this.

**PHILIP ALLAN**
UPDATES

# Student Unit Guides

- Focus your revision
- Build your confidence
- Strengthen your exam technique

**There are guides to help you in the following subjects:**

**Accounting** (AQA)
**Biology** (AQA, Edexcel, OCR)
**Business Studies** (AQA, Edexcel, OCR)
**Chemistry** (AQA, Edexcel, OCR (A), OCR (B) (Salters))
**Economics** (AQA, Edexcel, OCR)
**English Language** (AQA)
**English Language and Literature** (AQA)
**Geography** (AQA, Edexcel, OCR)
**Government & Politics** (AQA, Edexcel, OCR)
**History** (Edexcel, OCR)
**Law** (AQA, OCR)
**Mathematics** (AQA, Edexcel, OCR)
**Media Studies** (AQA, OCR)
**Physical Education** (AQA, Edexcel, OCR)
**Physics** (Edexcel, OCR)
**Psychology** (AQA (A), (AQA (B), Edexcel, OCR)
**Sociology** (AQA, OCR)

Visit **www.philipallan.co.uk** for the full list of unit guides and to order online, or telephone our Customer Services Department on **01235 827720**

PHILIP ALLAN
UPDATES

# EXAM *Revision* NOTES

- Revise core topics effectively
- Learn to identify what you are being asked to answer
- Prepare a thorough revision plan
- Improve your exam technique and ultimately your grade

Each title in the series is written by an experienced examiner, who highlights the key points for each topic area and identifies the common pitfalls you need to avoid.

**Titles available:**

Biology (2nd edition)
Business Studies (AQA)
Chemistry (2nd edition)
Critical Thinking (OCR)
Economics (2nd edition)
French (2nd edition)
German
16th Century British & European History
19th & 20th Century British History
19th & 20th Century European & World History
ICT
AS Law (2nd edition)
A2 Law: Criminal Law
A2 Law: Tort Law
Media Studies
PE/Sport Studies (2nd edition)
Physics (2nd edition)
AS UK Government & Politics (2nd edition)
A2 US Government & Politics (2nd edition)
A2 Political Ideologies
AS Psychology (AQA (A))
Religious Studies (2nd edition)
Spanish (2nd edition)

Visit **www.philipallan.co.uk** for more information and to order *Exam Revision Notes* online, or telephone our Customer Services Department on **01235 827720**